MODERN HUMANITIES RESEARCH ASSOCIATION
TUDOR AND STUART TRANSLATIONS
VOLUME 13

GENERAL EDITORS
ANDREW HADFIELD
NEIL RHODES

WILLIAM BARKER, *XENOPHON'S 'CYROPAEDIA'*

MODERN HUMANITIES RESEARCH ASSOCIATION
TUDOR AND STUART TRANSLATIONS

General Editors
Andrew Hadfield (University of Sussex)
Neil Rhodes (University of St Andrews)

Associate Editors
Guyda Armstrong (University of Manchester)
Fred Schurink (University of Manchester)
Louise Wilson (Liverpool Hope University)

Advisory Board
Warren Boutcher (Queen Mary, University of London);
Colin Burrow (All Souls College, Oxford);
A. E. B. Coldiron (Florida State University)
Patricia Demers (University of Alberta)
José Maria Pérez Fernández (University of Granada)
Robert S. Miola (Loyola College, Maryland)
Alessandra Petrina (University of Padua)
Anne Lake Prescott (Barnard College, Columbia University)
Quentin Skinner (Queen Mary, London)
Alan Stewart (Columbia University)

texts.mhra.org.uk

William Barker,
Xenophon's 'Cyropaedia'

Edited by Jane Grogan

Modern Humanities Research Association
Tudor and Stuart Translations 13
2020

Published by

The Modern Humanities Research Association
Salisbury House
Station Road
Cambridge CB1 2LA
United Kingdom

© Modern Humanities Research Association 2020

Jane Grogan has asserted her rights under the Copyright, Designs and Patents Act 1988 to be identified as the author of this work. Parts of this work may be reproduced as permitted under legal provisions for fair dealing (or fair use) for the purposes of research, private study, criticism, or review, or when a relevant collective licensing agreement is in place. All other reproduction requires the written permission of the copyright holder who may be contacted at rights@mhra.org.uk.

First published 2020

ISBN 978-1-78188-982-4 (hardback)
ISBN 978-1-907322-26-6 (paperback)

CONTENTS

	Acknowledgments	vii
	Introduction	1
	Textual Note	68
1	Dedication	73
2	Preface	77
3	The First Book	84
4	The Second Book	115
5	The Institution of Cyrus, the Third Book	133
6	The Discipline of Cyrus, the Fourth Book	153
7	The Discipline of Cyrus, the Fifth Book	175
8	The Discipline of Cyrus, the Sixth Book	201
9	The Seventh Book of the School of Cyrus's Institution	219
10	The Eighth Book of the School of Cyrus's Institution	237
	Glossary	265
	Neologisms	273
	Bibliography	274

ACKNOWLEDGMENTS

I have been extremely fortunate in the support of many scholars, colleagues and friends in preparing this volume, not least in the patience, generosity and excellent advice of the General Editors, Andrew Hadfield and Neil Rhodes, without which this would not have been completed. Their comments and support throughout have been invaluable; any errors are, of course, my own.

The text from which I worked is held at the Huntington Library, California, and I am very grateful to the Huntington Library for a Mayers Fellowship, which allowed me to complete the transcription work and early research on other editions. At the Huntington I am grateful to Steve Hindle, W. M. Keck Foundation Director of Research, and Stephen Tabor, Curator of Early Printed Books, for their advice and support, and to the many staff in the Ahmanson Reading Room and beyond who supported my research and fellowship there.

I also owe thanks to the librarians and staff at St John's College Archive (especially Felicity French and Fiona Colbert), at the Wren Library, Cambridge University Library, Arundel Castle, the Surrey History Centre and the British Library. In researching the Cheke circle at Cambridge, I am particularly grateful to Andrew Taylor, John McDiarmid and Richard Rex for sharing their research and deep knowledge of the world of the Tudor colleges, and to Lucy Nicholas and Ceri Law, who organized an excellent conference on Roger Ascham at St John's College, Cambridge. I also had the great good fortune to return to Churchill College, Cambridge, on a Visiting By-Fellowship, thanks to the kind support of Andrew Taylor, which was a great help in researching Barker at Cambridge. Some of the material in the Introduction has also been presented at research seminars at the University of Sussex, The Shakespeare Institute, the University of East Anglia, the British School at Rome, the University of Limerick and at the Freer | Sackler Gallery, Washington, DC. I am extremely grateful to all those who listened, questioned, and helped me with their comments and advice on the work.

Several scholars were good enough to share their research or expert advice at key points, and their contributions were more important than they know. These include Neil Rhodes, Micha Lazarus, Gabriel Heaton, Heather James, Tom Healy, Davide Amendola and Naomi McAreavey. Jason Powell gently steered me towards a more sophisticated understanding of the earlier Tudor period than my 1590s experience had prepared me for, and Andrew Hadfield, in turn, encouraged this.

I have been very lucky in the kindness and support of two exceptional Xenophon scholars, Noreen Humble and Norman Sandridge, whose work (and lives) continue to inspire me.

Finally, I thank my family, Frank and Eva, Nathan, Maya, my parents, siblings, and my very special nieces and nephews for their own great patience with me, this Xenophon and his 'old noble Persians'.

INTRODUCTION

Xenophon's *Cyropaedia* ('Education of Cyrus') can truly claim to be a forgotten classic. Written during the 360s BCE by a contemporary of Plato's, and a student of Socrates', it narrated the life of the Persian emperor Cyrus II (Cyrus the Great), considered the founder of the Achaemenid empire, adding fictional elements to the established story of a man and his empire. It became standard reading for the best-educated European boys from the fourteenth century until at least the eighteenth century, both within and beyond the schoolroom and university, whether in Greek, Latin or vernacular translation. Its cultural prestige and visibility were at their strongest during the fifteenth and sixteenth centuries, but its influence on poetic, educational and political thought extended well into the seventeenth century, certainly in Britain. The *editio princeps* was printed in Florence in 1516, but was preceded by several important editions of Xenophon's collected works translated into Latin — one of which may well lie behind the present translation as a consulted secondary source. Some of the leading humanists on both sides of the confessional divide edited and/or translated the *Cyropaedia*, including Francesco Filelfo, Henri Estienne, Johannes Camerarius and Philip Melanchthon. In Britain, Xenophon's detail-packed but always readable text influenced kings and schoolmasters, drama and poetry, educational theory and political thought, antiquarianism and travel writing. For early modern readers, the *Cyropaedia* was valued for its political and educational teachings, for its literary style and fictional enterprise, and, of course, as a source of information on the ancient Persian empire — all the more so while European nations sought to cultivate diplomatic and economic relations with its Safavid heirs.

Its very capaciousness and generic indeterminacy added to its attractions, and the early moderns read it as, variously, a mirror-for-princes, political treatise, heroic or panegyrical narrative, fictive history, or as a combination of some or all of those genres. Uniting all these readings, however, was a belief in its didactic purposes and effects. Structurally, the *Cyropaedia* first teaches its readers about the education of Cyrus and the methods and values of a Persian education in Book I, but continues by following Cyrus's career closely for the next seven books, presenting Cyrus's strategies and principles in building and maintaining the Persian empire, the culmination of which (in the *Cyropaedia*) is the capture of Babylon from the Assyrians. Bolstered by endorsements from Aulus Gellius, Cicero and Plutarch, the monarchical empire founded by Cyrus turned heads in early modern Britain, encumbered as it was with a sense of belatedness with respect to the Spanish, Ottoman, and other European and New World empires, but keen nonetheless to join in the global imperial competition. But the early modern reputation of Cyrus, as burnished in the *Cyropaedia*, also benefitted from the positive reports of Cyrus to be found in some of the books of the Old Testament, notably the books of Ezra, Isaiah and Daniel, which identified Cyrus as the conqueror of Babylon, and celebrated his allowing the Babylonian Jews to return to Jerusalem and to rebuild their temple. Unsurprisingly, then, the *Cyropaedia* was cherished by Protestant chroniclers and chronographers, who used it to verify events and dates in the Bible for their accounts of a universal human history, beginning with Adam and Eve. The combination of the biblical and Xenophontic Cyruses was a potent one, and figurations of Cyrus as an 'instrument of Gods power, used for the chastising of many Nations' endured into the seventeenth century, particularly in work of a Protestant polemical cast, such as Walter Ralegh's *History of the World*.[1]

This introduction begins with an overview of Xenophon's *Cyropaedia*, before examining its arrival in English Renaissance culture. The third section discusses this first English translation of it and its social, political and intellectual contexts, beginning with a closer look at the translator, hitherto a little-known figure but one who, this essay argues, was in the vanguard of early modern English Greek studies, specifically as a member of the loyal and enduring circle of scholars around Sir John Cheke. Finally, we will look at some of the uses to which the *Cyropaedia* was put by other writers in early modern England.

Xenophon's *Cyropaedia*

As a fellow student of Socrates and, alongside Plato, one of the main sources we have for the life and thought of Socrates, as well as the author of a string of histories, treatises, political biographies and handbooks, Xenophon had a stature over the centuries that can sometimes be difficult to appreciate today. (The parallel with Plato served Xenophon well until at least the eighteenth century, and an influential strand of the reception tradition (originating with Aulus Gellius and sustained by the likes of Edmund Spenser and John Milton) held that Xenophon was Plato's equal, or even his superior.)[2] The *Cyropaedia*

---

[1] See *The History of the World* (London: William Stansby for Walter Burre, 1614), sig. 4D2. See also Ralegh's Book III, chapters 2 and 3, for several other versions of this idea.
[2] Edmund Spenser, 'Letter to Raleigh' (1590), in *Edmund Spenser, The Faerie Queene*, ed. by A. C. Hamilton et al. (Harlow: Longman, 2007), pp. 713–18. Milton's declaration that Xenophon is Plato's equal appears in *Apology for Smectymnuus*, in Don M. Wolfe et al. (ed.), *Complete Prose Works of John Milton*, 8 vols (New Haven: Yale University Press, 1953–1982), II, p. 891; for similar statements, see also George Puttenham, *The Arte of English Poesie*, ed. G. D. Willcock and Alice Walker (Cambridge: Cambridge University Press, 1936), p. 41, and Sir John Harington's translation of Ariosto's *Orlando Furioso* (London: Richard Field, 1591), sig. ¶3. On Xenophon and Plato see Bodil Due, *The 'Cyropaedia': Xenophon's Aims and*

was, for much of its history, the most admired of Xenophon's works. He also had a reputation as a military general as well as a writer; the two came together most evocatively in his *Anabasis*, an account (in which he writes of himself in the third person) of the safe return of an army of ten thousand Greek mercenaries, under his charge, from Persia to Greece. Capitalizing on his own experiences of Persia, Xenophon must nonetheless have raised eyebrows with the *Cyropaedia*'s presentation of a Persian rather than Greek ruler as an ideal model, barely half a century after the battles of Salamis (480 BCE) and Plataea (479 BCE) had brought the Graeco-Persian wars to an end — the origins of which war Herodotus had ascribed to the rise of Cyrus. Certainly, others before Xenophon had written both of Cyrus and of Persia, but never in such an admiring vein. Xenophon must have known the more caustic account of Cyrus in Herodotus's *Histories*, and may also have used the *Persika* of the Greek doctor Ctesias, who had served the Persian king Artaxerxes from 404 to 398/7 BCE.[3] Perhaps, too, he knew Aeschylus's *Persians* (472 BCE) — or other plays on Persian themes that do not now survive — which treated of the Greek wars with Persia and presented the Greek victory as a political victory for democracy and liberty over Persian monarchy and slavery. Directly or indirectly, Xenophon probably also drew on Persian oral sources, perhaps even narratives he had heard on his own travels in Persia more than a century and a half after the death of Cyrus, when (as the *Anabasis* recounted) in 401 BCE he led an army of Greek mercenaries in support of Cyrus the Younger's attempt to oust his brother, the incumbent ruler Artaxerxes III.[4] Synthesizing these disparate sources and experiences in a highly readable, if generically hybrid, idealization of a Persian monarch was a bold move when the Greek wars with Persia were only a generation or two past. But that was, perhaps, the mark of the man. Despite his strong Athenian

---

Methods (Aarhus: Aarhus University Press, 1989), pp. 144–46.

[3] Although only fragments of it survive, and it has generally been deemed unreliable as a historical source, Ctesias's *Persika* was another major source of information about ancient Persia. Anthony Grafton terms Ctesias 'the first and greatest of Greek travel liars'. Grafton, *New Worlds, Ancient Texts: The Power of Tradition and the Shock of Discovery* (Cambridge, MA: Harvard University Press, 1995), p. 47. The Persian kings were traditionally keen on Greek doctors, and Ctesias had privileged access, as such. See Lloyd Llewellyn-Jones and James Robson, *Ctesias' History of Persia: Tales of the Orient* (London and New York: Routledge, 2010), pp. 1–7, 22–35. On Xenophon and Herodotus, see Due, pp. 17–35; on Xenophon and Ctesias, see Due, pp. 135–39; on Xenophon and Antisthenes see Due, pp, 139–41; on Xenophon's Persia sources, see Due, pp. 141–44.

[4] See Deborah Levine Gera, *Xenophon's 'Cyropaedia': Style, Genre, and Literary Technique* (Oxford: Clarendon Press, 1993), pp. 13–22. These include potential reworkings of Cyrus material in the *Shahnameh*, the Persian book of kings, the popularity of which was revived by the Safavids in sixteenth-century Persia. On a second attempt at 'Asiatic conquest' by Xenophon following his journey to Persia, see Pierre Carlier, 'The Idea of Imperial Monarchy in Xenophon's *Cyropaedia*', in *Xenophon*, ed. by Vivienne J. Gray (Oxford: Oxford University Press, 2010), pp. 327–66 (p. 335).

and Socratic credentials, Xenophon would also end up cultivating relations with that other great Athenian enemy, Sparta.[5] He would eventually be exiled by the Athenians, whether for his association with Cyrus the Younger or for his association with the Spartans soon after, as Diogenes reports, we cannot say.[6] Happily, his estate at Scyllus (on Spartan lands) became a productive and almost mythical space of reflection and writing for him.[7]

Although a classical theory of genre was yet to be fully unfolded, Xenophon shows a strong appreciation for what we might today call creative thinking, or scholarship through creativity. His prose writings are distinctly diverse, and the form of each seems carefully matched to its subject — the *Cyropaedia* most of all, perhaps. That diversity of forms (including Socratic dialogue, a symposiastic exercise, autobiography, military history, a treatise on horsemanship and several substantial explorations of political philosophy) became something for which he was noted, certainly in the early modern period, and it became something of a commonplace to note that in the *Cyropaedia* Xenophon synthesised the range of his thought as well as his forms.[8] Drawing on genres as disparate (and sometimes new) as novel, biography and treatise, the *Cyropaedia* must have been a ground-breaking work even in its own time. Its genre remains difficult to pin down. Although it concerns a historical figure and historical events, its self-evidently fictional moments and dialogue-rich narration (as if written by an embedded journalist, at times) distinguish it from Thucydides, Livy or other prominent historians of the ancient past. Modern critics have interpreted it either as biography, historical fiction, political treatise or novel. More helpful, perhaps, are those evaluations that accept its multiple and hybrid genres. Thus, Deborah Levine Gera also considers it in terms of encomium, romance, military handbook, guide to the political administration of an empire, and didactic work on ethics, morals and education, arguing that it is, in some respects, *all of those things*.[9] Christopher Tuplin, too, side-steps attempts to assign it to any one genre, suggesting instead that it draws on four distinct but familiar

---

[5] Apparently part of a Laconophile (pro-Spartan) circle in late fourth-century Athens, Xenophon also wrote a treatise on the *Spartan Constitution*, and an admiring political biography of Agesilaus, a very successful king of Sparta.
[6] Diogenes Laertius, *Lives of the Eminent Philosophers*, trans. by R. D. Hicks (Cambridge, MA: Harvard University Press, 1925), Book II, ch. 6.
[7] See Tim Rood, 'A Delightful Retreat: Xenophon and the Picturesque', in *Xenophon: Ethical Principles and Historical Enquiry*, ed. by Fiona Hobden and Christopher Tuplin (Leiden and Boston: Brill, 2012), pp. 89–121.
[8] Barker himself notes this: 'All these things which severally be scattered and sparsed in other be almost all in one gathered together in this book of Cyrus's bringing up and going forth, under this title, is indeed a pathway to wisdom, and for matter most fit to be read and known of all Gentlemen, and for fineness of style most pleasant and perfect in his own tongue.' See p. 81.
[9] Gera, *Xenophon's 'Cyropaedia'*, p. 1.

earlier genres (historiography, encomium, Socratic dialectic and technical treatise writing), in the service of didacticism.[10] The early moderns also read it as political biography and mirror-for-princes, in line with other staples of the humanist curriculum such as Isocrates's *To Nicocles* and Erasmus's *Institution of a Christian Prince*.

In other words, the *Cyropaedia* expanded the repertoire of classical genres of political and historical writing, and made questions about genre and the presentation of exemplars — now including foreign (even enemy) exemplars — central to the writing of history and political theory. Xenophon's early modern readers responded eagerly to these questions of genre, style and representation, as well as to his Persian subject. The English title of the first edition of William Barker's translation — *The bookes of Xenophon, contayning the Discipline, School and Education of Cyrus, the noble kyng of Persie* — makes its educational imperative clear, and it is alluded to in admiring terms in some of the major educational texts of the period, including Roger Ascham's *The Scholemaster* (1570). But didacticism extended beyond the schoolroom in humanist thinking, and the *Cyropaedia* inspired early modern writers of fiction and political theory as well. Northrop Frye was not far wrong when, writing on the humanist 'revolution' in education, he grouped together *The Faerie Queene*, Castiglione's *Il Cortegiano* and More's *Utopia* as what he called the 'cyropaedia' genre.[11] What drew the attention of the Spensers, Castigliones and Mores of the early modern world (and their readers) was less the specifics of Cyrus's Persian education, as described in Book I, and rather more the sequences of military and diplomatic successes with both allies and enemies that enabled him to build the Persian empire, culminating in the final defeat of the Assyrians — the major imperial power before Persia, according to biblical as well as historical accounts. Nor was Xenophon unaware of this kind of appeal to his idealized biography of Cyrus, as the much-quoted opening lines of Book I on the failures of so many human models of government testify:

> I have thought oftentimes with myself how many of the wealths hath been overthrown by them which would rather have any form of government than the commons. How oft the rule of one, the power of few, have been of the commons overthrown. How many attempting tyranny some forthwith have been deprived, some reigneth any time, be in admiration as men of rare wisdom and felicity [...] But when I remembered in my mind that Cyrus, being a Persian, had gotten so many sorts of men, so many sundry cities, and so many diverse nations obedient unto him, I was thereby enforced to

---

[10] Christopher Tuplin, 'Xenophon's *Cyropaedia*: Education and Fiction', in *Education in Greek Fiction*, ed. by Alan H. Sommerstein and Catherine Atherton (Bari: Levante Editori, 1996), pp. 65–122 (p. 67).
[11] Troni V. Grande and Garry Sherbert (eds), *Northrop Frye's Writings on Shakespeare and the Renaissance* (Toronto: University of Toronto Press, 2010), pp. 350–51.

forthink the same, because it is neither impossible nor yet greatly hard to have sovereignty over man if a man did it skilfully or wittily. For we know that men willingly have been obedient to Cyrus, whereof some have been distant many days' journey, some many months from him, some that never did see him, some that knew certainly they never should see him yet would become his liege men.

Cyrus's ability to win friends, to charm reluctant allies and even to convert enemies to his cause, his talent for determining resolutions to local geopolitical quarrels to everyone's advantage (including his own), and his military leadership and ability to inspire loyalty and, most of all, obedience, among his soldiers: all of these are winningly explored in Xenophon's text, through orations, exemplary narrative episodes and the larger narrative of Cyrus's coming of age as a leader. When the second, now complete edition of Barker's translation was printed in 1567, it bore a revised title: *The VIII. bookes of Xenophon, containinge the institutio[n], schole, and education of Cyrus, the noble Kynge of Persye: also his ciuill and princelye estate, his expedition into Babylon, Syria and Aegypt, and his exhortacion before his death, to his children*. Its own civil and princely estate in English Renaissance culture was now fully established.

Xenophon in Early Modern Europe

Xenophon's relegation to 'minor' or secondary status today is difficult to understand, considering the sheer command of literary style he achieves, the striking variety of complex political structures he explores, and the sophisticated and original historical analyses he produces, without even mentioning the wide range of his interests and experiences — qualities for which he earned centuries of admiration. He was much favoured in the second-century AD Hellenistic revival, earning commendations from Arrian as well as Plutarch, the latter of whom makes use of a range of Xenophon's writings in the *Moralia* and in his 'Lives' of Agesilaus and Lycurgus.[12] Aulus Gellius's inferences on the antagonistic relationship between Plato and Xenophon also date from this era (*Attic Nights*, 14. 3. 3–4). Early medieval Europe had very little access to Xenophon, however, and his work only re-emerged with any prominence in the late medieval period, travelling not from Greece but from Byzantium. Within the *translatio studii*, Xenophon was among the earliest classical authors to arrive in fourteenth-century Italy, through the efforts of scholars such as Manuel Chrysoloras (author of the most important Greek grammar of the fifteenth century).[13] Xenophon's *Hiero, Apologia Socratis, Hellenica, Anabasis*

---

[12] See Philip Stadter, 'Staying Up Late: Plutarch's Reading of Xenophon', in *Xenophon*, ed. by Hobden and Tuplin, pp. 43–62.

[13] See Paul Botley, *Learning Greek in Western Europe, 1396–1529: Grammars, Lexica, and Classroom Texts* (Philadelphia: Transactions of the American Philosophical Society, 2010),

and *Cynegeticus* were all relatively early arrivals and were quickly clothed in Latin garb, but the *Cyropaedia* was to prove the most appealing.[14]

A Greek manuscript of the *Cyropaedia* seems to have been in circulation in Italy in the first decades of the fifteenth century, but the *editio princeps* would not appear until 1516, from the Giunta press in Florence.[15] But even the *Cyropaedia* circulated more widely in Latin translation than in Greek, and one translation predominated across Europe: that completed by Francesco Filelfo in 1467, and first printed in Milan c. 1477.[16] It would become the standard edition of the *Cyropaedia* used in the popular collected works volumes ('Opera') in which Xenophon's work circulated for the next hundred years and more. The other important fifteenth-century Latin translation of the *Cyropaedia*, that of Poggio Bracciolini (c. 1446), predated Filelfo's, but was disseminated only in manuscript and took the unusual step of dividing Xenophon's eight books into six. Vernacular translations followed, most of which looked to Filelfo (and retained the eight-book structure), although Poggio's formed the copy-text of his son Jacopo's Italian translation in 1476, and of the French translation by Vasque de Lucène (c. 1470), as well as inspiring Lodovico Domenichi's six-book translation. By the mid-1540s, when William Barker began contemplating an English translation, the *Cyropaedia* was well-known and widely available: it could be read in five languages (Greek, Latin, Italian, French, German), and in numerous formats (manuscript and print, folio, quarto, octavo and duodecimo), both individually and in collections of the complete works of Xenophon, often Latin, sometimes Greek, but many in Latin/Greek parallel-text editions.[17] Those collected works did crucial work in establishing the reputation and influence of both Xenophon and the *Cyropaedia* in early modern Europe, by their provision of a range of Xenophon's already-translated texts, and even the

---

and Noreen Humble, 'Parallelism and the Humanists', in *Plutarch's Lives: Parallelism and Purpose*, ed. by Noreen Humble (Swansea: Classical Press of Wales, 2010), pp. 237–65.

[14] David Marsh, 'Xenophon', in *Catalogus Translationem et Commentariorum*, ed. by Virginia Brown (Washington, DC: Catholic University of America Press, 1992), VII, pp. 75–196 (p. 81).

[15] Botley notes Leonardo Bruni's 1407 letter to Pietro Miani seeking a Greek manuscript of the *Cyropaedia* which he believes Miani to possess (*Learning Greek*, p. 10).

[16] The first printed edition of Xenophon's work in Greek was the *Hiero*, a treatise on tyranny, edited by Janus Lascarus (Florence, 1495 or 1496). The *Hiero* was also the earliest of Xenophon's works to be translated into Latin; the *De tyranno* of Leonardo Bruni (pupil of Chrysoloras) was completed in manuscript by 1403, and printed in Venice in 1471. See Botley, *Learning Greek*, pp. 91–92, and Marsh, 'Xenophon', pp. 79–81.

[17] The use of parallel-text editions continued to be crucial to language instruction right into the seventeenth century, as Jason Lawrence points out, whether of Latin or Greek or vernacular languages such as Italian or French. *Who the Devil Taught Thee So Much Italian? Italian Language Learning and Literary Imitation in Early Modern England* (Manchester: Manchester University Press, 2005).

inclusion of biographical materials, on occasion.[18] It is worth bearing in mind, too, that those Continental editions had a long shelf-life, and the Cambridge scholar Gabriel Harvey is probably not untypical in acquiring in 1570 a 1545 Basle *Opera* (in Latin).[19]

The Giunta *editio princeps* (1516) had included most of Xenophon's works in Greek, and major editions of Xenophon's complete works in Latin or parallel-text Greek and Latin had been issued by presses in Milan (1501–1502), Bologna (1502), Lyon (1504), Florence (1516, 1522), Venice (1525), Louvain (1527), Basle (1534, 1545) and Paris, as well as Schwäbisch Hall (1540). The first Greek edition of the *Cyropaedia* to be printed in England, however, appeared in 1613 at Eton, edited by the accomplished scholar Sir Henry Savile (better known as the translator of Tacitus). Unlike the more scholarly Continental editions, this was designed for educational use, probably at Eton and similar schools. The lateness of this edition is perhaps surprising, given that the printer of Barker's English translation was the first printer in England to acquire a set of Greek type, and subsequently was granted the licence to print Greek, Latin and Hebrew books.[20] But only a small number of Greek texts had been printed in England, at least since the 1570s, and Savile's edition marks a new era for the *Cyropaedia* in England. In 1632, a second English translation, by Philemon Holland, was published, of which more later.

Not that vernacular translations of the *Cyropaedia* were hard to come by. Leaving aside the early manuscript translations, by the time Barker came to translate the text, there were at least four printed editions of the Italian translation by Jacopo Bracciolini in existence; de Lucène's French translation had just been bettered by that of Jacques de Vintimille (1547); and a German translation had already been printed in Augsburg (1540). Barker's incomplete English translation would appear in 1552, as would the first Castilian translation (in Salamanca).[21] Barker's complete translation was printed in 1567, and Holland's English translation would eventually be published in 1632, delayed by the sudden death of Prince Henry, its original dedicatee.

Thus, the *Cyropaedia* first reached England late, and in translation, both Latin and vernacular. Xenophon's place in the humanist pantheon of classical authors was by now firmly established, and the appeal of the *Cyropaedia* crossed

---

[18] There was also a flourishing European tradition of excerpting from Xenophon and other authors (e.g. Johannes Sambucus and the Englishman Thomas Beacon).
[19] Michael Isingrin was the printer. See G. C. Moore-Smith, *Gabriel Harvey's Marginalia* (Stratford-upon-Avon: Shakespeare Head Press, 1913), p. 125.
[20] Wolfe had acquired an Italian set of Greek type by the 1540s, and had begun printing with it both in technical books such as Robert Record's book of geometry, *Pathway of Knowledge* (1551), and in more substantial works such as Sir John Cheke's Greek/Latin edition of two sermons by St John Chrysostom (1543 and 1545).
[21] *Las Obras de Xenophon*, translated by Diego Gracián and dedicated to Philip II of Spain (Salamanca: Juan de Junta, 1552).

the scholarly with the political and the educational. Its protean genre(s) and its Persian hero captivated early modern readers, whose interests may also have been inspired by the new visibility of Persia in the early modern Mediterranean world: notably, the recent rise of the Safavids (1501–1722), who had restored the Persian and Median heartland of Cyrus's empire and found themselves locked in a much-discussed conflict with the Ottomans for much of the sixteenth century — a conflict from which Christian Europe sought to benefit. Indeed, accounts of fifteenth- and sixteenth-century European travel to Persia had also become newly and more widely available through print and translation, notably from Ramusio's three-volume collection of Venetian travels (1550–1559) and the early published accounts of Ludovico di Varthema's voyages to the near and Far East from 1502 to 1508.[22] (English travel to Persia was minimal before the Muscovy Company voyages of the late 1550s and 1560s, but some of the early reports were available from 1577, as we will see. But most attractive of all to early modern readers, as we will see, was the *Cyropaedia*'s careful delineation of how Cyrus built his empire, an explanation rooted in Cyrus's education, as Xenophon had it.

But the educational uses of the *Cyropaedia* went beyond the successes of its idealized hero, and its exploration of the link between education and empire-building. Another crucial factor of its appeal was its utility for teaching Attic Greek. There is strong evidence that the *Cyropaedia* was one of the 'elementary texts commonly used by students of Greek' in Europe in the late fifteenth and early sixteenth centuries.[23] Greek learners would have begun their language studies with rigorous study of grammar, aided by the grammars of Chrysoloras or Theodore Gaza, before moving onto texts proper. The Greek New Testament and other Greek scriptural works must have been among the earliest to which learners would be exposed, thanks to their close familiarity with the Latin text. But not long after would come Xenophon, Isocrates and the much-admired orations of Demosthenes, before the more challenging Plato and Aristotle. Some of Xenophon's appeal in this context can be ascribed to the relative simplicity of his language and the clarity of his style, which earned him the soubriquet of the 'Attic Muse' or 'Bee of Athens'. We find this compliment in the very first English translation of his work, Gentian Hervet's translation of the *Oeconomicus* (1532), which explains that 'the noble philosopher Xenophon, the scholer of Socrates, [...] for his swete eloque[n]ce and incredibile facilitie,

---

[22] Giovanni Ramusio (ed.), *Navigazioni e i viaggi*, 3 vols (Venice: Giunta, 1555–1559); di Varthema's voyages appeared in the first volume.
[23] Botley, *Learning Greek*, p. xii. Greek was taught at Eton, Winchester and St Paul's from the early sixteenth century, though not consistently. See also Neil Rhodes, 'Marlowe and the Greeks', *Renaissance Studies*, 27 (2013), 199–218, and Micha Lazarus, 'Greek Literacy in Sixteenth-Century England', *Renaissance Studies*, 29 (2014), 433–58.

was surnamed *Musa Attica*, that is to say, the songe of Athenes'.[24] But students of Greek may also have been exposed to Xenophon by way of Cicero, whose *De Senectute*, another popular teaching text in Latin, included a loose Latin translation of the *Cyropaedia*'s account of the dying Cyrus.[25] (Gaza's Greek grammar in turn provided a loose (Greek) translation of that same section.)[26]

Certainly, Xenophon's work became established in English educational institutions and curricula.[27] We know that the *Cyropaedia* was taught at the Merchant Taylors' school in London (attended by Spenser, Thomas Kyd, Lancelot Andrewes and Thomas Lodge) as well as in Shrewsbury School (attended by Philip Sidney), and Xenophon's work — most likely the *Cyropaedia* — at Westminster School, and Ruthin School in north Wales during the sixteenth century.[28] At Oxford, and especially at Cambridge, it was highly regarded, and found a place in private as well as college libraries, to judge by surviving booklists and probate inventories.[29] As Micha Lazarus and others have argued, Greek studies took root first in 1480s Oxford with Thomas Linacre (who would later teach Thomas More his Greek), but — after a brief period when Erasmus taught Greek there from 1511 until perhaps 1514 — Cambridge in the era of Sir John Cheke became the better-known flagship of Greek studies during the sixteenth century. Cheke, it turns out, proved to be a crucial figure behind the

---

[24] *Xenophons Treatise of Householde* [*Oeconomicus*], trans. by Gentian Hervet (London: Thomas Berthelet, 1534), sig. A1v. The tenth-century Byzantine Greek encyclopaedia, the *Suda*, describes Xenophon as 'Attic Bee', and his command of rhetoric is praised by Demetrius ('On Style'). See *Suda Online* <http://www.stoa.org/sol-entries/xi/47> and Vivienne J. Gray (ed.), *Xenophon On Government* (Cambridge: Cambridge University Press, 2007), pp. 14–20.

[25] See Noreen Humble, '"The Well-Thumbed Attic Muse": Cicero and the Reception of Xenophon's Persia in the Early Modern Period', in *Beyond Greece and Rome: The Ancient Near East in Early Modern Europe*, ed. by Jane Grogan (Oxford: Oxford University Press, 2020).

[26] See Botley, *Learning Greek*, p. 77, who suggests that the presence of the *Cyropaedia* in Cicero's text may well have been what motivated Gaza's version. See also Botley, pp. 91–93, on the use of Xenophon in the learning of Greek. The attractions of his dying words, largely thanks to Cicero, can be seen in other editions of Xenophon's work. For example, the 1582 French translation of Xenophon's Memorabilia made a point of adding that excerpt, and advertising it on its title-page: *Les Memoires de Xenofon* [...] *A la fin desquesls est ajouté le discours de la bien eureuse mort de Cyre l'ayné; Extraut dy mesme Xenofon, VIII. liure de sa 'Cyropedie'*, par 'Ian Doublet de Dieppe' (Paris: Denys du Val, 1582).

[27] A partial translation in manuscript of Xenophon's *Hiero*, once attributed to Queen Elizabeth, survives in Cambridge University Library. See Leicester Bradner, 'The Xenophon Translation Attributed to Queen Elizabeth', *Journal of the Warburg and Courtauld Institutes*, 27 (1964), 324–26.

[28] See T. W. Baldwin, *William Shakspere's Small Latine and Lesse Greeke*, 2 vols (Urbana: University of Illinois Press, 1944), I, p. 385, and Lazarus, 'Greek Literacy', p. 454.

[29] See Elisabeth Leedham-Green, *Books in Cambridge Inventories: Book-lists from Vice-Chancellors' Probate Court Probate Inventories in the Tudor and Stuart Periods*, 2 vols (Cambridge: Cambridge University Press, 1986).

popularity and prestige of the *Cyropaedia* in English educational and scholarly circles. Richard Mulcaster (innovative Master of the Merchant Taylors' school), for example, describes Cheke's interest in Xenophon, and his promulgation of Xenophon among his university students (as well as Mulcaster's own debts to Cheke and his teachings):

> My selfe am to honour the memorie of that learned knight, being partaker my selfe of his liberall distribution of those Euclides with whom he joyned Xenophon, which booke he wished, and caused to be red in the same house, and gave them to the studentes, to encourage them aswell to the greeke toungue, as he did to the mathematikes. He did I take it asmuch for the studentes in S. Johns colledge, whose pupill he had once bene, as he did for us of the kinges colledge whose provost he then was.[30]

The other major work of educational theory in the period, Roger Ascham's *The Schoolmaster* (1570), also had strong connections with Cheke, and originated (its preface informs us) in a 1563 conversation in the rooms of William Cecil, on the subject of contemporary young men's education: 'their to moch libertie, to live as they lust: of their letting louse to sone, to over moch experience of ill, contrarie to the good order of many good olde common welthes of the Persians and Grekes'.[31] Notably, it is Xenophon's Persian education in the *Cyropaedia* that sets Ascham's English agenda and pedagogic values, specifically in response to the contemporary state and values of education, and it is to Xenophon that Ascham returns again and again in *The Schoolmaster* — and even in *Toxophilus* (1545), his treatise on archery and the virtues of non-academic pursuits, where he writes that 'I wolde counsel al the yong gentlemen of this realme, never to lay out of theyr handes. ii. authors, Xenophon in Greke, and Caesar in Latyn, where in they shulde folowe noble Scipio Africanus, as Tullie doeth saye'.[32]

---

[30] Richard Mulcaster, *Positions (1581)*, ed. by Robert Hebert (London: Longman, 1887), p. 241. Neil Rhodes argues that the *Cyropaedia* was probably among the texts gifted by Sir John Cheke to King's College, Cambridge, after he took up his provostship there. See Rhodes, 'Marlowe and the Greeks', p. 207.

[31] Ascham's imperative to write, as he tells it, was augmented when he was reminded by Sir Richard Sackville that 'I heard you say, not long agoe, that you may thanke Syr John Cheke, for all the learninge you have [...] surelie, you should please God, benefite your countrie, and honest your owne name, if you would take the paines, to impart to others, what you learned of soch a Master, and how ye taught such a scholer.' *The Scholemaster* (London: John Day, 1570), sig. B2v. Not long after that conversation, in October 1564, Ascham presented a copy of the *Cyropaedia* to his friend Sir Walter Mildmay (another person present at Cecil's house on the occasion in question, and himself a Privy Councillor under Elizabeth; he would later establish Emmanuel College, Cambridge), along with a Greek copy of Xenophon, inscribing it on 28 October 1564. It was the edition printed by Christian Wechel in Paris (1538–1539), two volumes bound in one, and is now held at the Pierpont Morgan library (060841). Mildmay's support of Greek scholarship would extend to endowing Christ's College, Cambridge, with a Greek lectureship (1569), along with several Greek books (*ODNB*).

[32] Roger Ascham, *Toxophilus* (London: Edward Whitchurch, 1545), fol. 63.

The Schoolmaster was closely aligned with the Chekeian agenda, and attests further to Xenophon's high repute and currency in the Cheke circle, a particularly talented, well-travelled and successful group of scholars and courtiers — 'the goodly crop of Mr Cheke', as Ascham would write in 1553.[33] It was, moreover, a group for whom Greek studies became a vehicle connecting Cambridge — particularly St John's College — and the court: Cheke would be appointed Greek tutor to Prince Edward and Princess Elizabeth, probably on the basis of a series of New Year's Day gifts of Greek/Latin translations of St John Chrysostom he had presented to her father in the early 1540s, and following a series of university and parliamentary appointments, eventually (though briefly) secretary of state to Edward, before the young king's death.[34] William Cecil — who first married Cheke's sister, and after her death remarried Mildred Cooke, one of the famously learned Cooke sisters — would become Elizabeth's most trusted advisor.[35] (Cecil's subsequent seniority at court made him an important supporter of the college and patron of St John's alumni. Cheke was appointed to the visitations of the universities of Oxford and Cambridge in November 1548, for example, not long after Cecil was appointed secretary to Protector Somerset.) Ascham and Smith would also procure diplomatic or governmental positions — with Ascham, for example, boasting that he partook of near-daily discussions of Herodotus in Greek while on embassy to the court of Charles V with Richard Morison in 1550.[36] Even as late as 1570, in publishing his translation of some speeches by Demosthenes (with their significance to the present moment carefully highlighted), Thomas Wilson, another member of the group, would evoke Cheke's Greek scholarship in a dedication to Cecil.[37] For this group, an appreciation for Xenophon's *Cyropaedia* was a given, and was part of the ongoing 'project' of Greek scholarship they shared with Cheke. (I use here the useful vocabulary devised by Colin Burrow for 'reading Tudor writing politically', and specifically, for understanding 'why much early

---

[33] Roger Ascham, in a letter (dated 24 March 1553) to William Cecil seeking to be reinstated to pursue 'reading the Greek tongue in St John's' (p. 352), in *The Whole Works of Roger Ascham*, ed. by J. A. Giles (London: John Russell Smith, 1865), vol. I, part 2, pp. 349–55 (p. 351).

[34] See John F. McDiarmid, 'John Cheke's Preface to *De Superstitione*', *The Journal of Ecclesiastical History*, 48 (1997), 100–20 (p. 118), and on Cheke's Erasmian education of the young Edward, see Aysha Pollnitz, *Princely Education in Early Modern Britain* (Cambridge: Cambridge University Press, 2015), pp. 139–98.

[35] The moving epitaph Cecil wrote for Mildred's Westminster Abbey tomb specifically praises her Greek learning.

[36] See 'Life of Ascham', in *The Whole Workes of Roger Ascham*, ed. by Giles, I, part 1, p. lxviii. Himself another member of the Cheke circle, Morison had translated Frontinus's *Strategemata* (London: Thomas Berthelet, 1539) — which included some of Cyrus's military stratagems — and dedicated the translation to Henry VIII.

[37] Thomas Wilson (trans.), *The Three Orations of Demosthenes* (London: Henry Denham, 1570), sig. [π4]r–v.

modern writing might appear in various ways confused and conflicted about its politics'.³⁸ For Burrow, Tudor subjects 'subsisted within a complex web of what might be called, for shorthand, "networks and affinities", "juridical structures", and "projects"': overlapping and sometimes competing social, political and civic identity-structures, affiliations or interests.) Although Barker shared few 'affinities' or 'network' affiliations with Cheke and his supporters (using the sociopolitical categories as Burrow defines them), he and others developed Cheke's theories and practices in such a way that they might be identified as a diachronic (though not univocal) 'project' of Greek scholarship.³⁹ His career testifies to the sometimes extraordinarily powerful bonds of scholarship that traversed and even superseded confessional divides, and may even have offered protection against political persecution.

Roger Ascham, Richard Mulcaster, William Cecil — and William Barker — had one thing in common. All of them had studied under Cheke, whether at St John's (Ascham, Cecil, Barker) or King's College after he was appointed provost in 1548 (Mulcaster); some were fellows alongside him at St John's (Ascham, Barker) or at other Cambridge colleges (Wilson, Sir Thomas Smith, friends and supporters of Cheke's Greek studies and his promotion of a new method of Greek pronunciation). It is to Cambridge, and this group, that we can trace the inception of the first English translation of the *Cyropaedia*.

William Barker, Tudor Translator

Little of Barker's early or later life is known, but his long association with the Howard family has been key to scholarly surmises about his origins, with good reason.⁴⁰ Born probably in Norfolk during the 1520s, Barker's attendance at St John's College, Cambridge, was originally sponsored by Anne Boleyn, a fact he remembered to her daughter at a trickier moment later in his life.⁴¹ Her

---

³⁸ Colin Burrow, 'Reading Tudor Writing Politically: The Case of 2*Henry IV*', *Yearbook of English Studies*, 38 (2008), 234–50 (p. 234).
³⁹ Burrow defines 'project' as a diachronic collective enterprise, whether material or immaterial in its interests, but certainly 'intergenerational'. Burrow, 'Reading Tudor Writing', pp. 236–38.
⁴⁰ The dominant account of Barker's life thus far is that of R. Warwick Bond, who edited the Roxburghe Club edition of Barker's translation of Domenichi. William Barker (trans.), *The Nobility of Women*, ed. by R. W. Bond, 2 vols (London: Roxburghe Club, 1904–1905). See also the *ODNB*, and Roger Virgoe's biography of Barker in the *History of Parliament* <https://www.historyofparliamentonline.org/volume/1558–1603/member/barker-william-1520–1576>. George B. Parks, Kenneth Bartlett and Jonathan Woolfson also provide some biographical details in their essays or biographical entries on Barker. All of the above sources have various inaccuracies, however. More recently, Richard Rex identifies several important references to Barker in the College archives in his contribution to *St John's College, Cambridge: A History*, ed. by Peter Linehan (Woodbridge: Boydell, 2011), pp. 5–93.
⁴¹ Bond identifies numerous families named Barker living near Howard estates in Norfolk

support may well have been garnered through her Howard cousins and uncle in Norfolk, a theory Barker's subsequent career with Thomas Howard, fourth Duke of Norfolk, might corroborate. Or as one biographer of Boleyn surmises (improbably), it may have come through the recommendation of her chaplain, the physician William Butts (who was also a friend of Cheke's).[42] Either way, Barker probably matriculated at St John's in 1534 or 1535, and managed to stay on after Boleyn's 'crewell deathe' in May 1536 (as he later put it in a dedicatory preface to her mother, Queen Elizabeth).[43] Cheke was a senior fellow at St John's during this period, teaching since 1533 and becoming the first Regius professor in Greek in 1540. St John's had become the leading college for Greek learning, having hosted Erasmus, who lectured on Greek in 1511 until 1513 or 1514, later hiring Richard Croke as the first English fellow in Greek studies, and subsequently through Cheke's leadership and influence.[44] 'Nobody did more to develop Greek studies as a humane discipline in the sixteenth century', as Neil Rhodes has argued; certainly, Cheke's influence endured long after his death in 1557.[45] In other words, Barker studied at St John's at the height of its promulgation of Greek studies under Cheke. Moreover, there are strong indications that Barker was tutored by Cheke himself: the evidence lies in several letters from Ascham to Cheke, and in Cheke's connection with the printer who would subsequently print Barker's translation of Xenophon.[46]

(chiefly Blickling, Kenninghall and Framlingham). The fact that the Latin manuscript translation of Isocrates in the Lumley collection is dedicated to Henry Knyvet (of the powerful Norfolk family) also supports the theory of Barker's Norfolk origins.
[42] See Joanna Denny, *Anne Boleyn: A New Life of England's Tragic Queen* (Philadelphia: Da Capo Press, 2007), p. 215.
[43] '[A]fter that crewell deathe had beraft us / her most desyred lyffe, to the utter dyscoragement of o[u]r purpose begonne [...]' Barker, *Nobility*, p. 87. Before 1544 there were no formal matriculation requirements at Cambridge, so we have no records for this period.
[44] No foundation deed survives giving the precise date upon which the Regius professorships in Greek, Hebrew, civil law, divinity and medicine were established by Henry VIII. Recently, the leadership of St John's in Greek studies in England has been challenged by Micha Lazarus, who argues that Greek 'took root' in 1480s Oxford and soon became a regular part of the *studia humanitatis* in Oxford and Cambridge, partly through the teachings of Englishmen who had undertaken medical studies in Padua and returned proficient in Greek, but especially after Erasmus's lectures in Greek between 1511 and 1513 or 1514. Lazarus also pinpoints Cromwell's visitations in 1535, after which the colleges at both Oxford and Cambridge were expected to teach a reformed curriculum, with an 'immediate investment in Greek teaching from the wealthier colleges at least'. See Lazarus, 'Greek Literacy' (p. 438). See also Rhodes, 'Marlowe and the Greeks', pp. 201–04.
[45] Neil Rhodes, *Common: The Development of Literary Culture in Sixteenth-Century England* (Oxford: Oxford University Press, 2018), p. 40. Rhodes also describes Cheke as 'a principal agent in the translation culture that developed in England in the mid century', and a significant shaping force for 'the generation which supplied the teachers of many of the poets and dramatists who were to emerge during the Elizabethan era' (pp. 40–41).
[46] I am grateful to Richard Rex for this interpretation of a letter Ascham wrote (c. 13 September 1544) to Cheke regarding his hopes for the (fellowship) election of William

INTRODUCTION   15

Locating Barker in the Cheke circle gives his translation of the *Cyropaedia* much greater significance in the cultural history of the Tudor period than it has hitherto received, and reveals more about the connections between the worlds of scholarship, of court and of London printing during the turbulent years of the mid-sixteenth century. Most interesting, perhaps, is the strength of such connections across confessional lines, or during periods of confessional duress — and indeed the strength of conviction of the Cheke circle in Greek studies, even years later. But it also makes Barker's translation part of a larger 'project' of Greek studies and the promulgation of the humanities itself, in Tudor culture, one which undergirded the literary achievements of the era.

Barker's activities upon graduation were previously unclear, but recent scholarship confirms that he stayed on at Cambridge, becoming a fellow of St John's on 26 September 1539, although no details survive about who supported his election, unfortunately.[47] There are clues, however: early in 1540, in a letter to the Master of St John's seeking the election of his pupil John Thomson as a fellow, Roger Ascham cites in support the high opinion of Thomson shared by two other St John's fellows. 'I might bring many testimonies to his good conduct and learning, but I would rather ask you to lend your ear to Sir John Cheke and Barker's judgment in his favour.'[48] Ascham and Barker's careers at St John's, and perhaps their ambitions for life beyond the college, overlapped interestingly in these early days, though a 1544 letter implies that the alliance between them in 1540 had been broken by then. However, traces of it might yet be registered in the very contentious 1542 fellowship election, where Barker did not join the appellants (among whom Ascham was numbered) against the election of the evangelical Thomas Lever, whilst twenty fellows with conservative religious views like him did. Hinting perhaps at some financial need, Barker served for two years as 'lector' in Hebrew (although there is no surviving evidence of his proficiency in Hebrew, nor of others' who served in that role early on); during that time, Ascham was College lector in Greek.[49] By the end of his time at St John's, Barker had attained some degree of seniority within the College, acting

---

Grindall at St John's, in which he appears to invoke Barker and uses the usual form for addressing a fellow's pupil, 'tuus B---'. It is just one strand of several linking Cheke and Barker, as I argue. The letter is printed in *The Whole Works of Roger Ascham*, ed. by Giles, I, p. 54.

[47] Rex mentions Barker's appearance in the College archives, notably Barker's having been paid to travel to London in 1547 probably in connection with a controversial recent act of iconoclasm in the college chapel on 22 September. Rex, in Linehan (ed.), p. 46. Ascham's letters in the early 1540s also make several references to Barker.

[48] From Ascham's 'Letters', in *The Whole Workes*, ed. by Giles, I, pp. 6–9. Ascham's letter to the Master, John Taylor, is dated 9 March 1539.

[49] In 1547 and 1548; from the Bursar's accounts (St John's College Archives, D106/18, sigs 26r, 82v–83r). The accounts show that Barker also served as junior dean over several years. See also note 50.

as junior dean and examiner over several years, and he had been entrusted with College business in London and with collecting rents on College lands in the Huntingdon area.[50]

Barker's contemporaries at St John's in the 1540s included several major figures in Greek scholarship, including the fellows Ascham, Cheke, Thomas Watson and John Redman; other notable students of St John's during Barker's time there include William Cecil (a student from 1535 to 1541, making him an exact contemporary of Barker's), Thomas Wilson, Thomas Hoby and John Dee.[51] Despite the connections he forged with Cheke and his circle, Barker's time at St John's cannot have been entirely peaceful; the 1540s were a turbulent decade for the college.[52] The acrimonious debate surrounding the pronunciation of Greek had its origins in the mid-1530s, just as Barker arrived at St John's: in 1535, following his research with Thomas Smith, Cheke had begun to teach the Erasmian pronunciation of Greek, but this work attracted the censure of (among others) the (conservative) University chancellor, Stephen Gardiner, who in 1542 forbade the use of the new pronunciation.[53] Scholars have seen the pronunciation debates as, in part, a proxy for religious dissension during the difficult years of the 1530s and 1540s, quarrels that broke out at St John's with renewed vigour during the late 1540s, and that saw the college divided between conservatives and evangelicals, with the evangelicals strengthening their hand significantly by the end of the decade, unsurprisingly.[54] But Barker left St John's sometime during the first quarter of the 1549 financial year, college records attest; later that year, he arrived in Italy.[55]

Increasing friction around matters of religion at St John's (and the University) may have played a part in his move away from Cambridge.[56] Barker's own remarks on the subject are vague, and coloured by their new circumstances

---

[50] St John's College Archive, D106/18 fols 43, 99.
[51] The associations between Cambridge — especially St John's — and those who served Edward VI and Elizabeth were strong in the 1530s and 1540s. Dee was a student from 1542, before becoming a fellow and under-reader in Greek at the newly-founded Trinity College in 1546. (The establishment of Trinity College, and the movement of St John's scholars there is relevant to Barker's milieu in the late 1540s; I owe this point to Andrew Taylor.)
[52] See Rex, in Linehan (ed.).
[53] See Rhodes, *Common*, p. 42.
[54] Rex observes an 'evangelical turn' in St John's from the late 1530s onward, but notes that the 'religious strife' at St John's was 'not solely concerned with religion [...] College politics, personal ties, and academic commitments interacted to kaleidoscopic effect'. Rex, in Linehan (ed.), p. 40.
[55] It is surprisingly tricky to pin down the beginning of the financial year, partly because the role of Bursar rotated between the fellows, but the prevailing theory at the Archives is 1 January. This puts Barker out of Cambridge from approximately January 1549; our next record of him is Thomas Hoby's meeting him in Siena in early September 1549, where Barker seems to have been for some period of time.
[56] See Rex, in Linehan (ed.), especially pp. 30–48 (p. 46).

and addressee, appearing in a manuscript translation dedicated to the new queen Elizabeth in 1559: 'So I colde not leave that lyve [at Cambridge] entred by myne owne inclynacon and confyrmed by hyr ma[jes]tes [i.e. Anne Boleyn's] gratious goodnes but made myne habode a good tyme travelenge in sutche maner of Stodye, as then was theare approved. To this I thought good to add an experyence of travell and knowledge off more contris then myne owne.'[57] There may be further evidence to be found in Barker's translation of Gelli's *I Capricci del Bottaio*, where we find some echoes about the value given 'experyence' ahead of that ascribed to academia: as the cooper's Soul tells him, 'it wil not serve now a dayes, to say I have ben at stody, or at the Universitie, for men care not, till they see an experience thereof'.[58] But Barker's time in Cambridge was clearly important to him, and remained part of his scholarly identity: describing himself as 'a forlorn Scholar, not able to keep credit in learning' in the preface to the 1567 Xenophon translation, and even while appealing for pardon of Queen Elizabeth in the thick of the Ridolfi trial examinations in 1571: 'as by hir Majestie's Noble Mother I fyrst began at Cambridge tasting of hir Munificence, so by hir Majestie's Clemencie I may end the rest of my sorowful Dayes ther, (which I have long desired).'[59]

The early autumn of 1549 finds Barker in Siena amongst a small cluster of Englishmen encountered by Sir Thomas Hoby (who had studied with Cheke at St John's, and remained on good terms with him, and whom Barker likely already knew from there), probably studying, and spending time with the growing community of Englishmen abroad.[60] While Barker claims intellectual and cultural reasons for travelling to Italy ('an experyence of travell and knowledge off more contris then myne owne'), young Catholic Englishmen tended to find Italy a more hospitable home during the years of Edward VI's reign. Given his return to England only towards the end of Edward's life, this may also have

---

[57] These comments appear in in the dedication of his manuscript translation of Lodovico Domenichi's *Della Nobilita delle Donne* to the new Queen Elizabeth. Barker, *Nobility*, pp. 86-87. On Barker's reshaping of this translation for domestic audiences, see Brenda Hosington, '"A Poore Preasant off Ytalyan Costume": The Interplay of Travel and Translation in William Barker's *Dyssputacion off the Nobylytye off Wymen*', in *Travel and Translation in the Early Modern Period*, ed. by Carmen G. diBiase (Amsterdam: Rodopi, 2006), pp. 143-55.

[58] The *Fearfull Fansies of the Florentine Couper* (London: Henry Bynneman, 1568), fols 43-44.

[59] William Murdin et al. (ed.), *A Collection of State Papers Relating to Affairs in the Reign of Queen Elizabeth* (London: William Bowyer, 1759), p. 55.

[60] Our chief source here is Hoby's diary, which survives in manuscript (BL Egerton 2148); quotations here are from *The Travels and Life of Sir Thomas Hoby [...] 1547-1564*, ed. by Edgar Powell (London: Royal Historical Society, 1902). Among Hoby's companions during this particular Italian journey were several other translators: besides Barker, Peter Whytehorn (later translator of Machiavelli) and Henry Parker, son of the translator of Boccaccio.

been true of Barker. He spent approximately three years in Italy, travelling extensively but mostly based in Siena, it seems, 'the place of Curtesye'.[61] As Jason Lawrence reminds us, one of the attractions of travelling abroad for Tudor noblemen and those of scholarly inclinations was the opportunity to improve not just one's Italian or French, but also one's knowledge of Latin language and style; Barker certainly sought out scholars and translators of Latin as well as Greek, and brought back at least two Italian texts that he would later translate: Giambattista Gelli's *I Capprici del Bottaio* (1546) and Ludovico Domenichi's *La Nobiltà delle Donne* (1549).[62] He may well have met both Gelli and Domenichi (who had himself recently produced a vernacular translation of the *Cyropaedia* (1548)) in Florence; both were prominent members of the Accademia Fiorentina, 'the vulgar universitie of Florence, when I was ther' (as Barker calls it in his Gelli translation), an institution known both for its favouring of vernacular translation above Latin, and for its reformist tendencies.[63]

Hoby's diary records that he met Barker soon after his arrival in Siena on 3 September 1549, and that Barker joined his company when he travelled to Rome following the death of Pope Paul III in early November 1549, 'as well to the citie as to beholde the manner of the obsequies and the fasshion how they elect an other'.[64] But as events surrounding the election of a new pope dragged on, and having 'throwghlie searcht owt suche antiquities as were here to bee seene from place to place' (both Barker and Hoby show a particularly strong interest in classical inscriptions and epitaphs), the Englishmen moved onwards, sailing to Naples on 10 January 1550.[65] Although the architecture and governance of Naples evoked their admiration (governed, as it was, by the deputy for the Aragonese kings), Hoby decided to travel onwards without his English companions 'for the tungs sake'. But on his return to Naples, he found that Barker had returned to Siena, where Hoby would meet him again in the summer of 1550.[66] (Just a few years later, in 1554 and 1555, Thomas Hoby and his brother Philip would undertake new travels around Italy, this time with Cheke.)

---

[61] In his Domenichi translation; cited by Hosington, '"A Poore Preasant"', p. 144.
[62] The Domenichi text, translated as *A Dyssputacion off the Nobylytye off Wymen*, was only printed in 1904, but a manuscript text was presented to Queen Elizabeth in 1559.
[63] See Enrico Garavelli, 'Lodovico Domenichi, nicodemista?', in *Il Rinascimento italiano di fronte alla Riforma: Letteratura e Arte. Sixteenth-Century Italian Art and Literature and the Reformation. Atti del Convegno internazionale di Londra, The Warburg Institute*, ed. by C. Damianaki, P. Procaccioli and A. Romano (Manziana: Vecchiarelli, 2005), pp. 159–75. See also Jonathan Woolfson, *Padua and the Tudors: English Students in Italy, 1485–1603* (Toronto: University of Toronto Press, 1998), who in speculating on the visits of Thomas Hoby and William Thomas to the Accademia, points out that Gelli's works were on the Papal index of proscribed books, and that Domenichi was imprisoned on charges of heresy in the 1550s.
[64] Hoby, *The Travels*, pp.19–38 (p. 21).
[65] Hoby, *The Travels*, p. 25.
[66] Hoby, *The Travels*, pp. 52, 61.

From the evidence of the *Epitaphia*, the book of Latin epigraphs he collected in Italy, it is clear that Barker's travels brought him to all the major Italian cities north and south, as well as many of the sites of antiquity and tombs of great writers.[67] Published back in England long after his return, it stands as a travel record and an antiquarian record, as well as a record of the mark of his Italian travels on the man. In gathering epitaphs in this way, Barker was emulating an established Italian textual tradition; he likely also knew the living tradition of attaching paper epitaphs to the tombs of the great and the good from the worlds of Italian politics, scholarship and art. The printed marginalia to his 1578 translation of Appian also include personal observations on sites we know Barker to have visited: for example, 'Cuma was a goodly auntient Citie, not farre from Baie, nowe nothing is left but marvellous ruines'.[68] Barker retained an interest in Italy and Italian literature and affairs following his return, including contemporary events such as the Venetian success in reacquiring its former colony Durazzo (ancient Epidamnos) from the Ottomans a few months before the battle of Lepanto in 1571.[69] Long after his return, he retained his Italian interests and kept up his Italian language skills, using any opportunity to practise them — presumably with his avowed friend, the wealthy and well-connected Genoese merchant and banker Benedict Spinola, and less wisely, with another prominent and wealthy Italian banker in London, Roberto Ridolfi.[70] It was 'because he could speak Italian', according to the Bishop of Ross, that Barker was drawn into the thick of the Ridolfi plot.[71] Nor was Barker shy about his language skills, on one occasion asking Ridolfi to translate into Italian some tricky phrases in a letter written in French, in which language he protested less skill.[72] When in 1571 Thomas Howard complained that Barker was an 'Italianyfyd Inglischman', there was some truth to the charge.[73]

Barker returned to England in late 1552 or early 1553, and soon after took up employment in the house of Thomas Howard, Duke of Norfolk, as secretary and sometime tutor to his children.[74] Once again, his reasons for returning are

---

[67] *Epitaphia et inscriptiones lugubres* (London: John Cawood, 1566). On the relationship between Barker's *Epitaphia* and Hoby's diary, see Kenneth Bartlett, 'Thomas Hoby, Translator, Traveler', in *Travel and Translation*, ed. by diBiase, pp. 123–41.

[68] *An Auncient Historie and exquisite chronicle of the Romane warres*, trans. by W. B. (London: Raufe Newberry and Henry Bynneman, 1578), sig. [2X4]v.

[69] Barker (trans.), *An Auncient Historie*, sig. [O4]v.

[70] The evidence from 12 September 1571 has Barker attest that he did not like Ridolfi as he was 'quarrelus' and had dealt poorly with 'myn old Frend' Spinola. Murdin et al. (ed.), p. 92.

[71] From testimony of 6 November 1571; see Murdin et al. (ed.), p. 46.

[72] See Murdin et al. (ed.), p. 115; see also his 'confession' of 23 September avowing 'no great Knowledge' of French (p. 104).

[73] From one of Howard's letters to Queen Elizabeth, after he had been found guilty. Cited in Neville Williams, *A Tudor Tragedy: Thomas Howard, Fourth Duke of Norfolk* (London: Barrie & Jenkins, 1964), p. 247.

[74] Bond (in Barker, *Nobility*, p. 7) argues that the William Barker who appears in a list of

kept vague in the explanation to Queen Elizabeth appended to his manuscript translation of Domenichi:

> W[hi]ch [travelling to Italy], when I had donne my formor fancye of professenge nothinge partyculary was very mutche encreased. ffor theare the Stodye of a gentlema[n] is supposed to consyst in knowledge Suffitient for his owne contentac[i]on, and not to make a gayne thearof, and becom a Servaunt to every mannis Salarye. W[i]th this opynyon I retorned home and put my Selffe to attende uppon the Duke of Norfolke that nowe is, whose Synceritye and noble harte [...] I cannot reache to utter to yo[u]r highnes.[75]

Barker seems to have found himself in the predicament of many well-educated but low-born contemporaries: lacking opportunities for the kind of worldly and professional advancement he sought and saw others enjoy, with those frustrations exacerbated by his experience of gentlemanly foreign travel.[76] And yet Barker quickly became a senior and trusted member of the Howard household, after the death of the third Duke in 1554, and especially after the young Thomas Howard attained his majority in 1559. He was involved in a series of land deals Howard undertook in 1562 and 1563, and was himself granted a substantial leasehold of land, that of the former manor of Dorking in Surrey, in September 1562.[77] He also served as MP, as the 'servant to my lord of Norfolk' in Great Yarmouth (1558, 1559, 1571) and Bramber in Sussex (1563) — the latter very close to Dorking, and soon after his acquisition of land there.[78] As such, he was one of a relatively small number of MPs to have served in four parliaments during Elizabeth's reigns (111), and among another small group (6%) of MPs who were not country gentlemen, lawyers, government officials, courtiers or merchants, but rather 'servants of great men' — not to mention the even

---

28 subjects 'sworne to the Queen's Majestie' on 16 July 1553 — ten days after Edward's death, and when Mary was at Framlingham getting professions of support from her subjects — is likely to be the translator, recently returned from Italy, on the basis that another Howard family connection appears on the list the following day (p. 7, citing Acts of the Privy Council, IV, p. 431). Howard servants certainly appeared on these lists for 14 and 15 July, including Thomas Timperley (a relation of Howard's), Sir Thomas Cornwallis and John Blennerhassett. Timperley, Cornwallis and Barker would subsequently become three of six trustees Howard chose to protect the interest of his son Philip in the Norfolk Liberty, in 1569. See Williams, *A Tudor Tragedy*, pp. 119–20.

[75] *The Nobility of Women by William Bercher, 1559*, ed. by R. Warwick Bond, 2 vols (London: Roxburghe Club, 1904), I, p. 87.

[76] See Jonathan Woolfson, 'Thomas Hoby, William Thomas, and Mid-Tudor Travel to Italy', in *The Oxford Handbook of Tudor Literature*, ed. by Michael Pincombe and Cathy Shrank (Oxford: Oxford University Press, 2009), pp. 404–17.

[77] SD93, Arundel Castle Archives.

[78] See P. W. Hasler, 'Great Yarmouth', quoting the Great Yarmouth records on Barker's appointment in 1559, *History of Parliament* <http://www.historyofparliamentonline.org/volume/1558-1603/constituencies/great-yarmouth>.

smaller group of those who were Catholics, although the numbers are difficult to confirm.[79] But perhaps most tellingly, he was one of the six most trusted members of the Howard household engaged as trustees to the Norfolk Liberty in July 1569, when the fourth Duke took prudent action to ensure a smooth and cost-efficient transfer of the lands to his son Philip, even as he was involved in the risky and ill-starred plans involving Mary Queen of Scots.[80]

Barker may have had prior connections with the Howards, those that brought him the sponsorship of Anne Boleyn, the third Duke's niece. Certainly Barker's association with the Howards was strong, given his long career and senior position in the fourth Duke's household. But it is also clear that he found his employment unsatisfying, in some ways. On several occasions, he characterizes his translation activities as acts of truancy from his duties but in the irresistible service of learning: the second edition of the *Cyropaedia*, addressed to Howard's son, admits that 'for your lordship's further furtherance in learning, and for mine own poor estimation, I should rather have exhibited unto you some thing in Latin than in English. But as a forlorn Scholar, not able to keep credit in learning, I do yet entertain my selfe with studies not altogether devoid of learning, which I offer unto you'.[81] Under interrogation some years later, the sense of frustration turns to rancour: 'O hard Happe of Servants! for besyde the evyll Termes that are given them, they are eyther thought evyll of for their Masters, or evyll delt with for them selfs; and if they be faythfull, then be they Asses perpetuall, and must do as they be driven, or ells be beaten. In such sorte of Service I pore Wretche have ben never accoused of but in Tymes of Adversitie, and then put to do that I did detest.'[82] Exaggerated and defensive though this may sound, it resonates with Henry Woudhuysen's argument about the genuine challenges and intricacies of the lives of generations of tutors/secretaries at aristocratic households, their sense of scholarly ambition but arrested professional opportunity.[83] In his preface to the Gelli translation, Barker foregrounds his ambition, 'that my country men may see how learning may appere in all sortes of men, and they deserve praise whe[n] they will use it well'.[84] Yet the position was one that could bring a certain amount of influence and power as the guardians, advisers, agents and even brokers of their masters'

---

[79] See *Commons, 1558–1603* (in the History of Parliament series), ed. by P. W. Hasler (Woodbridge: Boydell and Brewer, 2006), I, p. 20. See also pp. 28–29. The Howard household records attest that he was a Catholic (see Bond).
[80] SD140/1, Arundel Castle Archives. See also footnote 74 (pp. 19–20).
[81] *The VIII bookes of Xenophon*, trans. by William Barker (1567), sig. A3v.
[82] This appears in an examination document dated 15 September 1571 (cited in Barker, *Nobility*, p. 33).
[83] Henry Woudhuysen, *Sir Philip Sidney and the Circulation of Manuscripts, 1558–1640* (Oxford: Clarendon Press, 1996), pp. 80–81.
[84] Barker, *Fearfull Fansies*, sig. ¶3v.

affairs, and Barker would have played these roles too.[85]

Barker's translation activity spans thirty years, from an early manuscript translation of Isocrates in the 1540s, to his final translation from the Greek (Appian, 1578). Translating from Greek and Italian, and primarily into English, his oeuvre encompasses translations from the classics, Church Fathers, and contemporary Italian scholars and writers. Most advertise his Continental experience to a greater or lesser extent. Although its content is entirely in Latin, the *Epitaphia et inscriptiones lugubres* (London: John Cawood, 1566) presents its author in Italianized rather than Latinized form, as 'Gulielmo Berchero', and presents a collection of Latin epitaphs collected and copied during his Italian travels. (Also in Latin is the undated manuscript translation of Isocrates's 'To Nicocles', dedicated to Henry Knyvet, which ended up in the Lumley collection.)[86] Cawood also printed another significant translation by Barker: his translation from the Greek of a sermon by the fourth-century Church Father St Basil of Caesarea, *An exhortation of holye Basilius Magnus to hys younge kynsemen styrynge theym to the studie of humaine lernynge that they might thereby be the more apt to attayne to the knowlege of diuine literature* (1557) (better known by its Latin title *De legendis gentilium libris*), a sermon advocating the study of ancient Greek authors as supports for Christian devotion. The homily is addressed to his nephews, defending the reading of classical texts as a key part of the preparation of the young Christian for the exegetical challenges of scripture. St Basil's sermon foregrounded the need for commitment to scholarship and 'humaine lernynge': 'yf there be no learnynge, there can be no religion, yf there be no religion there muste nedes be barbarousnes and confusion'.[87] Looking to the Church Fathers for support was a move made by both evangelicals and conservatives in the period, and Barker, for his part, claims St Basil for the Catholic side in a global battle for subjects as well as souls, contextualizing it for his readers as a defence of learning in the face of the recent 'diuisions and factions of religion, not only amonge the Mahomites and Christians, but also in the furthest and unknown partes of the

---

[85] Woudhuysen, *Sir Philip Sidney*, pp. 74–87.

[86] Although it is undated, the reference to 'nostri regis' suggests that it pre-dates 1553, but was more likely composed in the 1540s. The Knyvets were an important Norfolk family, with connections to both the Howards and Anne Boleyn, and the dedicatee may well be the ten-year-old son of Henry Knyvet (1510–1547), later Sir Henry Knyvet of Charlton (following his marriage to Elizabeth Stumpe in 1563), whose grandfather Sir Thomas Knyvet was master of the horse to Henry VIII, and married Muriel Howard, daughter of Thomas, second Duke of Norfolk. Thomas was Anne Boleyn's grandfather — and the Knyvets also had connections to the Boleyns; Henry's uncle Edmund Knyvet's wife Anne Shelton was also a first cousin of Anne Boleyn's on the maternal side.

[87] *An exhortation of holye Basilius Magnus to hys younge kynsemen* (London: John Cawood, 1557), sig. [A5]v.

earth'.[88] Chiding Christians by comparison with Muslims, Barker finds the Christians more 'wycked': 'for wher as they were contente to have one of the auncyent interpretours of the lawe, to be the staye of the same, we wuld have none at all, but that every manne shulde be a prophet at his pleasure'.[89] Detailing at length a prevailing Catholic conspiracy theory about the coincidence of the reformist movement in Germany with the factionalism within Islam that drew new strength from the rise of the (Shi'a) Safavids in Persia in 1501, he presents his translation as both counsel and service to 'the Prynces and states of Chrystendome'.[90] Cheke's translations of the sermons of St John Chrysostom for Henry VIII in the early 1540s, some of which were printed by Reyner Wolfe (printer of Barker's Xenophon), must have been an example for Barker. In 1559, shortly after Barker's translation of that homily, the recently returned Marian exile and staunch Protestant scholar Laurence Humphrey, soon to become President of Magdalen College, Oxford, would argue that translations of well-chosen classical works, especially 'of ethics and politics' were highly to be commended: 'taught privately to individuals, [...] they] bring the grace and order of good laws and practices to the nation as a whole'.[91] Beyond translations from the Greek, Barker also translated two Italian texts by scholars whom he probably met during his travels: Domenichi's *La Nobiltà delle Donne* (1549) and Gelli's *I Capricci del Bottaio* (1548). Both must have been newly-published when Barker encountered them, although it was years later that he undertook translations of them. His manuscript translation of Domenichi's dialogue as *A Dyssputacion off the Nobylytye off Wymen* was not printed until 1904, but was presented to the newly-crowned Elizabeth in 1559.[92]

Although he maintained his scholarly activities and publications, his later life cannot but have been overshadowed by his implication in the trial of Thomas

---

[88] *An exhortation*, sig. A2. Barker's was the first vernacular translation of this patristic text, and the only surviving copies of it in public hands are held, revealingly, in St John's College, Cambridge (where Barker studied), and Cambridge University Library.

[89] *An exhortation*, sigs A2–[A4]. From this Barker further derives '[th]e grosse errour' denigrating learning and scholarship as 'wycked and unprofitable', spurring him to undertake this translation, he writes (sigs [A4]r-v).

[90] 'Nowe for the tumultes that folowed in Alamania I wyll omytte to tell [...] only I will say that they proceded so far, as they raunged from Duchelande to Englande, where was practysed the like mater but wanted the like effecte, only by the myghty power of God, who preserved the royall bloude, from the crueltye of this factious deuyce'. *An exhortation*, sigs [A5]v, [A4].

[91] 'Interpretatio linguarum' ['The translation of languages'] (1559), in *English Renaissance Translation Theory*, ed. by Neil Rhodes, Gordon Kendal and Louise Wilson (London: MHRA, 2013), pp. 263–94 (p. 291).

[92] Hosington argues that Barker's translation omits any reference to its status as a translation, linking this strategy with the semi-fictional personalized framing of More's *Utopia* to inscribe expressions of loyalty to the Howard family into its highly Italianate form. See '"A Poore Preasant"'.

Howard in relation to the Ridolfi plot, and the related plans that Howard marry Mary Queen of Scots and ascend to the English throne alongside her. Arrested and interrogated at the Tower in September 1571, Barker gave evidence against Howard, who would subsequently be executed on his evidence and that of his confederate in the marriage plans, the Bishop of Ross — although the consensus today is that Howard was probably innocent of a full and knowing involvement in the plot itself. As Howard's linguistically-accomplished, longstanding and trusted secretary, however, Barker was in prime position to know of and participate in the plot.[93] Barker himself admitted as much, describing cyphered letters, secret meetings and payments, and even told his interrogators of a set of verses he had given the Bishop of Ross 'in Inglyshe meter', for Mary's eyes, and shared with them the letter of thanks that Mary had sent him in return![94] Most damningly, perhaps, the Bishop of Ross had stated (as we saw) that 'because he could speak Italian', Barker travelled with Ridolfi, 'that the letters might passe without Subscrypcyon of the Duke of Norfolk; abowte which Mattre this Examinat [Ross] and Barker weare twyse with the Spanish Ambassador for that Purpose'.[95] That is, without signing the letters of credit, Barker stood in for Howard in declaring Norfolk's consent to the plot. (In fact, in his own interrogation the Duke of Norfolk alleged that Barker had suggested this key manoeuvre whereby his assent to the plot was inveigled, or at least activated by Ridolfi and Barker, who may, he adds, have had 'sume newe forgyd Practysys' in mind.[96] Denying this charge, Barker would claim that he 'never was but a Messenger, no Persuader nor Practiser', however.)[97] Later bemoaning how he had been brought down by Ross ('a schameles Scot') and Barker, 'an Italianfyd Inglyschemane', Norfolk complained that 'thouh the one was my Mane, yet he wyll now count hymselfe my Master; and so in deade [deed] he maye, for he hathe, God forgyve hyme, maystrd me with hys Untrawthe'.[98]

And yet, despite the understanding of his interrogators that 'Barker was the common Doer in the Practise, as aperith' (as they wrote to Cecil early on), Barker was not submitted to the rack (as other suspects from Howard's household were), and was imprisoned and, ultimately, pardoned and released, with his goods restored to him — in stark contrast to Howard's fate. Closer scrutiny of the State Papers recounting the interrogation sheds some light on this curious leniency towards Howard's secretary in a plot against the queen's

---

[93] Others in Norfolk's service (notably the other secretary, Robert Higford, and Lawrence Bannister) identified Barker as the man who had most dealings with Ridolfi and the Bishop of Ross

[94] Murdin et al. (ed.), pp. 105–07.

[95] Testimony 6 November 1571; see Murdin et al. (ed.), p. 46.

[96] Murdin et al. (ed.), p. 170.

[97] Murdin et al. (ed.), p. 95.

[98] In a letter to Queen Elizabeth, 23 January 1571, in Murdin et al. (ed.), p. 170.

life that saw the execution of the highest-ranking aristocrat in the land — and returns us to Barker's formative years in Cambridge and his activities as a scholar and translator. For Barker's two principal interrogators, Sir Thomas Smith and Thomas Wilson, had both been close allies and friends of Cheke, and supporters of his Greek studies project, as well as being beneficiaries of the patronage of another St John's alumnus and former pupil of Cheke, Sir William Cecil, now Lord Burghley, Elizabeth's longstanding Secretary of State and chief advisor. Barely a year previously, Wilson had finally published English translations of a set of sermons from Demosthenes, dedicated to Cecil with pages of fulsome commendation of Cheke, their mutual friend and teacher.[99] Smith and Wilson were friends, and Smith had worked closely and prominently with Cheke in the project for the reform of Greek pronunciation that had proved so contentious in the 1540s, as well as retaining his interests in linguistic reform and classical political theory.[100] It seems highly likely that Wilson and Smith knew Barker as well as his Greek translating activities through Cheke — or certainly that they knew Barker's connection with Cheke. And it is also highly likely that Cecil knew Barker, as contemporaries at St John's, and perhaps selected Wilson and Smith for the task with precisely this knowledge in mind.

After their initial judgement of his guilt (and they wrote to Cecil several times about this), they began to nuance their assessment to present an incapacitated Barker. 'As for Barker', Smith continued, 'I think he hathe and will confess to so myche as his Wit will serve him; and yet, as it apearith, hath bene the most Doer betwixt the Duke and other Forene Practisers.'[101] Soon, Smith would push this narrative further by suggesting that Barker was 'rather, it may seme, chosen for Zele then for Wit'.[102] And yet, in an early letter to Cecil (and partly in response to letters received from Cecil enquiring specifically about Barker), his interrogators described his 'Folish Obstinacie': '[h]ow be it', they wrote, 'he will com of with the Trewth, so far as his Wit will serve hym, at the last, we suppose; especially seing the Duke confesseth so mych of hym, wherewith he may be charged'.[103] Barker certainly recovered his wits and memory sufficiently to give ample testimony against Howard in the months that followed — as

---

[99] *The Three Orations of Demosthenes*. Wilson also makes the contemporary political relevance clear, especially in the sermons arguing against Philip of Macedon (by which Cecil and other readers were to understand Philip of Spain).
[100] Smith's *De recta et emendata Linguae Graecae pronuntatione*, written in 1542, was first published in 1568.
[101] 17 September, Sir Thomas Smith's letter to Burghley; see Murdin et al. (ed.), p. 95.
[102] Smith continues immediately: 'As our Opinion was, so it remayneth: That only the Duke's folish Devocion to that Woman, kept the Fire kyndlyng still, although ones qwenched. They that should lay Sticks to it, were afraid, and durst not, although thei wold fayne.' Murdin et al. (ed.), pp. 101–02.
[103] Letter of 8 September from Ralph Sadler, Thomas Wilson and Thomas Smith; see Murdin et al. (ed.), p. 150.

Howard would remember to his children in one of his final letters to them, in which he exonerated both his other senior secretaries, Bannister and Higford, from blame, and instead laid it squarely at the door of Barker and the Bishop of Ross, Mary's intermediary: 'But the Bishop of Ross, and especially Barker, did falsely accuse me, and laid their own treasons upon my back. God forgive them as I do, and once again I will you to do; bear no malice in your mind'.[104]

It looks very much as if Barker had the support of his interrogators, was spared torture through their offices and agreed with them a line of defence that would exonerate him in return for betraying his employer. One must suspect some scholarly collusion in the way that Barker, a skilled linguist and translator from a small, and college-centred community of English scholars of Greek, was deemed by his examiners, themselves part of that community, to have been too foolish or witless to have been guilty of conspiracy. The prior affinities between Barker and his examiners, their shared involvement in the Chekeian project of the advancement of Greek learning, the likelihood that Cecil, too, knew him, and the astonishing in-joke — as it must surely have been — that a scholar who had already contributed so much to the Chekeian project of Greek studies lacked the 'Wit' to know or participate fully in the plot for which his employer was executed, presents astonishing proof of the power of those scholarly bonds forged at St John's College, Cambridge, and of the shared humanist commitment to Greek and translation studies, to influence and connect people even as pragmatically and politically polarised as a suspect and his examiners in a notorious case of treason, a plot against the queen's life.

Barker was eventually released, though not before spending two years in the Tower. His location and activities after the break with the Howards were previously unclear, though it now seems likely that Barker retired to his lands in Dorking; the lease ran its full course, and was next assigned to two of Howard's old retainers.[105] He was pardoned on 17 May 1574, and his goods restored to him a few months later; a 1576 case in the court of requests hints at his reduced circumstances.[106] One last translation from the Greek, this time of Appian, appeared in 1578, printed by Henry Bynneman, who had previously printed Barker's 1568 translation of Gelli's *I Capricci del Bottaio* (*The Fearefull Fansies of the Florentine Couper*). Signed only by W. B., the ESTC seems justified in ascribing it to Barker, both because of its profile and because of the printer — and, perhaps too, because of the text's subtle engagement with

---

[104] Cited in Williams, *A Tudor Tragedy*, p. 245. Higford (Norfolk's other secretary, who had, like Barker, served as MP in Norfolk's boroughs) was charged with complicity and sentenced to death.

[105] Howard's trusted surveyors William Dyx and William Cantrell. SD128, Arundel Castle Archives. A handsome 1566 New Testament, inscribed by Howard and given to Dyx shortly before his execution, is also held at Arundel Castle.

[106] See Virgoe.

Barker's circumstances. His paratextual presence is strikingly conspicuous here, with a flurry of printed marginal comments throughout, several replete with memories of his visits to sites Appian mentions. Yet there is no mention of the translator on the title-page, and instead Bynneman takes full control of the dedicatory epistle to Christopher Hatton, describing the subject of the work as follows: 'How God plagueth them that conspire against their Prince, this Historie declareth at the full.' Moreover, Bynneman writes, 'this Authoures only purpose is, to extoll the princely rule, and to procure the safetie of the people' (sig. A2v) — a nod, perhaps, for readers in the know. Certainly, some did; an epitome of Appian by Thomas Newton appeared just two years later, describing it as the work of 'a studious Gentleman of this our country in his trauaile into Italye there happilye founde and by him sensiblye translated', and discussing Newton's conference with Barker about it.[107]

We know almost nothing of the end of Barker's life; the name, unfortunately, is a common one. R. Warwick Bond has speculated about three likely William Barkers: one who died in Smithfield in 1597, one in Shropshire in 1595 and the William Barker granted a vicarage near Chester in 1585, but there are also William Barkers who die on likely dates in places more closely associated with our translator (i.e. Norwich, Great Yarmouth and northern Sussex, in the vicinity of Dorking).[108] Certainly, it seems that the lease of land in Dorking and Capel ran its course, and a new lease began exactly twenty-one years later, in May 1583, to lessees also drawn from within the Howard household. So it seems possible and perhaps even probable that Barker retired to a quiet life in Dorking with family, perhaps dying in the late 1570s or early 1580s, when he must have been in his late fifties. One way or another, there was merit in keeping a low profile, even after that one final translation made clear that Barker's 'wits' were in as fine working order as they had been throughout his life and career as a scholar and one of the most prolific and under-recognised English translators from Greek of his era.

The Text

Date and Dedication

No date appears on the title-page of the first edition of Barker's translation,

---

[107] *A View of Valyaunce* (London: Thomas East, 1580), sig. A4.
[108] The name is a common one; even in 1530s Cambridge there was another William Barker, a fellow at Gonville and Caius. Bond finds hints of state support in the situation of his three candidates, noting that in all cases 'in one way or another his old age was provided for', implying state favour, presumably for having given evidence against Howard. Barker, *Nobility*, p. 42.

a small-ish octavo titled *The bookes of Xenophon, contayning the Discipline, Schole, and Education of Cyrus the noble kyng of Persie*, with the running title 'The schole of Cyrus'. It was printed by Reyner Wolfe, a highly skilled Protestant immigrant printer whose previous work included Cheke's Chrysostom, who owned the first set of Greek type to be used in England, and who held the licence to print Greek, Latin and Hebrew texts from 1547 to 1553.[109] A reasonably large number of copies of the first edition survive, as the Textual Note explains. The ESTC editors suggest it may have been printed in 1552; this can now be refined further to sometime in the last few months of 1552 or the first five or six months of 1553. Dedicated to William Herbert, recently made Earl of Pembroke, it seems to have been a bid for patronage and employment during the final months of Edward VI's reign. Pembroke was one of the most important figures in Edward's court, the man primarily responsible for the toppling of Protector Somerset and who would soon join with the Earl of Warwick (later Northumberland) and Edward himself in attempting to divert the succession from Edward's half-sister Mary to his cousin, Lady Jane Grey. Given the titles by which Herbert is invoked in the dedicatory epistle, it must have appeared after 10 and 11 September 1551, when Herbert was made Baron Herbert of Cardiff and Earl of Pembroke, and before July 1553, when the new Queen Mary rescinded his presidency of Wales. Yet despite his awareness of Herbert's recent new titles, Barker makes no mention of several important events in Herbert's life in 1552 and 1553, which may narrow the possibilities a little further. On 15 May 1553 Herbert supported an attempt to block Mary's likely succession, when his son and heir Henry Herbert (mentioned in Barker's epistle) married Katherine Grey on the same day that her more famous sister, Lady Jane Grey, married the son of Herbert's ally, the Duke of Northumberland; this gives us a slightly earlier *terminus ante quem* for Barker's edition, I think. As for a *terminus post quem*, Herbert's wife Anne had died on 20 February 1552, and her funeral at St Paul's on 28 February had been notably grand; though she is the mother of the Herbert children referred to in Barker's epistle, the absence of any mention of her death or of Herbert's second marriage in May 1552 may indicate that it was not in the recent past (or not known to Barker, still abroad), perhaps bringing us into the later months of 1552 or early 1553. Another striking absence is Barker's failure to refer to Herbert's hosting of King Edward VI at Wilton in August 1552, particularly relevant for the text he was translating (at least to judge by the several copies of the *Cyropaedia* presented to Edward).[110] We can tentatively,

---

[109] On Reyner Wolfe, see Peter Blayney, *The Stationers' Company and the Printers of London, 1501–1557* (Cambridge: Cambridge University Press, 2013), Cyndia Susan Clegg, *Press Censorship in Elizabethan England* (Cambridge: Cambridge University Press, 2004), pp. 22–25, and Andrew Pettegree's entry on Wolfe in *ODNB*.
[110] These include the 1547 Paris translation by Jacques de Vintemille (BL Royal c. 48.f. 3), and Louis LeRoy's translation of a compilation of Isocrates and the *Cyropaedia* (presented in 1550).

I suggest, narrow the date of publication to sometime between September or October 1552 and 15 May 1553.[111]

This first translation of the *Cyropaedia* was incomplete: it contained only the first six books (of eight). There was already a Continental tradition that rendered the *Cyropaedia* in six books: Poggio Bracciolini's abridged Latin version, which had been translated into Italian in turn by his son Jacopo (1476). But Barker followed the standard eight-book model used by Filelfo, so although it was not acknowledged anywhere in the text or paratexts, the translation was incomplete. This in itself was not particularly unusual: William Watreman's 1555 translation of Johannes Boemus's *Omnium gentium mores, leges, et ritus* (1520) as *The Fardle of Facions* only translates the first two books, for example, as did the first English translation of Herodotus, by B. R. (1584); in each case the paratexts only glancingly acknowledged that the text was incomplete. It may have allowed the printer to hedge his bets about the potential sales, as well as creating a secondary market for the full edition. (An educational and popular rather than explicitly scholarly cast might be guessed from Wolfe's exclusion of any Greek type from either edition, despite having the resources.) However, Thomas Berthelet had done well with his editions of the first English translation of Xenophon's *Oeconomicus* (1532), issuing four editions before 1552, and the *Cyropaedia* surely promised to be even more popular, given its prominence; that Barker had not finished translating all eight books now seems more likely, and his explanation of precipitate publication in the dedicatory epistle is more believable despite the conventionality of such assertions.

Barker's readers would have to wait almost fifteen years for the complete text, also printed by Wolfe, in another sturdy octavo, in 1567, now titled *The VIII. bookes of Xenophon, containinge the institutio[n], schole, and education of Cyrus, the noble Kynge of Persye: also his ciuill and princelye estate, his expedition into Babylon, Syria and Aegypt, and his exhortacion before his death, to his children*. The additional details of Cyrus's campaign in Babylon and his death-bed advice to his children are in books VII and VIII, the latter of which was already a well-known passage through its use in Cicero's *De Senectute*. At this point Barker had been working for the Howard family for some time, so in dedicating the second edition to the ten-year-old Philip Howard, in an epistle signed from Howard House, he cements his connection with the Howards, and his senior position within the household.[112] (Although Thomas Howard professed Protestant beliefs (and had for a while had John Foxe as his tutor), the Howards were by tradition the most prominent and elevated aristocratic Catholic family in the land; Barker's young dedicatee would later be martyred,

---

[111] This dating late in Edward's reign also fits with the career of Wolfe, whose activity slowed down suddenly and significantly during Mary's reign.
[112] The original dedicatory epistle to William Herbert (who was still alive) was also reprinted alongside it.

following his conversion as an adult.) More copies survive of the 1567 edition, including (perhaps revealingly) in three Cambridge libraries: Trinity College and Christ's College libraries, as well as the University Library.

Barker's own account of the origins of his translation in the dedicatory epistle to the second edition is brief but more credible than many such assertions: 'Indeed I must confess this translation to be done before I went into Italy, finding six books of the same enprinted when I did return, not by my desire but only by the courtesy and goodwill of the Printer, a furtherer of good learning' (p. 75). Although Barker's profession of ignorance of the printing is a standard paratextual gambit, there is no reason not to believe that the first six books were translated before he left for Italy, particularly given Barker's position and intellectual circle at St John's College, Cambridge, during the 1540s; they were most likely begun, at least, while he was still at St John's, and printed (as we will see) through the offices of Cheke. Interestingly, the translation gets scrappier towards the very end of Book VI, perhaps a sign of it having been finished in haste — Barker may not have been entirely unaware of efforts to publish it as he travelled. We can also credit his further statement that the last two books were translated at a later stage, and not simply because Barker explains in 1567 that '[f]or these two later books I have often times been spoken to of diverse of my learned friends, whose requests at length I have satisfied'. The vocabulary of books VII and VIII differs markedly from the preceding six books, particularly the technical military terminology. Not only that, but some of the terms and phrases in the final two books bear strong marks of Barker's Continental experience (see Textual Note). The second edition shows clear signs of haste: the quality of the translations of books VII and VIII is significantly lower than that of the first six books, more compressed and more error-strewn; we also find a number of compositorial errors in the second edition, rare in the first (although Wolfe appears to have used some of the sheets from the 1552 edition in reprinting books I to VI in 1567).[113]

Printer

The identity of the Catholic Barker's first printer — a well-connected Dutch Protestant — is worth pausing over, and gives further insight into the ambitions and reach of the Cheke circle, as well as highlighting how early the kinds of cross-confessional alliances in the name of scholarship that have become more celebrated in regards to the Republic of Letters in the seventeenth century emerged.[114] Born in the Netherlands (Gelderland), Wolfe appears to have settled

---

[113] For example, the first edition has a mistaken catchword on sig. [J8]v, a mistake reproduced in copies of the second edition I've seen.
[114] See, for example, Carol Pal, *Republic of Women: Rethinking the Republic of Letters in*

in London with the support of Thomas Cranmer. But again there is a curious Anne Boleyn connection: Cranmer had served for a time as chaplain to the Boleyn family before becoming Archbishop of Canterbury in 1533, and it was through the support of Anne Boleyn in 1536 that Wolfe became a freeman of the Stationers' Company. Wolfe had an impressive career ahead of him: in 1547 he would acquire the royal patent to print Latin, Hebrew and Greek, a lucrative licence which included grammars and textbooks. Wolfe travelled frequently to Continental Europe: he acquired his Greek type from a foundry in Basle, for example, and regularly travelled to the Frankfurt Book Fair to sell and acquire books.[115] After the accession of Mary his press seems to have ground to a halt, presumably partly because of his connections with Cranmer (who is known to have used Wolfe as a messenger to Heinrich Bullinger in Zurich in 1536, for example, as well as procuring him books on the Continent). In fact, Cranmer's widow sought and found significant support from Reyner and Joan Wolfe after her husband's execution, and was still living in their household upon the death of both in the 1570s, attesting to the close relationship between Cranmer and Wolfe.[116] Wolfe was not idle during Mary's reign, though, and seems to have maintained good diplomatic relations with the regime, with New Year's gifts exchanged in 1557.[117] Working with John Cawood and others in the founding of the Stationers' Company, he became only its second Master, after its incorporation in 1557, serving three more terms (1564, 1567, 1572).

The connection between Barker and Wolfe was most likely facilitated by Cheke, Barker's sometime colleague at St John's (and another friend of Cranmer's during Cheke's time as tutor to Prince Edward). Cheke and Wolfe were friends, into the 1550s, despite Cheke's exile; Wolfe's first major venture as a printer was the 1540–1543 Greek/Latin edition of St John Chrysostom's sermons, translated (into Latin) by Cheke, and the first complete text published in Greek in England. It must have been a high-profile work at St John's in

---

the Seventeenth Century (Cambridge: Cambridge University Press, 2012), Kevin Sharpe, *Reading Revolutions: The Politics of Reading in Early Modern England* (New Haven: Yale University Press, 2000), and Anne Goldgar, *Impolite Learning: Conduct and Community in the Republic of Letters, 1680–1750* (New Haven: Yale University Press, 1995).

[115] See William H. Ingram, 'The Ligatures of Early Printed Greek', *Greek, Roman and Byzantine Studies*, 7 (1966), 371–89 (p. 376).

[116] See *ODNB* (Cranmer), Clegg, *Press Censorship*, p. 24, and Mary Prior, 'Reviled and Crucified Marriages: The Position of Tudor Bishops' Wives', in *Women in English Society, 1500–1800*, ed. by Mary Prior (London: Routledge, 1985), pp. 98–99.

[117] See Clegg, *Press Censorship*, p. 23, Ian A. Gadd, '"A Suitable Remedy?" Regulating the Printing Press, 1553–1558', in *Catholic Renewal and Protestant Resistance in Marian England*, ed. by Elizabeth Evenden and Vivienne Westbrook (Burlington, VT: Ashgate, 2015), pp. 127–42 (p. 138). The ESTC lists only three works published by Reyner Wolfe during Mary's reign, all in 1553 — that is, it is likely that they were printed in the first half of the year while Edward still reigned, and two of them were books he had already printed: Lily's *Grammar*, Record's *The Castle of Knowledge*, and a 1556 almanac.

the early 1540s, while Barker was a fellow there. Wolfe had strong interests in classical learning — Barker seems to acknowledge as much in calling him 'a furtherer of good learning'. So it seems highly likely that Cheke made the introduction or recommendation of Barker to Wolfe. Not only that, it was this crucial connection with Wolfe, probably brokered by Cheke, that furnished Barker with his publishing career as a translator: all of his printed translations can be traced back to this original connection with Wolfe. Although Wolfe seems to have published only three works during Mary's reign (and these possibly in the six months of 1553 before Mary's accession), John Cawood, the royal printer under Mary and a printer with whom Wolfe collaborated in setting up the Stationers' Company, printed Barker's 1557 translation of St Basil, as well as his 1566 *Epitaphia*. (Wolfe and Cawood remained close over the years: Cawood was granted the reversion of Wolfe's license for printing Latin and Greek books and grammars upon Wolfe's death, and Cawood's son Gabriel was a witness to Wolfe's widow's will.)[118] Barker's complete translation of the *Cyropaedia* was printed once again by Wolfe in 1567 — during which year Henry Bynneman is thought to have worked with Wolfe. And it was Bynneman who printed Barker's 1568 translation of Gelli's comic-philosophical dialogue (a work that fell outside Wolfe's usual interests), as well as the 1578 translation of Appian's *Iberika*, five years after Wolfe died.

In other words, Barker's entire print output of translations was produced by or through the offices of Protestant printers in London, a network he most likely first accessed through the patronage of Cheke. That crucial intellectual and pragmatic patronage continued to support Barker long after his Cambridge days, and indeed after Cheke's death in 1557. By contrast, at no point do Barker's print publications owe much to his position in the Howard household, beyond that dedication to Philip Howard of the second edition of his Xenophon. Howard connections are likely only in the two manuscript translations that survive (each in single copies): a presentation copy of a translation of Domenichi's *La Nobiltà delle Donne* which he presented to Queen Elizabeth in 1559 (presumably while Elizabeth was on summer progress at Nonsuch palace, then in the hands of Henry Fitzalan, Howard's father-in-law), and the Latin translation of Isocrates, dedicated to Henry Knyvet, which survives in the Royal collection at the BL.[119] Not only did Barker benefit from the skills of one of the best printers in London for his translations of Xenophon, then, but his whole career as a translator continued to be sustained by his membership of the Cheke circle as a young man in 1540s Cambridge.

---

[118] See H. R. Plomer (ed.), *Abstracts from the Wills of English Printers and Stationers, 1492–1630* (London: The Bibliographical Society, 1903), pp. 19–22 (p. 22).

[119] It is possible that that translation found its way into the Lumley papers through the fourth Duke's first wife, Mary Fitzalan — daughter of Henry Fitzalan, 12th earl of Arundel, and sister of Jane Lumley (who also, famously, completed a translation of both Euripides's *Iphigenia* and Isocrates's 'To Nicocles').

Copy-Text

From what language did Barker translate the *Cyropaedia*, and can his copy-text be identified? From his professional profile as both a scholar and a translator, it's clear that Barker was fully capable of working from the Greek, and that doing so complied with his scholarly principles and with those of Cheke and his circle. Barker's comment in the first edition that the translation can be used 'both to learn the matter, which is good and pleasant, and also to learn to turn Latin out of English' has been misinterpreted by R. W. Bond as a cover for his having translated from the Latin; Filelfo's Latin translation of the *Cyropaedia* was common enough to have been used alongside it, rather than indicating the kind of double-translation exercise that Ascham favoured.[120] (Double-translation was a language-learning exercise that involved students translating a text from the target language (Latin, for Ascham, expounding this method in *The Schoolmaster*) into their own tongue, and then retranslating that back into the target language.) Bond goes on to notice strong similarities between the later stages of Barker's Book VIII and Lodovico Domenichi's Italian translation of the *Cyropaedia* (1548) — perhaps partly inspired by Barker's likely encounter with Domenichi not long after, and his translation of another Domenichi work. Once again, however, the evidence is weak: although there are some verbal echoes, the passage in question (on the immortality of the soul) is particularly well-known and had been excerpted and re-translated into French by Louis Le Roy, for example, in his edition of Plato's *Phaedo* (as it does indeed bear comparison with Plato's theory of the soul), as well as having been loosely paraphrased by Cicero in *De Senectute*. So we cannot set too much store by such echoes.

But this is not to say that Barker did not use a Latin translation as part of his undertaking. Rather, it is most likely that he used a parallel-text Greek and Latin edition as his copy-text, the Latin text being that of Filelfo's translation. But Barker's syntactical structures, lexical choices and often word order reveal that Greek was the primary language from which he worked — even leaving aside his connections to Cheke and the Chekeian Greek project.[121] And translation itself interested him: he often shows an interest in other translations of the works he undertook. This is most evident in his Appian, which makes frequent and knowledgeable comments about the deviations from the Greek

---

[120] Sig. [A7] — p. 82. Bond (ed.), *The Nobility of Women*, I, p. 8. Filelfo's Latin translation would be 'thoroughly revised' by the French scholar-printer Henri Estienne in 1561 (Marsh, 'Xenophon', p. 125). On Filelfo's translation and the Greek texts he worked from, see Jeroen de Keyser (ed.), *Traduzioni da Senofonte* (Alessandria: Edizioni dell'Orso, 2012) and de Keyser, 'Elucidation and Self-Explanation in Filelfo's Marginalia', in *Self-Commentary in Early Modern European Literature, 1400–1700*, ed. by Francesco Venturi (Leiden: Brill, 2019), pp. 50–70.

[121] One very brief example: *Cyrop.* I. ii. 3: Barker translates τα τε βασιλεια literally as 'royal things' rather than the 'royal palace' found in Filelfo.

in current Italian and Latin translations. Nor was this necessarily unusual. Interestingly, when Philemon Holland came to translate the *Cyropaedia* years later, by request of King James himself, this highly respected translator of Plutarch and Suetonius (whose Xenophon translation has largely been preferred by scholars to that of Barker) seems to have been working closely with a copy of Barker's translation, as well as with Greek and Latin texts.[122] In other words, it seems likely — and not unusual — that Barker had the benefit of (Filelfo's) Latin as well as Greek texts of the *Cyropaedia* in translating, both probably within the very copy-text he was using: one of the many collected works of Xenophon printed on the Continent in the 1530s and 1540s. To venture one step further, it seems likely, on balance, that he was using the parallel-text Greek/Latin edition of Xenophon's *Opera* printed in Basle by Nikolaus Brylinger in 1545, for reasons detailed below.[123]

By the 1540s, a good number of editions of (more or less complete versions of) Xenophon's *Opera* had been printed, beginning with the Milanese edition of 1501–1502 (which included the *Cyropaedia*), then Bologna (1502), Lyon (1504, 1511, 1531), Florence (1522, 1527) and Venice (1525). But the largest number of editions of Xenophon's complete works in the period came from Basle, large, handsome folios including those printed by Cratander (1534), Brylinger (1545, 1555, 1568), Isingrin (1545, 1551) and Chateillon (1551, 1553).[124] Unfortunately, the copies surviving in the St John's College Library post-date Barker's translation, so we cannot identify his copy-text as one that survives there. But some intriguing traces of the availability of copies of Xenophon in Cambridge during the mid-sixteenth century do survive, and give a picture of a rich and varied set of offerings for would-be readers of the *Cyropaedia*, both individually and in collected works, in Greek, Latin and the vernacular, often in Continental editions. Editions of Xenophon's works would have been in demand in Cambridge, even if we acknowledge an element of boasting in Ascham's declaration to his friend John Brandisby in 1542 or 1543 that 'Herodotus, Thucydides and Xenophon are more

---

[122] See the notes to this edition. He also consulted John Bingham's translation of Xenophon's *Anabasis*, it seems, probably to help with some of the military vocabulary, as we see with a note on 'crest', glossed by Philemon Holland as 'Or plume, as saith Bingham', *Cyrupaedia, or The Institution and Life of Cyrus, King of Persians* (London: for Robert Allot, 1632), sig. [T3]v.

[123] Brylinger had some English connections, notably with John Foxe, who was in Basle, working for the city's printers, for a few years in the late 1550s: Brylinger would publish John Foxe's first attempt at an English martyrological history in 1559 and key reformist works such as Johannes Sleidan's *Four Empires* (1558), but he had also published parallel-text (Greek and Latin) editions of the Greek New Testament and Homer, and an important anthology of Latin drama (1540), which made its way to England; a performance of one of the plays at Christ's College Cambridge was dedicated to Cranmer. Cheke, too, would pass through Basle in 1554, during his Marian exile.

[124] See Marsh, 'Xenophon', especially p. 81.

read now than Livy was [five years previously]', and that Cambridge students and scholars 'talk now as much of Demosthenes as they did of Cicero at that time. There are more copies of Isocrates to be met with now than there were of Terence then'.[125] Certainly, we have evidence of plentiful holdings of Xenophon from the earliest Cambridge probate records. Although original records survive only from 1535, we find 'opera zenophontis grece' listed in formats ranging from folio to 16mo from 1537, 1542, 1546, 1546/7, 1548 and onwards, and most of these are marked as Greek editions.[126] Individually-named copies of the *Cyropaedia* appear in the probate records only from 1558 onward, suggesting, perhaps, that the primary demand for Xenophon during Barker's time was for Greek and Latin collected works. (We know, for example, that the edition of Xenophon acquired by Cambridge scholar Gabriel Harvey in 1570 was one of the 1545 Basle *Opera*, in Latin, printed by Michael Isingrin.)[127] Among the most interesting of these is the Latin collected works of Xenophon and the Greek *Cyropaedia* owned by Edward Raven, fellow of St John's and friend of Ascham's, who died in 1558. We might also note that upon his death in 1578, the bookseller John Denys had among his book-stock an octavo of the *Cyropaedia* in Greek, a folio of Xenophon's *Opera* in Latin and a 'Zenophon in French'. The details of the inventories are, unfortunately, too sparse to deduce the editions in question, except in a few cases, and the terminology itself can be deceptive: given that a good number of the collected works of Xenophon available were parallel-text editions, we cannot rule out the possibility that more of the 'Opera' noted were '*graecolatine*' than has been detailed in the records. But it is clear that while at Cambridge, Barker would have had ready access to editions of Xenophon's work through colleagues, libraries and booksellers.[128]

That Barker likely worked from a copy of Xenophon's *Opera*, rather than an individual copy of the *Cyropaedia*, is suggested by several things: firstly, Barker's references to other works by Xenophon — the *Anabasis*, *Memorabilia* or *Apology for Socrates*, *Agesilaus*, *On Horsemanship* — in the dedicatory epistle to the first edition suggests as much. Similarly, the details of Xenophon's life that Barker cites are likely derived partly from the *Anabasis*, and also from the short biography, ultimately derived from the *Suda*, which was often appended to these collected works.[129] Another feature of his translation which indicates that he used a collected works is his occasional recourse to Filelfo's Latin translation when translating obscure concepts or proper names, and, most significantly,

---

[125] Cited in the 'Life of Ascham', in *The Whole Works of Roger Ascham*, ed. by Giles, I, part 1, p. xxxvii.
[126] Details here come from Elizabeth Leedham-Green's *Books in Cambridge Inventories*.
[127] Moore-Smith, *Gabriel Harvey's Marginalia*, p. 125.
[128] It should not be ruled out either that the text he worked from came from Reyner Wolfe, given the latter's reputation and visits to Basle during the period in question.
[129] See note 24.

the location of one paragraph at the end of Book IV/beginning of Book V. Filelfo's was the most commonly-printed Latin edition before 1540. Poggio Bracciolini's earlier translation still had some currency, but all the collected works favour Filelfo's translation in eight books. Nonetheless, not all of the Filelfo translations appear in the same format in the various sixteenth-century editions: a notable difference is that what is now considered the first paragraph of Book V appears in certain editions as the final paragraph of Book IV (with the parallel-text Greek text following the same structure, necessarily). So, for example, the 1534 parallel-text edition printed by Andreas Cratander in Basle has the paragraph in question opening Book V, as does another Basle edition (that of Michael Isingrin), in 1545. But also in Basle in 1545, Nikolaus Brylinger's parallel-text edition (which, like Cratander and Isingrin, also uses Filelfo's Latin translation of the *Cyropaedia*) concludes Book IV with the paragraph in question. The paragraph pertains to a jocose request by Cyrus's men for the grant of two female musicians who have been taken captive, a request to which Cyrus accedes. The main effect of moving this paragraph to the end of Book IV is that it separates the narrative of Panthea from the run-of-the-mill treatment of captive women as booty of war, and lends more moral seriousness to the Panthea episode. Barker's edition includes the episode with the female musicians at the end of Book IV, preserving this distinction of seriousness, as does Philemon Holland, but the 1547 French edition of Jacques de Vintimille, for example, includes the female musicians in Book V.[130]

Other smaller indications suggest that Barker may have been working from Brylinger's edition. Visual clues from the mise-en-page of Brylinger's edition include the use of in-text subtitles (as opposed to the printed marginalia that appear in many other editions) for occasional subtitles such as 'The Parentage of Cyrus'. Similarly, the occasional use of in-text subtitles for 'Cyrus['s] Oration' follows Brylinger's practice (unlike that of Cratander or Isingrin, for example). An error that creeps into the Latin translation of the 'Magadidae' which sees it transcribed in Filelfo's translation as 'Mariandines' also appears in Barker — it is not the only time Filelfo's text becomes a resource where the Greek term refers to an obscure people.[131] On the other hand, it is not a given that he looks to Filelfo for help in a quandary: Barker never Englishes the Greek term for 'phalanx', for example, although it regularly appears in Filelfo's Latin as 'phalangem' (and John Brende, translating the Latin of Quintus Curtius in 1550 has no difficulty translating it as 'phalanx'). The question of what text Barker translated from shapes not only his translation, but the contexts in which he offers it to readers.

---

[130] Later, the editions of Henri Estienne (1561), Johannes Leunclavius (1569) and Johannes Caselius (1584, 1587) would put the female musicians at the end of Book IV.
[131] Filelfo seems to be substituting the name of a Bithynian people mentioned in Herodotus (III. 90) for the (still-unknown) 'Magadidae'.

In other words, Barker's translation — its subject, provenance and readership — bears scrutiny in several, sometimes overlapping contexts: Protestant intellectual circles at St John's College, Cambridge, particularly those invested in Greek learning; the emerging and cosmopolitan London print industry; and the court, particularly the tutors, counsellors and stewards of the young king Edward VI. (It is worth pointing out that Barker's Catholicism did not discernibly hold him back in any of these domains.) Finally, we should add another important context: the Continental scholarly engagements with and translation of classical and contemporary writings by young Englishmen such as Barker, Sir Thomas Hoby and Peter Whythorn on or after their European travels. Whatever his copy-text for books I to VI, evidence from the text corroborates Barker's statement that he completed books VII and VIII at a later date, certainly following his Italian travels, and the text of the second edition seeks to some extent to be understood as the product of those experiences. Before turning to the uses made of the *Cyropaedia*, and Barker's translation, by readers, we should pause to examine the contexts of its production.

Contexts

Barker's translation of the *Cyropaedia* appeared early in the print history of English translations of classical authors, and among the very earliest of the Greek authors.[132] Thanks to Barker and Gentian Hervet, Xenophon appears in English before Virgil, Ovid, Livy, Herodotus and the major works of Plutarch do, for example. Of Greek authors, only Lucian (1532) precedes Hervet's 1532 English translation (from the French) of Xenophon's *Oeconomicus*, which would soon be followed by Sir Thomas Elyot's translations of pseudo-Plutarch (1532) and Isocrates (1533), Nicoll's Thucydides (1550) and Lydgate's translation of the Troy book (1513) — but both Lydgate and Nicoll were translating from Latin and French rather than Greek.[133] Elyot was the first to translate directly from Greek to English, in his *A Dialogue Between Lucian and Diogenes* (1532?), and in *A Doctrinal of Princes* (1533), his version of Isocrates's influential oration 'To Nicocles', as Rhodes notes; interestingly, a Latin translation of the same text, by 'Gulielmus barkerus', survives in a Lumley manuscript at the British Library.[134]

---

[132] See also Kirsty Milne, 'The Forgotten Greek Books of Elizabethan England', *Literature Compass*, 4 (2007), 677–87.
[133] Lydgate was translating from the Latin intermediary of Guido delle Colonne, and Nicoll from the French of Claude de Seysell. There was also a small but growing tradition of Englishmen translating Greek to Latin, most famously More's collaborative translation with Erasmus of Lucian (1506).
[134] Rhodes, *Common*, p. 33. From 1530 until his death in 1546, Elyot was mostly based at his estate in Carleton, Cambridgeshire, fifteen miles from Cambridge, and he is known to have had contacts with scholars there, including Ascham. It is certainly conceivable that he met Barker. Elyot's success in making available important classical texts in accessible

In Elyot's *The Boke Named the Governour* (1531) — in which he recommends teaching Greek to boys from the age of three onwards — Elyot had also loosely translated and paraphrased sizeable passages from the *Cyropaedia*.[135] 'Xenophon', he wrote, 'condisciple of Plato, wrate the life of Cyrus kyng of Persia most elegantly, wherin he expresseth the figure of an excellent governour or capitayne.'[136]

In Isocrates and Xenophon, then, Elyot and Barker's translations address the education of the youth in specific moral virtues: those appropriate to a royal prince, and, secondarily, to the prince's subjects. Both texts were prominent in the early modern mirror-for-princes tradition, alongside Erasmus's *Institution of a Christian Prince*. Another important context for Barker's Greek translations was the scholarly context of St John's, but with an eye to the royal court, as epitomised by Cheke. If Elyot's translations of Lucian and Isocrates into English led the way, Cheke's Latin translations of selected sermons by St John Chrysostom as Christmas or New Year's gifts for Henry VIII comprised the other major achievement in English Greek studies during Henry's reign.[137] Chrysostom had a special place here, one curiously entwined with the English reception of the *Cyropaedia*. As we saw, Cheke's Chrysostom were printed by Reyner Wolfe — the printer who would subsequently print Barker's English *Cyropaedia*. In fact, Cheke's Greek/Latin parallel-text Chrysostom involved the first use of Greek type in England in a complete Greek text, an Italian-made set of type that Wolfe had acquired on his regular trips to the Continent.[138] In a curious coincidence, more than half a century later, Sir Henry Savile's eight-volume Greek edition of the complete Chrysostom was the first text to be issued from his press in Eton (1610–1613) — and may even have been printed with the

---

English may well have served as one model for Barker's *Oratio ad Nicoclem*, in BL MS Royal 15.A.xvii. (*c*. 1545). Nicocles was the newly-acceded successor to Evagoras, king of Salamis in Cyprus, one-time ally of Athens and an active proponent of Hellenizing Cyprus; he died a vassal-king to the Persians in 374 BCE. G. B. Parks notes that it pre-dates the reigns of Mary and Elizabeth (from the reference to 'nostri regis' on f. 1b). The manuscript is dedicated to Henry Knyvet, possibly the son or grandson of Muriel Howard and Sir Henry Knyvet (died 1546). Parks dates it to the 1540s, and suggests that it was dedicated to Sir Henry, though Henry's son (born 1537) is also a likely dedicatee. 'William Barker, Tudor Translator', *The Papers of the Bibliographical Society of America*, 51 (1957), 126–40.

[135] Elyot did not learn Greek at either Oxford or Cambridge, but was taught by Thomas Linacre, as part of the circle that gathered at the house of Thomas More.

[136] *The Book named The Governor*, with introduction by Foster Watson (London: J. M. Dent, 1907), p. 154.

[137] On Cheke's translation gifts for Henry from 1543 until his death, see McDiarmid, 'John Cheke's Preface', pp. 101–02.

[138] The first use of Greek type in England was in a 1521 edition of Lucian printed in Cambridge by John Siberch. See Chris Michaelides, 'Greek Printing in England, 1500–1900', in *Foreign Language Printing in Britain, 1500–1900*, ed. by Barry Taylor (London: British Library, 2002), pp. 203–26 (pp. 203–04).

same set of type that Wolfe had used.[139] This is notable because the second product of Savile's press was the first Greek edition of the *Cyropaedia* (1613) to be printed in England.

If Elyot was one kind of model for Barker (an educational agenda seeking a popular audience for Greek learning outside of the universities) the other was Cheke (an educational agenda seeking to promulgate the values of Greek scholarship within the universities, but also at court). And the choice of Xenophon (and Isocrates), while it resonates with Elyot, also came strongly recommended by Cheke too. Here is Ascham once again, summarizing Cheke's educational ideals: 'Yea, I have heard worthy Master Cheke many times say, "I would have a good student pass and journey through all authors both Greek and Latin, but he that will dwell in these few books only, first in God's holy Bible, and then join with it Tully in Latin, Plato, Aristotle, Xenophon, Isocrates and Demosthenes in Greek, must needs prove an excellent man".' Cheke led by example, translating the sermons of Chrysostom, as we saw, but also Plutarch's 'On Superstition' (1546–1547), Leo VI's *Taktika* (1544) and Maximus the Confessor's 'On the Ascetic Life' (1547) — acts Aysha Pollnitz describes as efforts at Erasmian self-fashioning.[140] For Cheke these were distinguished scholarly achievements — but politically motivated ones too: presentations of Greek learning designed for a courtly audience and imbued, however subtly, with Erasmian counsel, aimed at advising the monarch to whom they were presented.[141]

But Cheke also played a prominent role in the new religious settlement, working with Cranmer on the Book of Common Prayer he newly prepared, consulting on the composition of the 42 articles, and taking part in the two critical disputations on the sacrament hosted by Cecil and Sir Richard Morison in 1551.[142] Nor was this entirely separate from his project of Greek scholarship. Besides the humanist impetus to translate or study Greek authors, Greek learning was also a high-stakes activity for religious reformers, who used it to access the Greek New Testament and the writings of the early Church

---

[139] Henry Bynneman acquired Wolfe's Greek type after Wolfe's death in 1573, and after Bynneman it was acquired by the printers of the Eliot's Court Press in 1584 (see Michaelides, 'Greek Printing', pp. 203–04). Savile's printer, Melchisidec Bradwood, had become an Eliot's Court printer in 1602.

[140] Pollnitz, *Princely Education*, p. 144. Presenting Henry VIII with Greek-to-Latin translations, she argues, Cheke imitated Erasmus, who presented Charles V with Greek-to-Latin translations of Plutarch and Isocrates between 1505 and 1515. See also McDiarmid, 'John Cheke's Preface'.

[141] Pollnitz points out, for example, that the translation of Leo's *Taktika* coincided with Henry's military plans against France. *Princely Education*, p. 144.

[142] It is disputed, but there is some suggestion (by John Strype) that Cheke may have translated Cranmer's *A Defence of the True and Catholike* doctrine of the sacrament of the body (Emden, 1550) into Latin, or supervised its publication.

Fathers — *pace* Cheke's Chrysostom — for evidence of early church practices and beliefs, and/or to overgo partisan or corrupted Latin translations, as they argued. But conservatives, too, followed this course, again seeking authorities to corroborate their own position. As Neil Rhodes argues, the early Tudor period displayed a complex interweaving of Reformation and Renaissance principles, in which the 'common' emerged as a key value — one centred on the nature and status of Greek and Greek learning.[143] Barker's interest in the disputational potential of patristic authors is clear in his translation of St Basil, published during Mary's reign — but Basil was also one of the authors the evangelical Ascham had offered to translate for Archbishop Lee in the early 1540s, 'who though they speak elegantly enough, do not speak to us in safe and good Latin, seeing that they have come into the hands of men who were not altogether free from the charge of heresy'. (The second author Ascham mentioned to the archbishop was Chrysostom.) Although a religious conservative, Barker, like Cheke, would translate Greek to Latin (in the Isocrates manuscript), and would engage with the Greek Church Fathers, seeking guidance for the present moment of 'division and factions in religion', in his translation of the sermon of St Basil of Caesarea.[144] But if the interests of all three translators were partly confessional, they were primarily humanist in their motivations.

These early translators also theorised translation itself, and the relationship between Greek and English, again impelled both by humanist and confessional motivations. Elyot made a case for the proximity of ancient Greek and contemporary English culture at the level of language, even at the expense of Latin. Prefacing his translation of Isocrates (1533), Elyot writes that 'I have found (if I be not much deceived) that the form of speaking used of the Greeks called in Greek, and also in Latin, *phrasis*, much near approacheth to that which at this day we use than the order of the Latin tongue: I mean the sentences and not in the words'.[145] Barker may have taken Elyot's comments about the proximity of Greek and English to heart, to judge by the tendency to favour Greek word-order in his *Cyropaedia*, though in his epistle he also bemoans that English is a 'rude and a barren tongue, when it is compared with so flourishing and plentiful a tongue' (p. 81). Barker's first edition of the *Cyropaedia* favoured a plain, unvarnished vernacular. (Scholars have unduly tended to prefer Holland's later *Cyropaedia* translation (1632), simply on the basis of Holland's better-known reputation, and without recognizing Barker's achievement — and, indeed, Holland's use of his translation, as the present edition shows.) In this, he takes a different line to Cheke, whose best-known statement on translation into

---

[143] Barker's translation of the 'agora' as the 'common place' (I. ii. 4; p. 86) may support this argument. See Rhodes, *Common*.
[144] *An exhortation*, sig. A2.
[145] Continental translators commonly made these claims for their own language too. See Elyot in *English Renaissance Translation Theory*, ed. by Rhodes, p. 234.

English is that found in his 1557 commendatory epistle attached to (another St John's alumnus, and Barker's sometime travel-companion) Hoby's translation of Castiglione's *Il Cortegiano*: 'I am of this opinion that our own tonge should be written clean and pure, unmixed and unmangled with borrowing of other tongues, wherin if we take not heed, by time, ever borrowing and never paying, she shall be fain to keep her house as bankrupt.'[146] The economic metaphor gives way to a civic one closer, in fact, to the strain (and effects) of his teaching: 'that if either the mould of our own tung could serve us to fascion a woord of our own, or if the old denisoned wordes could content and ease this need, we wolde not boldly venture of unknowen wordes'.[147] (But Cheke's position changes, and this strongly-worded epistle contradicts his earlier thoughts on the vernacular, particularly in translating the New Testament (1551–1553), which favoured Latinate and French words above words with Saxon roots. As Rhodes writes, Cheke's Protestantism 'inspired what was a completely unsustainable agenda for a purified vernacular', but 'his teaching had the very different effect of developing an English culture of translation that fed directly into the vernacular literature of the final quarter of the century'.)[148]

Barker's translation of books VII and VIII for the second edition of his Xenophon changes tack and embraces and anglicizes 'unknowen wordes' from other languages, perhaps deliberately showcasing his Italian experiences: now using, for example, 'alpheres', a Spanish loan-word for a horseman that Barker must have encountered in Naples, with roots in the Arabic term ('al-faris'). Or in Book VIII, we find the term 'entrate' for revenues, from the Italian 'entrata', a very early usage and a recognisably Italianate term familiar, perhaps, to the merchant community. Certainly, the practice of translation itself interested him — as did the display of his own learning and languages. In his translation of Appian (1578), for example, he pays careful attention to other translations and editions, noting on several occasions where the Latin and Italian translations of Appian 'differeth from the Greek' (sig. B4v). The title-page makes a virtue of the translator's facility with editions in several languages. But the dedicatory epistles to each edition of the *Cyropaedia* present Barker's sense of divided duty, to scholarship (in the form of translation) and to his employer, although he tries hard to rationalise his Xenophon translation in terms of its utility to schoolboys learning Latin, as well as to those interested in governance and politics.

Barker's relationship with Cheke was key to all of his translation work,

---

[146] Cheke, in *English Renaissance Translation Theory*, ed. by Rhodes, pp. 303–04. Hoby matriculated (pensioner) in 1545.
[147] In his own translation work, in any case, Cheke trusted to Latin rather than producing vernacular translations.
[148] Rhodes, 'Pure and Common Greek in Early Tudor England', in *The Culture of Translation in Early Modern England and France, 1500–1660*, ed. by Tania Demetriou and Rowan Tomlinson (Basingstoke: Palgrave, 2015), pp. 54–70.

we can now say: he benefitted directly, significantly and enduringly from Cheke's patronage. Cheke tutored him, probably supported him in election to a fellowship at St John's, gave him a place in important friendship and scholarly networks, and probably introduced him to his printer, from which his career in print was launched and sustained. Yet Barker, unlike most of his educators, intellectual circle and fellow-translators, was a religious conservative, still a Catholic in later life under Queen Elizabeth, even if he sometimes supported the evangelical faction at university, and showed some inclinations towards radical thinkers during his time in Italy.

Hitherto a barely noticed figure in the English literary Renaissance, Barker's career as a scholar, translator, traveller, secretary and tutor gives new insight into early modern English cultures of translation and the not coincidental literary flourishing of the last quarter of the sixteenth century.[149] With a career traversing the reigns of Henry, Edward, Mary and Elizabeth, and encompassing experiences in Cambridge, Italy and the most prestigious aristocratic household in the land, Barker's translations reflect upon a period of great political and religious change, and trace an impressive trajectory of scholarship, linguistic skill, and a commitment to disseminating that skill and learning in print. As Helen Moore has argued, 'humanist translation was a social practice, embedded in and engaged with all realms of human activity'.[150] His translation of Xenophon's *Cyropaedia* is a major achievement, in the vanguard of early modern English translations, and it illustrates the cultural and political ambitions (and reach) of scholarly translation far beyond the educational sphere.

Early Modern Uses of the *Cyropaedia*

The influence of the *Cyropaedia* within Tudor and Stuart culture is predominantly felt in the domains of educational theory, political thought and literary theory. Dynamically engaged in its modelling of Cyrus and of a fictionalised biographical form, it benefitted from the self-styled authority of Xenophon himself as a classical soldier-author. Plots and characters from the *Cyropaedia* inspired plays and romances, and meaningful allusions to Xenophon's text criss-crossed popular and scholarly genres. A key text in the mirror-for-princes tradition, it attracted the attention of prominent European and English educationalists like Erasmus, Roger Ascham and Richard Mulcaster. It played a part in the education of early modern British

---

[149] On the connection between translation and literary writing in the late sixteenth century, see Rhodes, 'Pure and Common Greek'.

[150] Helen Moore, 'Gathering Fruit: The "Profitable" Translations of Thomas Paynell', in *Tudor Translation*, ed. by Fred Schurink (Basingstoke: Palgrave Macmillan, 2011), pp. 39–57 (p. 42).

princes, including the future King Edward VI, the future King James VI of Scotland and I of England, Prince Henry, and the future King Charles I. In political thought, Cyrus's success as an imperial monarch also earned him the attentions of key European theorists such as Niccolò Machiavelli and Jean Bodin. In literary theory, the didactic purposes of Xenophon's careful balance between historical 'truth' and fictive, idealizing embellishment gave rise to comparisons with Virgil's *Aeneid* in late medieval scholarly commentary; such comparisons were extended in early modern discussions of the role of fiction in Italian literary theory, and English literary theory after it.[151] But with leading literary figures such as Edmund Spenser and Sir Philip Sidney weighing in on these debates, early modern literary practices as well as theory were shaped by the *Cyropaedia*. In some ways, its influence, joining education, politics and poetics, was most powerful and most resonant with early modern cultural values, as Northrop Frye noted, linking it with More's *Utopia*, Spenser's *The Faerie Queene* and Castiglione's *Il Cortegiano*.[152] For the purposes of simplicity, I will discuss the influence of the *Cyropaedia* within political and educational thought, and then within literary theory and practice.

Before that, however, I should note that the *Cyropaedia* also exerted a notable influence in two other quite distinct domains, which I will treat briefly: biblical scholarship and chronography, and cultural geography. Its potential to corroborate biblical narratives, 'especially seeing he is that Cyrus the elder, of whom the holy Scripture maketh honourable mention', appealed to authors of chronicles and universal histories (such as Johannes Carion or James Ussher) seeking to date the (biblical) history of the world.[153] Cyrus makes brief but impressive appearances in the Old Testament books of Ezra, Isaiah and Daniel as the conqueror of Babylon who allowed the Babylonian Jews to return to Jerusalem and to rebuild their temple, earning him an important reputation as a good king.[154] And the *Cyropaedia* was used by by Protestant chroniclers and

---

[151] Landino's comparison between Cyrus and Aeneas appears in the 'Prohemium' (to Pietro de Medici, dated 14 March 1488) which precedes his commentary on the *Aeneid*, in Roberto Cardini (ed.), *Cristoforo Landino: Scritti Critici e teorici*, 2 vols (Roma: Bulzoni, 1974), I, p. 215. On Badius, see James Nohrnberg, *The Analogy of The Faerie Queene* (Princeton, NJ: Princeton University Press, 1976), p. 26.

[152] See Grande and Sherbert (eds), *Northrop Frye's Writings*, pp. 350–51. Hoby envisaged the ideal courtier presented in his translation of Castiglione's *Il Cortegiano* as exemplary for courtiers in the same way as Xenophon's Cyrus is exemplary for princes: 'there is no more imperfection in this Courtier, then in Cirus himselfe, in the translation of Xenophon into the Italian or any other tongue, the one as necessarie and proper for a Gentleman of the Court, as the other for a king.' In *English Renaissance Translation Theory*, p. 302.

[153] So writes Henry Holland, son of Philemon, introducing his father's *Cyrupaedia* to its dedicatee, King Charles, sig. ¶¶7v.

[154] On the rebuilding of the temple at Jerusalem: Ezra 1. 1–3, 1. 7, 3. 7, 5. 13, 6. 3; Isaiah 44. 28, 45. 1, 45. 13; and II Chronicles 36. 22–23; Josephus, *The Antiquities of the Jews*, XI. 1, also endorses Cyrus's support of the Babylonian Jews following his conquest of the city. On the

chronographers to verify events and dates in the Bible for their universal human histories and chronicles. In the English translation of the enormously popular Carion's *Chronicle* later continued by Thomas Cooper and Thomas Lanquet, Cyrus's stature — and Xenophon's influence — is clear: Cyrus is described as 'one among the most doughtyest kynges & lordes of the worlde. For besyde the manyfold excellent and very princely vertues, had God geve[n] and endued him wyth sundery luck and fortune in rulynge, and very excellent vyctoryes of hys enemies'. Not content with granting Cyrus God's favour, the *Chronicle* goes even further with its admiration, ascribing him proto-Christian inclinations, under the tutelage of the prophet Daniel (whose dream had foretold Cyrus's conquest of Babylon): 'yea he fortuned to be taught and instruct also by Daniel the prophet in godlynes and in the trew worshyp of God as holy scriptures do wytnesse.'[155] The idea of Cyrus as a godly liberator, or at least an 'instrument of Gods power, vsed for the chastising of many Nations', as Walter Ralegh put it, was cited by Protestant polemicists well into the seventeenth century.[156]

Ironically, that authority about the distant past was no bar to its contemporary relevance, for many early moderns. As Jonathan Woolfson writes, 'the pragmatic and the historical approaches to the classical past coexisted in Tudor England'.[157] Besides being the richest available European source of historical, cultural and ethnographic information about ancient Persia, such details were often assumed or redeployed to describe Safavid Persia, even after the availability of more recent accounts from travellers such as Ludovico di Varthema or the Venetian and Genoan travellers published in Ramusio's great collection of *Viaggi* (1550–1554). In England, too, the English Muscovy Company travellers' descriptions of Persia dating from the 1560s and 1570s first appeared in *The History of Travyle* (1577), and more would soon appear in Richard Hakluyt's *Principall Navigations, Voyages, and Discoveries of the English Nation* (1589; 1598–1600). But when Hakluyt grandly asks '[w]hich of [Elizabeth's predecessors] hath ever dealt with the Emperor of Persia, as her Majesty hath done, and obtained for her merchants large & loving privileges?', he relies on a sense of Persian empire more reflective of Achaemenid Persia than the Safavid Persia described by any of his authors.[158] Where Persia is a setting

other hand, the Protestant chronicler Johannes Sleidan cites Plato's critique of Cyrus for not taking sufficient care of the education of his sons, and a printed marginal note in the 1563 edition summarizes that 'the so[n]nes of Cyrus were yll instructed'. *A brief chronicle of the Four Principall Empyres* (London: Rouland Hall, 1563), sig. C2v.
[155] Carion, *The thre bokes of cronicles* (London: for Gwalter Lynne, 1550), fol. xxxi (sig. [D7]).
[156] See *History of the World*, sig. 4D2.
[157] In Introduction to *Reassessing Tudor Humanism*, ed. by Jonathan Woolfson (Basingstoke: Palgrave Macmillan, 2002), p. 12.
[158] Hakluyt, *Principall Navigations, Traffiques and Discoveries of the English Nation* (London: George Bishop and Ralph Newberie, 1589), sig. *2v. Ultimately, English trade

in the plays or prose of the period, once again it is ancient rather than Safavid Persia that is depicted, even where the setting is a modern one.[159] Despite its relative paucity of geographical or antiquarian detail, then, the *Cyropaedia* remained a touchstone for English and European travel writers such as John Cartwright and Nicholas de Nicolay, and even a traveller as astute as Pietro della Valle, who spent nearly six years in Persia, drew on the *Cyropaedia* when publishing his letters and diaries.[160] In other words, Xenophon's Achaemenid Persia under Cyrus remained a powerful and vivid English image of Persia long into the seventeenth century.

Political and Pedagogic Thought

The *Cyropaedia* was actively mined for lessons in politics, literature, education as well as history in early modern England, particularly during the sixteenth century. In his long dedicatory epistle to William Herbert in the first edition, Barker explicitly promotes it as a book suitable for teaching subjects as well as princes. 'Of all books which philosophers have written with judgement, and others hath translated with labour, no book there is which containeth better matter for life, order for war lines, policy for courtliness, wisdom for government, temperance for subjects, obedience for all states' (pp. 82). The duality of its teachings about governance — teaching paradigms of civic obedience as well as strategies of rule — was crucial to its reception in early modern England, as Barker foresaw. It was a combination of social and political lessons that had already been articulated to some degree in Elyot's *Governour*, but that overlapped with the principles and readerly dynamics of the early modern *speculum principis* (mirror-for-princes) tradition within which the *Cyropaedia* took strong root.

Perhaps the most characteristic humanist genre, mirrors-for-princes

---

with Persia fell away in the 1580s, which probably gave the *Cyropaedia* a longer life as a geographical and ethnographic account of Persia than it would have had had the stream of contemporary accounts continued.

[159] The rhetoric around being king of Persia and riding in triumph through Persepolis, in Marlowe's *Tamburlaine*, is a good example, but the habit endures even into later plays such as William Cartwright's *The Royal Slave* (1636). See Chloë Houston, 'Persia and Kingship in William Cartwright's *The Royal Slave* (1636)', *SEL*, 54 (2014), 455–73.

[160] Cartwright's *A Preacher's Travels* (1611) drew heavily on Xenophon and Strabo, as well as contemporary authors such as Giovanni-Tommaso Minadoi, in his account of his early seventeenth-century travels in the Middle East. On Delle Valle, see Sonja Brentjes and Volkmar Schueller, 'Pietro Della Valle's Latin Geography of Safavid Iran (1624–1628)', *Journal of Early Modern History*, 10 (2006), 169–219. On the antiquarian interests of travellers to Persia, centred on Persepolis, see Lindsay Allen, 'Chilminar *Olim* Persepolis: European Reception of a Persian Ruin', in *Persian Responses: Political and Cultural Interaction with(in) the Achaemenid Empire*, ed. by Christopher Tuplin (Swansea: Classical Press of Wales, 2007), pp. 313–42.

combined an educational agenda with political instruction and counsel in an aspirational and tactically idealizing form. While Erasmus's *Institution of a Christian Prince* is the most important early modern example (and the key text of Frye's 'cyropaedia genre'), the most important classical example was the *Cyropaedia* (although Isocrates's speech 'To Nicocles' and, to a lesser extent, 'Evagoras' are often cited too). Xenophon's Cyrus stood out as a princely ideal, with lessons and attractions for both rulers and subjects: the vicarious pleasures for non-royal readers had always been a part of the success of published mirrors-for-princes. For a typical expression of the stature of Xenophon's Cyrus thanks to his association with the mirror-for-princes tradition, we might look to Richard Mulcaster, headmaster of the Merchant Taylors' school, who writes of his own pedagogic practices that he honours especially 'Xenopho[n] in the person of Cyrus, who[m] he deviseth so perfit, as the best boy for a patern to bring up, & the best pri[n]ce for a preside[n]t to princes'.[161] Or, to appreciate its familiarity within the domain of educational and political thought, consider Bryskett's remarks on it in his translation of parts of Cinthio's *Tre dialoghi della vita civile*. Bryskett shrugs off a request to discuss 'the instruction and training up of the children of [...] Princes', and refers his audience instead to 'what *Xenophon* in his *Ciropedia* hath left written of that subject, having learnedly and diligently under the person of *Cirus*, framed an idea or perfect patterne of an excellent Prince'.[162] (The identification of Cyrus as a perfect pattern of princehood, or words to that effect, is utterly commonplace in the period, and heavily influenced by a compliment from Cicero, to be discussed in more detail further on.)

The mirror-for-princes could also be read as a political treatise: a theory of kingship or rule, all the more persuasive for being exemplified by its historical exemplar. Machiavelli read the *Cyropaedia* in this way, citing Cyrus's actions in support of certain of his own recommendations for *realpolitik* in the *Discorsi* and *Il Principe*, as did King James VI of Scotland, rather differently, in his *Basilikon Doron* (1599).[163] Machiavelli's commentary on Cyrus in both *The Prince* (where he commends Cyrus for using fraud and deceit as a ruler) and the *Discourses* (which further develop his sharp reading of the *Cyropaedia*) reveal the violence underlying Cyrus's practice of absolute rule in this way.[164] But for the most part,

---

[161] Mulcaster, *The First Part of the Elementary* (Menston: Scolar Press, 1970), p. 15. Under Mulcaster's charismatic leadership, both Hebrew and Greek were taught at the Merchant Taylors' school.

[162] Bryskett, *A Discourse of Civill Life* (London: for Edward Blount, 1606), sig. I3, p. 61.

[163] A treatise on government, and specifically his own personal values and principles of rule, it was written in the form of a letter to his son and heir, Prince Henry, but published strategically in Edinburgh and London in 1599, as a means of cultivating support for his potential succession to the English throne.

[164] On Machiavelli's use of Xenophon's *Cyropaedia*, see, for example, Christopher Nadon, *Xenophon's Prince: Republic and Empire in the 'Cyropaedia'* (Berkeley: University of California Press, 2001).

Machiavelli's version of Xenophon's Cyrus as governor-turned-autocrat is less often reflected in other early modern engagements with the *Cyropaedia*. The idealized Cyrus of the mirror-for-princes, however, is alive and well, even in the late days of the genre. James VI's *Basilikon Doron* (1599), addressed to his son and heir, Prince Henry, was, in effect, a mirror-for-princes written not just for, but also *by* a prince. Xenophon ('an old and famous writer') looms large in it, partly through direct allusion (where he is called upon to endorse the traditional royal sport of hunting with hounds, and to recommend moderation in appetites and banqueting in particular), but especially Xenophon's broader representation of a charismatic imperial monarch.[165] As James Cramsie has shown, James makes careful use of the episode in which a young Cyrus, being trained up in justice, learns the deontic principles of equity and strict application of the country's laws, when he is chastised for giving a large coat belonging to a small boy to a larger boy, and the smaller coat to the smaller boy.[166] For James, the episode illustrates the principle that princes as well as subjects must obey the laws of the land, and not rule or judge by fiat or favour or any other principle, but by and through the laws of the land:

> remember the throne is Gods and not yours, that ye sit in, and let no favour, nor whatsoever respects moove you from the right. Ye sit not there, as I shewe before, for rewarding of friends or seruvnts, nor for crossing of contemners, but onely for doing of Justice. Learne also wisely to discerne betwixt Justice and equitie; and for pitie of the poore, rob not the rich, because he may better spare it, but give the little man the larger coat if it be his; eschewing the errour of young Cyrus therein: For Justice, by the Law, giveth every man his owne; and equitie in things arbitrall, giveth every one that which is meetest for him.[167]

James Cleland's sycophantic *Heropaideia* (1607) recognized James's debts to the *Cyropaedia*, and sought to privilege the king's work ahead of that of Xenophon by citing the Machiavellian reading of Cyrus's deceptions and 'treasons':

You shal not find the like of the least of these faultes in his Majesties instructions, which have worne *Xenophon* out of credit in al other Countries, where they are trulie translated and read unto all Noble mens children, the

---

[165] 'But because I would not be thought a partiall praiser of this sport, I remit yo[u] to Xenophon, an olde and famous writer, who had no minde of flattering you or me in this purpose: and who also setteth downe a faire paterne, for the education of a yong king, under the supposed name of Cyrus.' *Basilikon Doron* (London: Edward Allde for Edward White, 1603), sigs H2r–v. The marginal notes printed in the London editions make clear James's reliance on the *Cyropaedia* (e.g. on kingship during war (sig. E3), but also on moderation in diet 'as yong Cyrus did' (sig. [G4]), on honouring one's parents (sig. G1v) and on the rule of law (sig. [C4]v)).

[166] James Cramsie, 'The Philosophy of Imperial Kingship and the Interpretation of James VI and I', in *James VI and I: Ideas, Authority, and Government*, ed. by Ralph Houlbroke (Vermont: Ashgate, 2006), pp. 43–60.

[167] *Basilikon Doron*, sig. [F5]v.

fathers themselves not disdaining to keep a booke of them in their owne bosome; as I councel you especiallie to do, who do daily see the practice of these precepts by the Pupil, unto whom they were first taught.[168]

So appreciative of the *Cyropaedia* was James that he apparently commissioned a new English translation of it from the prolific and accomplished translator Philemon Holland, for the benefit of his son and heir, Prince Henry. Unfortunately, the translation stalled following Henry's precipitate death in 1612, but was eventually published by Holland's son Henry in 1632, now tactfully re-dedicated to King Charles I.[169] The association with Prince Henry was sufficiently well-known to be invoked strongly in William Alexander's 'A Paraenesis to the Prince' (1604), in which he encouraged Henry's military and chivalric career to be modelled on that of Cyrus, and following Henry's death, Cyrus was invoked again in several funeral elegies, including Henry Peacham's 'An Epicedium mourning Prince Henry', and another by Christopher Brooke, who wrote,

> And who (in his Praeludium) did not see
> (Pent in the CHAOS of his manly Frame)
> The spirit of Cyrus in Minoritie,
> In boundlesse hope, and in a soundlesse Aime.[170]

A new Restoration translation by John Norris and Francis Digby (1685) cements the Stuart connection with the *Cyropaedia* still further: prefacing their translation, they declare that

> the great end [Xenophon] design'd it for, which was, (by laying down such an exact Plat-form of an Empire) at once to free his Country from the Insolencies of a *Popular*, and the Inconveniencies of an *Aristocratical* State; I mean *Monarchy*; which he has so admirably contriv'd, and so effectually recommended, that ever since, that kind of Government has been held most perfect, which has come up nearest to his *Model* and *Design*.[171]

(Digby and Norris's translation was probably also bolstered by the royalist colouring of Madeleine de Scudéry's blockbuster romance *Le Grand Cyrus*

---

[168] *Heropaideia, or the Institution of a Yong Noble Man* (Oxford: Joseph Barnes, 1607), sigs T3v–[T4] (p.151).
[169] The title-page styling of 'Cyrus' and 'Carolus', in an engraving by William Marshall, is particularly noteworthy. A further link with James was the publication alongside Holland's translation of Henry Holland's *Naumachia* — itself a tribute to James's minor epic, *Lepanto* (1591).
[170] Henry Peacham, *The Period of Mourning* (London: Thomas Snodham for John Helme, 1613), and Brooke, 'A Funerall Elegie on the Prince', in *Two Elegies* (London: Thomas Snodham for Richard More, 1613). Accessed at <http://spenserians.cath.vt.edu/TextRecord.php?action=GET&textsid=36992>.
[171] *Kyrou paideia, or The Institution and Life of Cyrus the Great* (London: for Matthew Gilliflower and James Norris, 1685), sig. [A7]v.

(1650–1653), which embellished narratives of Cyrus from a range of sources, including Xenophon.) A good English example of the interest of Cyrus for seventeenth-century romance is John Bulteel's prose romance *Birinthea* (1664), which also reimagines figures and narratives from the *Cyropaedia* in warmly royalist terms. Indeed, the Restoration saw a marked increase in interest in Xenophon's Cyrus: among its other fruits are a new Greek edition of the *Cyropaedia* (1660), and plays such as John Banks's *Cyrus the Great; or, the tragedy of love* (1696) and John Dryden's *Secret-love, or the Maiden Queen* (1691).[172]

Whether the *Cyropaedia* provided a prescription for good governors, or for good princes (the majority view), had more at stake than some of its early supporters acknowledged. With the notion of governorship came accountability to a higher power, but with that of princeliness came the possibility of absolute imperial authority.[173] Xenophon's Cyrus pulls off quite the tightrope act of, on the one hand, observing his lifelong subservience to parental authority and (apparently) the will of the people, qualities that have led to his rule being figured as republican or, at least, republican in its origins.[174] On the other hand, as King James VI was quick to see, Cyrus skilfully instates himself as an absolute ruler, responsible *for* his people but not *to* them. Supporting this are the many moments when Cyrus cultivates a princely camaraderie with his higher-ranking (and usually Persian or Median) soldiers — but sets loyalty and obedience as their price. One of the most commonly cited stories about Cyrus, and which originated in Xenophon, is the notion that Cyrus remembered the names of all of his soldiers. Thus, John Florio praises Montaigne for his ability to 'out of question like Cyrus or Cæsar call any of his armie by his name and condition'. That it is his generals whose names he remembers, rather than all of his army, is clear in the *Cyropaedia*, but the idea is of a piece with Cyrus's reputation for charismatic leadership and his talent for friendship.[175]

On the whole, early sixteenth-century presentations of Xenophon's Cyrus as

---

[172] Dryden's play, like Bulteel's romance, is heavily indebted to *Le Grand Cyrus* (1649–1653), which was quickly translated into English (*Artamenes, or The Grand Cyrus*, trans. by F. G. (London: for Humphrey Mosely, 1653)).

[173] This is precisely the issue Queen Elizabeth sought to negotiate, and which was partially played out in the 1559 Book of Common Prayer and its denomination of Elizabeth as 'our quene and Governoure' (in the communion service). I am grateful to Thomas Healy for this point.

[174] Nadon argues that Xenophon presents Cyrus moving from republican to imperial, universal rule, 'a movement one is hard pressed simply to regard as progress', in *Xenophon's Prince*, p. 23.

[175] It also earns Cyrus a place in the gallery of heroes of mnemonics. For examples, writing on 'The devision of Memorie' in *The Arte of Rhetorique*, Thomas Wilson writes: 'Likewise Cyrus King of the Persians, having a great armie of men, knewe the names of all his Souldiers.' *Wilson's Arte of Rhetorique (1560)*, ed. by G. H. Mair (Oxford: Clarendon Press, 1909), p. 211.

a model governor give way to interpretations of his imperial rule within a model of absolute monarchy; the emphasis now falls instead on the self-governance of the ruler and the dangers of falling into tyranny. This danger is nicely illustrated in a presentation copy of Jacques de Vintimille's 1547 French translation of the *Cyropaedia* held in the British Library.[176] It was presented to King Edward VI, who had begun learning French in 1546 and was apparently relatively proficient by 1550 when he received several embassies from France following the signing over of Boulogne to Henri II. During one of these embassies, he was presented with a stunning illuminated manuscript of Louis LeRoy's French translations of Isocrates' mirrors-for-princes together with a translated excerpt of the *Cyropaedia*: Cyrus's paternal advice to his sons and heirs from Book VIII (Royal 16 E. xxxii, f. 1v).[177] The handsomely-bound presentation copy of the printed edition of de Vintimille's translation Edward also received from the French bears a salutary inscription for the young king, a story derived from the *Suda* (Alpha 3909) in which the Cyrenaic philosopher Aristippus, having successfully appealed to Dionysius of Syracuse on behalf of a friend by throwing himself onto the ground and embracing the tyrant's knees, told his happy friend not to attribute his success to the dubious means of flattery but rather to 'ce Tirant qui a les oreilles aux genoux' [this Tyrant, who has his ears in his knees].[178] The choice of Aristippus to deliver a message against tyranny was probably not accidental: Diogenes Laertius had reported Xenophon's antipathy to the free-living philosopher, so the donor (or some tutor's?) framing of this royal copy of the *Cyropaedia* as a guide to young princes redoubles its warning against the kind of tyranny into which an adherent of the *Cyropaedia* might well fall. A mirror for princes, and Xenophon's *Cyropaedia* in particular, could very easily become an instruction-manual for tyrants. This anonymous mid-sixteenth-century commentator had already seen Cyrus's potentially tyrannical habits, though it is a lonely voice of warning in a tide of early modern approbation of Xenophon's Cyrus.

The protean character of the *Cyropaedia* meant that it was also associated with other genres of political writing and political thought. A frequent comparison promulgated by early modern authors put it in company with some or all of Plato's *Republic*, Virgil's *Aeneid*, Thomas More's *Utopia* (1516), Edmund

---

[176] Vintemille's translation of the *Cyropaedia* was commissioned by François I for his son, Henri II, who would accede to the throne the same year Vintemille's translation came out. Just a year earlier, Jacques de Vintemille had produced the first French translation of Machiavelli's *Il Principe* (1546).

[177] Le Roy would soon publish these in Paris (1551), the first of his many vernacular translations. Le Roy had already presented a copy of two of the Isocrates translations to the new French king Henri II in 1547, soon after his accession. See Werner L. Gundersheimer, *The Life and Works of Louis Le Roy* (Geneva: Librairie Droz, 1966), pp. 11–13. The Paris edition was reprinted in 1568.

[178] In BL Royal c. 48.f. 3 (the 1547 Paris edition).

Spenser's epic romance *The Faerie Queene* (1590–1596) and Castiglione's *Il Cortegiano* (1528). Marking out his own *De Republica Anglorum* (1583) as new territory, Sir Thomas Smith (another member of the Cheke circle) makes the striking declaration that the commonwealth he described was real, 'not in that sort as Plato made his common wealth, of Zenophon his kingdome of Persia, nor as Syr Thomas More his Utopia being feigned common wealths, such as never was nor never shall be, vaine imaginations, phantasies of Philosophers to occupie the time and to exercise their wittes'.[179] On the other hand, as we will see, Sir Philip Sidney characterized More, Virgil and Xenophon as providing the best kind of philosophical counsel for a prince, locating their virtues precisely in their fictiveness: 'But even in the most excellent determination of goodness, what philosopher's counsel can so readily direct a prince, as the feigned Cyrus in Xenophon; or a virtuous man in all fortunes, as Aeneas in Virgil; or a whole commonwealth, as the way of Sir Thomas More's *Utopia*?'.[180] We will return to early modern literary theory and practice in the next section. But the didacticism Sidney here elucidates was already a strong part of the reception tradition of the *Cyropaedia*.

Beyond its royal readers, and beyond royal tutors (such as Cheke) who espoused it, the *Cyropaedia* was judged to encapsulate positive educational practices more broadly, as one might guess from Barker's new title, 'The Schole of Cyrus'. Those practices were principally (but not exclusively) articulated in Book I, but the didactic and exemplary character of Cyrus in his activities beyond his education were also absorbed as part of the educational theory Xenophon offered. Two key principles of Persian education impressed themselves on early modern educationalists: firstly, the special place of justice in Persian education, one not found to the same extent in the English curriculum. As Mulcaster put it, 'justice was the Persian grammar'.[181] Secondly, there was the commitment to moderation (in appetites) shown by Xenophon's Cyrus, whether in relation to diet, furnishings or sexuality. Supporting these was a common formulation of the tenets of Persian education — 'to ride, to shoot, to tell truth and never lie' — first found in Herodotus (1.136) but also supported by the emphasis on the ability 'to shoot and dart' in Cyrus's Persian education, and of truth-telling in the *Cyropaedia*. Even in a text as distant as John Bulteel's *Birinthea* (1664), we find fulsome praise for Cyrus's Persian education:

> You cannot but have heard of those celebrous Academies in Persia, where

---

[179] *De Republica Anglorum*, ed. by Leonard Alston (Cambridge: Cambridge University Press, 1906), p. 142.

[180] Sidney, *Apology for Poetry*, ed. by Geoffrey Shepherd (Manchester: Manchester University Press, 1977), p. 108. Gabriel Harvey would concur, in almost the same words (now in Latin), in marginal notes on one of his books (J. Foorth's *Synopsis Politica* (1582)). See Moore-Smith, *Gabriel Harvey's Marginalia*, p. 197.

[181] Richard Mulcaster, *Positions (1561)* (London: Harrison & Sons, 1887), p. 278.

vertue alone presides, and where they are so well taught to practice it [...] 'Twas in those learned schooles, Our Prince was bred and instructed, whose condition did not dispense him from the severity of those lawes which they observe, they gave him no other but the ordinary course nourishment of bread and cresses, and satisfied his thirst with nature's plain beverage, a dish of water, thereby to accustome him to undergo hardship when he should come to be more necessarily acquainted with it in time of war: they taught him likewise to shoot exactly with a bow ...[182]

Some of the most prominent books of sixteenth-century educational theory — Ascham's *The Schoolmaster* (1570) and Mulcaster's *Positions Concerning the Training Up of Children* (1581) and *The First Part of the Elementary* (1582) — are works indebted to the Chekeian agenda, so it is not surprising to find the *Cyropaedia* loudly approved in them. Ascham's *The Schoolmaster*, as mentioned, originated in a 1563 discussion at the rooms of William Cecil. Queen Elizabeth herself must have encountered Xenophon through Ascham, while he served as her Greek tutor in her younger days (on Cheke's recommendation). Writing to Archbishop Thomas Cranmer in early 1545, Ascham describes what's being read at the university in revealing terms: 'Herodotus, Thucydides, and Xenophon, the three lights of chronology, truth, and Greek eloquence bring a great splendor to the rest of our studies'.[183] Ascham, in particular, shows a deep and engaged interest in Xenophon's educational models of exemplary behaviour in Book I, including in his own treatise the Persian strategies Xenophon describes of curbing youthful appetites and passions and educating young men living in the company of well-minded adult men until the age of 21. Ascham, of course, was wholly supportive of the Chekeian agenda, and in his letters provides our best evidence of the popularity of Xenophon in 1540s Cambridge.

Mulcaster, it is agreed, was the most innovative educationalist of his age, a practitioner as well as a theorist — and a great admirer of the *Cyropaedia*. *Positions Concerning the Training Up of Children* (1581) and *The First Part of the Elementary* (1582), in which he promulgated his programme for English education, showed his absorption of many of its principles.[184] Both were published while Mulcaster held the position of the first headmaster of the

---

[182] Bulteel, *Birinthea: A Romance* (London: Thomas Mabbe for John Playfere, 1664), sig. [H6] (p. 107). See also Richard Robinson's emphasis on Cyrus's archery, explicitly linking it to Cicero's reported statement that Xenophon showed 'not onely ... | What Cyrus did, but what a Prince by dewty ought to doo, | Both in pastimes for pleasure, and in seryous matters'. Robinson, *The Auncient Order, Societie, and Unitie Laudable of Prince Arthure* (London: John Wolfe, 1583), sig. L2v.

[183] John Strype recounts this in *Memorials of* [...] *Thomas Cranmer* (London: for Richard Chiswell, 1664), p. 169; Strype also confirms that Cheke was 'the great setter on foot of this ingenuous Learning in the University' (p. 170).

[184] Mulcaster had attended King's College, Cambridge, while it was under Cheke's provostship (1548–1553), and Cheke's influence was strongly felt in the curriculum at his schools, notably in the teaching of Greek.

Merchant Taylors' School, a position he held from 1561 to 1586. Later he would take up the mastership of St Paul's (1596–1608). Mulcaster's educational writings show strong traces of his favouring of Xenophon, which began during his university days. One of the more interesting aspects of Mulcaster's engagement with the *Cyropaedia* is his interest in the descriptions of the space in which Persian boys were educated (the 'free square'). Mulcaster writes that the schoolroom must be 'commodious for situacion', and he develops Xenophon's description of the proximity of elders who might serve as exemplars, by advocating lifelong careers for schoolmasters that they might become proficient in 'judgement, cunning and discretion' and, thereby, models for their charges.[185] For Mulcaster, Xenophon's text is not so much an historical account as a 'devise', a carefully-assembled prescriptive exemplar — and all the more valuable for it. In the *Positions*, for example, Mulcaster cited at length the story of Cyrus's being punished during his training on justice for making the incorrect judgement about the coats of the small and tall boys.[186] The same episode drew King James's attention in the *Basilikon Doron*, of course, but where James used it to discuss the discharge of royal justice, Mulcaster uses it to demonstrate the need for masters to be invested with ungainsayable powers of correction, and for students to be engaged: 'Xenophon maketh Cyrus be beaten of his maister, even where he makes him the paterne of the best Prince, as Tullie sayeth, and mindes not the trueth of the storie, but the perfitnesse of his devise'. Mulcaster goes on to re-tell the story in all its detail as 'a matter of the Persian learning', and despite his professed belief in 'gentlenesse and curtesie towarde children' rather than beating, he finds merit in Xenophon's 'devise' (or prescription) of Cyrus being beaten by his master for not learning properly:

> For a soule there could not be one less servile then he, which was pictured out beyond exception: for impunitie, there could not be more hope, then in a Prince enheritour, and that is more, set forth for a paterne to Princes. And yet this Princes child in the absolutenesse of devise, was beaten by his devise, which could not devise any good traine exempt from beating beinge yet the second ornament of Socrates his schoole.

Mulcaster also highlights Cyrus's tactical munificence towards the conquered Armenians, and Xenophon's opposition between weeping and laughing, in which he presents a strikingly sharp reading of the *Cyropaedia*'s politics: the court of Cyrus finds a place for weeping, 'because awe, feare, correction, punishments, which commonly have weeping, either companion, or consequent, be used in pollicy, to kepe good orders in state, and good manners in stay, wheras laughing is never, but upon some foolish ground'.[187] (On the other hand, Cyrus's

---

[185] *Positions*, p. 230
[186] *Positions*, p. 278; see also Rebecca Bushnell, *A Culture of Teaching: Early Modern Humanism in Theory and Practice* (Ithaca: Cornell University Press, 1996), pp. 51–53.
[187] *Positions*, p. 66.

willingness to laugh at himself is praised in the *Elementary*, as a self-amending exercise still opposed to weeping which 'might bewray a pusillanimity and a faint of stomach'.)[188]

Relevant, too, to these didactic contexts is an early modern tradition of excerpting sections from the *Cyropaedia*, especially Cyrus's paternal advice to his sons at the end of Book VIII, for inclusion in collections of classical wisdom (such as the *Demogoria* of Johannes Sambucus (1552), which excerpted no fewer than twelve 'orations', or the two speeches from the *Cyropaedia* included in the *Conciones* (1570) of the great scholar-printer Henri Estienne), or alongside works of political theory (such as those of Le Roy, who added sections from the *Cyropaedia* to his French translations of Aristotle's *Politics* and Plato's *Phaedo* as well as his 'To Nicocles').[189] Similarly, as Noreen Humble has pointed out, Cicero's use of a passage from Cyrus's death-bed in *De Senectute* ensured its visibility in the early stages of a student's Greek studies.[190] The excerpted *Cyropaedia* had its own wide influence, though it is trickier to track. Before moving onto the uses of the *Cyropaedia* in early modern poetics and literary endeavour, however, I should point out that one final important aspect of the *Cyropaedia*'s influence in the educational sphere was the biographical *ethos* of the author himself, and a related tradition in which the *Cyropaedia* was recommended as a *vade mecum* for would-be imperial soldiers and generals.

A certain glamour and authority were evinced by the figure of Xenophon himself. For Mulcaster as for Barker, the *Cyropaedia* was all the more to be attended to for the sake of its author, a man both bookish and full of worldly experience. 'Xenophon this philosopher hath not only travailed in the general knowledge of true reason to have right understanding what is good and bad in life and what is true and false in nature', Barker writes, 'but also travailed by experience to see the diversities of men's manners, and to acquaint himself with right order of civil government' (p. 79). The 'Life' of Xenophon offered by Diogenes Laertius was appended to most sixteenth-century editions of the collected works of Xenophon, but he also provided his own publicity: his Persian travels as the leader of an army of Greek mercenaries in support of Cyrus the Younger, volubly described in the *Anabasis*, allowed him to be presented as an author who bridged the dicey gulf (as humanists presented it) between scholarly learning and worldly experience. Xenophon's support of Cyrus the Younger — a relationship the *Anabasis* framed in terms of a ruler and a wise counsellor — also lent him the air of an Isocrates to a Nicocles, an Aristotle to an Alexander, a Solon to a Croesus (if not quite a Ulysses to an

---

[188] *First Part of the Elementary*, p. 15.
[189] See Marsh, 'Xenophon', pp. 124–25.
[190] See Humble, 'The Well-Thumbed Attic Muse'. As Botley notes, this gave students of Greek an example of Cicero's own translation work in practice. *Learning Greek*, p. 77.

Agamemnon). That self-styled reputation as a great military leader endured: translating parts of Xenophon's treatise on horsemanship in 1584, the courtier John Astley declares that 'this Xenophon was not onelie a great Philosopher, but also an excellent Captaine, speciallie over the horssemen'.[191] A century later, such endorsements of Xenophon's combination of the active and contemplative life were still standard: for the translators of the *Cyropaedia* in 1685, Xenophon was 'a Man no less famous in an Active than in a Contemplative Life; and perhaps the only Person upon Record whose Words and Actions so highly adorn'd the Philosophy he profess'd'.[192] Cementing this sense of Xenophon as part of that 'poetry' that Sidney decreed to be 'the companion of the camps', was an established tradition of the *Cyropaedia* serving as *vade mecum*, particularly for the Roman hero Scipio Africanus, on the model of Alexander the Great's much-travelled copy of the *Iliad*.[193] A typical example is the Count's comment, in Castiglione's *Il Cortegiano* that (in Hoby's translation), 'Alexander had Homer in such reverence, that he laide his *Ilias* always under his beddes head: and he applied diligentlye not these studies onely, but also the speculations of Philosophye under the discipline of Aristotle'. In similar fashion, he notes, '[i]t is said that Scipio Affricanus carried alwaies in his hand the bookes of Xenophon, wherein under the name of Cyrus he instructeth a perfect king'.[194]

Thus, it was not just the Persian king Cyrus who became an attractive and familiar exemplary figure in early modern England, but the philosopher, author and well-travelled military man Xenophon too. And we see those striking features of Xenophon's achievement in its original moment endure into the early modern era: a compelling interweaving of a striking, charismatic Persian hero and a striking, charismatic literary-historical-military Greek author.

Poetics and Literary Uses

While *paideia* (education) is signalled in Barker's title, 'The School of Cyrus', arguably the *Cyropaedia*'s most valued teachings were political — about the acquisition and maintenance of empire, the virtues and exercise of kingship, the public and private values of justice, self-governance and obedience. Those lessons were explored as much in early modern literature as they were in political or pedagogic genres. Moreover, early modern literary theory and

---

[191] *The Art of Riding* (London: Henry Denham, 1584), sig. C1v.
[192] These are the opening words of the Francis Digby and John Norris's translation: *Kyrou Paideia: or, The Institution and life of Cyrus the Great* (London: for Matthew Gilliflower, 1685).
[193] Sidney, *An Apology for Poetry*, ed. by Shepherd, p. 127.
[194] *The Courtyer of Count Baldessar Castilio*, trans. by Thomas Hoby (London: William Seres, 1561), sig. H3. Machiavelli also mentioned this tradition (ch. 14), as did numerous others.

practice sought to engage with Xenophon's literary-historical method itself, and lessons from the *Cyropaedia* became key to the new Protestant poetic theory promoted by Philip Sidney, William Scott and Edmund Spenser. This was partly because of the respected place of the *Cyropaedia* in Italian poetic theory, particularly in scholarly commentary on the *Aeneid*. But it was a statement by Cicero, in one of his letters to his brother Quintus, recently appointed to govern the province of Asia, that gave rise to the most energised literary approach to the *Cyropaedia*, and that became the most rehearsed idea about Xenophon's Cyrus in the early modern period.

Cicero's letter reflected on the potential dangers of one man's rule over so vast a province, with little opportunity for recourse by citizens. It is worth quoting the passage in full, although early modern responses concentrated on one key phrase:

> Wherefore it requires an exalted character, a man who is not only equitable from natural impulse, but who has also been trained by study and the refinements of a liberal education, so to conduct himself while in the possession of such immense power, that those over whom he rules should not feel the want of any other.
>
> Take the case of the famous Cyrus, portrayed by Xenophon, not as an historical character, but as a model of righteous government, the serious dignity of whose character is represented by that philosopher as combined with a peculiar courtesy. And indeed it is not without reason that our hero Africanus used perpetually to have those books in his hands, for there is no duty pertaining to a careful and equitable governor which is not to be found in them [...] In my opinion, all who govern others are bound to regard as the object of all their actions the greatest happiness of the governed.[195]

Read in context, Cicero's advice seems less concerned with endorsing a Persian political model than with providing sensible advice to his not always sensible brother as he took on a famously unruly but lucrative province — at least given the letter's purported function. All the same, a Persian reputation for justice as well as empire had come through from classical antiquity (not least from the *Cyropaedia* itself), and from the seeds of Cicero's brief example, a commonplace grew, to the benefit of Xenophon's imperial ruler. (Interestingly, a 1561 translation of Cicero's letter to Quintus compresses this passage so reductively as to confuse Cyrus and Scipio, but the accompanying marginal note clarifies the republican character of Cicero's thought: 'the felicity of the subjects is the

---

[195] *The Letters of Cicero*, trans. by Evelyn S. Shuckburgh, 4 vols (London. George Bell and Sons, 1908–1909), I, pp. 78–79; see also Cicero's familiar letter to L. Lucceius, in which he declares the power of the *Cyropaedia* in disseminating a good reputation: that 'a single pamphlet of Xenophon's in praise of that king has proved much more effective than all the portraits and statues of them all'.

end of government'.[196] And yet, this would not become the dominant reading of the *Cyropaedia* during the early modern period.)

It was Sidney who brought Cicero's ostensible approval squarely into English poetic theory, and who shaped its influence on early modern English understandings of Cyrus as the ultimate exemplar of the ultimate empire, strategically portrayed by Xenophon for precisely those ends and whose literary techniques were to be commended accordingly. 'For Xenophon', he writes, 'who did imitate so excellently as to give us *effigiem justi imperii*, "the portraiture of a just empire," under the name of Cyrus (as Cicero saith of him), made therein an absolute heroical poem.'[197] The interpretation of the *Cyropaedia* as 'heroical' or epic in nature comes largely from the tradition of commentary on Virgil's *Aeneid*, and from an interest in promoting its epideictic cast and Cyrus as a model for emulation.[198] In the *Defence of Poesy*, therefore, Xenophon's Cyrus keeps good company, appearing alongside Virgil's Aeneas, sometimes Ariosto's Orlando, and Heliodorus's Theagenes. Most commonly, Cyrus and Aeneas stand together as models for princes and princely behaviour: 'The poet nameth Cyrus or Aeneas no other way than to show what men of their fames, fortunes, and estates should do.'[199] It is this literary emphasis on heroic princely models that makes the *Cyropaedia* an easy reach for Shakespeare (and his audience and readers) when representing English princes, as we will see. But it is also what allows Marlowe to allocate an ancient Persian princely model to his would-be Persian princely parvenu in the *Tamburlaine* plays: Marlowe looks to Xenophon's Cyrus, Rhodes argues, 'for the pattern of relentless conquest', even as he looks to Lucian 'for the ironic colouring of the pattern'.[200] Moreover, the well-established tradition of the *Cyropaedia*'s uses as a *vade mecum*, and the echo of Alexander the Great's carrying Homer's epic *Iliad* with him, resonates strongly with Sidney's infamous declaration about poetry being the 'companion of the camps'. But Sidney's powerful phrase (and self-serving translation) '*portraiture* of a *just empire*' resonated throughout early modern literary and political thought, and added force to arguments in favour of English (and later

---

[196] 'If Cyrus who knew he shulde never be a privat man so diligently observed these things w[ith] what care oght they to kepe and observe them which beare rule with this condition that they must depart from it againe and returne under obedience of those lawes by order of th[e] which the governaunce was committed unto them.' *An Epistle or Letter of Exhortation*, trans. by Goddred Gilby (London: Rouland Hall, 1561), sig. B5v.
[197] Some critics (e.g. S. K. Heninger) explain this claim in terms of Sidney's Platonism, as a universal abstraction from a specific example.
[198] See O. B. Hardison, *The Enduring Monument: A Study of the Idea of Praise in Renaissance Literary Theory and Practice* (Chapel Hill: University of North Carolina Press, 1962), pp. 72–77, Nohrnberg, *Analogy*, p. 268, and Brian Vickers, 'Epideictic and Epic in the Renaissance', *New Literary History*, 14 (1983), 497–537.
[199] Sidney, *Apology*, ed. by Shepherd, pp. 124–25.
[200] Rhodes, *Common*, p. 272.

British) empire, particularly on the model of Cyrus.[201]

However, we could also note that the view of Xenophon's Cyrus as an exemplary 'pattern for princes' was already present in early sixteenth-century pedagogical and political traditions. For Sidney, Xenophon's fictiveness in the service of the didacticism of his text was not to be impugned, but instead admired and emulated. But note his use of the visual term 'portraiture' (rather than the term 'model' which most modern editions use), and his insistence on 'empire' rather than 'governance'. With that, the phrasing also endorses empire as a desirable political model, 'under the name of' a singular epic hero who establishes and embodies its virtues. Sidney's recasting of Cicero's terms is notable for making more of 'empire' and of Xenophon's literary efforts in 'portra[ying]' him — but not without contradiction. Cicero's point to Quintus is about moderation, temperance, self-restraint in public office, something that Xenophon's Cyrus conspicuously performs — but not once he actually rules an empire. Sidney's emphasis on empire, with its seemingly unending appetite for expansion, exposes a fundamental tension in Xenophon's text that has long drawn comment. In the nineteenth and twentieth centuries, such commentary tended to centre on the sceptical-sounding Epilogue, and whether it might be original to Xenophon's text; such doubts have now been allayed. Yet Leo Strauss's more searching 'ironic' reading of the text as a whole remains current, though it is toned down in the work of scholars such as Vivienne J. Gray, who contest the 'dark' aspect of Xenophon's Cyrus, or those such as Christopher Nadon, who see the text moving across republican and imperial values, in critique as well as exposition.[202]

The tensions are easy to spot, whether locally or more broadly. For example, what is the relationship between the principles of frugality and moderation characterizing the Persians early on to Cyrus's deceptions during the campaign, and his adoption of the very principles of conspicuous luxury (including the wearing of make-up) that he had earlier rejected, once Babylon has been conquered? What are we to make of Cyrus's Median education and treatment of his Median allies when his virtues (and education) are extolled under the sign of his Persian identity? And what virtues of Cyrus's, precisely, are readers to emulate, when they so often seem double-edged, or achieved at the expense of some other party — as often friends as enemies? Or are readers to emulate only the loyal obedience of his subjects? (That same challenge is acknowledged by Spenser (of whom more later) when he notes the exemplary value not just of Cyrus but of 'Cyrus and his Persians'.) In the final book of the *Cyropaedia*, one of Cyrus's subjects discusses the route to empire, and confirms Xenophon's

---

[201] See Jane Grogan, *The Persian Empire in English Renaissance Writing, 1549–1622* (Basingstoke: Palgrave Macmillan, 2014), pp. 32–69.

[202] See note 231 (p. 66).

adumbration of obedience as the cardinal virtue of subjects:

> We that now be come to wealth, whereby have we attained to the same but by obedience to our prince? [...] Things that have been commanded us, we have done them at full, him we have followed and idle contentation we have eschewed, and thereby have we finished our enterprises. Then if to obey the prince be the only way to get lordship and empire, think there is none other way to save the same but that self obedience.

Certainly, obedience is the touchstone of at least one early modern reading of the *Cyropaedia*: that of a late Tudor reader, busily annotating a copy of the 1567 edition now held at the Huntington Library.[203] The flourishing of Cyrus's imperial virtue, it seems, depends upon the cardinal virtue of his subjects and allies: total obedience.

All of these issues are implicit in Sidney's use of the *Cyropaedia*, and, indeed, in his exploration of the virtues (and vices) of kingship in his *Arcadia* — where even Cyrus's deceptions and 'stratagems' are referenced, and perhaps even paralleled with the careful fictional stratagems of the Protestant writer.[204] The *Cyropaedia* is pressed into service at several crucial points of Sidney's poetics: not just exemplifying principles such as the 'Idea or fore-conceit' or the superiority of poetry to history or philosophy but developing them further, often on lines already established by Italian theorists such as Scaliger and Castelvetro. The references are often brief but hard-working. Sidney names Cyrus thirteen times; Aeneas, for comparison, is named only ten times. So in stating that poetry should not just 'make a Cyrus' but 'make many Cyruses', the seriousness of Sidney's literary-political vision should not be underestimated. Yet that depends on a recognition by readers of Xenophon's fictive methods: 'if they will learn aright why and how that maker made him'.[205] Sidney's poetic theory is a social and political vision, concerned not just with improving individuals but with reforming whole societies through the ameliorative effects of reading 'speaking pictures' of heroical virtue, preferably false (i.e. fictions) rather

---

[203] See Jane Grogan, 'Ancient Persia, Early Modern England, and the Labours of Reception', in *Eastern Resonances in Early Modern England: Receptions and Transformations from the Renaissance to the Romantic Period*, ed. by Claire Gallien and Ladan Niayesh (Basingstoke: Palgrave Macmillan, 2019).

[204] The slightly inaccurate excursus on Abradatas having 'feigned' a 'stratagem' on behalf of Cyrus, and the encouragement that the reader 'learn it of Xenophon's fiction', 'if occasion be presented unto you to serve your prince by such an honest dissimulation', makes it clear that the issue is one of 'counterfeit[ing]' and when it can be licensed. *Apology*, ed. by Shepherd, p. 111.

[205] Sidney proposes that writers 'not only [can] make a Cyrus, which had been but a particular excellency as Nature might have done, but [can] bestow a Cyrus upon the world to make many Cyruses, if they will learn aright why and how that maker made him'. *Apology*, ed. by Shepherd, p. 101.

than true 'histories'.[206] And where Sidney leads, others follow. Francis Meres borrows Sidney's phrasing almost word for word, in his derivative *Palladis Tamia* (1598). George Puttenham summarises Sidney's view, acknowledging that the *Cyropaedia* is 'fained and untrue' but written 'for example and good information of the posteritie'.[207]

Edmund Spenser, author of the great unfinished epic romance *The Faerie Queene*, follows suit. But he puts Sidney's appreciation for Xenophon's *Cyropaedia* into practice by instating the structure of Xenophontic rather than Platonic political ideals at the heart of his poetic theory.[208] An alumnus of the Merchant Taylors' school under Mulcaster, Spenser writes that he modelled the virtuous knightly exemplars of *The Faerie Queene* after the 'doctrine by ensample' of Xenophon's *Cyropaedia* (and specifically in place of any kind of prescriptive 'doctrine by rule'), aiming to 'mirrour' and 'fashion' not just Queen Elizabeth herself (in the idealizing fashion of a mirror-for-princes), but also any 'gentleman or noble person' reading it.[209] His quest-bound knights, whose allegorical paths towards virtue enable and stand in for the reader's path to virtue, thus gain their Xenophontic didactic power not as ideal embodiments but rather as strategically flawed exemplars, even carefully fictionalised exemplars. Thus, the stumbling Redcrosse knight of Book I, who will eventually become St George, is in many ways the least Xenophontic of Spenser's knights. But Spenser's writing of him, and presentation of him continuing to err in later books, makes clear that he is neither perfected nor perfectible, at least within human culture.[210] But rather than pursue the Xenophontic shades of Spenser's knights, I will conclude by looking at the poetic treatise by William Scott, who follows Sidney closely but also turns away from the Sidneyan agenda in revealing ways. Scott, too, uses visual terms to understand the poetic work of the *Cyropaedia*, and retains an imperial emphasis, but he marks himself as both Sidneyan and as moving away from Sidney through his treatment of the *Cyropaedia*.

---

[206] For a different argument about Sidney's social and political vision, which sees the *Defence* providing not just the orthodox humanist position about the role of poetry but also a more radical voice of critique, see Catherine Bates, *On Not Defending Poetry: Defence and Indefensibility in Sidney's 'Defence of Poesy'* (Oxford: Oxford University Press, 2017).

[207] 'Also as *Theucidides* wrate a worthy and veritable historie, of the warres betwixt the *Athenians* and the *Pelopones*: so did *Zenophon*, a most grave Philosopher, and well trained courtier and counsellour make another (but fained and untrue) of the childhood of *Cyrus* king of *Persia*, neverthelesse both to one effect, that is for example and good information of the posteritie.' Puttenham, *Arte*, ed. by Willcock and Walker, pp. 40–41.

[208] Described in the Letter to Ralegh that accompanies the first edition of *The Faerie Queene*.

[209] *The Faerie Queene*, ed. by Hamilton, p. 716.

[210] See Jane Grogan, *Exemplary Spenser: Visual and Verbal Pedagogy in 'The Faerie Queene'* (Aldershot: Ashgate, 2009).

Scott's *Model of Poesy*, a manuscript treatise on poetics written in the summer of 1599, was only rediscovered in recent years.[211] An insider in literary London, as his editor Gavin Alexander shows, Scott's treatise is a fascinating and scholarly document full of allusions to contemporary work by Spenser, Shakespeare, Jonson and others. First and foremost, though, it addresses the work of Sidney: Alexander describes it as in many ways a commentary on the *Defence of Poesy*, but also 'a much more ambitious and comprehensive exercise inspired by the *Defence* but not bounded or constrained by it'.[212] We see that appraising attitude in action in Scott's careful rewriting of Sidney on the *Cyropaedia*, a reworking of terms that reveals, perhaps, some dwindling in its stature — or perhaps even the belatedness of Sidney's own appreciation of it. Unlike Sidney's thirteen evocations of Cyrus, Scott only mentions him twice. Once again, Scott's references to Xenophon's Cyrus appear in a discussion of heroic poetry (and like Sidney, Scott allows that 'heroical' literature can be written either in poetry 'or else in a grave prose'), in which category he includes the traditional epics of Homer, Virgil, Lucan and Tasso, but also the romances or mixed romances of Ariosto, Heliodorus and Sidney himself, as well as More's *Utopia*, the 'moral invention' of Spenser's *The Faerie Queene* — and Xenophon's *Cyropaedia*.[213] Like Sidney, Scott sees the purpose of heroical writings as being 'to direct and move us to virtue in particular or general', and his catalogue of such works closely resembles Sidney's. (But where Sidney's taxonomies of genre tend to be exclusive, Scott's are much more inclusive; his category of the heroical is clearly very broad, and encompasses minor epic such as Spenser's *Muioptomos*, complaint such as Daniel's *Rosamond*, blustering patriotic romances such as William Warner's ever-expanding *Albion's England* and even the *Mirror for Magistrates*.) Scott also uses a strongly visual language to describe the work of poetry, and he picks up on Sidney's visual framing of the *Cyropaedia*'s didactic, political and epideictic value, and even his key phrase, 'effigiem iusti imperii' — but with a crucially different translation. 'In some example or precedent, feigned or true', he continues, 'they all endeavour by an admiring emulation to direct and move us to virtue in particular or general. Xenophon (as Tully acknowledgeth) in his Cyrus hath given us "effigiem iusti imperii", the true scantling of an happy estate of government.'[214] The invocation of Sidney is as clear in Scott's phrasing as his deviation from it. Scott supplies his own paraphrase in place of Sidney's translation: 'the true scantling of an happy estate of government'. That Scott continues in Sidneyan vein by praising Aeneas as 'a perfect man for wisdom, valour, and piety, as far

[211] It is now available in Gavin Alexander's edition for Cambridge University Press (2013).
[212] From Alexander's Introduction, p. liii.
[213] Frye likely did not know Scott's treatise, but his theorisation of a 'cyropaedia genre' is strengthened by Scott's association of Spenser and More in this way.
[214] Scott, *Model of Poesy*, ed. by Alexander, pp. 19–20.

as Virgil could imagine; Orlando of bold hardiness' and so on, only compounds the sense of difference. A 'scantling' is a measure or pattern, used in carpentry, ship-building or other such crafts. A visual term, like so many of Sidney's preferred metaphors for poetry, it is less ambitiously or convincingly applied by Scott: unlike the Sidneyan lexicon of portraiture or example, a scantling has no independent value outside of measuring, and no particularly positive or heuristic charge like them. Other contemporary uses of 'scantling' confirm this: in fact, most writers who use it also take their cue from 'scant' to imply the poverty or slightness of what it measures.[215] (So, for example, Joshua Sylvester worries that his translation of Du Bartas's *Seconde Sepmaine* loses its richness and gives English readers only a 'scantling' of the original.)[216] There may be another buried criticism too in Scott's revaluation of 'trueness' — evoking accuracy as well as truth: to term it a 'true scantling' rather than a 'portraiture' deals a further blow, scored against Sidney's insistence on the superiority of Xenophon's 'feigned Cyrus' to the 'true Cyrus in Justin', as he had it. More striking still than this snub to Sidneyan poetics, though, is the rejection of Sidney's 'just empire' translation for the much less partisan, more republican-sounding 'happy estate of government'. Rather than focalize the imperial monarch, Scott offers instead a vision of political stability, with no royal or imperial endorsement.[217] That these two allusions comprise the sum total of Scott's references to the *Cyropaedia*, direct or indirect, may also hint at Scott's being significantly less enamoured than Sidney was by its politics. This is, of course, only one moment of Scott's response to Sidney. But it is useful for demonstrating one early modern writer's alertness to the political programme and imperial values at the heart of Sidney's poetics, by way of the *Cyropaedia* and its central place in Sidney's programme, and finding a way of gently challenging them.

Literature

Beyond poetic theory, the strong influence of the *Cyropaedia* can be tricky to track in the literature of the period. The difficulty emerges, ironically, from its very familiarity. One result of the broad reach of the *Cyropaedia* (from chronography to poetics, from political treatises to travel writing) was its

---

[215] For example, Barnabe Riche's romance *Brusanus* (London: for J. Oxenbridge, 1592) sees the eponymous princely hero's courtesan lover lament upon his departure, 'Alas my Lord [...] and can you bestow nothing for a farewell, if you bee driven to so narrowe a scantling, the paringes of your nayles shall suffyce to content your lover [P]etrona' (ch. 3).

[216] Guillaume Du Bartas, *The Triumph of Faith, The Sacrifice of Isaac. The Ship-Wreck of Jonas*, trans. by Joshua Sylvester (London: Richard Yardley and Peter Short, 1592), sig. A3.

[217] It may refer directly to Xenophon's Proem, in which he admires the stability of the Persian empire under Cyrus's sovereignty.

permeation of both scholarly and more popular discourses as narratives or received ideas and beliefs, often already shaped by the Ciceronian view of Xenophon's Cyrus. Cyrus was, therefore, both a familiar and respected figure in the popular imagination, just as he was respected in more prestigious literary, political and educational writing. A full analysis of the influence of the *Cyropaedia* in early modern English literature remains to be completed; I will confine myself to a few illustrative examples here, choosing examples from poetry, drama and prose to indicate the breadth and popularity of Xenophon's Cyrus in early modern English literary culture.

Unsurprisingly, many of the early modern literary engagements with the *Cyropaedia* feature the virtues of Cyrus, or colourful narratives associated with him. As noted above, the heroic Cyrus was invoked by numerous writers of elegies on the death of Prince Henry in 1612, but he also featured as an example of 'continencie' in Lyly's popular romance *Euphues* (1578). The biblical Cyrus and Herodotean Cyrus also made their presence known: apocalyptic verse such as that of Francis Quarles' *Hadassa* (1621) cited Cyrus alongside Nebuchadnezzar and Belshazzar, while the bloody fate of Herodotus's Cyrus, aided by the rising popularity of biblical and classical queens such as Tomyris and Semiramis, was remembered elsewhere.[218] (Thus it is that the Countess of Auvergne wishes to emulate Tomyris's 'famous' defeat of Cyrus in Shakespeare's *1 Henry VI* (II. 3. 5-6), when she in turn meets the English hero Talbot.) Sir John Denham, on the other hand, reimagined 'the noble speech the dying Cyrus made', rewriting it in iambic pentameter, in *Cato Major: Of Old Age*, his 1648 translation of Cicero's *De Senectute*, which had already been important to the good reputation of Xenophon's Cyrus.[219] Cyrus appeared in various dictionaries, epitomes and chronicles in the period, which also promoted his familiarity. It was from Xenophon, not Herodotus, Justin or Diodorus, that Cyrus received his best press, and entries for him in texts such as Thomas Cooper's *Dictionary* or Carion's *Chronicle* tended to foreground the Cyrus of the *Cyropaedia*. For example, Cooper's second edition of Thomas Elyot's *Dictionary* (*Bibliotheca Eliotae* (1552)) refers readers onward to Justin, Herodotus, Solinus and Valerius Maximus but gives pride of place to Xenophon in the entry itself: 'This man excelled all men of his time in goodly personage, gentleness, prowess, liberality, wisdom and memory [...] The residue of his wonderful virtues be written by Xenophon most eloquently in Greek.'[220] Not that the grisly end afforded Cyrus in the Herodotean account was neglected: it tended to appear in moralising collections such as Lodowick Lloyd's *The Pilgrimage of Princes* (1573) or indeed

---

[218] On Quarles's poem, see Adrian Streete, 'Francis Quarles' Early Poetry and the Discourses of Jacobean Spenserianism', *Journal of the Northern Renaissance*, 1 (2009).
[219] Denham, *Cato-Major: Of Old Age* (London: for Henry Herringman, 1669).
[220] Thomas Cooper (ed.), *Bibliotheca Eliotae* (London: Thomas Berthelet, 1552), sig. X6.

in the *Mirror for Magistrates*. But it was thanks to Xenophon that Cyrus was such a familiar and appealing figure, even for critical purposes. Traces of the *Cyropaedia* can be found in Marlowe's First Part of *Tamburlaine*, and in the representations of kingship in Shakespeare's history plays, notably *Henry V*.[221] Shakespeare is notable for apparently glancing but particularly revealing allusions to the *Cyropaedia* , though those significances often remain hidden to readers, even of modern editions. For example, Hal's declaration that he is 'sworn brother to a leash of drawers and can call them all by their Christian names' (II. 4. 7–8) recalls Cyrus's carefully performed amity with his troops — but also Hal's larger military ambitions and strategy by that amity. Even more significantly, perhaps, is the buried allusion in the infamous last words of Shakespeare's Richard III, too often read as a mere sign of desperation, even ridiculousness, on the part of this complex king. But so well-known was Xenophon's Cyrus that Shakespeare could not just invoke him, but could give a depth of historical irony to those desperate last moments by having Richard call out 'my kingdom for a horse!'. Shakespeare's king — and, presumably, his audiences and readers — were recalling a short episode buried in the middle of Book VIII of the *Cyropaedia*, which set about exemplifying the extreme loyalty of Cyrus's troops, and its strategic significance to Cyrus's imperial conquests.[222] Through this retrospective allusion, the extent of Richard's ambitions are finally revealed, even in the teeth of his own failure, and the abiding usefulness of the *Cyropaedia* signalled.

It was not only Xenophon's flattering tales of Cyrus that circulated in early modern culture: the story of Panthea, Abradatas and Araspes in Book V was one of the most readily excerpted or re-narrated. It appeared, for example, in Richard Taverner's *The Second Boke of the Garden of Wysdom* (1542) and at more length in William Painter's *The Pallace of Pleasure* (1566).[223] Where Taverner drew a moral lesson ('Let Chrystiane magistrates and rulers take here an holsom document and lesson of a panym prynce'), Painter's moral framing of the collection was not enough to disguise the more salacious and sensational flavour of his collection. The constant lovers Argalus and Parthenia in Sidney's *Arcadia* evoke Xenophon's Araspes and Panthea, both by their names and by their unbesmirched character in Sidney's romance.[224] They found expression

---

[221] See Rhodes, 'Marlowe and the Greeks', *Renaissance Studies*, 27 (2013), 199–218, and Jane Grogan, '"A Warre ... Commodious": Dramatizing Islamic Schism in and after *Tamburlaine*', *Texas Studies in Language and Literature*, 54 (2012), 45–78.
[222] See pp. 247–8 here, and Paolo Cherchi, 'My Kingdom for a Horse', *Notes and Queries*, 46 (1999), 206–07.
[223] Taverner, *The Second Boke of the Garden of Wysdom* (London: for Richard Banks, 1542), sig. B5.
[224] Sidney, *The Countess of Pembroke's Arcadia*, ed. by Maurice Evans (New York: Penguin, 1977).

in drama, too, in *The Warres of Cyrus* (1594, but likely written in the late 1570s), a romance-play probably written by Richard Farrant for the Children of the Chapel Royal, which takes Xenophon's Panthea, Abradatas and Araspes subplot as its main plot. Beaumont and Fletcher take liberties with Xenophon's account of the lovers in *A King and No King* (1619, but first performed 1611), relocating the narrative to 'Iberia' and setting the virtuous Panthea at the heart of an incest plot. Still beloved of two men (here, the man she thinks is her brother, Arbaces, and Tigranes, defeated king of Armenia), Beaumont and Fletcher combine the two loyal marriages seen in the *Cyropaedia* (that of Tigranes and his wife, and of Panthea and Abradatas) in a tragicomedy about a succession crisis. (There are further ironies and echoes for those familiar with the *Cyropaedia* in the choice of 'Gobrias' as the name of the king's regent who sought to become king, or in observing Arbaces's merciful treatment of Tigranes.) But in omitting a Cyrus-figure, the play signals its more flexible uses of the *Cyropaedia*, perhaps even shifting its political allegiances far enough to explore (as Zachary Lesser has argued) the question of mixed government under King James I.[225] The deck of characters and untoward love-plots would be shuffled once more in John Bulteel's prose romance *Birinthea* (1664), which also involves Tigranes. (Tigranes and Cyrus, of course, are friends, 'having had their breeding together in the Persian Academies').[226] In *Birinthea*, Cyrus, too, falls victim to love-sickness for the eponymous Birinthea, Bulteel's (newly-invented) sister of Tigranes. As noted, the success of Scudèry's *Le Grand Cyrus* in the mid-seventeenth century likely played a part in popularising romance versions of Cyrus, gleaned from Xenophon and then gleefully reworked. And early in the eighteenth century, Octavia Walsh wrote a poetic version of Xenophon's Panthea and Araspes narrative, which survives in a manuscript miscellany at the Bodleian Library.[227] But by the later decades of the seventeenth century, the playful appropriations and knowing reworkings of the *Cyropaedia* hint that the very interest of Xenophon's text may, in fact, have become over-familiar and under-valued. With this came a retrenchment into the less subtle royalist readings favoured by the Stuart kings and celebrated anew with the restoration of King Charles II, as the Restoration translation of the *Cyropaedia* shows.

Conclusion

Despite his popularity and prestige in late medieval and early modern Europe,

---

[225] Lesser, *Renaissance Drama and the Politics of Publication: Readings in the English Book Trade* (Cambridge: Cambridge University Press, 2004), pp. 165–90.
[226] Bulteel, *Birinthea*, p. 123.
[227] 'The Princely Persian led his warlike Host', in MS ENG. poet e. 31 (Item 49 (Verse), fols 131v–122r). See the Perdita Project entry for it at <https://web.warwick.ac.uk/english/perdita/html/pw_WALS01.htm>. I am grateful to Danielle Clarke for this reference.

by the mid-eighteenth century Xenophon's status had fallen to that of a minor writer, a once-entertaining visitor who had outstayed his welcome.[228] By the early eighteenth century, the familiarity and decline in prestige of the *Cyropaedia* made it an easy target for Laurence Sterne, who generated plenty of steam out of having Tristram's father neglect his son's very education in a misguided attempt to write a 'Tristra-paideia' on Xenophon's model. An added sting to Sterne's satire comes from the note that in so doing, Tristram's father aims to save his son from being educated by women — precisely the terms of Plato's critique of (Xenophon's) Cyrus in the *Laws*.[229] As James Tatum writes, '[i]f it were not for footnotes, today's reader of *Tristram Shandy* might never smile at an account of Mr Shandy's attempt to undertake his son's education'.[230]

The clarity and relative simplicity of Xenophon's language is sometimes given as a factor in this decline in his reputation — other Greek thinkers now displaced the 'Attic bee' with their heftier reputations and more challenging, sophisticated Greek — but the narrowing political horizons of the *Cyropaedia*, and its association with royalism, also contributed. Appreciation of Xenophon today still bears the traces of this decline, and its only superficially investigated 'dark' or 'ironic' character. Much current scholarship on Xenophon sets itself the impossible task of reconciling his diverse work into one coherent body of writing and thought, and therefore finds it either disarmingly simple or devilishly clever and camouflaged. Apart from Leo Strauss's important attempt to argue for a complex irony running through Xenophon's thought (and he drew heavily on Niccolò Machiavelli's self-serving reading of Xenophon, but also saw Xenophon less interested in Persia than in Sparta), few political philosophers have shown much interest in his work.[231] But the modern decline

---

[228] See James Tatum, *Xenophon's Imperial Fiction: On 'The Education of Cyrus'* (Princeton, NJ: Princeton University Press, 1989); but see also Doohwan Ahn on the recuperation of Xenophon's thought on leadership in the works of Archbishop Fénelon, Andrew Michael Ramsay and Henry St John Viscount Bolingbroke, in 'The Politics of Royal Education: Xenophon's *Education of Cyrus* in Early Eighteenth-Century Europe', *Leadership Quarterly*, 19 (2008), 439–52.

[229] Plato blames Cyrus's poor education on 'a womanish rearing by royal women lately grown rich, who, while the men were absent, detained by many dangers and wars, reared up the children' (*Laws*, III. 694–95). Cited from *Plato in Twelve Volumes, Vols. 10 & 11*, trans. by R. G. Bury (Cambridge, MA: Harvard University Press; London: William Heinemann Ltd, 1967 & 1968).

[230] Tatum, *Xenophon's Imperial Fiction*, p. 3.

[231] On Strauss's contribution to Xenophon studies, see the introduction and overview to the *Leo Strauss Transcripts* project, which has a helpful focus on the *Cyropaedia* (upon which Strauss, in fact, published little directly): <http://leostrausstranscripts.uchicago.edu/navigate/8/?byte=547471>. The legacy of Strauss's 'ironic' readings of Xenophon endures, especially in recent scholarship on Xenophon's engagement with leadership: its ideals, challenges and the personal virtues that make strong public leaders. See especially Higgins, Nadon, Gray and Sandridge.

in its fortunes has obscured not just its lessons and influences on early modern education, politics and poetics, but also a great deal of early modern thought on Persia and the world east of Europe, whether ancient or modern. I hope that this edition will inspire further research on Xenophon in early modern Europe, and specifically on early modern approaches to the *Cyropaedia* which foreground questions of power, empire, education, geopolitics, rhetoric, poetics, genre and the still under-studied concept of 'classical reception' itself.

TEXTUAL NOTE

There are two editions of Barker's translation of the *Cyropaedia*: STC 26066, *The bookes of Xenophon* ... (no date, but estimated as 1552 by the STC; see Introduction), and STC 26067, *The VIII. bookes of Xenophon* ... (1567). The first edition contained only books I to VI of Xenophon's eight books and epilogue. The second edition is complete, and includes the dedicatory epistle from the first edition along with a new dedication for the second. Both editions were printed by Reyner Wolfe (see Introduction). The STC editors note two variants of 26067; from copies I have seen, it seems that in some, a number of sheets from the 1552 edition (26066) were used in copies of the 1567 edition (26067). The majority were reset, however.

The copy-text for this edition is the 1567 edition of Barker's translation held at the Henry E. Huntington Library (79935), a well-preserved copy with relevant ownership marks from the early modern period. This copy was owned by the London mercer Nicholas Moxsay, who seems to have been reading it in 1604, as an adult. I chose the 1567 text for its completeness, as well as for the ease of comparison to the rarer first edition and the later Philemon Holland translation while transcribing and editing. Moxsay's annotations are few but intriguing. As well as these, an inscription on the title-page which appears to be in a slightly later hand than Moxsay's lifts a choice quote from Virgil's well-known second eclogue, detailing Corydon's love for a slave-boy Alexis who is introduced as 'delicias domini', the darling of the master; in borrowing precisely this description for Barker's translation of Xenophon's *Cyropaedia*, the reader may be referring to the several homoerotic moments in Xenophon's text, notably when a Median falls in love with Cyrus and finds excuses to kiss him.

Moxsay takes advantage of a blank page to write out some spiritual reflections on the exodus of the children of Israel over the Red Sea. The biblical Cyrus, who would become the liberator of the Jews of Babylon, restoring to them their temple, is clearly in mind here. Otherwise, apart from some descriptive marginalia early on in Book 1, most of the text is free of annotation. On the other hand, the Huntington copy (79939) of the first edition of Barker's translation (1552?) is graced from beginning to end with the assiduous annotation of a reflective and thorough sixteenth- or early seventeenth-century reader, one who shows awareness of other accounts of the life of Cyrus, and who has some acquaintance with Greek and Hebrew. Intriguingly, this annotator has added a date of 1550 to the printer's colophon on the title-page (no date is printed, but the STC estimate the date of publication as 1552), and even administered the initials of the translator to the conclusion of his dedicatory epistle. I have incorporated comments on the annotations of this reader in the notes to this edition.

In the footnotes and Introduction, I have also included some comparisons with the better-known translation of Philemon Holland (1632), whose translation was commissioned by King James, though publication was delayed by twenty years owing to the precipitate death of its dedicatee, Prince Henry. An accomplished translator of Suetonius, Plutarch, Camden and other prestigious authors, Holland had a copy of Barker's translation close to hand during his own translation, somewhat surprisingly; his points of contact and divergence from Barker's text are helpfully revealing of Barker's values and style.

Source Text

It seems highly likely that Barker was working from a parallel-text Latin and Greek composite edition of the works ('Opera') of Xenophon, and I suggest in the Introduction that it may have been one of the 1545 Basle editions printed by Nikolaus Brylinger. This may have been procured for him by Wolfe (who travelled often to the Frankfurt Book Fair) or been accessible to him at Cambridge, where he was a fellow at St John's; unfortunately no surviving copy at Cambridge stands as a possible candidate. Barker worked primarily from the Greek, but occasionally had recourse to the Latin translation of Francisco Filelfo included in these composite editions, for example when he encountered the name of an unfamiliar people.

Besides evidence such as matching internal sub-headings, one helpful guide to Barker's copy-text is an editorial habit found in some Continental editions that he follows, whereby the first paragraph of Book v is moved to the end of Book IV, with the effect of sequestering some lighter material at the end of Book IV (relating to female captives) from the much-loved narrative of Panthea and Araspes in Book v. This makes Brylinger's edition much more likely as a source than Michael Isingrin's (also printed in Basle in 1545), which does not make this change. (Holland, interestingly, follows Barker in this, rather than take up the much more common and recent habit of prestigious European editors/translators (Estienne, Leunclavius, Caselius) of leaving the material in question in Book v, where most modern editions also place it.)

One near-contemporary vernacular translation which Barker may have known was that of Lodovico Domenichi (1547); Barker translated another work by Domenichi and probably met him during his Italian travels of 1549 to 1552. However, it is not a source-text for Barker (despite Barker's appreciation for the Italian language, and the likelihood that he took part in discussions about translation with Domenichi at the Accademia Fiorentina; see Introduction), as Domenichi follows Poggio Bracciolini's Latin translation of the *Cyropaedia* in six books, with crucial differences. Barker's translation is in eight books and follows the structure of the Greek editions, and the much more common Filelfo Latin translation.

There is a noticeable difference in the quality and nature of the translation between the first and second editions. The translation work in books VII and VIII, printed for the first time in the second edition, is rushed — it tends to conflate or omit sentences, or compress large chunks of text; inaccuracies result. More positively, the language changes somewhat (for example, we find 'God' more often than 'the gods' and 'norishe' for nurse, throughout books VII and VIII, unlike in the first edition), and we find several instances of Barker's Italian travels evidenced in his lexical choices (some of which are the first appearances of these Italianate words in English). Barker tends to shift direct to indirect speech in books VII and VIII, unlike previously. There are also more compositorial errors in the second edition than the first, particularly in books VII and VIII, where the compositors, would not have had the neat first edition to work from.

In his edition of another translation by Barker (this time from Italian), R. W. Bond described Barker's translation of the *Cyropaedia* as follows: 'fairly accurate, perhaps for its date even scholarly, rendering of Xenophon's sense but it sometimes omits a word or two, occasionally mistranslates, and often misses fine grammatical points. I note no special felicities of rendering; but on the other hand he possesses some gift in the manipulation of clauses to suit the flow of his English. His inaccuracies may be due to is Latin original.'[1] Bond is mistaken in thinking Barker was working from a Latin original, however, and the word-order seems much closer to Greek word-order than Bond credits. The full argument for Barker's translation from the Greek is provided in my Introduction.

While there are few surviving witnesses of the first edition of Barker's translation (the ESTC lists only seven: two at the British Library, and one each at Glasgow, Ripon Cathedral, the Folger, Huntington and University of Illinois), more survive of the second edition. Eleven copies of this are listed by the ESTC: one at the British Library, three in Cambridge (Christ's College, Trinity College, Cambridge University Library), one each at the Bodleian, St Andrews, the Huntington, Newberry, Harvard, Yale and Illinois. (The Introduction also discusses several Continental vernacular translations and presentation manuscripts of the text which were given to King Edward VII, roughly contemporaneously with Barker's translation.)

There is no substantive modern critical edition of Barker's translation, though the text of Barker's translation has been edited with a brief introduction by James Tatum (1987) in Garland's 'Renaissance Imagination' series, and there is a good modern English translation of the *Cyropaedia*, by Wayne Ambler (2001).

---

[1] R. W. Bond, *Addenda, Glossary, and Index to William Barker's 'Nobility of Women'* (London: Roxburghe Club, 1905), pp. 8–9, note 2.

Contractions and conventions

I have expanded all contractions (e.g. M^r to Master) and ampersands, and reintroduced the definite article for clarity — e.g. thoccasion' and 'Thassyrians' have been changed to 'the occasion' and 'the Assyrians'. I have regularized names — e.g. 'Aniball' (of Carthage) to 'Hannibal' — and Cyrus to Cyrus's, where the possessive is indicated. I have removed capitalizations of occasional nouns (e.g. 'policy for Courtliness' in Herbert dedicatory epistle). While the spelling is modernized, the text can still be tricky to understand, so I have also added and removed punctuation for the sake of clarity. I have expanded Roman numerals to written-out numbers. On occasion, where the passage allows it, I have sometimes made conjunctions of two words in more familiar ways, where there is a chance of confusion or an obvious need for balance — e.g. in the dedicatory epistle to the second edition, I have changed 'labour worthy' to 'labourworthy' to match 'praiseworthy' a few words earlier; or on p. 12, I have 'hunteth himself' rather than the confusing suggestion that the king 'hunteth him self'. I have changed the past tense 'rid' for the more modern 'rode', and where it clarified the sense, 'an other' has been changed to 'another'. Obvious typographic or compositorial mistakes have been silently corrected. Marginal notes in the original are noted in the footnotes. All page signatures are recto unless otherwise indicated. Finally, the degree symbol (°) marks words to be found in the Glossary at the end of the volume.

The VIII. bookes | OF XENOPHON | CONTAININGE THE | institutio[n], schole, and education | of Cyrus, the noble Kynge of Persye: also his | ciuill and princelye estate, his | expedition into Babylon, Syria and | Aegypt, and his exhortation | before his death, to his | children.[1]

Translated out of Greeke into Englishe by M. William Bercker.

Imprinted Anno Domini | M. D. LXVII

---

[1] The VIII. Bookes] The title of the (incomplete) 1552[?] edition (STC 26066) is *The bookes of Xenophon, contayning the Discipline, Schole, and Education of Cyrus the noble kyng of Persie*. All further references to the 1552[?] edition will use the STC number, as will all further references to the 1567 edition (STC 26067).

To the right honourable my singular good Lord, Philip, Earl of Surrey,[2] son and heir to my Lord and master the Duke of Norfolk's grace, William Barker wisheth furtherance in forwardness of learning with continuance of virtue and honour.

When Alexander the Great did pass by the place where Achilles was buried, he said these words: O happy Achilles, that haddest such a trumpet as Homer to sound thy glory to the world. Of this saying did grow a disputation, whether the valiant captain that by courage and policy attaineth to same, or the skilful writer that by learning and cunning maketh report thereof is worthy more commendation. For as the doer of noble deeds giveth matter to the writer of goodly books, so those deeds should soon die if they did not live by writ.[3] When Zopyrus, a noble man of Persia, had disfigured his body and thereby won the City of Babylon, Darius the King of that country said: I had rather have one such faithful subject as Zopyrus was than ten such cities as Babylon is.[4] Of which sentence riseth this question: whether the mighty prince that commandeth what he will have done, or the worthy subject that executeth the prince's pleasure, deserveth greater praise. I will leave the matter in suspense, and suffer by silence the sentence to be given where it ought. And to your Lordship this I have to say: there is no gentleman alive hath more occasion to be stirred by his ancestors' virtues than you. For if I may remember unto you the noble acts that they have done and singular services that they have showed, then must I say that even from my Lord your great-great-grandfather's to my Lord's grace your father, you have to receive examples of rare virtue as well of warlike affairs done abroad as of civil wisdom showed at home, whose steps to follow you have two ways: the one is by learning, whereunto I rejoice to see you so well given.[5] For by it shall you receive such lessons in your youth as the same shall be instructions to you at more years. The other is experience,

---

[2] Philip] The ten-year-old Philip Howard, whom Barker likely tutored at one point. Philip was named after his godfather, Philip of Spain, and was to have a turbulent life; he would eventually be executed for cleaving to Catholicism, following a mid-life conversion. He was canonized in 1970 as St Philip Howard, one of the Forty English Martyrs.

[3] live by writ] i.e. knowledge of these deeds would perish were they not written down. A commonplace of Renaissance epic theory.

[4] Zopyrus] Herodotus (*Histories*, III. 153–60) rather than Xenophon had included the story of Zopyrus, a Persian who was instrumental in Darius I's capture of Babylon. Upon the failure of Darius's siege of the city (even using stratagems once used by Cyrus), Zopyrus took matters into his own hands. He cut off his own nose and ears and posed as a defector to the Babylonians, before opening the gates to the city for the Persian attack.

[5] your great-great-grandfather's] Thomas Howard, second Duke of Norfolk, a military man and diplomat close to Henry VII and Henry VIII, who led the army that defeated the Scots at Flodden Field in 1513. (He was also Queen Elizabeth I's great-grandfather on her mother's side; Anne Boleyn was a cousin of Philip's father Thomas Howard, fourth Duke of Norfolk, and Barker's 'master' and employer.) On the Howards, see Introduction, pp. 19–21.

DEDICATION

to the which I hope you will give yourself when time shall come. For as the one without the other hath a want, so both being joined together maketh a marvellous perfection. In the first you are yet to be trained with as good inducements as may be, and better can there none be than the reading of such authors as for the matter be most worthy, and for the manner be most skilful. Which being granted, I dare affirm this Xenophon, whom I now present unto you, to be most fit for you. For he treateth of a prince that in his time exceeded all other, and in him he showeth a plat° of perfect and princely education.[6] The handling of it is such as for the excellency both in learning and experience can not be amended. For this Xenophon was scholar to Socrates, and proved so singular as he was accounted concurrent with his schoolfellow Plato who for his knowledge was surnamed Divine.[7] This Xenophon was he that after Cyrus the Younger was slain in the expedition he made into Asia, brought home the Grecians that served in that voyage, amidst so many fierce enemies, over so many huge mountains, and through so many dangerous passages.[8] And this was the Xenophon whom Scipio, the singular Roman that overcame the valiant Hannibal of Carthage, had ever at his pillow to receive instructions by night that he would practise by day.[9] So as for both considerations, few or none have been found the like. Which although it be true, yet is there one thing that hath a while withdrawn me from that I now am a-doing. And that is that for your lordship's further furtherance in learning, and for mine own poor estimation, I should rather have exhibited unto you something in Latin than in English. But as a forlorn Scholar, not able to keep credit in learning, I do yet entertain myself with studies not altogether devoid of learning, which I offer unto you. Indeed I must confess this translation to be done before I went into Italy, finding six books of the same enprinted° when I did return, not by my desire but only by the courtesy and goodwill of the Printer, a furtherer of good learning.[10] For

---

[6] perfect and princely education] Barker reorients the Renaissance commonplace that Cyrus is a perfect prince to foreground his education. Castiglione, for example, compares Xenophon's perfect prince to Cicero's perfect orator (in *De Oratore*) to claim in turn that his *cortegiano* is the perfect courtier. Castiglione's epistle, where this claim appears, is translated as part of Thomas Hoby's *The Courtyer of Count Baldassar Castilio* (1561).
[7] concurrent with his schoolfellow Plato] On the comparison between Xenophon and Plato as contemporaries and fellow disciples of Socrates, and its currency in Renaissance writing, see Introduction, p. 75.
[8] This Xenophon] In the *Anabasis*, Xenophon described (albeit in the third person) how he led an army of Greek mercenaries back through hostile Persian territory following the precipitate fall of the Persian king's brother, Cyrus the Younger, whose attempted coup they were supporting. The *Anabasis* was translated into English by John Bingham (1623); on the familiarity of the *Anabasis* in the Renaissance, see Introduction, pp. 6–7, 35.
[9] had ever at his pillow] Barker refers to the much-cited assertion that Scipio Africanus carried Xenophon's *Cyropaedia* with him as a *vade mecum* on campaign, even as Alexander the Great is said to have carried Homer's *Iliad* with him.
[10] finding six books of the same enprinted] Unusually, we can trust Barker's chronology

these two later books I have often times been spoken to of diverse of my learned friends, whose requests at length I have satisfied. And because the only intent of the book is to show what a noble man by good education may prove unto, I have both by duty and skill made election of your lordship to be the last patron of it, as I made my very good Lord, the Earl of Pembroke, the first.[11] To your lordship the reading of such matter is convenient, to his lordship the judgement is to be referred. Your lordship must talk of your book, his lordship of his experience. For the which, joining him with you, as it were in commission for the goodwill he hath borne to my lord your grandfather and for the friendship he beareth to my Lord your father, I dare say he will be both a father and a grandfather to you, if cause should require.[12] I shall desire your lordship when you read it to think the time will come when you shall be called of your prince to take such journeys as you shall see that Cyrus appointeth to such as you are, and to do such service as your most noble progenitors have done by the commandment of their princes, whose great glory shall ever so shine before your eyes as you must needs foresee yourself to follow the same to the contentation of your prince, the benefit of your country, the joy of your parents, and comfort of all your friends and servants, the which I among the rest do wish and trust to see.[13] And so most humbly I take my leave of your Lordship. From my chamber at Howard's house, the viii day of this new year. 1567.

---

here. On Reyner Wolfe, printer of both editions, and on the dating of Barker's translations, see Introduction, pp. 28–9.

[11] the first] William Herbert, first Earl of Pembroke, was the dedicatee of the translation of the first six books (STC 26066).

[12] both a father and a grandfather to you] William Herbert would later support Philip's father Thomas Howard in the Ridolfi plot. On the dedications, see Introduction, pp. 28–9.

[13] to take such journeys] Barker may have been thinking of the diplomatic embassies of Thomas Howard second Duke of Norfolk, which included the negotiations for the marriage of Prince Arthur with Katherine of Aragon.

A Preface to the right honourable William Earl of Pembroke, Lord Herbert of Cardiff, knight of the honourable Order of the Garter and President of the King's Highness' Council in the marches of Wales,[1] William Barker wisheth health and honour.

Those authors be chiefly to be read which have not only by fineness of wit and diligence of study attained to an excellency, but also have had the experience of manners of men, and diversity of places, and have with wisdom and eloquence joined those two together. For as general things and order of nature can not be perceived but by them whose natural sharpness of wit is holpen° with earnest and continual painfulness of study, so be private doings and dispositions of men only known by daily use and trial of them. And there be many skilful in the one that be in the other kind very simple, and can say much of generalities but in particularities be utterly ignorant, and other again who can talk well and wisely in singular points wherein they be experienced but in the other kind they be in a manner without understanding. For they who have been brought up in study and know no more than they have attained unto by reading be in general things laboured in by other, and found out by much debating of common reason, skilfuller than the common sort, and therefore called better learned.[2] And they who have whet the fine edge of their wit, and peered the doings and inclinations of other with diligent marking of the seen and remembering the marked, be called witty and wise men, and have good praise of their sayings and doings in common life. And hereby happeneth that which is commonly said, 'The best learned men be not the wisest', other for that they can not tell particular things which be in daily and common use of life; or else for cause, although their reason be well furnished with reading and understanding what is best, yet their affections and moods be not hardened enough, nor strengthened with experience and trial of things, and therefore be in their doings many times unadvised and simple. And because each of these things require an whole man's life to grow to any perfectness therein, and it seldom chanceth and once in a man's age that perfect study and perfect experience meet together in one man, and few painful wits be good and fewer good wits be painful, therefore cometh it seldom to pass that there be many thoroughly wise men at one time

---

[1] marches of Wales] William Herbert had reaped the fruits of his activities of 1549 and 1550 when he switched his loyalty from Protector Somerset to the Earl of Warwick (later Northumberland), and had offices, lands and sinecures granted him for his support. Among them were the offices of Lord President of the Council in the Marches of Wales and Earl of Pembroke, both titles he received in late 1551 and the titles by which he is addressed here by Barker.

[2] in by other] A case of eye-skip here by the compositor. Suggested sense: 'For they who have been brought up in study and know no more than they have attained unto by reading be in general things laboured, and found out by much debating of common reason by other skilfuller than the common sort (and therefore called better learned).'

and be commonlier talked of than seen, and more looked for than found, and wished for rather than had. And this maketh that in all the course of learning and experience there be very few who satisfy goodly and well-judging wits, and whom they would, that seek the price° of fame, labour to follow in their writings whose wits they marvel at in writing.³

Some there be who by diligence and nature have goodly understanding of praiseworthy things, and can find out well what is best to be done, and wittiest to be reasoned, but they lack the stream of eloquence which floweth with delight to please the dainty ears, and can roughly hew the matter to serve for good purpose, but yet lack the swift violence of sweet running talk to carry away the indifferent mind to their intented° purpose. Other there be whose wit melteth words sufficient to serve, and gusheth with abundance when they turn their cock°, but it is muddy and troubled for lack of fined° reason, and so serveth not the purpose well, although it be plentiful, but better unoccupied than spent in weighty causes. Thus Nature playeth well where she purposeth her show, and showeth what she liketh to open her diversity, and is fruitful to weeds if she lie untilled, and overgroweth herself with her own plenty, and by fruitfulness is unfruitful except her fruitfulness be ordered, and wisdom rule Nature and pare away her excess wherewith she is overcharged when she is unordered.⁴ The barren ground sometime° with diligence is tilled, and bringeth forth such fruit as such a ground can serve for, and what cunning can do where nature will not help, she showeth by her burden and telleth us this lesson: that nature's want is holpen where good husbandry is used, and ill grounds well looked to be of like value to the good grounds ill ordered and overgrown by sloth.⁵

Such hardness is it for good things well made to meet all in one man, and matchly° to be coupled, for nature and diligence to serve experience and study, all which things lightly fall not well together except° some godly grace frame some diligent nature, which being well brought up and well disposed to, do furnish nature's beauty with the favour of good learning, and mark well in travail° the common doings of men, and apply well together his learning and experience, and labour thereunto to join wisdom in talk by following of the wise, and raising out his words of the nature of the matter, and driving to the end the order of his reason, and measuring by discretion the affection of the

---

³ in writing] i.e. that there are few whose writings please all good wits, and many more who seek the prize of fame but who struggle to follow the writings of those whose wits they praise.
⁴ unordered] Barker's chiastic phrasing works hard to advertise itself as 'fined reason'.
⁵ overgrown by sloth] This parable of the necessity of putting order on nature where she is most abundant savours strongly of husbandry manuals and may serve to recall Xenophon's influential husbandry manual, the *Oeconomicus*, the first of his works to be translated into English (1532). On its influence, see Hutson, *The Usurer's Daughter: Male Friendship and Fictions of Women in Sixteenth-Century England* (London: Routledge, 1994), pp. 17–51.

hearer and draw him to the matter by cunning in conveyance,° and not the matter unto him, to serve his desire.

But Xenophon this philosopher hath not only travailed in the general knowledge of true reason to have right understanding what is good and bad in life and what is true and false in nature, but also travailed[6] by experience to see the diversities of men's manners, and to acquaint himself with right order of civil government, and thereby hath attained to a great estimation of worthiness among the wise and learned, and judged a man most worthy, whose writings should be read with diligence and travailed in for the fruits of wisdom. For he was Socrates' scholar, out of whose school came first the excellent philosophers, who were afterwards divided into certain sects and filled all Greece with manifold knowledge, and being joined with the most notable men in schoolfellowship, got equal praise with the chiefest, and hath learnedly entreated the sum of well-doings in his book that he wrote of Socrates' worthy remembrances.[7] For government and order of policy, he first travelled through not only Greece but also remained with great estimation in the King of Persia's court,[8] and understood not only the natures of men, the usages of orders, the devices of counsel, the engines of war, but also the sports and pastimes most convenient for a leisureful life,[9] and hath sorted with skill that was engrossed by experience, and hath given rules of peace and war no learned man more, and furnisheth a gentleman with much goodly knowledge so much more to be commended than the other, that his rules be in practice for common life and not sought out of the depths of nature, whose perfectness as it is most commendable, so can it not best agree with the common use of life.[10] But what

---

[6] travailed] I have preserved the pun on travel/travail here as the text seems to be evoking both Xenophon's travels in Persia as well as his labours, a pun Barker also recommends to his readers by extension.

[7] Socrates' scholar] Both Xenophon and Plato were scholars of Socrates and wrote about him: Xenophon in his *Memorabilia*, *Apology* and *Symposium*, Plato across his various dialogues, as well as his own *Apology of Socrates*. On the tradition of a supposed rivalry between Xenophon and Plato dating back to Aulus Gellius, see Introduction, pp. 2, 6.

[8] King of Persia's court] Given that Xenophon led an army of Greek mercenaries preparing to oust the incumbent King of Persia, Artaxerxes II, on behalf of his brother Cyrus the Younger, a welcoming reception at the King of Persia's court is very doubtful. Xenophon's *Anabasis* did mention one Greek author welcomed at the King of Persia's court, the physician Ctesias. But Ctesias's *Persika* would not achieve anything like the readership or authority of Xenophon's *Anabasis*. See Rood, 'A Delightful Retreat', on Xenophon's later reputation as a retired general at his estate at Scyllus.

[9] leisureful life] There may be a distant echo here of a saying attributed to Scipio Africanus and reported by Cicero, via Cato, in *De Officiis*, at the beginning of his third letter (here, in Nicholas Grimald's 1556 translation, *Marcus Tullius Ciceroes thre bokes of duties* (London: Richard Tottel, 1556), fol. 110: 'He was never more leasurelesse, than whan he was leasurefull: and never lesse alone, than whan he was all alone').

[10] the common use of life] Barker's emphasis on the 'common use of life' and 'practice for common life' is part of his larger project to present the usefulness of Cyrus as a model not

is there that a wise man can with honesty desire, whereof not only the sparkles be scattered in him but also the great beams be largely set, that in such variety and plentifulness of good things, as it is not hard to choose the good, so is it very hard to choose the best? If knowledge of war be sought for, is there any that giveth truer and wiser rules both for the captain to govern by and the soldier to be ruled after? Did not Scipio, as Tully citeth out of Polybius, think the books of Cyrus's bringing up so full of good instructions and warlike wisdom that a good captain should never go without them?[11] Was not Cyrus so well taught himself that he learned not only obedience[12] like a soldier but government like a captain, and afterwards was fulfilled with all the noble virtues that may be wished with excellency in any ruler? And all those good lessons that other Cyrus[13] learned, or Scipio praised, be contained in this treatise, and fit to be known at this time, not for that the kinds of war be not changed,[14] but forcause° those precepts which he gathered out of the everlasting and unchangeable right of Nature's laws do serve all men at all times and come amiss to no country. The miseries and misfortunes of war, the shifts° and escapes from the enemies, the foresight of dangers and avoiding of perils, be they anywhere more grievous or more manifold than in younger Cyrus going up against the King and in Xenophon's return again to Greece?[15] If peace and quietness be looked for, can there be any better rules given for every man's private life than the worthy remembrances of Socrates?[16] Which books contain a sum of manners and life and what is to be followed as good and avoided as evil, and what honesty and philosophy doth look for, and what nature uncorrupted can naturally require, and which is the right and easy way to the true and reasonable happiness. If

---

just for princes but for aspiring young gentlemen (such as Philip Howard) and respected generals (such as William Herbert). It may also intersect with Barker's habit of translating πολιτεία (*politeía*) and δημοκρατία (*dēmokratía*) as 'common' rather than 'public', as later translators often do. See Introduction, p. 40 and note 143.

[11] never go without them] See note 194 (p. 55) on this commonplace about Scipio's endorsement of the *Cyropaedia* as a book to be brought on campaign. ('Tully' is Cicero.)

[12] obedience] See Introduction on Xenophon's emphasis on the quality of obedience taught by the *Cyropaedia*, not just military but social. Roger Ascham made much of 'this obedience that was in great King Cyrus and stout Samson' in *The Schoolmaster* (1570), citing Cyrus's deferral to his parents' wishes in the matter of his marriage, in Book VIII: 'And see the great obedience that was used in old time to fathers and governors. No son, were he never so old of years, never so great of birth, though he were a king's son, might not marry but by his father's, and mother's also, consent'. Ascham, *The Schoolmaster* (1570), ed. by Lawrence V. Ryan (Washington, DC: Folger/University Press of Virginia, 1974), p. 39.

[13] that other Cyrus] Cyrus the Younger.

[14] be not changed] The value of ancient military theory was widely accepted. Bingham's translation of the *Anabasis* (1623) professed the utility of Xenophon's text to his dedicatee precisely because 'there is no difference to be found betwixt us and Antiquitie in the universall course Militarie, save only in the use of Gunnes' (sig. π3).

[15] return again to Greece] As described in Xenophon's *Anabasis*.

[16] of Socrates] The rules for private life expounded in dialogue with Socrates in Xenophon's *Oeconomicus* and, perhaps, the *Memorabilia*.

government and order of commonwealth be sought, can we have a perfecter example of a good ruler than the praise of Agesilaus is?¹⁷ Which hath prescribed all the worthy virtues that a man can praisably° devise, to furnish a ruler, which hath not hereon° all the incommodities that longeth° to governers, and plain demonstrations how in seeking for pleasures they be furthest from pleasures and last to attain that wherein they labour first. Be not these books like true glasses,¹⁸ that will show none other favour and beauty of conditions than be in the owners in deed? Nor will not by flattery make mean things great and great vices small but according to the true proportion of the qualities, show the visage of the same? If hunting, riding,¹⁹ and other chosen pastimes be fit to be learned of Gentlemen and taught of skilful men, who did experience them more naturally and write of them more cunningly than Xenophon hath done? The matters whereof be neither unpleasant to be known nor unhandsome to be practised. And yet the chief groundworks of riding be so naturally laid by him that he is at this day counted the best horseman that keepeth his orders in riding best, and goeth nighest that true ways which he by wisdom hath of long time prescribed.²⁰ All these things which severally be scattered and sparsed° in other be almost all in one gathered together in this book of Cyrus's bringing up and going forth, under this title, is indeed a pathway to wisdom, and for matter most fit to be read and known of all Gentlemen, and for fineness of style most pleasant and perfect in his own tongue. And although herein I have a goodly occasion to commend the writer, that in the most eloquent and excellent tongue hath written most purely, yet because it carryeth the matter whole into another tongue, and keepeth his own fineness still in his own tongue, and our gross tongue is a rude and a barren tongue, when it is compared with so flourishing and plentiful a tongue,²¹ I will pass over this praise, with touching only the remembrance of it, and leave so large a matter until a better time, lest in

---

¹⁷ Agesilaus is] The third century BCE Spartan king, subject of Xenophon's *Agesilaus*. Not published in English translation until centuries later, it was nonetheless widely available in the composite 'Works' of Xenophon popular on the Continent and in England.

¹⁸ like true glasses] A popular rhetoric of 'glasses' and mirrors, both true and distorting ones, animated humanist exemplary rhetoric and genres. It was also co-opted for hortatory or cautionary genres such as the *speculum principis* (mirror-for-princes) and the *Mirrour for Magistrates*, and even for an epic romance such as *The Faerie Queene*, in which Edmund Spenser instructed his dedicatee, Queen Elizabeth, 'in mirrours more then one her selfe to see' (III. Pr. 5). On the *Cyropaedia* within the mirror-for-princes tradition, see Introduction, pp. 45–7.

¹⁹ hunting, riding] Xenophon wrote two treatises on horsemanship: *On Horsemanship* and *Hipparchicus*.

²⁰ of long time prescribed] In Xenophon's *On Horsemanship*.

²¹ so flourishing and plentiful a tongue] English apologetics about the inferiority of English as a literary language on a par with Greek or Latin was a widespread mid-century phenomenon, though it would soon be tackled by poets and critics such as Edmund Spenser in *The Shepheardes Calender* (1579) and George Gascoigne in *Certayne Notes of Instruction* (1575).

commending his writing I might dispraise mine own, or else in an unneedful matter spend too many words. But shortly to conclude: of all books which philosophers have written with judgement, and others hath translated with labour, no book there is which containeth better matter for life, order for war lines, policy for courtliness, wisdom for government, temperance for subjects, obedience for all states. I seem to praise this book too much: to the ignorant I may do, who can not judge, and therefore I pardon him, and yet least worthy pardon to rule over that he knoweth not and be most busy where he hath least skill. But to the wise I cannot, who weighing the matter and judging the examples and examining the rules, shall find as much as plentiful wisdom wittily framed in this short treatise, as in other great volumes, having as expressly every part of wisdom as well set together as a little tablet containeth the lively face by cunning of workmanship, which the great table[22] for want of cunning sometime doth miss. But because I thought it praiseworthy I thought it labourworthy also, and began my travail of this good opinion, supposing that which of reason contented me might by the same reason content others too. And besides the honest contenting which must needs be in well-minded men, if any man learn anything that he is the better for, I trust he will yield me some thanks, by whose means he hath met with a good counsellor and learned plainly that he might long else have sought for, and therefore thank me for my pains herein at the least if he further require me not to go on with the like. Therefore in devising to whom I might offer this honest travail of mine, well, I trust, bestowed although of every noble man well, yet of no man better than of your good Lordship, whose virtues be better known unto me than you yourself are, and therefore thought it fit to offer written virtues where lively virtues dwell, to be better accepted where they see report of their ancient fame and honour much esteemed. And if this thing moved me not, yet another might: your children whom ye love and bring them up in learning, and have chosen them of late a good schoolmaster,[23] as I hear, whose diligence and discretion hath much always commended the good learning he hath and other good qualities. The reading hereof to them may double profit them, both to learn the matter which is good and pleasant, and also to learn to turn Latin out of

---

[22] little tablet ... great table] Contrasting the artistry of a miniature and a large painted portrait.

[23] a good schoolmaster] This may be Henry Iden, who translated Giovanni Battista Gelli's *Circe* (1557), and also dedicated it to William Herbert and his two sons. Iden writes of his dedicatees that 'I have of long time heretofore served in your educatio[n]', and refers to their 'conference' in Italian, presumably taught by him (sig. a2v). Barker would later translate Gelli's *Capricci del Bottaio* as *The Fearfull Fansies of the Florentyne Couper* (1568), and it is likely that he was among the 'divers frendes' who encouraged Iden to undertake his translation of Gelli's *Circe* from the Italian. Barker and Iden also shared a printer in the late 1550s: Iden's translation was printed by John Cawood in 1558 or 1559; Cawood had printed Barker's translation of St Basil's homily on classical learning in 1557.

English, which way although it seem trifling to some, yet is it the readiest exercise that ever I could find, to make a child easily to attain to that profit which else with labour they shall not hit at all.[24] These things make me bold, although not much acquainted, to present to your Lordship the honour of my pains, most humbly desiring you to accept my boldness, moved yet with reason, and where the goodness of the matter, your Lordship's noble virtues, your children's bringing up, hath moved me thereunto, ye will for these causes accept well my good will, and I shall hereby think myself so bound to you, as other must to me that hereby profiteth ought,[25] and desire the living LORD, whose rule goeth through all, to increase your lordship's honour and nobleness always.

---

[24] hit at all] Barker describes the common pedagogical practice of double translation, whereby students translated from Latin to English and then back into Latin, comparing their results with the original. Although Xenophon is a Greek writer (whose style was much admired), his work is nonetheless deemed an appropriate subject for translation into Latin from English, probably because of the ready availability of Francesco Filelfo's Latin translation of the text in numerous Continental editions of Xenophon's work.

[25] ought] i.e. anything; 'oughtes' in both 26066 and 26067.

The Proem of Xenophon

I have thought oftentimes with myself how many of the wealths[1] hath been overthrown by them which would rather have any form of government than the commons.[2] How oft the rule of one, the power of few,[3] have been of the commons overthrown. How many attempting tyranny some forthwith have been deprived, some reigneth any time, be in admiration as men of rare wisdom and felicity. Methought also I had learned that among many masters of private families, some have had many servants, some very few, which few notwithstanding they could never very well break and have at commandment. I perceive furthermore that neatherds be rulers of neat°, and horsekeepers of horses, and that all other which be called herdmen be semblably reputed rulers of the cattle that they keep. I thought also I saw all herds more willing to obey their keepers than men their governors. For the herds going whither the keepers driveth, feeding on that pasture which they appoint, departing from the same when they compel, and suffering them to take at their pleasures all such profits as of them ariseth. I never yet heard any herd to be rebellious or disobedient or denying their keeper the fruit of their increase, but rather to be more untractable to all other than to them which receiveth profit by them; but men do withstand none so much as them whom they perceive do go about to have dominion over them. When I had thus debated these things, I gave this sentence of them: that it is naturally given to man to have more easily of all other creatures the sovereignty than of only man.[4] But when I remembered in my mind that Cyrus, being a Persian, had gotten so many sorts of men, so many sundry cities, and so many diverse nations obedient unto him, I was thereby enforced to forthink° the same, because it is neither impossible nor yet greatly hard to have sovereignty over man if a man did it skilfully or wittily. For we know that men willingly have been obedient to Cyrus, whereof some have been distant many days' journey, some many months from him, some that never did see him, some that knew certainly they never should see him yet would become his liege men. So much did he exceed all kings as well inheritors to their fathers' kingdoms as them which by their industry achieved the same. For the Scythian king, albeit the Scyths be in number great, can get dominion over

---

[1] wealths] i.e. commonwealths. (This is added as a marginal gloss by the reader of the Huntington copy, for example.) In the copy-text it is usually rendered as two words ('common wealths'), but for the sake of clarity 'commonwealths' will be used in this edition.

[2] the commons] Barker translates δημοκρατία (*dēmokratía*) as 'the commons' (although in the same sentence, he translates the plural form as 'the wealths'). By choosing 'commons', Barker may be seeking to avoid the absolutist tradition of anti-democratic thought which often conceptualized democratic rule as rule by a monstrous, many-headed hydra.

[3] power of few] oligarchy.

[4] of only man] That is, that it is easier for humans to rule over non-humans than over humans.

none other nation, but is well apaid° if he can govern his own country.⁵ And the Thracian the Thraces, the Illyrians the Illyries. And of other nations we hear the like thing. And truly the countries of Europe be yet, as they say, free, and one of them disseuered from the other. But Cyrus beginning his reign after this sort, and invading the nations of Asia, being of separate regiment with a small army of Persians, ruled the Medes, and Hyrcanians, they frankly giving it him. He conquered the Syrians, the Assyrians, the Arabians, the Cappadocians, both Phrygians, the Lydians, the Carians, the Phoenicians, the Babylonians. He ruled the Bactrians, the Indes, the Cilicians. Likewise the Sacians, the Paphlagonians, and Mariandines with other very many nations whose names a man could not well rehearse.⁶ He governed also the Greeks that be in Asia, and making a voyage to the sea side he subdued the Cyprians⁷ and Egyptians. Thus he had dominion over these nations which in language agreed neither with him nor with themselves. Notwithstanding so great a portion of the earth could he go throughout by fear of his prowess that he astonished all men, and none durst enterprise anything against him, yet he could imprint so great desire in all mens' hearts to be thankful to him that they thought good evermore to be governed by his pleasure. He got the friendship of so many nations as were a pain to number whether so ever a man will travel from his palace, either east, west, north, or south. We therefore have considered this man as worthy estimation, what kindred, what natural inclination, what form of bringing up he had, whereby he did which passed so far all other living men in princely dominion. As much then as I have either heard or known of him, so much I purpose to declare.

The Parentage of Cyrus⁸

Cambyses⁹ king of Persia was father to Cyrus. This Cambyses was of the Perses

---

⁵ country] Philemon Holland tends to use 'state' rather than Barker's 'country' or 'nation', though at other moments (e.g. 'apaid' here) Holland looks to be consulting Barker's translation.
⁶ rehearse] Barker's 'Mariandines' provides a clue to his copy-text; Holland uses 'Megadines'. Modern editions use 'Magadidae'. See Textual Note.
⁷ Cyprians] Cypriots.
⁸ Parentage of Cyrus] Apart from the frequent use of 'Oration' as a subtitle or printed marginal note, 'The Parentage of Cyrus' is a rare subtitle within the books, and follows Continental editions such as Nicholas Brylinger's 1555 Basle edition. Besides subtitling the Proem, the 'Parentage of Cyrus' and the interspersed Orations, Barker uses no sub-divisions within the books, unlike later translators such as Philemon Holland, who divides the books into chapters.
⁹ Cambyses] The son of Cyrus was also named Cambyses, and it is he who is the subject of Thomas Preston's eponymous play, the style of which Falstaff parodies in *1 Henry IV*, Act II, scene 4. Ladan Niayesh suggests that the rude mechanicals' play in *A Midsummer Night's Dream*, 'The most lamentable comedy and most cruel death of Pyramus and Thisbe' (I. 2.

family, who have their name of Perseus.[10] Mandane was his mother,[11] the daughter of Astyages, king of Media. The saying is, and yet reported among the barbarians,[12] that Cyrus by nature was of most goodly shape, in heart most gentle, of learning most studious, and of honour most desirous, in so much that for glory or praise sake he would endure any pain and abide any peril. This is recorded of the nature both of his mind and of his favour°. He was brought up in the Persians' laws; these laws[13] as it appeareth hath in their beginning some respect of the commonwealth, for they go not that way to work that many other cities do. For the most part of cities suffereth every man as he list to bring up his children, and the ancients° to lead what life they will. Then they enjoin them neither to steal, to rob, to enter any house by violence, to strike any man unlawfully, to commit adultery, to be disobedient to their rulers, and all such other things after like sort. If any do offend in these, a pain is appointed for the same. But the Persians' laws proved by foresight that from the beginning none of their countrymen might be such in time to come as should desire any evil or dishonesty. And this is their provision. They have a common place of free resort, as they name it, where the palace and all other royal things[14] be placed, from whence all buying and selling, all market men with their noise and rudeness, is rejected to another place, that the pureness of good nurture[15] should not be intermeddled with the base multitude.

This common place, compassing the palace, is divided into four parts.

11–12), later described to Theseus as 'very tragical mirth' (v. 1. 52), may also be inspired by the long title of Preston's play, *A lamentable tragedy mixed full of pleasant mirth, containing the life of Cambyses, king of Persia*. Niayesh, 'Shakespeare's Persians', *Shakespeare*, 4 (2), 127–36 (p. 130).

[10] have their name of Perseus] Xenophon probably derived this detail from Herodotus, *Histories*, VII. 61.

[11] Mandane was his mother] Xenophon omits Herodotus's account of the prophetic dream of Astyages regarding Mandane's child, which causes him to order the killing of his baby grandson. In the Herodotean account, Cyrus is instead raised by shepherds and the prophecy of Cyrus's conquest of Astyages eventually proves true.

[12] Barbarians] 'By the barbarians' is an addition by Barker. On the Greek coining of the term βάρβαροι (*bárbaroi*) to refer to their enemy, the gathered peoples of the Persian army, see (among others) Edith Hall, *Inventing the Barbarian: Greek Self-Definition through Tragedy* (Oxford: Clarendon Press, 1989).

[13] these laws] The stability of Persian laws and Persian justice is celebrated by Xenophon, unlike Herodotus, who critiques them for instability.

[14] other royal things] An awkward translation of τὰ βασίλεια (*tà basíleia*), which refers to the buildings of the palace. Holland has 'the Kings Palace with the other stately Courts', and gives more detail on the spatial organization and character of the 'place of free resort' (as he also translates it), 'from whence, all Merchandizing, al mercate folke with their clamorous noises and trifling fooleries, are driven into another place; to the end, that the unruly and base multitude of such as they are, might not be intermingled with the civill order of those, who have had good breeding' (sig. A2).

[15] pureness of good nurture] Holland makes the differentiation of class more explicit, with 'the civill order of those, who have had good breeding' (sig. A2).

Whereof one is for children, another for young men, the third for them that be at the full state of men, the fourth for them which for their years be pardoned from wars. And by the law every one of these is present at their place, children by break of day and likewise they that be at the full age or estate of men; the ancients when they may, except at days appointed when as they must needs be there. But the young sort lie also about the palace in warlike armour, except married men, which be not required, unless they be afore commanded to be present. Yet to be oft away, it is not good. And of every of these parts, there be twelve governors: for the Persians be divided into twelve families. And they of the ancients be governors to the children, which be thought able to make them most honest; over the young men, such of them of middle age as seemeth to bring the young sort to best proof; over them of perfect age they which be thought most meet to cause them best to do such things as be institute and commanded of the chief ruler. There be also lieutenants or governors chosen over the ancient sort which do command that they also perform their duty. Now what is appointed to every age to do we will declare, that it may be the more manifest what diligence they take to make the citizens most honest men. Children that come to the schools spend their time in learning justice, and as men say, they go as diligently to this as with us to learn their letters. Their governors consume the most part of the day in giving judgement among them. For there be, as well among children as men, accusements° one against the other, of theft, robbery, force, sleight or deceit, slander, and such other like. And whom they know to offend in any of these, they punish. They chastise also such as they find accusing without just cause; they give judgement also of quarrelling or complaining, for the which men do hate one another most of all.[16] They be also sore in the judgement of unthankfulness. And whom they know able to requite thanks and do it not, him they punish sharply, for they judge the unthankful to be most negligent, both toward God, their parents, country, and friends. For of unthankfulness seemeth to follow unshamefastness°,[17] which, as it appeareth, to all mischief, is the chief mistress. They teach their children soberness, and they be much furthered in learning to be sober because they see the very ancients every day live so soberly.[18] They teach them to obey their rulers. And in this also it much

---

[16] most of all] Some misreading of the Greek here, where what men hate most is ingratitude or unthankfulness, not quarrelling and complaining. Holland does a better job: 'Moreover, they call judicially into question that crime, for which, men indeed hate each other most, yet never question any therefore. And that is Ingratitude' (sig. A2v).

[17] unshamefastness] Holland has 'unshamefacednesse', which he glosses as 'impudence', but Barker probably has in mind the virtue of 'shamefastness' that Sir Thomas Elyot praised in his *Boke Named the Governour* (1531). Roger Ascham enthusiastically repeats this point, 'as Xenophon doth most truly and most wittily mark', in *The Schoolmaster (1570)*, ed. by Lawrence V. Ryan, p. 35

[18] live so soberly] Continuing the idea of exemplary pedagogy, the proximity of the older people ('ancients') to the young itself parallels Xenophon's provision of a 'glass' or 'mirror'

availeth them because they behold the ancients very obedient to their rulers. They teach them to be moderate in diet, to the which also they be much moved both because they see the ancients not to go to meat before the rulers give them leave, and because the children be not fed before their mothers, but before their masters,° and that when the governors do appoint. They bring from home for their sustenance bread, for their meat cresses°. And if any lust to drink, he hath an earthen pot to draw him water of the river. Over and beside all these they learn to shoot and dart.[19] And till the sixteen[th] or seventeen[th] year of their age, these things the children practise. After this time they come among the young men, which lead their life or be brought up on this wise.[20] Ten year[s] after their childhood, they lie about the palace as it is said tofore°, both for the custody of the city and also of temperancy,[21] for this age seemeth to have most need of good governance. They give attendance on the day upon the princes, if they will have their service in any matter of the commonwealth. And when any need is, they all remain about the palace. When the king goeth on hunting, which he doeth oft every month, he leaveth at home half the guard. They that attend upon him must have a bow and arrows with a quiver, a short sword or a wood-knife in a sheath, a target and two darts, the one to pick at large°, the other to use, if need be, at hand-strokes.

Why they give diligence° to common hunting,[22] the king being their captain, as it were in war, which both hunteth himself and provideth that other may hunt also, is because it seemeth a very true practice or exercise of warlike affairs: for he accustometh them to rise early to endure cold and heat. He exerciseth them in going afoot, and running: and of necessity they must shoot and dart at the deer, where so ever he cometh. And the mind in hunting must needs be quickened, when any cruel or fierce beast maketh against them. For when it approacheth, strike he must, and avoid the assault of it. Wherefore a man shall not lightly find in war that doth not chance in wild chase.[23] Going on hunting, they may not dine. If there be any cause of long tarrying, either for the game or that otherwise, they will continue the hunting or chase and sup with their dinner and all the next day hunt till night. Then they account these two days but one because they spend but one day's diet. Thus they do for their

---

of Cyrus for his young readers.

[19] to shoot and dart] Persian skill in archery, and its importance in Persian education, are often remarked upon by later writers — including Ascham, who published *Toxophilus* (1545), a rather unusual treatise in the form of a dialogue extolling archery especially for students.

[20] on this wise] in this way.

[21] temperancy] Barker is here translating Xenophon's σωφροσύνη (*sōphrosýne*), the well-known Greek doctrine of self-control and moderation.

[22] common hunting] Again, Barker's emphasis on the 'common' is striking. Holland has 'hunting in publike' (sig. A3), but the Greek text simply has 'hunting'.

[23] in wild chase] i.e. the man who has hunted will not encounter anything in war that he has not already met in hunting.

exercise, that if any like thing should happen in war, they might be able to do the same. And what game the young men killeth, that have they for their repast; if none, cresses.[24] If any man think they have little pleasure in eating because cresses is their only meat, and as little in drinking because water is their drink, let him remember how pleasant it is to eat coarse bread and gruel[25] in hunger, and how sweet to drink water in thirst.

The other companies which remain at home diligently exerciseth both all other things learned in their childhood and also to shoot and dart. And contending in these, one with another, they spend their time. There be also of these feats common[26] games or gifts and rewards ordained or chosen for the same. And in which family be most cunning and forward, the teacher not only that now is but also that was in their childhood is greatly praised and honoured of the people. The rulers useth the youth remaining at home if any need be of guard, of searching out transgressors, pursuing thieves, or any other thing wherein quickness and strength is required. And thus the young men pass their time. After they have lived ten years, they be placed among them of perfect age, and from the time of their youth, they spend twenty-five years after this sort, first after the manner of their youth, they give attendance upon the high rulers,[27] if any common cause needeth feats either of knowledge or courage. If at any time they must go to war, they that be thus taught occupy in warfare neither bows nor darts but such as they call armour for hand stripes°, that is, a breastplate afore° their breast, a target in the left hand, even such as the Persians have in painture°, in the right hand, a sword or arming dagger.[28] And of these men be made all magistrates, except the children's governors.[29]

After they have spent these twenty-five years they, being somewhat more than fifty years of age, be received among them which both be indeed, and also called, ancients. These ancients go not to war out of their own country, but remaineth at home discharging or dispatching all common and private causes, and judging matters of life and death. And they also do choose all other officers. If any of the young company, or of the other of perfect age, do in any thing transgress the laws, the rulers of every family or any other, do accuse the same.

The ancients hearing the cause, give judgement; he that is condemned liveth

---

[24] cresses] The frugality of the young Persian men's diet is much remarked by early moderns.
[25] coarse bread and gruel] The Greek term Barker translates is μᾶζα καὶ ἄρτος (*mâza kaì ártos*), the latter later the name of the unleavened bread used in the Eastern church.
[26] common] Again, Holland translates this as 'publike'.
[27] high rulers] Holland has 'Magistrates'.
[28] arming dagger] The word 'scimitar' does not appear in Barker's text; Holland here uses 'a sword or Cymiter' (sig. A3v).
[29] governors] Earlier Barker had translated (οἱ) τῶν παίδων διδάσκαλοι ((*hoi*) *tôn paídōn didáskaloi*) as 'masters'. On the *Cyropaedia*'s connections with governorship, see Introduction.

all his life in shame. Now that the whole Persian commonwealth may be made evident, we will a little repeat the same, being thus briefly expressed by this former declaration.

The Persians (as it is said) be in number one hundred and twenty thousand and none of all these is debarred by the law from honour and offices. It is lawful for all the Persians to send their children to the common schools of justice.[30] But they only send which are able to find them with ease,[31] they that be not able send not. They that have been taught in their childhood of the common schoolmasters may with the young sort learn the young feats. They that have not been so taught may not. They that perform so much as the law requireth of the young men proceed among them that be at full age and be partakers of honours and offices. But they that continue not out in the young men's trade may not come among the perfect aged men. And they that remain their time without reproof among the men be made ancients, so such be made ancients as have proceeded through all goodness. And this form of commonwealth they have which, they using, be reputed best men. And yet a witness remaineth of their sober diet, and also of labouring out the same. For at this day, it is shame among the Persians to spit, to snite° the nose, or to be puffed up with wind.[32] It is also a rebuke if any man be seen openly going to make water, or any other such thing.[33] Which they could never do if they kept not both a moderate diet and also did so waste their moisture by much labour that it is conveyed some other way. Thus much thought we good to speak of all the Persians. Now we will declare the noble acts of Cyrus, even from his childhood, for whose cause we have begun this treatise.

Cyrus being trained in this discipline till the twelf[th] year of his age and upward did excel all his schoolfellows both in quickness of learning and also in handsome and courageous doing of every thing. At this time, Astyages king of Media, sent for his daughter Mandane, and her son, whom he greatly desired to see, because he had heard that he was of no less beauty than honesty.[34] She

---

[30] common schools of justice] See Introduction, pp. 51-2. The ancient Persian reputation for justice was another much-cited topos in the early modern period, mostly thanks to this description of Persian schooling.
[31] find them with ease] i.e. only children whose parents can afford to spare them (from other labour) are sent to the common schools of justice. This is not, properly, an educational or political system open to all, nor is it simply meritocratic: only those who can afford to spare their children from other work can have them educated, and only the educated can subsequently take up offices or honours.
[32] puffed up with wind] fart.
[33] make water] urinating. Persian social decorum was much remarked upon in early modern England.
[34] no less beauty than honesty] The Greek text uses καλὸν κἀγαθὸν *kalòn kagathón* — beauty and goodness, a formula also used to describe the nobility. However, Barker's choice of 'honesty' may further indicate his Ciceronian interests. (Holland, by contrast, notes 'what a goodly and towardly Youth he was' (sig. [A4]).)

went to her father, taking with her her son Cyrus, to whom when they were come with speed and Cyrus knew Astyages to be his grandfather, forthwith as a child full of natural nurture, he did salute him as one that had been of old acquaintance, and embrace him as an ancient friend, and beholding his princely estate[35] by the painting of his eyes, the setting on or rubbing on of colour, and by his made hair which be lawful among the Medes (and other attirements, as purple coats and garments, and chains about their necks, and bracelets on their arms), whereas the Persians at this day, being at home, use very coarse array and thin diet. Cyrus seeing this rich array of his grandfather, and looking upon him, said to his mother, 'O Mother, how goodly is my grandfather'. His mother then asking of him whether his father or grandfather seemed the goodlier, he answered thus: 'Mother, of all the Persians my father is goodliest, but of all the Medes that I have either seen by the way or at men's doors, my grandfather is far the goodliest.' Astyages then welcoming him again arrayed him with a robe of honour and honourably apparelled him with chains and bracelets. And if he did ride to any place he was set upon a horse trapped with gold, even as Astyages was wont to ride himself. Cyrus being a child desirous of honesty and honour was delighted with his robe, and glad that he learned the feat of riding for in Persia, because it is hard to keep horses and to use riding by reason the country is full of hills, it is seldom that a man shall see an horse.[36] Astyages being at supper with his daughter and nephew, and minding that the child should have a pleasant supper, that he should the less long to go home, served him with all kinds of dishes, sauces and fine fare. And Cyrus (as they report) said thus: 'Grandfather, what a business have you to do in this supper, if ye must move your hand to every dish and taste of so many sundry meats?' Then said Astyages, 'Doth not this supper (think ye) pass far your suppers in Persia?' To whom Cyrus thus answered: 'No, Grandfather, for we go a more plain and straight way to suffice our selves than you do. For bread and flesh bringeth us to that, but you desiring that very thing which we have, wandering up and down, as it were in a maze, do scarcely at length come to that whereunto we attained long before.' 'But we, O son' (said Astyages), 'be not grieved when we do wander, and when ye have tasted ye shall know how sweet they be.' 'But methinketh, Grandfather' (said Cyrus), 'that ye be loathed with these meats.' 'Whereby conject° ye that?' said Astyages. 'Because' (said he), 'when you touch bread, you do not wipe your hand. But when you touch any of these, forthwith you make clean your hands with a napkin, as though you were much grieved with the encumbrance of your excessive meats.' 'If ye think so, Son' (said Astyages), 'yet

---

[35] his princely estate] i.e. that of Astyages.
[36] see an horse] Historically untrue; horses from the Persian hills were famed throughout the ancient world and were likely to have been an important factor in their ascendancy in the region in the earliest times of human habitation.

assay° of the flesh that you may go home a lusty young man.' And after he had said thus, he caused all kind of flesh, both wild and tame, to be brought to the table. And Cyrus beholding so much meat said, 'Grandfather, do ye give me all this meat to do with it what I list?' 'I give it thee, son' (said Astyages), 'certainly.' Cyrus taking the meat did distribute it among his Grandfather's servants, saying thus to every one: 'Take thou this, because thou gladly teachest me to ride. Take thou this, because thou gavest me a dart, for that I have yet. Take thou this, because thou doest honourably serve my Grandfather. Take thou this because thou dost reverence my mother.'[37] And thus he did, till he had given away all the meat that he had. 'But ye give nothing' (said Astyages), 'to Sacas my cupbearer whom I esteem most.' This Sacas was a goodly fellow, and had the office to admit all them that had to do with Astyages, and keep back such as he thought to come out of season. And Cyrus, quickly as a child, nothing afraid, asked, 'Why do ye (Grandfather) set so much by him?' And Astyages dallying with him said: 'Do ye not see how neatly and comely he poureth wine?' For these kings' cupbearers be most neat in giving wine and pure handling of the same. They bear the cup and give it with three fingers, and so bring it as they may most easily deliver it him that shall drink. 'Command, grandfather' (said he), 'Sacas to give me the cup, that I serving you of drink cleanly may, if I can, get your favour.' Astyages commandeth the cup to be given him. Cyrus taking it, did so cleanse it as he had seen Sacas done, and with a stable countenance, so prettily and seemly bring and give it to his Grandfather that he made both him and his mother to laugh heartily. And Cyrus, laughing for good company, ran to his Grandfather and embraced him, saying: 'O Sacas, ye be undone. I am like to thrust you out of your office. For I can give wine as well as you and yet drink none myself.' For kings' cupbearers, when they bear the cup, drawing off it into a piece°, they pour some into their left hand, which they drink lest poison might be mixed, and they escape harmless.

Then Astyages merrily said, 'Why do ye (Cyrus) follow Sacas in all other things and do not drink the wine as he does?' 'Because' (said he), 'I feared that poison was mixed in the cup. For when you on your birthday did feast your friends, I knew well that he gave you poison.' 'And how, Son' (said he) 'did you know that?' 'Because' (said he), 'I did see you distempered both in body and mind. For first, that that you would not suffer us children to do, you did the same your selves: ye cried out all at once, one of you could not understand another, ye sang, and that very foolishly. And whom he heard not sing, him would ye swear sang best, every one of you bragging of his strength, and rising to dance; in dancing ye could not only keep no measure but scarcely stand right up, so did every [one] of you forget what he was, you that ye were king,

---

[37] reverence my mother] An early example of Cyrus's later strategy of binding people to him by gifts, and an example of his avoidance of unthankfulness.

and they that they were subjects. And then did I first learn that it was a very confused talk which you did use, for ye could never leave.'³⁸ And Astyages said, 'Son, when your father drinketh wine, is he not drunken?' 'No truly', said he. 'How doth he order the matter?' 'He leaveth with thirst, other pain he feeleth none. For I think, Grandfather, that this Sacas doth never give him wine.' Then his mother said: 'What is the matter, son, that ye be so heavy master to Sacas?' Cyrus said, 'Because I have cause to fall out with him. For many times when I am desirous to come to my grandfather, he like an unkind fellow keepeth me back. But I beseech you, good grandfather, give me authority over him but three days.' Astyages asked, 'And how will ye order him?' Cyrus said, 'Standing in the entry where he is wont to stand, I when he would come in to dinner, will say, "Back sir, my grandfather is busied with certain men". And when he would come to supper, I will say, "He is bathing of him". And when he would very fain eat, I will say, "He is with women", till I have put him off, as he hath delayed and kept me back from you.' And such pastance° Cyrus did minister at that supper. And from time to time, if he perceived any man having any suit to his grandfather or his uncle, it grieved him that any should prevent him in promoting their suits. And he was glad to do men pleasures to his power.³⁹

When Mandane had prepared to return to her husband, Astyages prayed her to leave Cyrus with him; who answered that she in all things would gratify her father. But she thought it would be hard to leave the child there against his will. Then said Astyages to Cyrus: 'Son, if ye will tarry with me, you shall be master of my suitors, and not Sacas. And when you will you shall come to me, and the oftener that you come, the more thank[s] you shall have; my horses also shall be at your pleasure, and what you will beside. And when you shall depart, take with you which of them you list. And because ye love thin diet, you shall have it as you will.⁴⁰ Moreover, I will give you in hand the wild beasts in my gardens, and all that otherwise I can get for you. Which when you can ride perfectly, ye shall chase: and by shooting and darting, overthrow them, as big men do. I will appoint also children to be your playfellows, and all other things that you will, ask and have of me.' After that Astyages had thus said unto Cyrus, his mother did ask of him whether he would tarry or depart. Who without any study answered shortly that he would tarry. She asking him again, 'For what cause?'

---

³⁸ leave] i.e. 'leave off'/keep silent.
³⁹ pleasures to his power] A mistranslation here: the pleasures Cyrus seeks to do are to his uncle and grandfather rather than to those needing an audience with them.
⁴⁰ as you will] The point about the Persians' spare diet and its centrality to their way of living and martial prowess is repeatedly made by Xenophon and his early modern readers. (This occasions several marginal notes praising the Persians' 'dieate' in the Huntington copy, for example.) In this scene of family conviviality and warmth, Xenophon works hard to counter Herodotus's account of Astyages' order that his grandson be murdered so that he not usurp him.

He answered: 'Mother, because at home I am counted and am indeed best in shooting and darting of my companions. But here in riding I know well I am inferior to my fellows. Which thing, Mother, as ye know right well, doth not a little grieve me. Now if ye leave me here that I may get the feat of riding when I am among the Persians, I trust ye think I shall easily pass them that be good on foot. And resorting to the Medes and being most excellent in riding, I will endeavour my self to aid my Grandfather in war.' Then said his mother: 'But how (Son) shall ye hereafter learn justice, seeing your teachers be in Persia?' Cyrus answered: 'I am, mother, very perfect in that.' 'How know ye that?', said his mother. 'For my schoolmaster' (said he), 'did appoint me a judge over other, as one that in justice was most cunning. And in judging one thing, I was beaten for judging it not right, and this was the cause.

The Judgement of Cyrus[41]

'A great boy having a little coat did unclothe a little boy having a great coat, and caused that the one did wear the other's garment. I being judge in this matter did give sentence that it was best for both parties either to have his coat meeter for him.[42] At which sentence my master did beat me, saying, When you are judge in a controversy of fitness and convenience, then must ye judge after this sort. But when ye must determine whose is the coat, then ye must consider who hath right possession, whether he that taketh away a coat by violence, or he that hath caused it to be made for him or else hath bought it. For that is just which is lawful, that that is not lawful is violent. Wherefore sentence must be given always of the judge according to the law. Therefore, mother, I am perfect enough in justice and if I lack anything, my Grandfather shall teach me.' 'But son' (said she), 'the justice of your grandfather and of the Persians do not agree. For he, here in Media, hath made him self lord of all: amongst the Persians to have equality is thought just. And your father first maketh the laws that he maketh for the city, but he also receiveth laws. He measureth things not by lust but by law.[43] How then can it be but that you shall be undone with beating at your return if you for kingdom have learned tyranny, whose nature is to have more than all other.' 'But my Grandfather, Mother' (said Cyrus), 'is so wise that he can teach men to have rather less than more. Do ye not see how he hath

---

[41] Judgement of Cyrus] A favourite episode from the *Cyropaedia*. On the conflicting principles of equity and justice at stake in this episode, see Gabriel Danzig, 'Big Boys and Little Boys: Justice and Law in Xenophon's *Cyropaedia* and *Memorabilia*', *Polis*, 26 (2009), 271–95; on the prominence of this lesson in King James's *Basilikon Doron* and the influence of this reasoning on James's economic policies, see Cramsie. Among early modern treatments of it, see the episode of the Giant of the Scales in *The Faerie Queene* (v. ii. 30–50).
[42] meeter for him] i.e. that each should have the coat that fit him best.
[43] not by lust but by law] Median tyranny contrasted with Persian justice.

taught all the Medes to have less than himself? Therefore fear ye not, mother, but he will so instruct both me and other too that when I shall depart, I shall not have more than he.'

Cyrus after this sort spake many things. In conclusion, his mother departed. He remained and was brought up there, being soon acquainted with his companions, as with his familiar fellows.[44] And he did straight ways get the love of their fathers in going to them and signifying how much he loved their children, in so much that if they had any suit to the king, they would bid their children desire Cyrus to do it for them. Cyrus, when the children did desire or require him, of his singular humanity and desire of renown had no greater pleasure than to speed their suit. And Astyages could deny no request that Cyrus made but gratify him in the same. For when it chanced that he was sick, Cyrus would never depart from him, never leave weeping, that every man might perceive how fearful he was of his Grandfather's death. For in the night if Astyages called for anything, Cyrus would first hear him and of all other most readily make haste to minister such things as he thought might please his grandfather. Whereby he was in most high favour with Astyages. But peradventure Cyrus was somewhat full of talk. For both by his education wherein he was compelled of his schoolmaster to render cause of all that he did when he was in judgement, and also because he was desirous of learning, he did ever ask many questions of such as were present, how the world went with them. And what so ever other did demand of him, he for his quick wit would give ready answer. By reason of all which things, a certain liberal talk was reputed in him. But as in young men whose bodies be of great growth, there appeareth some young shape that doth disclose their tender age: so of Cyrus's liberal talk, no boldness did appear, but a soft and gentle haviour°. Whereby every man desired rather to hear him speak much than to be in silence. But in continuance of time, growing in body and years to young man's estate, he used fewer words and less noise. He was also so bashful that he would blush when he met with any ancient man. And his rudeness to press in every company after a wanton fashion he did no more use but became very quiet.

Also with his equals he was most acceptable.[45] For truly in such exercises as his companions did oft use, he never would challenge his fellows in that he was superior. But wherein he well knew he was too weak, therein would he assay him self, affirming that he, one day, would do it better than they. And he began now to leap on horseback, to shoot and dart on horseback before he could well sit his horse. When he was overcome, he would be most merry with himself and

---

[44] familiar fellows] The addition of 'familiar fellows' to his 'companions' may present Barker's attempt to render οἰκείως [*oikeios*], domestic/of the household, with the bedfellow implications of 'familiar fellows'.
[45] most acceptable] i.e. well liked.

not shrinking though he were overcome to practise those feats wherein he was inferior, but eftsoons° enforcing himself in assaying to do them better, in short time he was as good in riding as his fellows, and in short space by reason of his fervent desire of the feat, he did excel them all. In short time with chasing and shooting at the wild beasts in the park he wasted and destroyed them all, in so much as Astyages could not provide him game. And Cyrus perceiving that his Grandfather being very desirous could not provide them alive, oft said unto him: 'Grandfather, why do ye trouble your self so much in seeking for these wild beasts? If ye will let me go on hunting with my uncle, I will think every wild beast that I see to be kept up for me.' And being very desirous to go on hunting, he could not now desire it wantonly, as when he was a child, but was somewhat afraid to go about it: and wherein he before did reprehend Sacas, which would not suffer him to go to his grandfather, he was now become a Sacas to himself. For he would not come except time served him, and desired Sacas to show him when it were time convenient to go and when not. Wherefore this Sacas, as well as all other, did wonderfully love him.

After that Astyages knew he was so desirous to go on hunting abroad he sent him forth with his uncle, appointing a certain guard of ancient horsemen to keep him out of dangerous places and from the wild beasts that should be put up°. Cyrus then asked earnestly of his waiters[46] which beasts were not for him to meddle with and which he might boldly chase. They answered that bears, boars, lions and leopards have slain many approaching too nigh. 'But harts, goats, wild sheep and wild asses be not so dangerous.' And this they said more, that the danger of the place was as well to be regarded as the very beasts. 'For many men, horse and all, have been hurled down headlong.' Cyrus diligently marked these words. But when he saw a hind afoot, he forgetting all that he had heard, did pursue her, looking to nothing else but whether she fled. In so much that his horse leapt and fell on his knees and had like to have cast him over his neck; nevertheless he with much ado did sit him and the horse recovered. Being come in to the plain, he picked his dart and overthrew the hind, a fair beast and a large, and he did not a little rejoice. But his rulers and tutors riding to him did rebuke him, showing in what peril he was, affirming that they would tell his Grandfather. Cyrus stayed and alighted, being much grieved to hear such words. But when he heard any halloing, he as past himself[47] leapt eftsoons on horseback, and seeing a boar chased, he rid against it and threw so right that he hit it in the face and made the boar to stay. Then his uncle, seeing his rashness, rebuked him who, notwithstanding his rebukes, desired him that

---

[46] waiters] Those who attended him.
[47] as past himself] Barker shifts the Greek word ἐνθουσιῶν (*enthousiôn* — present participle singular nominative masculine of ἐνθουσιάω *enthousiáō* 'to be possessed by a god') into a secular register to show Cyrus enraptured in the hunt.

he might present his Grandfather with those that he had taken. To whom his uncle answered: 'if he should know that you have chased he would not alonely be angry with you but also with me for suffering you.' 'Let him beat me' (said he), 'if it be his pleasure, so I may present them to him. And you, uncle, beat me too as ye will, so ye do me this pleasure.' And his uncle at length said, 'Do as ye list, for you are now as a king among us'. So Cyrus presented the deer and gave them to his Grandfather, and said that he had hunted these for him. His darts he did not show but left them bloody in such place as he thought his Grandfather should see them. Astyages said unto him: 'I accept (Son) gladly, what so ever ye give me. But I have no such need of them that ye should put your self in jeopardy.' 'If you have no need' (said Cyrus), 'I pray you, Grandfather, give me them to distribute among my companions.' 'Take them', said Astyages, 'and give them to whom ye will and anything else that ye will desire.'

Cyrus took them and gave them to the children, saying thus: 'O children, how did we trifle when that we hunted deer in the parks it is like, I think, as if a man would hunt beasts in prison. For first they were in strait place then both little and unlusty, some of them halt°, some lame. But the deer that be in mountains and forests, how fair, how fresh, and great they seem? The harts as swift as birds flying up to heaven, the boars assaulting as they say valiant men do.[48] Whom, being so broad, a man cannot lightly miss. Wherefore, I think, that these be fairer being dead than the other enclosed in house[49] yet being alive. But will your fathers' (said he), 'give you leave to go on hunting?' 'Readily' (said they), 'if Astyages command.' 'And who' (said Cyrus), 'shall be a mean for you to Astyages?' 'Who', said they, 'can better speed this purpose than you?' 'But I' (said Cyrus), 'cannot tell in what case I am.[50] For I can neither speak nor look on my grandfather as I was wont to do. If I grow on this fashion, I am afraid I shall prove an ass or a fool. When I was a little boy methought I had tongue enough.' 'Marry', said the children, 'ye tell a shrewd tale for us, if you when we have need can do no thing for us but must desire another to do for us that you may best do.' Cyrus hearing this was much grieved, and departing in silence and enforcing him self to be bold, went forth and, waiting how he might without displeasure speak to his Grandfather and obtain his and the children's request, began thus: 'Tell me, grandfather, if any of your servants did run away and you should take him again, how would ye handle him?' 'How else', said he, 'but imprison him, and make him a slave.' 'If he did return of his own mind, what would ye then do?' 'What' (said he), 'but after sharp correction that he

---

[48] valiant men do] i.e. the boars are as fierce as valiant men in battle.
[49] enclosed in house] i.e. penned in.
[50] case I am] Here, Barker omits μὰ τὸν Δία [*ma ton Día*]. In Philemon Holland, we have 'By Juno' [i.e. Hera] (sig. B3v). But he displaces the phrase to the children in the next line, now rendered as 'Marry'. Elsewhere he substitutes 'Marry' or 'by Mary' for *ma ton Día*; see Introduction.

might no more so do, use him as I did before.' 'Then it is time' (quod Cyrus), 'for you to provide sharply to punish me. For I purpose to run from you and take my fellows with me on hunting.' 'It is honestly done' (said Astyages), 'that ye give me warning. But I command you not to stir one foot out of the doors. Were it not a pretty pastime if I for a little benison° should lose my daughter's son?' Which thing Cyrus hearing obeyed, and abode at home. And being heavy and sad kept himself in silence. Astyages perceiving him very sad, intending to please him again, had him forth to hunt, assembling many both foot and horsemen and the little boys too. And gathering the deer into the plains, he made a goodly hunting and being him self present in royal manner, commanded that no man should shoot before Cyrus had his fill therein. But Cyrus did not suffer them to be forbidden but said: 'Grandfather, if ye will have me hunt pleasantly, suffer all these that be with me to chase and travail and do the best that they can.' Then Astyages gave them all leave and himself stood still, beholding how they encountered with the deer and contended in chasing and darting at the same. Being much delighted in Cyrus, which for pleasure could not keep his tongue but, as a whelp of good kind, made a noise when he drew nigh the game, and did encourage every man by name,[51] rejoicing furthermore to see him laugh at one, to hear him praise another, repining° at no man, at length having great prey. Astyages departed and had from thenceforth such pleasure in this pastime that at other times when he had leisure he would go abroad° with Cyrus, taking with him the other boys for Cyrus's sake. After this sort Cyrus continued a long season, to all men cause of goodness and pleasure, of hurt to no man.

And when he was about the age of fifteen or sixteen year[s], the king's son of Assyria,[52] which should marry, had great desire to hunt at that time. And hearing much deer to be in the marches° of them and the Medes, which had been spared by occasion of war, he coveted to hunt the same, and that he might hunt in safety he took with him men of arms and light horses which should drive the deer to him into the plains and champaign° ground. And being come to the places where his castles and garrisons were, he did there sup, that he might early hunt the day following. And when it was night, there came out of the city that succeeded the former garrison both of horsemen and footmen, wherefore he thought him self to have a great army. These two garrisons being joined, having himself many horsemen and footmen that came with him, he thought it therefore best to make a drove out of the Medes' ground, both that the pastime of his hunt should be the more notable, and also did think to have

---

[51] encourage every man by name] Prefiguring Cyrus's fame for remembering the names of all his soldiers — e.g. Thomas Wilson, writing of the role of memory in rhetoric, commends Cyrus who, 'having a great armie of men, knewe the names of all his Souldiers' (*The Arte of Rhetorique*, Book III (sig. 2F1)).
[52] Assyria] The first mention of the great enemies to Persia (and Media) throughout the *Cyropaedia*, which builds towards Cyrus's siege of (Assyrian-held) Babylon in Book VII.

the more abundance to make sacrifice. So rising early, he set forth his host° and leaving ambushments° of footmen in the borders, he with the horsemen, which he hath both very good and many, did ride to the fortresses of the Medes and there remain, that the garrisons should not rescue them that were chased. Then he sent bands° forth of the most forward men to chase, some one way, some another, commanding that with what so ever they met in their compass, they should drive the same to him. And so they did.

When it was reported to Astyages that enemies were in his land, he with such as he had about him went to help the marches, and his son likewise with the horsemen that were present, and gave warning to all other to come in aid. When they saw many of the Assyrians in good order and the horsemen not stirring, the Medes also stayed. Cyrus seeing other[s] making them ready on every side did so himself likewise. And that was the first time that he put on harness° unlooked for, so desirous was he to be in arms with them, and truly they were very goodly and meet which his grandfather had do make[53] for his body. Being thus harnessed, he took his horse and rid forth. Astyages, seeing him, much marvelled at whose motion he came and commanded him to abide with him. When Cyrus saw many horsemen on the contrary part, he asked: 'Be yonder horsemen, Grandfather, our enemies, that stand on horseback so quietly?' 'They be our enemies', said he. 'And they too, that drive the prey?' 'And they.' 'Now surely, Grandfather' (said he), 'they look like cowards and being horsed with jades°, they drive away our goods. Is it not meet that some of us make after them?' 'What, son' (said he), 'do ye not see what a troop of horsemen stand in good array? If we chase them, they shall enclose us, or compass in, and our strength is not yet come.' 'Yet', said Cyrus, 'if you tarry here and repair your force, they being in fear shall not move and they that drive the prey shall let go the same when they see the onset given them.' When he had said thus, he seemed to Astyages to speak somewhat, and marvelling at his prudence and forecast, commanded his son to take a band of horsemen and pursue them that drive the prey. 'And I', said he, 'shall set upon the other if they move toward you. Wherefore they shall be enforced to have watchful eye at us.' So Cyaxares taking the strongest horse and men set forward against them, and when Cyrus perceived them marching forward, he marched forth among them, and being the foremost he led them a great pace. Cyaxares followed, and the other were not behind. The prey-drivers, seeing them approach, left their booty and fled. Cyrus's company did enclose and hurt them that they overtook, Cyrus being the foremost, and so many as had escaped and prevented them, they chased and pursued and did not cease till they had taken some of them. And even as a dog of a good kind, uncunning,[54] rashly runneth on the boar, so Cyrus

---

[53] had do make] i.e. had had made.
[54] uncunning] The point is that Cyrus has great spirit but is still inexperienced or untrained.

rushed among them, only looking how he might strike him that was overtaken, regarding nothing else.

Their enemies seeing their men in jeopardy moved forth the troop of horsemen, thinking that the chase would cease if they see them once to march forward. But Cyrus staying never the more, and for joy calling upon his uncle, followed the chase, and handling his enemies hard, made great slaughter among them. Cyaxares followed truly, perchance for fear and shame of his father. The other followed also, being thereby the more encouraged to pursue, yet in force and power inferior to their enemies. Astyages perceiving them rashly to pursue and his enemies both in number great and in good array making toward them, being afraid both for his son and nephew lest they, so scattered, falling in danger of their enemies well appointed should be in peril, marched straight forth against his enemies, who, seeing the Medes making toward them, holding forth some their darts, some their bows, kept their place as though they would resist them being come within arrowshot, as oft they were wont to do. For approaching somewhat nigh together, they skirmish with shot at large,[55] many times till night. When they saw their men flee toward them so fast and them with Cyrus following so fiercely, and Astyages with his horsemen like shortly to be within arrowshot, they recoiled and fled, the other pursued with all their might, and took, hurt, and slew many valiantly, both horse and man, not ceasing till they came to the Assyrians' footmen; there fearing lest some greater ambushment might be in covert,[56] they stayed. And Astyages returning with his army was very joyful of his victory of horsemen and of Cyrus could not speak too much, whom he knew to be chief cause of this feat, perceiving him to be hardy and fierce.

And whereas other returned home, only he could do nothing but ride about, beholding them that were overthrown. And they that were appointed to bring him to Astyages had much ado to get him away; he causing the same to go a good way afore him, because he saw by his Grandfather's countenance that he was moved in beholding of him.[57]

These things were thus done in Media, and as all other men set forth Cyrus in word, report, and song, so Astyages, highly tofore regarding him, had him now in more estimation. Cambyses, Cyrus's father, hearing this report, was very joyful and understanding that Cyrus played manly parts, sent for him that he might be fully furnished with the discipline[58] of the Persians. And Cyrus (as they report) said he would depart, both that his father should not be displeased nor his country reprove him, wherefore Astyages thought it necessary to send

[55] at large] from a distance.
[56] in covert] i.e. hidden from them.
[57] moved in beholding of him] Holland describes Astyages' face as 'stern and terrible' at witnessing Cyrus's gloating over the dead Assyrians.
[58] discipline] i.e. education.

him home. And giving him such horses as he desired to have, honourably dismissed him, all things for that purpose being prepared, because he both loved him and had also great hope that he should prove such a man as might be able to do his friends good and his enemies hurt. Cyrus at his departure was accompanied of all states,[59] children, his equal, men, and ancients on horseback, and also Astyages himself, and as they say, there was no man but that wept at that departure. And Cyrus himself, as it is reported, departed with much weeping, giving many gifts among his equals which Astyages had given him; in conclusion, putting off the Medish robe that he wore, gave it to one, declaring that he most entirely loved him. When they had taken and received these gifts, they did (as men say) show them to Astyages, who took and sent them again to Cyrus, which sent them quickly to the Medes with these words: 'O Grandfather, if ye will have me repair to you without shame, suffer them to have my gifts to whom I have given the same.' Astyages, hearing this, fulfilled Cyrus's request. And if I may recount somewhat of amorous talk,[60] it is report, that at his departure, taking leave one of the other, his kinsman kissed his mouth, dismissing him according to the Persians' law, for the Persians at this day use so to do.

And one of the Medes, a man of much goodness and honesty, had long time marvelled of Cyrus's estate, beholding his kinsmen kissing him, he stood still and when all the others were departed, he went to Cyrus saying, 'Be ye ignorant, Cyrus, that only I am your kinsman?'[61] 'What, are you my kinsman also?' 'Yea surely', said the other. 'Is that the cause', said Cyrus, 'that you have so countenanced° me? For I have marked you oft so to do.' 'Truly', said the other, 'being very desirous to come unto you, as God save me,[62] I ever was too bashful.' 'But so you should not have been', said Cyrus, 'being my cousin°': and coming straight to him, he did kiss him. The Mede being kissed asked, 'Is this a law of Persia for friends to kiss one another?' 'It is indeed' (quoth Cyrus), 'when they have not seen one another a certain space, or when one do depart from another.' 'Then is it now the time', said the Mede, 'when you must kiss me again for I must, as ye see, depart from you.' And Cyrus kissing him eftsoons left him and departed. They had not ridden very far but the Mede returned again to him, his horse all in a sweat, whom Cyrus seeing asked, 'Have you forgotten anything that you would have spoken?' 'No truly' (said he), 'but I am come again after a long while.' 'Indeed, cousin' (said Cyrus), 'it is but a very short while.' 'What,

---

[59] all states] people of all ranks and ages. Xenophon here mentions the four categories of Persian (male) society: children, young men, adults and elders.

[60] amorous talk] Translating παιδικὸς λόγος (*paidikòs lógos*), a word that was also used for the younger partner in a paederastic relationship.

[61] your kinsman] Later identified as Artabasus, a key figure in Cyrus's army in Book IV and Book VI.

[62] God save me] Translating ναὶ μὰ τοὺς θεούς (*naì mà toùs theoús*).

short?' quoth the Mede. 'Do ye not know, Cyrus, that when I wink never so little time, it seemeth to me very long if I do not behold you, being such a gentleman?' Cyrus then after his former weeping first began to laugh, saying: 'Depart and be of good cheer, for it will chance in short time that you may behold me, if ye will, and wink not.'

Cyrus being returned into Persia, was one year more among the children, who at his coming scoffed with him at his pleasant life that he learned in Media: but after they saw him eat and drink as heartily as themselves, and in a feastful day when they had good cheer, perceiving that he would rather give away some of his part than desire any of theirs, and also saw that he in all other feats excelled them all, they had him in estimation again.

Being perfect in this trade of learning, he entered among the young men in the which he appeared also to pass other, exercising all things requisite, endeavouring every thing that was his duty, reverencing his seniors, and obedient to his governors. In continuance of time, Astyages King of Media died, whose son Cyaxares and brother to Cyrus's mother received the dominion of the Medes. The king of Assyria subduing the Syrians, no small nation having the Arabian king and the Hyrcanians subject unto him and now besieging the Bactrians, though[t] if he might weaken the Medes' state, being the most strong nation of all his borderers, that he should easily achieve the dominion of all the country about him. Wherefore sending both to his subjects, and also to Croesus, king of Lydia, to the king of Cappadocia, and to both the Phrygians, to the Paphlagonians, to the Indians, the Carians, and Cilicians, and accusing to all these the Medes and Persians, declaring how these nations were great and strong, confederated and allied in marriage and perpetual league, in so much that except some man did by forecast abate their force,[63] they were like, by invasion to subdue all other nations, one after another. Some persuaded by his allegations, some inveigled by gifts and money wherein he was most wealthy, joined with him in league. Cyaxares, Astyages his son perceiving their trains and purveyance° made against him, gathered straight of his own strength so much as he could, and also sent for aid to the Persians as well the council, as to Cambyses his brother-in-law king of Persia. He sent also to his nephew Cyrus, praying him that if the council did send any aid that he would labour to be captain of the same. At this time Cyrus had spent ten years with the young sort, and was in the company of men whom, when he approved the thing, the council after consultation chose captain of the army into Media. They also licensed him to choose two hundred of them that be equal in honour, and to every one of the two hundred they gave the election of four of the same peers, which number maketh one thousand, and to every one of this thousand they gave leave to choose of the commons ten darters°, ten slingers°, and ten archers, which

---

[63] did by forecast abate their force] i.e. attacked them first.

amounteth to ten thousand archers, ten thousand throwers of darts, and ten thousand slingers, beside the thousand noble men. And this so great an army was committed to Cyrus, which being chosen, forthwith made his beginning of God, and having prosperous sacrifice,[64] did elect the two hundred, and when they also had chosen four more, Cyrus assembled them, and thus he first spake unto them.

Cyrus's Oration[65]

'Friends, I have chosen you, not now having the first experience of you, but beholding that from your childhood ye have with much quickness and lustiness travailed in those things which the city reputed honest, and utterly abandoned those which it judgeth unhonest. Now for what cause I, not unwillingly, am appointed to this business, and why I have assembled you, I will declare unto you. I have considered that our ancestors have in nothing been inferior to us, for they have travailed to accomplish all such things as be reputed the works of virtue; but what good they, being of this sort, have exploited, either for the commonwealth of the Persians or for themselves, that can I not yet perceive. Surely I think therefore that virtue is not put in use among men that good men should not be preferred to the [e]vil. They that refrain from present pleasures do it not because they would never more be in rejoice,[66] but that at length by such temperance they might the rather attain to many sundry delights and pleasures. And they that study to excel in eloquence do it not that they should never cease and stay from pleading of causes but because they trust that by persuading many men by their eloquence they shall purchase themselves great avails°. They that travail in feats of chivalry do it not that they should never leave off fighting, but because they think that if they excel in martial prowess, they shall get both themselves and their country great riches, much felicity and high honour. And if some men, after such pains taken before they can receive any fruit of the same, perceive themselves to be made impotent by age, they as I think be in case like the husbandman which would fain be cunning, soweth well and planteth diligently, yet when he hath need to take fruit of the same suffereth it ungathered to fall to the ground.[67] And if a champion, after

---

[64] prosperous sacrifice] Holland omits any mention of Cyrus's sacrifice to the gods before this, his first military campaign as an adult and general, and before this first important oration to his troops.
[65] Cyrus's Oration] Typically, Cyrus's speeches are marked off with in-text subtitles such as this one, though occasionally shorter annotations are identified with printed marginal annotations instead (e.g. 'Oratio').
[66] in rejoice] i.e. enjoying it.
[67] to the ground] i.e. that men who allow themselves to grow old and weak without having reaped the fruits of their labours in youth are like the farmer who sows well but instead of gathering the fruits at harvest-time, leaves them to rot on the ground.

intolerable pains and many guerdons° of victory worthily won would end his life as one that never assayed feats of strength, he were not worthy, as I think, to be excused to his foolishness. But friends, let not us be in this case, but seeing we all do testify with ourselves that from our childhood we have travailed in good and noble feats, let us go against our enemies whom, I certainly know by that I have myself seen, be unexpert men of war in comparison to us, for such be too weak to match with us, which though they can shoot, dart and ride perfectly, they quail when labour is required; but our enemies cannot away with labours, neither such as when they ought to watch be overcome with the same, but our enemies cannot lack their sleep, neither though they be in these things able men which be untaught how to use their aiders[68] and now their enemies. But it is evident that our enemies be to learn[69] in those disciplines that be most expedient in war.

But as for you, ye can away with night[70] as well as other with day: you repute pains the guides to pleasant life. You take hunger instead of meat, and you can away with water, drinking as well as lions. You have also laid up within your hearts the most precious treasure of the commonwealth, for you be more in love with renown than all other men, and they that be lovers of renown must needs gladly for it endure all pains and perils.

If I should thus speak of you, thinking otherwise, I should deceive myself. For if by you no such thing could come to pass, the less should redound° to me. But I trust that by your experience and benevolence toward me, and by simplicity of our enemies, that these good hopes shall not deceive me but that we may boldly set upon them. And where we have abhorred to be reputed unjustly to covet other men's [goods], our enemies at this time be authors of doing this injury, our friends call on us for aid. What is there either more just than to resist injury or more honourable than to help our friends? And I think that you have not the less confidence because that I have not been negligent to make my beginning of God. For you being privy of many things with me do know that as well in weighty as small affairs, I use always to begin of God. To conclude: what should I say more? When you have chosen your men, and have them ready in all other things, being well appointed, set forth into Media. I do return to my father, that when I have learned with all speed the state of our enemies, I may make the best provision for you that I can, that we may with God's help most honourably go forward with this enterprise.'

They prepared themselves: Cyrus being come home, and his prayers made to Vesta and Jupiter, his country patrons,[71] and the other gods, he set forth toward

[68] aiders] i.e. friends, supporters. 'Away with labours' implies 'manage' labours.
[69] be to learn] i.e. have yet to learn.
[70] away with night] i.e. can use the night.
[71] His country patrons] Vesta (Roman goddess of the hearth) and Jupiter (ruler of the gods) are deemed 'ancestral' gods of Persia here. Historically, it is more likely that Cyrus invoked

the army, his father bringing him on the way. And when they were come forth of the house, it thundered and lightned on his lucky side. And when that was done, they using none other token did set forward, as who would say, The high God did signify no thing else. As Cyrus set forward, his father began to speak unto him on this wise.[72] 'It is evident, O Son, as well by sacrifices as celestial tokens that the gods send thee forth with their help and favour as thou thy self doest well know. For I have diligently taught that these things that thou not through others' interpretation mightst know the will of God, but that thy self seeing the sights and hearing the noises mightst perceive it, and not go to soothsayers which if they would might deceive ye, showing thee otherwise than were signified of God. And that at no time thou shouldst be without an interpreter, or be in doubt what God meaneth by his signs, but knowing by divination what God his will and pleasure is, thou mightst obey the same.' 'Surely father' (quoth Cyrus), 'I will not cease to do mine endeavour, to the uttermost of my power according to your advertisement, that God may the rather be favourable and inclined to do us good. For I remember that I heard you once say that of congruence he obtaineth more as well of God as man, which doth not flatter when he is in need, but when he is in his chief wealth, then doth most remember God.[73] And the same consideration you said, ought to be had of friends.' 'Verily, Son' (said he), 'thou at this time, being so affected, dost come to God with more delight, by reason of the same regard. And thou dost trust to obtain the better thy want, because thou art certain in thy conscience never to have been negligent in the same.' 'Without doubt, father' (said he), 'I am so affected toward God as to my most assured.' 'What Son' (said he), 'dost thou remember what we once concluded? For men, which learn what God at any time give them, and take diligent pains, do speed better than they that be idle. And they that provide afore, behaving themselves as they ought to do, liveth more in safety than they that care for nothing. After this sort, we thought expedient, that men should make request to God for all good things.' 'Truly, father' (said Cyrus), 'I remember; I have heard this lesson of you, wherefore I am enforced to follow the same. And I know that you be of this mind, that it is not lawful for them that have not learned to ride, to ask of God victory on horseback; nor for them that be uncunning in shooting to desire better hand of them that be expert in the feat; nor for the ignorant of sailing to wish the safeguard of ships that they take in hand to govern; nor that they which soweth no corn should desire they might have good corn to grow; neither the unware° in war to make prayer to be in surety. For all such things be against God's ordinance. You said likewise that

---

the Zoroastrian god Ahura Mazda.
[72] on this wise] i.e. in this way.
[73] most remember God] i.e. that one's chances of success with the gods are better if one calls on them not only in the hour of need but remembers them in the good times too.

they that ask of God ungodly things were as well worthy to be said nay of God as they to be denied which make unlawful request of men.'

'But have you, son, forgotten those things which we did devise? That it is for a man a sufficient and honest part if he can procure to be in deed in very good and honest case himself, and also in provision of necessary things, to be so diligent that he and his family may have sufficient. But to rule other men, and to sustain the labour thereof, it being so weighty, that they might have abundantly all things necessary, and that they might all prove as they ought to do, this seemed to us a thing of admiration.' 'Truly, father' (said he), 'I remember that you did so say. And it seemed to me likewise a thing of much importance to rule well: and now it seemeth no less unto me when I consider and muse with myself what it is to rule. But when I behold other men and do consider what they be that are in rule and the condition of them that shall be our enemies, I think it a very great rebuke to me to be afraid, they being of such sort and not willingly to go with such companions who, as I suppose, to begin with these our friends, be of this opinion: that it behoved a ruler to exceed his subjects in plentiful diet, in abundant treasure, in longer rest, and in all things to take less pains than his subjects. But I think', quoth he, 'that it becometh a ruler to exceed his subjects not in easiness of life but in the care of provision, and prest° courage of travail.' 'But son' (said he), 'there be certain things wherewith we strive not so much against men as against the things themselves, which we cannot lightly overcome with ease. And ye know', quoth he, 'that if your army have not out of hand° sufficient purveyance°, your rule will soon decay.' 'Marry father' (quoth he), 'Cyaxares said he will provide for all that shall go hence, how many so ever they be.' 'And will you, Son', quoth he, 'go forward trusting to Cyaxares' habilite°?' 'I will', said Cyrus. 'What?', quoth he, 'know ye how able he is?' 'No surely', quoth Cyrus. 'And do you give credit to things uncertain? Do ye not know that ye shall have need of many things? And that ye shall even now be enforced to spend much, other ways?' 'I know', said Cyrus.

'Then', said he, 'if he lacketh money or peradventure should dissemble of purpose, in what case then shall your army be?' 'In no good case, as it appeareth. Therefore, father', quoth he, 'if you see how I might make provision for money, show it now whiles we be among our friends.' 'You ask, Son, if any provision of money should be made by you. Of whom is it more meet that money should be provided for then of him that hath power? You have, son, a company of footmen to go forth with you, as I know you would not change for a far greater number. And as for horsemen, you shall among the Medes have the best aid with you. Then what country, think you, that is nigh such power will not both be glad to aid and succour you, but also fear some displeasure by you? Which things you, jointly with Cyaxares, must devise that at no time ye lack anything that ought to be had. And a revenue of money must be found out to accustom you to it. But of all other, remember this, that in no wise you do not defer the provision of it till that need enforceth you, but when you have most plenty, then ratherest provide against want. For you shall the sooner relieve your lack of them that you do ask if you seem to have no need, and furthermore, your own soldiers shall have no cause to complain of you, but shall thereby cause other to have you in the more reverency. And if you desire with your power to do pleasure or displeasure to any man, your men shall be the more ready to serve you, so long as they have all things necessary. And your words, as ye well know, shall have the more pith to persuade if you can evidently show that you are both able to do pleasure and displeasure.' 'Methinketh father', said he, 'that ye have spoken all other things very well, and that the soldiers will give me no thank[s] for that they shall now receive because they know for what cause Cyaxares hath sent for their succour. But what any shall receive beside this tofore spoke, that they will think honesty to themselves and render great thanks, as reason is, to the giver. He that hath a great company with the which he may help his friends by doing them good and his enemies, if he have any, he may go about to get something from them, and then will be negligent in getting of it, think ye it to be a less shame than if a man had both land and tillmen wherewith to work, and yet would suffer his ground to be untilled without profit? Therefore, have this opinion of me that I will never be negligent in studying for my soldiers' provision, neither being with my friends nor with mine enemies.' 'Keep that mind still' (quoth he). 'But do ye not remember, Son, what other things we thought necessary to be cared for?' 'I remember indeed' (said he), 'when I came unto you for a reward, to be given him that said he had taught me the feats of chivalry, which you giving me did thus ask of me, "Did this man, son, to whom you bear this reward, among his matters of war, make any mention of household governance?"[74] For no less need have the soldiers of things necessary to live in the camp than servants in the house. I, showing you the truth, that he made mention of no such matter, you did ask me again if he said anything of health and of strength, which should no less be cared for of a captain than anything that belong[s] to a captain's office. And when I had also said "nay" hereunto, ye asked more, if he taught me any way how to make my men most expert and courageous in every feat of war? Which thing I denying also, ye required eftsoons whether he had given me any precept how to encourage and make hearty my soldiers, affirming that quick courage did in all things far exceed slothful hearts. When I had denied this too, ye did demand if he had taught me any way how to persuade an army, which thing a man must most diligently assay? I utterly denying any such word to be spoken. Finally ye asked me in what point he had taught me the knowledge of governing an host. I then answered, "In setting an army in array". Whereat you smiling showed me by conferring one thing with another that ordering an army

---

[74] household governance] The subject of Xenophon's *Oeconomicus*.

should little profit without the purveyance, without health, without knowledge of feats of war tofore mentioned and without obedience, in so much as ye made it plain unto me that ordering of array was but a little part of governing an army. I then desiring you to instruct me in these things, ye commanded me to resort to men of most experience in war, and with them to debate and learn how all these things might best be done. Since which time, I have been conversant with them that have been reputed most politic in such affairs.⁷⁵

'As concerning victual at this time I believe there is sufficient purveyance because Cyaxares must find us the same for preservation of health, because I both have heard and seen that cities which regard health maintain physicians, and that captains for their soldiers' sake lead physicians with them, even so I, being appointed to like office, will have diligent regard of it. And I hope, father, I have such men with me, as be very expert in physic.' Whereunto his father said:

'These physicians, son, that you now speak of, be like unto butchers, and clouters° of torn and ragged garments. For when men be sick, then they cure them. But you must have a more honourable and decent regard of health than this, wherefore you must provide at the beginning that your army fall not into sickness.' 'What way shall I go to work, father, to be able to accomplish this?' 'If you shall foresee that the place wherein you shall be long in camp be of good and wholesome soil, wherein you shall not err if you take heed. For men commonly report which places be healthsome, which unhealthsome: and men's bodies and colours be evident witnesses of both. Furthermore it is not enough to consider that the place be sufficient, but ye must remember to have regard that your self may be in health.' 'Then', Cyrus said, 'I do first beware that I surfeit not, for that grieveth me much. Then with labour, I consume that I receive. So methink I have the better health and stronger body.'⁷⁶ 'Likewise, son' (said he), 'you must provide for all other.' 'May soldiers, father, have leisure to exercise their bodies?' 'They may not only', said his father, 'but be of necessity enforced to the same. For an army that shall do that it ought to do must never rest but be doing either some hurt to his enemies or good to him self. For it is evil to nourish an idle man and worse, son, to nourish an idle household, but to keep an whole army at idleness, it is a thing importable°: much it is that an army spendeth and what it hath it wasteth excessively. Wherefore it is not in any ways expedient that an army should be idle.' 'Your saying, father, as I can guess, is this, that as of an idle husbandman cometh no profit, so of an idle captain cometh no good.' 'I allow' (said he), 'him for a travailous° captain which, God not hindering, can provide

---

⁷⁵ in such affairs] Holland has 'military men, that were reputed best Commaunders', further describing the art of generalship as the 'art Imperatorie' (sig. D1v).

⁷⁶ surfeit not ... stronger body] The Persian doctrine of moderation and exercise in their bodily regimen was much admired in Greek writing, according with the Greek emphasis on moderation or temperance.

both that his army have things needful abundantly and also prepare that their bodies be strong and lusty.' 'Therefore, father, that they might have assay of every feat of war methinketh if I did proclaim common games and appoint rewards for the same, I should best cause them to have a proof in every thing, that when need shall require, I might have them prest and ready.' 'That is very well said, son', quoth he, 'for in doing this be ye well assured you shall perceive your bands of men, studying to keep their order, as it were in a dance.' 'Verily', said Cyrus, 'concerning the encouragement of soldiers, I think nothing so good as if a man could put them in hope of great avails.' 'That is like, son' (said he), 'as if a man in hunting would always hallow° his hounds with the noise which he useth when they see the deer, at the first they will quickly hearken to it. But if he so deceive them oft, the end will be that they will not then believe him when the deer is up indeed. Likewise it is in hope. If a man many times put them in hope of gains and deceive them, it will come to pass that when he showeth the certain hope in deed they will not give credit to him. Therefore ye must, son, refrain to speak that[77] you do not certainly know. For though some men, sometime perform like promise yet, let that encouragement be reserved till greatest dangers that it may the rather continue in credit.' 'Truly father', said Cyrus, 'methink ye speak very well, and this way delighteth me much. But to make my men obedient to me, methink, father, I am not to learn. For you, even from my childhood, have taught me this, compelling me to obey you. Afterward, ye recommended me to schoolmasters which did so likewise use me to the same. And being among young men, our governor was most diligent in this: and many of our laws seemed to teach most these two things, To rule, and to be ruled.[78] And therefore, pondering thoroughly all these things, I think I see that this were the best exhortation to make obedient men: to praise and advance him that doth obey, and the contrary to punish and condemn.' 'To make them', said he, 'to obey by constraint, this is the readiest way, son, but to make them freely to obey, which is much better, there is a readier way than this, for whom men think wiser than themselves, for their avails, him they gladly will obey. And as ye may know, that this is true in many other things, so in sick men which very gladly do call on them which do appoint and enjoin what they ought to do. How carefully in the sea do the sailors obey the shipmasters? And whom men think to know the way better than themselves, from them they will not gladly be departed. But when they think that by obeying they shall take hurt, neither will they be enforced for pain, nor allured for reward. For no man willingly will take reward to do himself hurt.' 'Then, father' (quoth he), 'your sentence is, that there is no readier way to have obedience than to appear wiser than his

---

[77] to speak that] i.e. to speak of that
[78] To rule and to be ruled] See Introduction, pp. 58–9.

subjects.'[79] 'It is so indeed', said he. 'And how, father, may a man soonest bring to pass that opinion of him?' 'There is, son, said he, no readier way than in those things to be wise indeed in which you would appear to be wise. And marking this in every particular thing, you shall find that I say true. For if you would seem a good husbandman, a good horseman, a good physician, a good minstrel, or any other like, and be not, consider what shifts° ye must make to maintain this appearance. And if you persuade your self that many men do praise you and think to get glory thereby, and have laid good foundations in every man, you do deceive them presently. But when you shall come to the trial, you shall bewray° yourself, and so forever be taken as a vain boaster.' 'But how can a man, father, presently be wise in foreseeing profit to come?' 'It is evident, son, that so many things as can be known by learning you may by study attain to, as you did learn the ordering of an army. But such as men cannot learn nor yet be foreseen by man's wisdom, if you can understand them by divination and God's oracles, you shall be thought to be wiser than other men. And when you know what is best to be done, if you will be careful to do it. For to be careful for things needful is a point of a wiser man, than to be altogether careless. Furthermore, to be beloved of his subjects, which thing I think one of the chief, a like way is evident, as if a man would desire to be beloved of his friends. For I think surely that he that doth well must needs be notable, but this, son, is hard: always to be able to show pleasures to whom a man would. But to show himself to rejoice with them at their good chance, to lament with them at their hurts, and to be ready to relieve their lacks, to provide that they take not hurt, to foresee that they be not deceived, and also how they may most gladly accompany him.

'And in doing feats if it be in summer, the captain must manifestly suffer most heat; if in winter, most cold; and if labours must be endured, most pains. All these things be most available° to get the love of subjects.' 'Do ye say, father, that a captain must be in all things more painful[80] than his subjects?' 'Yea, son, so I say. But be not dismayed of that. For you know well that the labours of like bodies be not alike painful in a ruler and in a private man. For honour in a ruler maketh the labour lighter. And because he knoweth that what so ever he doth, it shall be notable.' 'But father, when an army hath sufficient appointment°, is in good lust, able to travail, exercised in feats of war, desirous to declare manhood, gladder to obey than to be stubborn, do you not think him wise which at that instant would encounter with his enemies?' 'Yes truly', said he, 'if he may have the better hand. If not, as I think myself, to be in better state and my men also better appointed, so much the more ware° shall I be, even as those things which

---

[79] to appear wiser than his subjects] A principle Machiavelli carefully noted and reworked in his own advice to princes.
[80] more painful] i.e. suffer more pain, be more industrious.

I think to be of most price, them will I covet, to be in most surety.'[81] 'But how can a man soonest have the better hand of his enemies?' 'It is no trifling matter, son, nor light thing that you do ask of me. But know for certainty that he that shall bring this to pass must be politic,[82] close, subtle, taking his advantage, privily catching, cloining°, and in every thing aforehand with his enemies.' And Cyrus, smiling, said: 'O Hercules, what manner a man, Father, do ye describe me to be?' 'Such one, son, as you may be a most just man, and keeper of the law.' 'Why then', said he, 'when we were children and young men, did ye teach us the contrary?' 'So truly do we now', said he, 'toward our friends and countrymen. But do ye not know that ye have learned many subtleties how ye may do hurt to your enemies?' 'No truly, father.' 'For what purpose', said he then, 'did ye learn to shoot? For what purpose to dart? For what purpose to catch wild boars with nets and pits? Wherefore harts with snares and traps? Why lions, bears and lybards°? Ye did not match with them of even hand[83] but always laboured to encounter with them, you having the advantage. Do ye not know that all these things be e[q]ual parts deceits, crafts and getting of advantage?' 'Yes truly, father', quod Cyrus, 'concerning wild beasts. But if I were but suspect[ed] to go about to deceive any man, I remember full well that I had many a stripe.' 'Indeed, son', said he, 'we did not, as I think, trade[84] you to pick a dart at a man, but we taught you to drive it to the prick.[85] And now ye may not hurt your friends in no wise. But if war did chance that ye might be able to hit, to deceive, and get the advantage of men, we taught not you these feats in arms but in beasts because you should not hurt your friends. Nevertheless in time of war, ye should not be [loth] to seek in such feats.'[86] 'Then, father, if it be profitable to know the way both to do good and hurt also to men, it had been meet we had been traded in the use of both in men.' 'There is a saying, son, among our ancestors, that there was sometime a schoolmaster that taught children justice, even as you now would have it. Not to lie and to lie, not to deceive and to deceive, not to slander and to slander. Not to oppress and to oppress. And did divide, which should be done to friends, which to enemies. And went so far that he taught to be lawful to deceive friends for a good purpose, to steal friends' goods for a good purpose. Children, being thus taught, must needs practise to do the same, one against another, as yet the Greeks, men say, teach their children in the common

---

[81] most surety] i.e. just as the things we count most precious are kept under the most security.
[82] politic] The word, with its implications of cunning self-advancement, was closely linked with the theories of Machiavelli.
[83] of even hand] i.e. equally matched.
[84] trade] train you up.
[85] prick] the mark (in archery).
[86] in such feats] The term is missing in both 26066 and 26067.

school to deceive, and exercise them to be able to do it, one against another.[87] Therefore, son, being very toward to deceive cunningly and to get advantage cunningly and peradventure not untoward in coveting riches, did not spare their friends, but attempted to be enriched by them. By which occasion a law was made, which we use at this day, that children should one way be taught as we do now teach our servants, To do truly, not to deceive, not to steal, not to be aforehand,[88] which things if they transgress, we punish them. That thus being accustomed to this trade, they might be made the milder men. But being at that age which you now be, it was thought they might safely be taught what was lawful against enemies. For being trained in mutual shamefastness, it was not thought that you would go so far as to prove wild citizens. Even as we do not make any mention of natural pleasure to very young men, lest ease, joined to the vehement desire, might provoke the same to unreasonable lust.'

'Yet, father, if ye can show any way how I may get advantage of mine enemies, be not afraid to teach me, as one somewhat dull in the other.'

'You must then endeavour', said he, 'with all your strength, well appointed, to assail your enemies unprepared. You being armed, they unarmed. You watching, they sleeping, they espied of you, you not of them, you being in sure place, receiving them in straits°.' 'But how, father, can a man take his adversaries in such errors?' 'Because, son, both you and your enemies shall of necessity suffer many such things. Ye must both needs send a foraging, both needs have herbigage°, both needs in the morning stray out for necessaries, and with such way as it happeth ye must be content, all which things ye must consider afore. And in what thing you know your men to be most weak, in that must ye be most ware. In what things you know your enemies to be most easy to be vanquished, in that ye must fiercely set upon them.' 'Whether must be', quoth Cyrus, 'get the advantage in these only, or in some others too?' 'Yea, much more, son', quoth he, 'in other. For commonly in these all men use to keep sure watch and ward°, knowing their own lack. If they that will deceive their enemies can make them have good comfort in themselves, and so unlooked for assail them and negligently pursuing them make them to disparple°, and by retiring bring them into straits, then it is good to set upon them. And son, you must be desirous to learn all these things, not that when you have learned you that practice only these but of your own policy, you must be inventing of sleights against your enemies, even as musicians do not only use the measures which they have learned but also study to invent every day new harmony. And as in music, new and fresh stuff is had in most price, so much more in war, new policies be most set by, because they may soonest deceive your enemies. And son, if you would turn those sleights upon men which you devised in catching of little wild beasts,

---

[87] one against another] The critique of Greek education here seems directed at the sophists.
[88] be aforehand] take (unfair) advantage.

do you not think that you shall have advantage to set upon your enemies? For you to take fowl have risen in the most bitter cold weather and gone forth in the night. And before the fowl could stir, your snares for that purpose were set for them. And the ground, that was moved was like a thing not movable.[89] And birds were caught to serve your turn, and to deceive their own kind. You lay in covert that you saw them and they not you. All your purpose was to prevent the same before they should flee away. And for the hare, which feedeth at night and fleeth the day, you kept hounds that find him out by scent, and because when he is found, he swiftly fleeth, you had greyhounds taught to overtake him by footmanship, and lest he should escape them, you learned the course and place whither the hare coveted to flee. And there set privy nets that he in his most fleeing might fall in them, and trap him self. And that he should not here escape, you set watches for it, which being nigh might straight come upon him. And these which on the fore part[90] you taught to lie in wait, ye made to be in covert. And you on the back half with an hallo made in time, so astonished the hare with the noise that he was taken, as it were, in amaze. Therefore, as I said tofore, if ye will practise these feats against men, I know not what you should need in feats of war. If it shall at any time so chance that ye are enforced both to fight in plain ground and in open field, being both thoroughly apparelled, then, son, your things better appointed afore, doth much prevail. Which I say be these: if your men's bodies be well exercised; if their hearts be courageous and well instruct in martial feats. This also you must well know, that so many as ye think worthy to be obedient to you, they all will think you worthy to be a ruler to them. And you must never be negligent but foresee over night what your men must do in the day, and in the day that things be well at night. How the army may best be appointed to fight, how ye may convey it in the day, how in the night, how in straits, how in the plains, how in the hills, how in dales, how to camp, how to appoint the watch and ward, both in night and day, how to advance against your enemies. How to retreat from them, how to bring your army to a city being your foe, how to march to the walls or recoil from the same. How to pass forests, floods, how to order your horsemen, how darters and archers. Or when you lead your army against the wing and your enemies set upon you, how you must array your men. If you set forth against the main battle and your enemies appear in any other place, rather than at the front, how you may encounter with them. Also, how a man may best know what his enemies intend or how they shall have little knowledge what you intend. Why do I now rehearse all these things to you? For what is there that I know but you have full oft heard? Specially if any other seemeth to have knowledge in any of

---

[89] not movable] i.e. that the earth disturbed in setting the snares looked as if it hadn't been touched.
[90] on the fore part] i.e. in front.

these things, you have not condemned any of them, nor have been ignorant in the same. Wherefore you must, I think, when anything chanceth, use such of these remedies as you suppose may ever do you good. And learn these things of me, son, as chiefest: against sacrifices and tokens, enterprise nothing.[91] Neither alone, nor adventuring with your army remembering that men by conjectures take matters in hand, not knowing which shall redound to their wealth. But you may know by that that chanceth.

'For many men, being reputed most wise, have persuaded cities to make war against them of whom they have been vanquished, when by persuasion they have invaded.[92] Many have increased both cities and private men by whom, being increased, they have come to extreme displeasure. Many, which might have used their friends, both doing and receiving pleasures, choosing rather to use them like servants than like friends, have been by them brought to nought. Some men not being content with sufficient pleasure and happy life, but coveting to be lords of all, have thereby lost that they have afore had. Many possessing great treasure of gold have by the same lost their lives. So men's wisdom do no more know how to choose the chief good than he that goeth by lot when he cast the same.

'But the gods, O son, which be immortal, knoweth all things, both past, present and what shall of every thing come. And to men, that make request to them, if they favour, they do declare what they ought to do and they ought not. And though they do not show so much to every man, marvel not. For there is no necessity can compel them to regard that they will not.'

The end of the first book.

---

[91] against sacrifices] i.e. against the warnings of sacrifices.
[92] by persuasion they have invaded] Xenophon prefigures Cyrus's later victory over Croesus, whose arrogance effectively persuades Cyrus to attack Lydia.

The School or Discipline of Cyrus, the Second Book

Devising thus together, they came to the end of Persia. Whereas an eagle appearing unto them with lucky token became their guide in the way. They, making prayers to the gods, patrons and defenders of Persia, favourably and mercifully to dismiss them, passed the marches° of the same.¹ Being past, they made eftsoons their prayer to the gods, avowers of Media, as favourably and mercifully to receive them. This done, and after comely manner embracing one the other, they departed, the father returning in to Persia, the son marching forward in Media to his uncle Cyaxares. Whither when he was come at their meeting they embraced one the other, as was decent. Then Cyaxares demanded of Cyrus, what manner of army he had brought. He answered, 'I have twenty thousand of them, which heretofore have been in wages with you. And certain other of the nobility which never yet came abroad be now come with me.' 'How many be they?', quoth Cyaxares. 'As for the number' (said Cyrus), 'it will not greatly delight ye to hear, but this ye must learn: that a few of these whom we call peers or men of equal honour² do far pass a great many of other Persians. But have ye any need of them? Do ye not fear in vain? Do your enemies come?' 'Yea surely' (quoth he), 'and that very many.' 'How know ye that?' 'Because' (quoth he), 'many that come from thence do diversely report, but all to one purpose.' 'Must we then match with men?' 'There is no remedy.' 'Why then' (quoth Cyrus), 'have ye not told me what ye know of their power? How great a company cometh? And likewise of your own force that both being known we may devise how we shall best join with them.' 'Then hark' (quoth Cyaxares), 'Croesus the king of Lydia bringeth (they say) ten thousand horsemen, targetmen and archers more than forty thousand. Artacaman the prince of great Phrygia, bringeth about eight thousand horsemen; spearmen and targetmen, no less than forty thousand. Aribeus, the king of Cappadocia, about six thousand horsemen; archers and darters no fewer than thirty thousand. Maragdus the king of Arabia, ten thousand horsemen, one hundred chariots, and slingers an huge multitude: but it is not yet certainly told, whether the Greeks that inhabit Asia do follow or no. But the Phrygians that join upon Hellespont do accompany Gabeus, having in the plain of Caustre six thousand horsemen and ten thousand targetmen. The Carians, the Cilicians, and Paphlagonians being called do not follow, as they say. The Assyrian himself, which is king

---

¹ of the same] i.e. they sought the help of the gods as they passed beyond the bounds of Persia.

² men of equal honour] Modern editions translate the Greek word (οἱ) ὁμότιμοι ((hoi) homótimoi, literally 'those who are equally valued') as 'peers', meaning that class of Persians who did not have to work the land and could devote themselves to war and self-advancement. Azoulay argues that as his empire grows and his allies diversify, Cyrus switches from this language of Persian class to κοινωνέ [koinone], a language of commonality (in Tuplin (ed.), pp. 158–60).

of Babylon and all Assyria, hath (as I think) no less than twenty thousand horsemen, chariots (I am sure) not above two hundred, and footmen (as I guess) an infinite sort. For so is he wont when he marcheth hither.' 'Then' (said Cyrus), 'you have declared our enemies to be in horsemen three score thousand,[3] in targetmen and archers above two hundred thousand. Now, what number have ye of your own power?' 'There be' (quoth he), 'of Median horsemen more than ten thousand, of targetmen and marchers may be made in our dominion sixty thousand. Of the Armenians our neighbours shall come four thousand horsemen, and twenty thousand footmen.' 'Then ye say' (quoth Cyrus), 'that our horsemen be less than the third part of our enemy's. And our foootmen almost half so many as they.' Then said Cyaxares, 'Do ye account the Persians so few, which you say ye have brought?' 'Whether we have' (quoth Cyrus), 'any need of men or not, we shall consult hereafter. Now tell me the manner of your several fight.' 'The fight' (quoth Cyaxares), 'is of all almost alike, for there be archers and darters as well of them as of us.' 'If they be' (quod Cyrus), 'thus appointed, must there not needs be skirmishing with arrow shots?' 'Of necessity', said Cyaxares. 'Then' (quoth Cyrus), 'the greater number must needs get the victory. For a few be sooner hurt and destroyed of many than many of a few.' 'If the case standeth so' (quoth Cyaxares), 'what device were better than to send to the Persians, declaring that the Medes' loss must needs redound to them, and requesting to have more aid of them?' 'Ye say well', quod Cyrus, 'but ye shall know that if all the Persians should come hither, they were not able to countervail our enemies in number.' 'Do you' (quoth Cyaxares), 'espy any better way than this?' 'I would' (said Cyrus), 'if I could, with all speed provide for all the Persians that shall come hither such armour as they have which with us be called men of equal honour or peers. That is, a curet° before the breast, a light target in the left hand, an arming blade or curtolax°[4] in the right hand. These, if ye can provide us, ye shall cause us to join with our enemies with most security, and then rather desiring to flee than abide the Persians, shall couple with them that tarry, and if any flee we shall commit them to you and your horsemen that they shall not be able neither to retire nor eftsoons to march.' Thus Cyrus said, and seemed to Cyaxares to say well, in so much as he made no more mention of sending for more men. This armour rehearsed tofore was speedily prepared, and when it was well nigh ready, the noble men of Persia were come with the army of the same. When as Cyrus calling them together, spake on this wise.

---

[3] three score thousand] sixty thousand.
[4] curtolax] 'Curtolays' in the text. Translating σάγαρις (*ságaris*), a Persian or Scythian axe-like weapon with a single-edged blade, this precedes the *OED*'s first use of 'curtolax' in Sir Thomas North's translation of Plutarch's *Lives of the Ancient Grecians and Romans*.

The Oration of Cyrus

'When as I (dear friends) perceived you to be so armed, and in hearts so appointed as is meet to match with our enemies at hand, and the residue of the Persians that follow to be so apparelled as serveth to fight at large,[5] I was not a little afraid lest you, being few, and abiding the brunt without succour, might haply fall in the danger of your enemies that be so many, and by occasion thereof be in no small jeopardy. But now, seeing you be come with tall men's bodies and no refuse,[6] and they shall have even the same armour that you have, it must be your part to quicken and encourage their hearts. For it is the office of a captain not only to be good himself but also to care that his men be very good too.'

Thus he said; they were all glad, because they thought they should be well accompanied at the battle. And one of them[7] spake after this sort:

'I shall peradventure seem to speak strangely if I should exhort Cyrus to say somewhat of us to them that shall be our war-fellows, when they shall receive their armour. But I surely know that they which be most able to do good or hurt do most prevail in words, and soonest persuade the hearts of the hearers. And when such men giveth any gifts, though of less price than their families do, yet the receivers do much more esteem the same. Wherefore if the Persians were now exhorted of Cyrus, they would much more rejoice and regard it than if they were to the like admonished of us. And when they shall be appointed to be of the nobility, they shall esteem the matter to be of more weight, being assigned of a king's son and grand captain, than if they were of us moved to the same. Nevertheless, our parts may not be behind, but with all means we must encourage and quicken the hearts of our men. For if they be good and valiant, it shall be to us profitable and commodious.'

When Cyrus, according to this device, had brought the armour into the middest of them and assembled all the Persian soldiers, he spake unto them after this sort.

'Friends Persians, you were born and bred in the same place that we were.[8] You have bodies nothing inferior to ours, and your hearts ought to be no worse than ours, being of this sort, yet in our country ye have not equally been partakers with us, not of us repelled but enforced of necessity to seek for your living. But now that ye may have even the like, I (with God's help) will provide ye may, if ye will, have the same armour that we have, to endure the same peril

---

[5] fight at large] fight from a distance.
[6] no refuse] No worthless people (*OED* 1.b) among you. Holland concentrates on the positive: 'as cannot be found fault with'.
[7] one of them] A Median.
[8] Marg] Oration.

that we shall, and to be advanced equally with us, if any of you shall become valiant and hardy. Heretofore as well you as we have been archers and darters and though ye do the feat worse than we, it is no marvel, for you have had no such opportunity to put the thing in use as we. But in this armature,[9] we shall not be any deal better than you. For every man shall have a meet curet for his breast, a target in his left hand, as we all are wont to bear, an arming sword or curtolax in his right hand, wherewith we must needs hit our enemies and not fear to miss when we strike. Then, wherein do one of us pass another but in valiant courage? Which you ought no less to declare than we? And for to desire victory, the which possesseth and saveth all wealth and felicity, why ought we more than you? Finally, to be conquerors, which giveth all that the conquery[10] hath, why is it more expedient for us than for you? To make an end, ye have heard all. Ye see this armour. Take every man that is meet for him and give his name to a captain of a crew°, to be in like array with us. He that is content with the place of a stipendiary soldier,[11] let him remain and minister harness.' Thus he said. The Persians hearing thus thought themselves worthy all their life to live a wretched life if they, being called to like avails, would not be willing to take like pains. Wherefore they gave their names and took every man the harness. All that time that it was said their enemies came, and did not, Cyrus travailed to exercise their bodies in feats of strength, teaching them to keep array and quickening their courage against their enemies. And having ministers° of Cyaxares, he commanded them to give to the soldiers all things that they should need. And by this mean[s], he left them nothing to do but the only exercise of martial feats, supposing learning taught him that men be made in every feat most excellent when they leave all other things and set their minds upon one only. Dismissing also part of their warlike exercise and taking from them the use of bow and dart, he left this only to them: to fight with sword, target and breastplate. Whereby he fashioned their hearts to join with their enemies at hand-strokes, or else to confess that they were unprofitable war-fellows. But that were a grief for them to confess, knowing that they were found for none other purpose but to fight for them that gave them wages. Furthermore perceiving that men be most willing to exercise those things wherein is contention and desire of victory, he proclaimed prizes or games of all things that were meet for the soldiers to put in use. And those that he did proclaim were these: that the private man should show himself obedient to the rulers; being ready to labour and forward to adventure with modesty, expert in things belonging to the army; brave in wearing his harness, and in all these, to seek for honour. To the

---

[9] armature] An early use of this term (for armour). The *OED* notes a first use in 1542, with this and other examples found especially in theological writing (Wyclif 'armure'; Tyndale 'armoure').
[10] conquery] Middle English form of 'conquer'.
[11] stipendiary soldier] mercenary.

quincurion or captain of five, to behave them self as becometh an honest private man, doing to his power all things belonging to the office of that number; to the decurion or captain of ten, the like in his number, even so the band of twenty-four to the band leader, to the centurion or captain of a crew, and to every other ruler, after like sort, being careful to perform the captains' commandments, they again might provide for them, doing their office accordingly. The rewards of good captains of a crew, which did best frame their men, was to be made a tribune or captain of a thousand. The band leaders, that best did teach their bands, did ascend to the place of a centurion. The best decurions or captains of ten were appointed to rooms of bandleaders. The captain of five to the captainship of ten. The private sort that most excelled to the captainship of five. The chief regard of these captains was to be honoured of their men, the which being obtained, other advancements followed every man in comely wise. Furthermore, he proposed° greater hope to them that were worthy praise if any greater commodity should appear in time to come. He proclaimed rewards of victory to the whole crews, to the whole bands, likewise to the whole number of ten and five as they appeared most faithful to their captains and ready to exercise these things tofore rehearsed, and such rewards were appointed to them as is meet for the multitude. These things were proclaimed and put in practise in the host. Furthermore he provided pavilions for them according to the number of captains of crews, and so big as was able to receive a crew. And in every crew was one hundred men, and so they had their tents according to their crews. In camping thus together, he thought this commodity would ensue for the battle that should be, because he perceived that they being kept together should have no pretence of cowardice that one was better or worse taught than another; concerning the coupling with their enemies, it seemed also to profit in that they should know one another being camped together and in knowing one another, they should be more ashamed one of another. For when they know not one another they seem to be the more given to sloth, as men living in darkness. Wherefore he thought that this camping together should much profit to the perfect struction of his men. The centurions had their crews so lying as every crew might march by him self, the bandleaders, the captains of ten, the captains of five after the same manner. And this order of every band seemed very profitable as well not to be disarrayed as if it should so chance to be soon in order again, even as wood and stones which must be framed, though they lie cast hand over head,[12] be easily set together if they have notes whereby it may be perceived for which place every one serveth. It seemed also profitable to be the less willing to forsake one another, because he saw that beasts feeding together had great desire of them that chanced to stray away.

Cyrus had regard of this also, that none should go to dinner or supper except

[12] hand over head] recklessly, carelessly.

they had laboured and sweat tofore: for either he led them on hunting, and so caused them to sweat, or else devised such pastimes as might move them to the same. And if it chanced anything to be done, he would begin the feat that they should not return without sweat. For he supposed this to be profitable as well to the better lust to meat and health of body as to the enduring of pain, and to be the more gentle one to the other. For horses accustomed to like labours stand the more quietly together. And soldiers be made the more courageous against their enemies, if they be assured to be well exercised. Cyrus prepared for himself a tent that might be sufficient for the receipt of them whom he called to feast. He called commonly such captains of crews as seemed meet to him, and sometime bandleaders, sometime captains of tens and five, sometime soldiers, sometime the whole number of five and ten, sometime a band and a crew. He called and advanced such as he saw doing that he would have all to do. His service was ever equal and all one for himself and his guests. And the ministers about the army he made partakers of every thing. For he judged those ministers of the camp to be no less worthy advancement than heralds and orators.[13] Wherefore he would have them expert and cunning in things belonging to the army and also hardy, quick, ready, and stable. And he appointeth that they should have even as much as they that were reputed best, and so to use themselves as they should refuse no labour, but think it their duty to do whatsoever the general did command them. Cyrus also had regard that when they made merry, such talk should be ministered as was pleasant and might stir them to manhood. And on a time he chanced to talk on this wise. 'Friends' (quoth he), 'doth other men[14] seem inferiors to us because they be not trained after our sort? Or is there no difference at all betwixt them and us, neither in behaviour nor in things appertaining to the trade of war?'

Hystaspas answered and said: 'What they be in warlike matters, I can not tell, but in behaviour and company they be some (by my say) rude enough. For of late Cyaxares sent to every band and company sacred meat, and we had three dishes of flesh every man or more. The cook began the first meat at me. And when he came the second time, I had him begin again at the hindermost. Wherefore one of the soldiers that sat in the middest cried out and said: "By God this gear° goeth not indifferently, if no man shall begin at us that be in the middest". Which when I heard I was grieved that he should think he had too little and called him unto me. He very modestly obeyed me. When the meat came at us and the lowest had taken their part, there was, I think, but little left. Whereas he was again grieved as he did plainly express, and said to himself: "What ill luck had I to come hither when I was called?" And I said, "Take no

---

[13] orators] Holland has the more usual translation: ambassadors.
[14] other men] Specifically, Cyrus refers to the Persians' comrades (or perhaps the cavalry — (οἱ) ἑταῖροι ((hoi) hetaîroi) and allies, the Medes.

care for the matter, for he shall straight begin at us and you shall be first and take the most". And with that he brought in the third and last course. And this fellow took next unto me. When the third man had taken, and seemed to take more than he, he laid aside that he had taken, intending to take another. The cook, thinking he had no list to meat, bare it away before he could take another piece. Then he was grieved at his evil chance, because that that he had taken was eaten up. Wherefore being in a rage and fury for so evil fortune, he overthrew the sauce that was left him. Which when the bandleader that sat next unto me saw, clapped his hands and laughed heartily. And I made as I had had the cough, for I could not refrain from laughter. Such one of your soldiers can I show you (Cyrus)', quoth he. At the which tale they laughed, as they might well. Another of the captains said, 'This man (Cyrus) as it seemeth was not well contented, but I, when you had taught us and sent us forth to our crews, commanding every man to teach his company as you had taught us, did my devoir° as other men did, so I came to teach one band. I placed the bandleader first, next him a lusty young fellow, and then other as I thought good: then standing afore and looking to the band, when I saw my time, I bade the band march. And this fellow, your lusty young man, coming before the bandleader marched foremost. And when I saw him I said: "Good fellow, what dost thou?" "I march" (quoth he), "as you command". Then I said: "I did not thee alone, but I bid all to march". And he hearing this, turned to his fellows and said: "Do ye not hear that he biddeth us all march?" And they all going before the bandleader came about me. And when the bandleader had brought them again to their places, they grudged and said: "which must we obey? Now the one commandeth us to march, the other will not let us." I took the matter in good part and placed them eftsoons in order, saying that none of the hindermost should move till the former did set forth, and that they all should have regard at this, to follow the former. When it chanced that one went into Persia, he came unto me and bade me give him letters which I had written home. And I bade the bandleader, which knew where the letters lay, to run and fetch the same. He ran forth. This young fellow followed the bandleader with his breastplate and arming blade: all the remnant of the band, seeing him run, followed, and fetched my letters. Thus hath my band' (quoth he), 'perfectly learned all that you have taught them.' The other that were there laughed at the warlike bringing of these letters, but Cyrus said: 'O Jupiter, and other gods, what fellows have we to our friends? They be so tractable that some of them will be won with a little meat, some be so obedient that before they know what is commanded them, they obey the same. I cannot tell what kind of soldiers a man ought rather wish to have than such.' Cyrus laughing with them thus praised the soldiers. It chanced that at this feast there was one of the Captains named Aglaitadas, a man in manners like to testy and froward men, who said on this wise: 'Do you think, Cyrus' (quoth he), 'that these fellows say true?' 'Why should they' (quoth Cyrus), 'desire to lie?' 'Why' (quoth he), 'but because they would move laughter, and therefore speak after this sort to avaunt° themselves.' 'Speak honestly' (quoth Cyrus), 'and call them not avaunters: for the name of an avaunter seemeth to be made, as I think, of them that pretend to be richer than they be, valianter than they be, and not able to perform that they take in hand: and that be evidently known to do this for lucre° and advantage sake. But they that move laughter in company, neither for their own advantage nor the hearers' hurt neither for any other kind of displeasure, they ought of right rather to be called pleasant and fine than avaunters.' Thus Cyrus answered in their defence that moved laughter. Then the bandleader that told the merry tale of his band said: 'Aglaitadas, if we should make you to weep, ye might right well blame us. As some men in their verses and orations recite lamentable matter to provoke weeping. And now when we, as you know, would have you merry, doing no man hurt, you have us for the same in much disdain.' 'Yea, by God', quoth Aglaitadas, 'and that justly. For he that maketh his friends to weep doth, as I think, a great deal better than he that maketh the same to laugh. And you shall find, if ye weigh the matter well, that I speak rightly. For by weeping, fathers make their children sober, and the schoolmasters their scholars well learned, and the laws enforceth citizens by making them to weep to keep justice. But wherein can ye say that they which move laughter do profit either the body or mind to be the more apt to govern families of common wealth?' Then said Hystaspas: 'Aglaitadas, if ye will follow my counsel, among your enemies be bold to be liberal in this as in a very precious thing and do your best to make them weep. But with us your friends, I pray you be more liberal of laughter, because it is a thing of little price. For you have neither spent it yourself, neither willingly amongst your friends or acquaintance uttered the same, so that you can make none excuse but that ye have a great deal of laughter in you.' And Aglaitadas said: 'Do you think, Hystaspas, to move laughter of me?' And the bandleader said: 'Marry, then he were a fool. For I think a man shall sooner beat fire out of thee than get laughter.' At this all the other laughed, considering the manners of Aglaitadas, and he him self also smiled. Cyrus seeing him somewhat merry said: 'Ye do not well to corrupt this our sober man in moving him to laugh, he being such an adversary against all laughter.' When this was spoken, Chrysantas said thus:

'Cyrus and all you here present, I think that there be come with us some of more price, some of less. But if any good luck shall hap unto us, they will all think themselves worthy to have like avail. And I judge nothing to be among men so unequal as that the good and the bad should be reputed alike.'

To this Cyrus said: 'Friends, we could not do better than propound this matter to be debated of the army, whether if God giveth us any good of our travail, the feats of every man being considered, according to the same the rewards to be employed.' 'What need you' (quod Chrysantas), 'propound this to be reasoned, and not rather proclaim that so you will do? Have ye not already proclaimed common games and rewards for the same?' 'Yes, certainly' (quod Cyrus), 'but they be not like. For what as they shall get in their soldierfare°,[15] that (I think) they will take to be common to them. As for the governance of the army, they peradventure thought to be in me before they came forth. Therefore though I appoint the order of the same, I suppose they think I do them no wrong.' 'And do you think' (quod Chrysantas), 'that the multitude will decree every man not to have equally but the best to be preferred in honours and advancements?' 'I think so' (quoth Cyrus), 'partly by your exhortation and partly because it will be a shame to speak against it, that he which travaileth most and profiteth the common should not be worthy most reward. And I think' (quoth he), 'that the very worst and refuse will suppose the best to be preferred.' And Cyrus was the more willing that this decree should be made, for the noble men's sakes. For he thought they would do the better if they knew their travails should be considered and their worthiness regarded. Wherefore he thought the time meet to have this decree made, because the noble men repined at the equal reward of the commons. Every man at this feast thought it meet to be debated, and that every manly man should accord unto it.

One of the captains smiled and said: 'I know one of the common sort which will agree that equal reward shall not be had.' Another asked who it was. 'It is' (quoth he), 'my tent-fellow, which in all things requireth to have more.' 'What' (quoth another), 'in labours too?' 'Nay, by my say' (quoth he), 'there I lied. For in labours and such other he is always very gentle to let him that will have more than himself.' 'But I' (quoth Cyrus), 'do determine such fellows as he now speaketh of to be banished our army if we intend to have a valiant and obedient army. For I think it the part of the soldiers one to induce another. And the good will do their devoir to induce to goodness, the evil to lewdness°. And for the most part, the lewd have more agreeing to them than the good. For lewdness coming with present pleasures hath the same, as joint persuaders, to allure the multitude; but virtue, leading to hardness, is not able to draw unto it out of hand,[16] especially where other do incite to ease and pleasure. There be also some which only be evil in sluggardy° and loitering, whom I repute as drones[17] hurting the common weal, only be wasting.[18] But they that in labours be lewd and stout and vehement to have with the most, they be also leaders to lewdness. For many times they may boast and show that their lewdness prevaileth.

---

[15] soldierfare] military service or experience. Holland also uses this phrase, one of only two examples cited in the *OED* for this obsolete word, for which Barker's is the earliest use.
[16] out of hand] Here, at once, immediately.
[17] drones] 'draues' in the text (a turned 'n'); the drone, or male honeybee, is not a worker-bee, and thought to be indolent or sluggish.
[18] only be wasting] i.e. that they damage others by wasting common resources etc.

Wherefore, in any wise, see that they be banished from us. And do not regard to fulfil your number with your own countrymen, but as in horses ye seek them that be least[19] not of your country, even so in men, of all other, take them which seemeth most meet for the strength and honour of yourselves. This also witnesseth with me for the best, that neither a cart can be swift which hath slow horses nor a house well governed where be lewd servants. And less loss it were to have no servants than be troubled with evil servants. Ye know well, friends, that this profit shall not only come by weeding out the lewd that all lewdness shall cease, but also they that remain and were infected with others' lewdness shall eftsoons be purged of the same. And the good seeing the evil rebuked shall with the more courage embrace virtue.' Thus he said, which pleased all his friends, and did accordingly.

Then Cyrus began to jest again: for perceiving that one of the captains had brought a guest to make merry, which was a man hairy and deformed, he called the captain by his name and said thus: 'Sambaulas, do you after the Greek fashion, which is commendable, lead about that young man which sitteth next you?' 'Yea surely', quoth Sambaulas, 'for I have a pleasure to be in his company and behold his countenance.' When the other at the table heard this, they looked upon him, and when they saw his face so evil favoured, they all laughed and one said: 'Good lord, Sambaulas, by what mean hath this man won your favour?' 'Marry I will tell ye' (quoth he), 'when so ever I call him, either by night or by day, he never maketh any excuse for his ease nor obeyeth me slowly, but ever runneth when I bid him do anything: and I never see him labour but he sweateth. And doth declare not in word but in deed how all the other like companies should behave themselves.' And one said, 'If he be such, why do ye not kiss him as your kinsman?' To this the foul fellow answered, 'By God, because he listeth not to take the pain: for if he would kiss me it were enough for all his other exercises'.[20] Such matters both of mirth and importance were ministered at this feast. In the end making thrice oblation, and praying God to send them good chance, they brake up the feast and went to bed. The day following, Cyrus assembled all the soldiers, and said thus.

'Friends, the battle is at hand: for our enemies cometh.[21] The rewards of victory if we overcome, certainly our enemies be ours, and all our enemies' goods. But if we be overcome (for this must we ever both speak and practise), all the goods of them that be overcome to be evermore present rewards to the conquerors. This ye must think. When men that indifferently be doers in this war shall assure themselves to have no commodity except they play the valiant

---

[19] least] best; a mistake in both 26066 and 26067.
[20] exercises] Even here, in the comic cameo of Sambaulus and the hints at Greek paederasty, obedience is cherished.
[21] **Marg**] Oration.

man, then they will without delay do many valiant feats, for they will not bear anything undone that ought to be done. But when every man shall think that another may travail and fight and he take his ease, through such (be you sure) all kind of displeasure shall redound to all. And God worketh after this sort, for to such as will not appoint themselves to do good, he hath made other their rulers.

'Therefore now let some man arise and say his mind of this matter, whether he thinketh that virtue shall the rather be put in use among us, if he that shall most travail and adventure shall have also most advancement, or if we perceive that it maketh no matter to be a coward, because all shall have equal reward.' Then Chrysantas arose, one of the nobles, no big man nor strong to see to, but of singular wisdom, and spake thus unto them:

The Oration of Chrysantas

'I think, Cyrus, you do not propound this case because ye think it meet that the evil should have equally with the good, but to prove whether any man will show him self to be of this opinion, that doing no good nor laudable feat would have equal part with them that shall achieve honour by their virtue.[22] I am neither swift in feet nor strong in hands. And I am sure, if I be judged by that I shall my body do, I shall neither be the first nor second: no, not the thousand, as I guess, and peradventure not the ten thousand, yet this I know for certain: if they that be valiant shall receive for their travails any commodity, my part shall be so much as right requireth. But if the evil do nothing and the good be out of courage, I fear me lest I shall be partaker of more than I would of anything rather than of good.' Thus Chrysantas said.[23]

After him Pheraulas, one of the Persian commons and to Cyrus at home familiar and pleasant in body, not unbeautiful and in mind not unlike a gentleman,[24] arose and said thus:

The Oration of Pheraulas

'I suppose, Cyrus and all your Persians here present, that we all equally be moved to the trade of virtue.[25] For I see that we all do nourish our bodies with like diet, and all be entertained in like companies, like commodities being

---

[22] **Marg**] Oration.
[23] Thus Chrysantas said.] Even as he takes Cyrus's cue and fulfils his agenda, Chrysantas recognizes Cyrus's own strategic dissembling by making this request.
[24] a gentleman] Pheraulas, a commoner (unlike Chrysantas), will later (Book VIII) be the subject of the story of utmost obedience from which Shakespeare would borrow the infamous line 'A kingdom for a horse!' for his *Richard III*. See note 43 (p. 247).
[25] trade of virtue] 'triall of vertue' in Holland.

laid before us all. For to obey the rulers is indifferently appointed. And he that seemeth to do the same without grudge, I see that he doth get honour at Cyrus's hand. And to be valiant against our enemies is not propounded to some as the goodliest thing and to some not, but indifferently to all. Now battle is declared to be at hand, in the which I see that courageous men be made cunning by nature, even as other creatures hath each learned a certain fight of none other schoolmaster than of nature, as the cow to strike with the horn, the horse with the hoof, the dog with the mouth, and the boar with the tooth. And they know to avoid all things of the which they ought most to beware. And these they learn without any schoolmaster at all.[26] I being a child knew straight how to defend myself against him of whom I thought I should be beaten, and if I had nothing, I would hold forth my hands and as much as I could let him that beat me. And this I did, not taught, but was beaten for the self same, if I did defend myself. And being a very child, I would get a sword when I could see it, learning this neither now to take it of none other but of nature, as I say. And this I did forbidden, not taught, as other things, which being restrained of father and mother, I did being enforced of nature. And truly I would privily strike with the sword all that I could. For it was not only natural unto me as to go and run, but methought I had a certain sweetness in doing the thing that nature moved. Seeing therefore that all one fight is left unto us, in the which rather courage than cunning is required, why should not we with pleasure contend with noble men? For the rewards of virtue be equally propounded. And if we be compared together, we be not like in adventures. For they live an honourable life which is pleasant, and we a painful life without honour which is displeasurable. But, friends, this doth most encourage me to fight, that Cyrus is the judge, which doth not judge partially but, as God knoweth and I dare swear, whom he seeth valiant, them he loveth no less than himself. To them I see he hath more pleasure to give than him self to keep. I know these gentlemen be high-stomached° because they have been brought up to endure hunger, thirst and cold, ill perceiving that we be taught the same of a better schoolmaster than they. For there is no schoolmaster so good as necessity, which hath taught us to be very perfect in the same. They learn to labour when they bear their harness, which all men have devised to make most light and easy to bear. But we have been compelled to go and run with great burdens, in so much as the bearing of harness seemeth to me at this time more like feathers than burdens. Therefore, Cyrus, so take me as one that will do my best, and whatsoever I be, think it meet that according to their worthiness so men shall be advanced. And friends of the commons, I do exhort ye, that ye will encourage your selves to contend in this fight with these well brought-up gentlemen. For now men be taken to a fight

---

[26] schoolmaster at all] Pheraulas is one of the Persians who was not educated in the 'place of free resort' described in Book i.

of[27] the commons.' Thus Pheraulas said. And many other arose and accorded with them both. Wherefore it was decreed that every man should be rewarded after his worthiness and that Cyrus should be the judge of the same. Thus his matters went forward.

Cyrus on a time, called an whole crew of men with their captain to supper. He saw him[28] place the one half of his crew against the other meet to fight, both having breastplates and targets in their left hands: in their right hands he gave the one half good round wasters°, the other had take up clods and throw when they saw time. When they stood in order of battle, he gave a token to fight. Then they threw their clods and hit some on the breastplate, some on the target, and some on the shins and legs. But when they came together, they that had the wasters struck some on the legs, some on the hands, some on the thighs. And as they stooped to take up more clods, they hit them on the backs and necks. At length they were put to flight, and the waster-bearers chased them, and struck them with much sport and laughter. Cyrus being delighted at this witty device of the captain, and the due obedience of the other because they were exercised and also recreated, and they did overcome which counterfeited the Persian armour, being at this delighted, he called them all to supper. And when he saw in his tents some having their legs, some their hands bound up, he asked what they ailed. They answered that they were hit with clods. Then he asked them again whether it was when they met together, or when they were asunder. They answered, 'When they were asunder'. For when they met together the waster-bearers said it was a pleasant pastime, but they that were stricken with the wasters cried that it was no pastime to them when they met together, and showed the stripes of the wasters, some in their hands, some in their necks, some in their faces. And thus one laughed at another, as they might right well. The day following, the plain was full of all the host, counterfeiting these.[29] And ever when they had no weightier thing to do, they used this pastime. He saw at another time a captain leading his crew from a river on the right hand one by one, and when he saw his time, commanded the hindermost band to lead the third and fourth into the front, when the bandleaders were in the front, he commanded to lead every band two by two, then the captains of ten lead into the front. When again he saw it time, he commanded to lead a band by four a rank, then the captains of five were the leaders, and every band went four by four when he was at the tenth gate, commanding them to go two by two, he led in the first band and commanded the second to follow at the tail of it. So likewise the third and fourth he led them all in. And so sat at supper as they entered.

---

[27] a fight of] i.e. to contend with.
[28] him] i.e. the captain.
[29] counterfeiting these] Cyrus's encouragement of imitation, in keeping with the exemplary principles of Persian education.

Cyrus being delighted with their mildness, device and practice, called this crew to supper with their captain again. There was another captain at supper which said: 'Cyrus, ye call not my crew to your tent, which when it cometh to supper do even the like? And when supper is done, the tail leader of the last band leadeth the band, having the last first in ray to fight. Then after them the tail leader of the other band and the third and fourth after like sort, whereby they know how to go back, when they shall retreat from the battle. If we be appointed to walk a course, and it be in the morning, I lead and the first band is first, the second, third and fourth followeth, as they ought, so long as I command. When it is night, the tail leader and the last goeth first, and nevertheless obeyeth me coming last that so they might be accustomed both to follow and to lead, being alike obedient.' Cyrus said, 'Do ye this always?' 'So oft' (quoth he), 'as we go to supper.' 'Then I bid you to come' (quoth he), 'both because ye trade your men going and coming, night and day, and also exercise your bodies by walking, and profit your minds by learning. And because ye do all things double, it is right we make you double cheer.' 'For God's sake' (quoth the captain), 'not in one day, except ye also give us double bellies.' And thus they made an end of the feast. The next day Cyrus called that crew to his tent, as he had said overnight, which other perceiving from that time forth all followed these.

As Cyrus was mustering his men in harness and setting them in order, there came a messenger from Cyaxares, saying that an embassage° was come from the Indians, 'wherefore Cyaxares would that ye should come with all speed. I have brought you a goodly robe from him, that you should come most comely and civil, because the Indians shall behold ye when ye come.' When Cyrus heard this, he commanded the captain that was first in array to stand at the front, leading his crew one by one, placing himself in the right hand, and commanded him to give the like charge to the next, and so throughout. They obeyed him, and warned the other, so that shortly the charge was given. And in a while there was in the front about two hundred (for there were so many captains) and in breadth, one hundred. When they were placed, he had them follow as he marched, and went on a good pace. But after he knew the way which went to the palace to be more streight° than all could go in the front, he commanded the first thousand to follow in place, and the second at the tail of it. When it was so done throughout, he marched forth without stop, the other thousands followed every one at the tail of the former. He sent two ministers at the entry of the path, that if any man were to seek they should tell what ought to be done. When they came to the gates of Cyaxares, he commanded the first captain to lead his men by twelve a rank. And the leaders of every twelve to stand in the front about the place and commanded like charge to be given to the next, and so throughout all, and they did accordingly. He came to Cyaxares in a Persian robe, not of the worst sort.³⁰ When he saw him he was glad of his speedy repair, but offended with the baseness of his garment and said: 'Why have ye done thus, Cyrus, so to appear to the Indians? I would ye should have been seen in most goodly wise. For this had been an honour to me, to have had my sister's son set forth most royally.'

To this Cyrus said, 'Whether should it have been more to your honour if I, being clad with purple and dashed with bracelets and chains and ruffling in my robe, should have accomplished your will, or as I now have with so great a power and so speedily performed the same, to your high honour, garnishing myself with sweat and diligence³¹ and honouring you by teaching other[s] how to be obedient to you?' Thus Cyrus said. And Cyaxares thinking that he had said well, commanded the Indians to be brought in. Being come in, they said the Indian king had sent them and commanded to enquire the cause of the war between the Medes and Assyrians. 'And your answers heard, to go to the Assyrian king to make the like demand of him. And in fine,³² thus to say unto you both: the king of India sayeth, he will stick to him that hath the wrong.' To this Cyaxares answered, 'Then this is mine answer: I have not done any wrong at all to the Assyrian. Now go to him and learn what he sayeth.' Cyrus being there said: 'May I, Cyaxares, speak anything?' And Cyaxares bade him speak his mind. 'You then' (quoth he), 'shall thus say to the king: that we, except it seemeth otherwise to Cyaxares, make this answer: if the Assyrian shall say he hath wrong by us, we choose the king of India judge thereof.' When they heard this answer they departed. When the Indians were gone, Cyrus began thus to talk with Cyaxares: 'Sir, I came from home with no great store of money beside mine own: and how much so ever it was, there is but a little left, for I have spent it upon my soldiers: whereat you may marvel how I have spent it, seeing [how] you find us. But ye shall well understand that it is employed upon none other thing but upon the advancement and encouraging of my soldiers by some benefit. For I think it is better for him that will have at all hands good helpers in any matter, to incite the same by well speaking and well doing rather than by cruelty and compulsion. Likewise, he that will make courageous travellers³³ in warlike matters must (I think) allure the same with good words and works. For they must be friends, not foes, which shall be unfeigned fellows in war, neither envying their captain in wealth nor betraying him in woe. Which thing I considering, perceive I have need of money. And that you should care of all, whom I perceive liberally to give so much, I think it not convenient. Wherefore

---

³⁰ not of the worst sort] A confusing translation: Cyrus's robe is not showy or extravagant in the way Cyaxares would like. Holland has 'nothing proud nor sumptuous' (sig. G1v).
³¹ sweat and diligence] Another example of Cyrus's Persian moderation and discipline contrasted with Cyaxares' Median taste for pomp and luxury.
³² in fine] in the end.
³³ travellers] i.e. travailers, undertakers of.

it is meet that you and I indifferently should devise that money do not fail us. For if you have plenty, I know I shall have part at my need, specially if I take it for such purpose as may profit you by the expense thereof. I remember I heard you say of late that the Armenians despiseth you, neither sending you an army nor paying you your tribute which he oweth.' 'He doth even so, Cyrus' (quoth he), 'wherefore I am in doubt whether it were better for me to make him war and compel him to pay me, or more for my profit to let him alone at this present, lest I should increase mine enemies by him.' Then Cyrus asked, 'Be his houses in sure places or easy to come to?' Cyaxares said: 'They be in no very sure places, for I have marked that. But there be hills, whither if he can come he is straight in safety from being taken, himself, and all that he bringeth with him, except a man would lie at long siege, as my father sometime hath done.' Then Cyrus said, 'If ye will send me, and appoint me so many horsemen as shall seem sufficient, I trust with God's help to make him send you an army, and also pay your tribute. And I trust further that he shall be more assured to you than he now is.' And Cyaxares said, 'But I think they had rather come to you than to us. For I hear say there be some which were your companions in hunting when ye were children which peradventure had rather come again to you, but if we can make some sure, our will shall be fulfilled.' 'Then' (quoth Cyrus), 'is it not good to keep this device close?' 'The sooner' (quoth Cyaxares), 'should some come into our hands: and if a man would go against them, he should take them unwares°.' 'Then hark' (quoth Cyrus), 'what I say:

'I have many times with all the Persians which were with me hunted about the borders of your ground and the Armenians' and have taken horses of my friends there and gone forth. Wherefore if I did the like now, I should not be suspected. But if my company be more now than it was wont to be in hunting, it shall be suspected. But we may make a shift[34] for this, that shall seem somewhat true. That is, if some man would report among them that I intend to make a great hunting, and have made an open request to you for horsemen.' 'Ye say well' (quoth Cyaxares), 'and that I will give you but a few, because I will go to my forts which be near Assyria. For so I will in deed' (quoth he), 'to make them so sure as I can. And when you be gone with the power you have, and hunt, I shall send ye within two days sufficient horse and footmen which I have gathered, whom ye shall take and then invade. And I having another power shall do my devoir[35] not to be far from you, that when time requireth I may show myself.' So out of hand, Cyaxares gathered horsemen and footmen for his forts and sent wagons with victuals the way that went to the same. Cyrus made sacrifice for his journey and desired Cyaxares to have his younger horsemen,

[34] make a shift] manage by contrivance.
[35] devoir] duty.

and he granted him but few, very many being willing to go.³⁶ Cyaxares being gone his journey to his forts with power of foot and horsemen, Cyrus had lucky sacrifice to go against the Armenians, and so marcheth forth as appointed to hunt. Going forth in the first field, an hare was sterte,³⁷ and an eagle flying on the lucky side, and espying the hare running, made his flight and struck him, took him up and bare him away, and going to the next hilltop, seasoned on his prey as he would. Cyrus seeing this sign rejoiced and thanked Jupiter king, and said to them that were present, 'Friends, this shall be a pleasant hunting, I trust in God'. When he was come to the borders, straight he hunted as he was wont. And the multitude of footmen and horsemen coursed to and fro to put the deer up. The best of the foot and horsemen were divided, to stand at receipt of the deer put up, who chased and killed many boars, harts, goats and wild asses. For in those places there be many asses at this day. When he had done hunting and drew near the marches of Armenia, he supped, and the next day early hunted again, going nigh the hills which he coveted to have. When he had done, he supped. And hearing that Cyaxares' host was at hand, he sent unto them, bidding them keep two Persian miles³⁸ off, foreseeing the commodity of closeness.³⁹ When they had supped, he had their captain to repair to him. When he himself had supped, he called his captains unto him and said: 'Friends, the Armenian heretofore hath been confederate and tributary to Cyaxares, but now hearing of the coming of our enemies, he despiseth us and neither sendeth army nor payeth his tribute.⁴⁰ Now therefore we must hunt him, if we can. And thus I think good to do. You, Chrysantas, shall go into his land so far as ye may, and take with you half the Persians. You must walk over the hills and take the same, whither they say he fleeth when he is in fear. I shall give you guides. And they say the hills be thick, so that I hope ye shall not be seen. Ye shall also send before your army quick fellows like to these both in number and array. And they, if they chance upon any of the Armenians, shall take them and keep them from telling tales: and whom they cannot take, they shall drive them so far off as they shall not espy the whole army, but shall make provision as it were against thieves. Thus shall you do: I, by the break of day, having half the footmen, and all the horsemen, will go by the plain straight to the palace. If he do make resistance, then belike we must fight. If he conveyeth himself from the plain, it is like we will follow him. If he fleeth to the hills, then must your part be played

---

³⁶ willing to go] The increasingly tense issue of Cyrus's greater popularity than Cyaxares among the army, something Xenophon shows Cyrus to have cultivated by his strategic generosity, hospitality and communal games.
³⁷ sterte] jumped up suddenly (here). Another Middle English word.
³⁸ two Persian miles] two parasangs. The term 'parasang' was commonly used in classical writing on Persia, but Barker chooses to English it.
³⁹ commodity of closeness] Here, the advantage of secrecy.
⁴⁰ Marg] Oration.

that none escapeth that cometh to you. Think ye were on hunting, and that we be the hounds and you keep the nets.[41] Then ye must remember to prevent and stop the ways before the deer be up, and they must be in covert that shall be appointed to it, that they may prevent the deer before they come. But you may not do, Chrysantas, as many doth which loveth hunting: for they many times spend the whole night without sleep. But now men must have measurable° rest, that they may be able to resist sleep, nor ye may not wander in the mountains as one that had no guides but ye must run to that place whither the deer maketh. Nor ye may not go in places hard to pass but command your guides (except the way be much shorter) to lead you the easiest way. For an army that goeth easily goeth speedily. Nor you may not lead your men running though you be wont to run up the hills, but you must lead a measurable pace, that your army may conveniently follow. And it were good that some of the best sort and forward men should sometime stay and encourage the other. And the forward must so pass as all the other may seem to run.'

Chrysantas hearing this, and being glad of Cyrus's instruction, took his guides and departed. When he had told them that should go with him what to do, he went to rest. When he had rested so much as seemed convenient, he marched to the hills. When day was come, Cyrus sent a messenger to the king of Armenia, willing him to say thus:

'"Cyrus commandeth you, O king of Armenia, thus to do, that with all speed ye come unto him, bringing both an army and your tribute." If he demand where I am, say as the truth is: in the marches. If he do ask whether I will come myself, say and that truth: that you know not. If he ask how many we be, bid him send some man and learn.' Thus he sent a messenger with this commission, thinking it to be more princely[42] than to come upon him without warning. He being thoroughly appointed both to go the journey and also to fight if need were, marched forth. He gave a commandment to his soldiers that they should do no man wrong. And if any of Armenia chanced to meet them, to bid them be of good comfort, and every man that would to come and sell at his pleasure either meat or drink,

The end of the second book.

---

[41] nets] Hunting with nets was a Persian sport during the Achaemenid period.
[42] princely] Holland has 'with courtesie and humanitie' (sig. [G3]v).

The Institution of Cyrus, the Third Book

Cyrus thus did. The king of Armenia, hearing Cyrus his ambassage, was astonished, remembering that he had done wrong both in withholding his tribute and in not sending aid, being most of all in fear because it should be espied that he had begun to edify his palace so that he was able to keep out his adversaries. Being troubled with all these things, he sent out to gather his strength and also conveyed his youngest son Sabaris to the mountains, and the wives and daughters, both his and his sons', with all their ornaments and jewels of much value, appointing men to conduct them safe. He also sent forth other to espy what Cyrus did, and also made in a readiness those Armenians that were present; and forthwith other came to him, saying that Cyrus was at hand. Then he being afraid to try it by fight conveyed him self away. Which the other Armenians perceiving, fled every man home, intending to carry away such things as they had.

Cyrus beholding the field full of them that ran away and fled to save themselves, he sent them word that he would hurt none which did tarry, but if he took any fleeing away him he said he would handle as his enemy. Whereby many stayed. And all they that privily fled were with the king. And when as they which went afore with the women fell in their hands, which lay privily in the mountains,[1] they made by and by great escries° and fled, and were very many taken. The king hearing of these things, doubting what he should do, fled into an hill top. Which Cyrus seeing, did besiege the hill with the army that he had, and sent to Chrysantas, commanding him to leave the custody of the mountains and come to him. And when Cyrus had all his army together, he sent a messenger to the king, asking him these questions. 'Tell me, king of Armenia, whether ye will remain there and fight with hunger and thirst, or come down to the plain and fight it out with us?' The king answered that he would fight with neither. Then Cyrus sent again, and asked, 'Why then do you lurk there and will not come down?' 'Because I doubt' (said he), 'what to do.' 'Ye need not doubt' (said Cyrus), 'for you may come down and answer for yourself.' 'But who shall be judge?' said he. 'Truly' (said Cyrus), 'even he to whom God have given without judgement to use ye as he list.'[2] Then the king perceiving this necessity descended. Cyrus bringing him and all his into the middest did enclose him with his camp, having with him all his force.

In the meantime, Tigranes, the king's eldest son, which afore had accompanied

---

[1] in the mountains] i.e. fell into the hands of those (of Cyrus's army) who lay in wait in the mountains.
[2] as he list] i.e. he into whose power God has delivered you.

Cyrus on hunting,[3] was come from a certain progress.[4] And hearing what was done, went straight to Cyrus to know the matter. But perceiving his father, mother, brother and sisters, yea his own wife to be captives, he could not refrain weeping. Cyrus seeing him used none other friendly entertainment but said: 'Ye are come in good season, that you being present may hear your father's cause.' And straight way calling the captains together both of the Persians and Medes, and assembling also the noblemen of Armenia, which were present and not rejecting the women being in their chariots but suffering them to hear when he thought it time, thus he began to speak.

'I do first give you counsel, O king of Armenia, in this cause to speak nothing but truth, that you may be clear of that one thing which is of all other most hateful. For to be taken with a lie, it is as you well know, the greatest impediment to men to attain pardon.[5] Your children, your wives, and all the Armenians being present be privy to that you have done, which hearing you speak otherwise than the truth, shall think that you do judge yourself to suffer all extremity, if I do hear the truth.'[6] 'Then ask what you list, Cyrus' (said he), 'that for the truth's sake, which you require, you may obtain what you will.' 'Then answer me', said Cyrus: 'Did you make war against Astyages, my mother's father, and the other Medes?' 'I did', said he. 'Being overcome of him, did ye not covenant to yield him tribute, to find him men when he should warn you, and to have no fortresses in your land?' 'It is true', said he. 'Now, then, why have you neither paid your tribute nor sent him men but have immured fortresses?'[7] 'Because' (said he), 'I was desirous of liberty and thought it a noble thing both to be myself at liberty and also to leave the same to my children.' 'It is a noble thing' (said Cyrus), 'to fight that a man may for ever escape bondage. But if one being overcome by war or made captive by any other mean should be espied to go about to revolt from his lord, tell me first yourself, would you, if you took any such, advance him with honours as a man of price, or punish him as a transgressor?' 'I would punish him' (said he), 'for you will not have me to lie.' 'Then answer plainly to every thing', said Cyrus: 'if any of your officers should

---

[3] hunting] Tigranes had been part of the hunting parties Cyrus had enjoyed during his time in Media.

[4] progress] Translating ἀποδημία τις (*apodēmía tis*), 'a certain journey' in Holland. Barker employs the term used for travel generally, but also for official travels or progresses by the monarch or nobility.

[5] attain pardon] Cyrus upholds the Persian emphasis on the necessity of truth-telling — another feature of ancient Persian life early moderns were fond of citing: for example, a 'lawe' instated by Cyrus for the education of Persians from the ages of five until twenty was, according to Richard Robinson, to 'Learne three thyngs well, To ryde. To shoot. Tell truth and never lye' (*The Auncient Order, Societie, and Unitie Laudable of Prince Arthure* (London: John Wolfe, 1583), sig. L3).

[6] if I do hear the truth] i.e. if ever I discover the truth (if the king of Armenia had lied).

[7] immured fortresses] 'enmured' in Barker's text, that is, fortified.

use himself unjustly, whether would ye suffer him to be in authority still or place another in his room?'[8] 'I would place another' (said he). 'If he had money, would ye suffer him to wax rich, or make him poor?' 'I would take from him' (said he), 'that he had.' 'If he would go to your enemy's part, what would ye do?' 'I would kill him' (said he), 'for why should I, being reproved as a liar, rather die than showing the truth?' The which word his son hearing threw off the attirements of his head[9] and tore his garments, the women shrieked and rent their faces, as though the king had now been dead, and they all even then destroyed. But Cyrus commanding them to cease said, 'We have enough. These be rightful, you say (O king of Armenia). Now what counsel will you give us to do in the same?' The king kept silence, doubting whether he should counsel Cyrus to put him to death or teach contrary to that he said tofore.[10] Then his son Tigranes asked Cyrus, saying: 'Show me, O Cyrus, because my father is like a man amazed, if I may give you counsel concerning him, what I think best for you to do?' And Cyrus because he knew that what time[11] Tigranes was his companion in hunting, he had a subtle sophister[12] attendant upon him whom he had in great reputation, was very desirous to hear what he could say, and bade him boldly speak what he thought. 'Aye then', said Tigranes, 'if you do allow both that [which] my father hath spoken and also done, I will give you counsel to follow the same. But if ye think he hath done evil in all, I advise you not to follow him.' Then said Cyrus: 'If I will do right, I may not follow him that doth evil.' 'It is true', said he. 'Then must I punish your father according to your own sentence, if it be just to punish the unjust.' 'Whether think ye Cyrus', said he, 'to be better for you to punish with your profit or with your damage?'[13] 'I should so punish myself', said he. 'Yea, and you should' (quoth Tigranes), 'much hinder yourself if then ye would kill any of your men when it were more meet for you to have them alive.' 'How can they be' (quoth Cyrus), 'more meet for me, which be found unjust?[14] Can I think that they will be made sober?' 'I think (Cyrus), that so it is. For without soberness, other virtues little avail. For what

---

[8] room] Here, an office or position.
[9] attirements of his head] Holland has 'Turbant' (turban), but Barker's acquaintance with the Islamic world is not sufficiently well developed for him to use this term.
[10] said tofore] On Cyrus mastering and even 'enslaving' the king of Armenia in this dialogue, see Danzig, *Apologizing for Socrates*, pp. 194–95.
[11] what time] when.
[12] sophister] Holland has 'a certain learned man'. A longstanding critical tradition, originating in the early modern period, holds that Xenophon is writing glancingly about Socrates here. On Xenophon's Socrates, and for an argument comparing Xenophon's Socrates with his Cyrus in their each being a 'supreme master of the art of politics [... i.e.] the art of acquiring devoted followers', see Danzig, *Apologizing for Socrates*, p. 194.
[13] with your damage] Tigranes switches the question from one of justice and equity to advantage and power, a lesson Cyrus has already learned from his father in Book I.
[14] found unjust] i.e. how can men who have been found unjust be useful to me?

profit shall a man have of a strong, a valiant man, and an horseman, not being sober? What of a rich man, what of a man of power in a city? But with soberness, every friend is profitable and every servant good.' 'Then thus ye mean' (quoth Cyrus), 'that your father is made in one day of an unsober a sober man.' 'Yea truly' (quoth he). 'Then you do say, that soberness is an affection of the mind, as dolour, not a discipline. For if he that shall be sober must be made wise, he is not therefore made by and by a sober man of an unwise man.' 'What, Cyrus' (said he), 'have ye not yet learned that one man enterprising through want of soberness to fight with his better when he hath been overcome hath straight way ceased from his unsoberness? Again, have ye not yet seen a city moving war against another city, which being overcome, forthwith instead of fighting would use obedience?' 'But what overthrow of your father' (said Cyrus), 'can ye show, whereby ye may prove that he is made sober?' 'Truly because he feeleth it in himself that for coveting liberty he is made so thrall as he never was to before.[15] And things that he thought expedient to have been close, to have prevented or defeated, he was able to accomplish none of all. He knoweth that you, wherein ye intended to deceive him, have so deceived him as a man might deceive the blind or dumb, and not men which had any wareness or wisdom. And where you thought closeness should be used, he knoweth you have so closely dealt with him that such places as be counted most secret for his refuge, you closely had before made his prison, and in swiftness you have so passed him that you prevented him, being come with a strong army before he could gather his power together.' 'Do ye then certainly think' (said Cyrus), 'that such overthrows be sufficient to make men sober, and to acknowledge their superiors?' 'Yea, surely' (said Tigranes), 'much more than when a man is overthrown by fight. For he that is overcome by strength thinketh that his body being better appointed he may try it again. And cities being taken, getting others' aid, think they may eftsoons renew the fight. But whom they shall judge to be stronger than themselves, them many times they will without compulsion obey.' 'Then' (said Cyrus), 'you think that despiteful° men do not acknowledge them which be soberer than they, nor thieves true men, nor liars truth-speakers, nor the unjust them that doth justice. Do ye now know that your father hath lied and not performed covenants made with us, knowing that we have transgressed no point of the conditions made by Astyages?' 'I do not' (said he), 'mean that it maketh sober men only to know their betters without some pain done them of their betters, as now is done to my father.' 'As for your father' (said Cyrus), 'as yet he hath felt no pain. But he is in much fear (I know well) lest he should suffer extreme pain.' 'And do you think' (said Tigranes), 'that anything doth more reclaim men than great fear?[16] Do ye not know that men being stricken with

---

[15] to before] i.e. heretofore.
[16] great fear] One of the points that catches the eye of Machiavelli: the political effectiveness

sword, which is counted most sharp punishment, will eftsoons fight against their enemies? But whom men do much fear, them though they put them in good comfort they can not look on.' 'Then you say' (quod Cyrus), 'that fear do more punish men than to be ill handled in deed.' 'You know' (quod he), 'that I say truth, for they which be in fear to be exiled their country, and they that would fight and dare not lest they should be overcome, live most pensively. Also they that sail fearing shipwreck and they that fear slavery and bondage, for such can neither eat nor sleep for fear. But they that be already banished, overcome and bound, may sometime eat and sleep more than they that be in happy estate. Furthermore, it is manifest in some what a burden fear is, for some fearing least being captives, they should be put to death, dieth afore for fear, some throw themselves down headlong, some hang, some choke themselves. So of all terrible things, fear doth most torment men's minds. And how is my father, think ye, now troubled in his mind, which is in fear not only of his own captivity but also of mine, of his wife's and all his children's thralldom?' 'I can easily believe' (said Cyrus), 'that he is thus troubled, for it is one man's part to be despiteful in prosperity and soon desperate in adversity. And when he can recover, wax eftsoons proud again and stir up new trouble.' 'Truly' (said he), 'our offence is the cause why we be out of credit. But you may both make fortresses and retain them that be already fortified, or take any other assurance or pledge what you will, yea and ye take our own selves we will not greatly be grieved, remembering that we be causes of our own displeasures. But if you betake this kingdom to any that have not yet offended, appearing to be distrustful, take heed lest ye do them a pleasure which do not take you for their friend. And if you to avoid hatred do put no yoke upon them to keep them under, take heed lest hereafter ye shall have more need to restrain them than ye now have us.' 'Be ye sure' (said Cyrus), 'I will not gladly put such ministers in trust as shall serve me by constraint, but such as I perceive of good will and benevolence toward me do their duties, them (methink) I may more easily suffer, though they do offend, than they that hate me by compulsion, doing never so well.' Whereat Tigranes said, 'Of whom can ye get so much friendship as ye now may of us?' 'Of them, I think' (said he) 'which were never mine enemies, if I will be beneficial unto them, as ye would have me now be to you.' 'Can ye find' (quoth he), 'any man at this present to whom ye may be more beneficial than to my father? Again, if ye would suffer a man to live which hath done you no displeasure, what thank, think ye, would he give you? What if ye do not make captive his wife and children, who will for this thing love you more than he which thinketh his deserts hath brought the same to captivity? If he have not the kingdom of Armenia, who, think ye, will be so sorrowful as we? Therefore it is evident that to whom greatest anguish shall redound, if he be not

of fear in gaining obedience or support.

king, the same receiving his kingdom by you must needs give you most high thanks. And if you be desirous to leave these things in most quiet state after your departure, consider whether you think it shall be more quiet the kingdom being changed or the old received manner remain still. And if you desire to have at any time a great army, who think ye can so well prepare it as he that oftenest hath used to do it? Finally, if ye have need of money, who think you can better purvey the same than he which both knoweth and hath all the store? Therefore (noble Cyrus) beware lest in destroying us, you shall sustain more hindrance than my father could do you.' Thus he spake.

Cyrus hearing him was glad, because he thought all things would come to pass which he had promised Cyaxares to do, remembering that he had said he would make the king more assured to him than he was before. Then he asked the king: 'If I shall give credit to you, tell me king of Armenia, how great an army will ye send with me, and how much money will ye give me toward this war?' Whereunto the king answered thus: 'I can show you nothing more plainly nor more justly than to declare unto you my whole power, that you knowing what it is may take with you as much as you list, leaving some for the defence of this country. Likewise concerning my money, it is my part to show you all that I have that you, knowing what it is, may take at your pleasure and leave what you list.' Then Cyrus said: 'show me then both what power and also what money ye have.' The king said: 'I have now eight thousand horsemen, and forty thousand footmen of Armenia. In money, with the treasure that my father did leave me, I have numbered in silver more than three thousand talents.' Then Cyrus without delay said, 'You shall then because that the Chaldees, your borderers, do make you war, send with me half your army. And for withholding of Cyaxares' tribute, for fifty talents you shall pay him double. And me ye shall lend one hundred talents, which I promise you, God sending me good luck, either to repay you if I be able or else do you great pleasures. But if I be not able, I trust I shall be rather thought unable than rightly be judged unjust.' 'For God's sake' (said the king), 'speak not so, Cyrus, for else you shall make me distrust you. But think surely this, what so ever ye leave behind you it shall be as certainly yours as that ye take with you.' 'Be it so' (said Cyrus). 'But what will ye give me to have your wife again?' 'As much' (said he), 'as I am able.' 'What for your children?' 'As much for them also as I can make.' 'Then', said Cyrus, 'these be double so much as you have. But tell me Tigranes, what will you give to receive your wife again?' He was new-married and entirely loved his wife, and said: 'I Cyrus would redeem her with my life, that she might not become a thrall.' Then said Cyrus, 'Take her unto you, for I did not intend to make her captive, seeing you never fled from me. And you also (O king) take your wife and children, leaving none behind you, that they may know they depart free. And at this time sup with us, and when supper is ended, go whither ye list.'

And so they tarried. Being set at supper, Cyrus said: 'Tell me, Tigranes, where is he become which was wont to hunt with us, whom you, as it appeared, did much esteem?' 'My father' (said he), 'hath put him to death.' 'For what offence?' 'He said that he did corrupt me,[17] which notwithstanding (Cyrus) was so good and honest that when he should die, he sent for me and said, "Be not, Tigranes, grieved with your father because he doth kill me, for he doth it not of malice but of ignorance. And what as men offend of ignorance, that I think to be done unwillingly".' 'Alas good fellow' (said Cyrus). Then the king said thus: 'They that take their wives having to do with other men do not therefore sue them to death because they do disparage their wives but because they think that they do quench the love which they owe to their husbands, and therefore they use them as their enemies. Even so I put that fellow to death because methought he made my son more to regard him than me.' And Cyrus said, 'Surely your offence (as I think) was a gentle fault. Therefore, Tigranes, do you forgive your father.' Thus talking with gentle entertainments (as meet was) after their atonement they went gladly with their wives into their chariots and so departed. Being come home, some praised Cyrus his wisdom, some his constancy, some his gentleness, some his beauty and goodly shape. Then Tigranes asked his wife: 'Did Cyrus seem so goodly to you?' 'By my troth' (said she), 'I did not look on him.' 'On whom then?' (said Tigranes). 'Marry, on him' (quoth she), 'which said he would redeem my captivity with his life.' So ceasing of their talk they were at quiet among themselves, as they might.

The day following, the king sent to Cyrus and the whole army gifts of friendship, and commanded them that should go to the war to be ready the third day, and sent Cyrus twice so much money as he required. Of the which Cyrus taking so much as he appointed, sent the other again. Then he demanded whether of them should lead the army, himself or his son, which made both this answer, the father thus: 'which you will command'; the son thus, 'I will not forsake you (Cyrus) though I should be a drudge and follow you'. And Cyrus smiling said, 'What would you think if your wife should hear that you should become a drudge and slave?' 'She shall not need', said he, 'to hear of it for I will do it, that she may see what I do.' 'It is time' (said Cyrus), 'for you to furnish your men.' 'I think' (said he), 'that they shall be furnished whom my father will send you.' Then gifts given among the soldiers, they went to rest.

The next day, Cyrus taking with him Tigranes and the best of the Medes' horsemen, with so many of his friends as seemed convenient, did ride abroad to view the country, devising where he might build a fortress, and mounting to an hilltop, he asked of Tigranes which were the hills from whence the Chaldeans

---

[17] corrupt me] Again, the Socratic parallels of Tigranes' tutor are evoked (Socrates was put to death on charges of corrupting the youth).

did use to seek their preys. Which being showed of Tigranes, he asked again, 'Be the hills now without company?' 'No', said he, 'but always there be espies° which do signify to other what they see.' 'What do they when they perceive anything?' 'Every man come to the height of the hills to help that he may.' Cyrus hearing these things, and beholding the country, did perceive that there was much waste ground and unprofitable in Armenia, by reason of the war. Then they came down to their camp and supped and went to rest. The day ensuing, Tigranes well appointed, came with four thousand horsemen, ten thousand archers and as many targetmen. Whiles these were gathered together, Cyrus made his sacrifice and called the captains both of the Persians and Medes, to whom being assembled, he spake in this wise:

'These mountains (well beloved friends) which ye see, be the Chaldeans, which if we may take, and in the height of them build a fortress, both the Chaldean and Armenians shall be enforced to be at quiet with us.[18] Our sacrifice hath good tokens and man's boldness shall not be so available to us to accomplish the same as quickness and celerity.[19] If we can prevent our enemies before their power is gathered and ascended, we shall get the hilltop, either without resistance or if any be made, it shall be but small and weak. And no labour is more easy nor more in surety than with constant courage to make speed. Therefore, harness yourself. And you the Medes shall go on the left side, and you the Armenians, being divided, shall go the half on our right hand and the other half shall lead the vaward°. And you the horsemen in the rearward shall incite and provoke us forward. And if any man waxeth faint, let him have no favour.' Thus said Cyrus. And so marched that his bands went in length. The Chaldeans perceiving the assault in the mountains did signify it to other and making shouts one to another assembled themselves. And Cyrus exhorted his men saying, 'It is time (O Persians) that we make speed. For if we may prevent our enemies, they can do us little hurt'. The Chaldeans had every man a buckler and two darts, being counted the most martial men of all that region, and be ever in wages[20] when any need is, because they be both poor and also valiant. For their country is full of hills, and small wealth they have. As Cyrus approached nigh the height of the hills, Tigranes being with him said, 'Do ye not know, Cyrus, that you must give the onset?[21] For the Armenians are not able to abide their enemies.' Cyrus answered that for that cause he had placed the Persians next, that they might out of hand give the onset if the Armenians should haply retire. So the Armenians had the forward. The Chaldeans being

---

[18] **Marg]** Oration.
[19] quickness and celerity] i.e. nothing will help our ambitions to succeed more than quickness and alacrity.
[20] in wages] for hire. Commonly used in the fifteenth century to refer specifically to a soldier's pay.
[21] give the onset] attack.

ready so soon as the Armenians were at hand, they suddenly shouting after their manner rushed upon them. The Armenians, as they were wont, recoiled. The Chaldeans chased them, and perceiving their enemies advancing up toward them with sword in hand some tarried and were slain, some fled, some were taken. And thus shortly the hilltops were gotten. When as they were on the hills and did behold the houses of the Chaldeans, they perceived them to flee away from all the nigh habitations. Cyrus when his soldiers were come together commanded them to take their dinner. Dinner being ended and learning where the espies of the Chaldeans were, he did by and by immure[22] a fortress in a place strong and full of water, commanding Tigranes to send to his father in his name to come and bring with him all masons and carpenters that he could. Straight a messenger went to the king. And Cyrus began his building with such as he had. At which time, captives were brought unto him, some bound, some wounded. Whom Cyrus seeing, commanded the bound to be loosed and the wounded to be cured. Then he said unto them, that he came not desiring their destruction or stirring up war, but because he would make peace betwixt the Armenians and Chaldeans. 'But' (quoth he), 'before I had gotten these mountains, I knew that you had no need of peace. For you yourselves were in safeguard, and the Armenians ye did reave° and rob. I therefore do dismiss you and all other captives, giving you and all the other Chaldeans space to consult whether ye will be our adversaries or friends. If that ye choose war, come not hither again, if ye be wise, unarmed. If ye choose peace, come at your pleasure and I will see that your goods shall be in safety, you being our friends.' The Chaldeans hearing this, after great praises of Cyrus and many embracings, they departed home.

The king of Armenia, hearing of Cyrus his commandment and purpose, taking all the artificers[23] and other necessary things which he thought to be good, came to Cyrus with all celerity. Whom when he saw he said, 'O Cyrus, how little is it that men can foresee of things to come, and how much is it that they will enterprise? For I now enterprising to get liberty was made such a thrall as I never was to before. And when I thought that by this captivity I should utterly have been lost, I am so preserved as I never was tofore. For the Chaldeans which have always continually molested me, I see now to be in such case as I would have wished. And this I would ye should believe (O Cyrus), that I to have driven the Chaldeans from these mountains would have given much more money than you have now of me. And all the commodities which you promised us when ye received the money be now performed of you. Wherefore we do acknowledge

---

[22] immure] 'enmure' in the text.
[23] artificers] Translating (οἱ) τέκτονες ((hoi) téktones, carpenters), Barker uses the more general word for artisans or craftsmen, though 'artificers' could also refer to military engineers.

ourselves to owe you yet other thanks, which if we will be honest, it will be a shame if we do not requite. And we cannot so requite as shall be worthy so beneficial a friend.' Thus said the king. The Chaldeans came to Cyrus for peace, whom Cyrus asked thus: 'Do ye require peace for any other purpose than this, that you think you may live more safely in peace than in war?' 'For this only purpose', said they. 'Then', said Cyrus, 'what if ye have any other commodity by it?' 'We would be the more glad', said they. 'Do you think your self poor for any other thing than for the lack of good ground?' 'For this lack' (said they). 'Would ye' (said Cyrus), 'pay so much tribute as the Armenians do if ye might lawfully occupy the waste ground of Armenia?' 'Yea', said they, 'if we thereby should sustain no damage.' 'What say you, king of Armenia?' (said Cyrus). 'Will ye give them the occupying of your waste ground, paying you tribute as we shall appoint?' 'I would gladly purchase this thing' (said the king), 'for my revenue thereby should be augmented.' 'What say you, Chaldeans, because ye have goodly mountains will ye suffer the Armenians to use the same for pasture, paying you therefore accordingly?' 'Gladly', said the Chaldeans. 'For we without our travail should receive much profit.' 'Would you, king of Armenia, occupy this as pasture to some profit of the Chaldeans, to much more of your own?' 'Very gladly' (said he), 'if I might use them without danger.' 'Should ye not use them without danger, if you might have possession of the mountain tops?' 'Yes', said the king. 'But we surely' (said the Chaldeans), 'shall not safely occupy our own ground, much less theirs, they being possessed of the mountains.' 'But what' (said Cyrus), 'if the mountains might help you?' 'Then it were well', said they. 'But it were not well for us' (said the king), 'that they should have the mountains, specially being thus fortified.' 'Then', said Cyrus, 'thus will I do: neither of you shall have the strength of the mountains, but I will keep them in my hand, and if you vex one another, I will aid him that suffereth wrong.' They hearing this did both parties praise it, affirming that by this only mean, peace should be satisfied. And to observe these things, they gave and took hostages on either parts, and did agree that one should be free with the other, the one should marry with the other, they should use tillage and pasture indifferently, and one aid the other if any did molest either of them. Thus they agreed. And at this day that league remaineth which then was made betwixt the Chaldeans and the king of Armenia. These conditions being confirmed, either parts by and by did help the building of the fortress as a common defence, bringing thereunto all things necessary. The night approaching, Cyrus called both parties, as friends, to supper. Being at supper, one of the Chaldeans said: 'this concord to all other shall be acceptable but[24] to such only of the Chaldeans as live by robbery, which neither know the feat of tillage nor can labour, being always wont to lead their lives in war, seeking always their prey, being in wages and that very oft with the

---

[24] but] except.

king of India, who is (as they say) most wealthy and many times with Astyages.' And Cyrus said, 'Will they not now take wages of me? I will give them as much as ever any man gave.' They answered that many would be very willing. And thus they accorded. Cyrus hearing that the Chaldeans had oft recourse to the Indian king, remembering that he had sent messengers into Media to explore their purpose, and the same also to their enemies to espy their intent likewise, he was desirous that the king of India might know what he there had done. Therefore he began thus for to speak:

'Tell me (O king of Armenia, and you Chaldeans) if I would send any messengers to the king of India, would you send any of yours to conduct him, and help to bring to pass those things that I would have of the king? For I would have plenty of money that both I might give my soldiers good wages when they need, and also set forth and advance such as were worthy. For this cause I would have money plenty. For I think we shall have need, and it were pleasure to me to spare your money, you being friends, as I take you. But of the Indian I would gladly take if he will give me. And the messenger to whom I move you to appoint a guide and helper in the journey shall at his coming thither say thus:

'"Cyrus hath sent me to you, king of India, saying that he hath need of money because he looketh for another army to come out of Persia" (for so I do in deed, said Cyrus); "therefore if you will send him so much as you may well forbear, he, God giving him good success, will so behave himself toward you that ye shall think ye had good counsel when ye were moved to show him pleasure." Thus shall he say from me. Command them, whom ye will send, to do as you think good. And if we shall have money of him, we shall be the more liberal, if not we shall have no cause to thank him but may do all things for our profit.' Thus (said Cyrus), thinking that the messengers of Armenia and Chaldea should so report of him as he would every man should both speak and hear of him. And thus things being well stated and the feast ended, they went to rest.

The day following, Cyrus sent forth the ambassador with such message as he had showed before. The king and the Chaldeans appointed such men to this journey as they thought were most meet both to do and speak of Cyrus as should be convenient. After that Cyrus had finished this fortress and left both sufficient garrison and things necessary, appointing a Median captain, such one as he thought would be most thankful to Cyaxares,[25] he departed. And gathered another army, both so many as he brought and had received of the Armenians, and also four thousand of the Chaldeans, which were thought better than all the other. And being come into the inhabited places, there was none of the Armenians, neither man nor woman, but that came forth rejoicing

---

[25] thankful to Cyaxares] The tensions that will later emerge between Cyaxares and Cyrus, which Xenophon presents as differences both of talent and of power, are hinted at here in Cyrus's care to choose a commander acceptable to Cyaxares.

at this peace, bringing and presenting the best jewel that any of them had. And the king was not grieved with this, thinking that Cyrus should be the more encouraged, being thus honoured of all men. And finally came forth the queen with her daughters and young son, offering with other gifts that money which Cyrus before had refused. Which when he saw, he said: 'you shall not make me for money's sake to do you pleasures. Therefore, woman, depart hence with all thy money, and give it no more to the king to be hidden, but bestow it upon apparelling of your son, and send him honourably into the host. That that remaineth, keep for yourself, your husband, daughters and sons, that by the having thereof, ye may adorn yourself the better and live the more at quiet and pleasure.[26] And let the earth serve to cover men's bodies being dead.' Thus speaking, he rid forth. The king and all other waiting upon him, oft calling him a man of most bounty and benevolence. And thus they did, till they had brought him out of their country. After which time, the king sent him a greater army, because he had peace at home. Thus Cyrus departed being glad not only of the present money, which he had received, but because he had gotten such estimation as he might have much more when he should need. And then he did camp within the borders. The day ensuing, he sent his army and money to Cyaxares, which was at hand, as he promised. And he with Tigranes and other the gentlemen of Persia went to hunt the wild deer, and had good sport. And being come among the Medes, he gave the captains sufficient for every one, that they might advance such of their men as seemed most forward; thinking that if every several part did things worthy praise, the whole should be the better appointed. And he seeing at any time any things that might encourage his host, that if he had, he would give to the most worthy, thinking that he himself was adorned with all such things as were to the ornament and beautifying of his army. After he had given them that he had received, and assembled the captains and bandleaders, and whom he esteemed, he said thus:

'A certain gladness, friends, seemeth to be among us, both because we have abundance and also be able to honour them that we think worthy, and be honoured of them which be advanced of us.[27] We must always remember what feats have been the cause of these good things, and pondering with yourselves, ye shall find that to watch in time, to be painful, to make speed and not to give place to our enemies, hath wrought this thing. After this sort therefore, you must continue like valiant men, knowing that your obedience, your constancy, your labours in convenient time, your taking pains shall purchase you great pleasures and commodities.'

---

[26] quiet and pleasure] An early example of Cyrus's tendency (most infamously in regards to the rebellious Lydians, as reported by Herodotus) to encourage the peoples he subjugated to live the lives of luxury and ease he denies himself and the Persians, at least until after their success in the Assyrian campaign.

[27] **Marg**] Oration.

Cyrus perceiving how fresh his soldiers were to endure the labours of war, how lusty their hearts to despise their enemies, how cunning to handle every man his armour, and seeing them to be well instruct, concerning the obedience to their rulers, he was desirous to do some feat against his enemies, knowing that by delays many times good policies of princes lack their effect. Perceiving also that in their contentions, every one was so desirous of praise that they began the one to envy the other. He was desirous that they should march forward against their enemies, because common peril maketh common love among confederates. And in this case, they neither hate them that be more gallant in armour, nor them that be more worthy honour, than themselves, but rather do both praise and love all such, reputing them as furtherers of a common wealth.[28] So afore all things, he did harness his army, and appoint them as orderly and comely as he could. And then he did call together the praetors, the tribunes, the captains, the bandleaders, and these were free not to be counted in the ordinary number of soldiers.[29] Yet when it was requisite that the grand captain[30] should know or command anything, no part was left without a governor. But if anything needed, it was appointed by captains of twelve and captains of six. When these were come together in good season, Cyrus led them and showed them what was well done and taught them how every thing might be made most sure for the aid of the whole. And when he had brought to pass that they desired to do some feat, he said unto them: 'Now go among your crews, and teach them to do as I have taught you, encouraging them to novel feats, that every man may with prest heart advance forward, and the next morning to be present at the court.' They departed, and did as they were commanded. The next day they were in good season all about the court, and Cyrus coming with them to Cyaxares, began to speak thus:

'I know, Cyaxares, that those things which I shall speak have heretofore been no less considered of you than of me.[31] But peradventure you be abashed to speak anything of departure, lest you should be thought weary of keeping us so long. Therefore because ye speak nothing, I will speak for us both. We all think it good that, being well prepared, we should not defer the battle till your enemies invade your country, we remaining as it were idle in our friends' land, but with all speed invade them; for now being in your country, we do against

---

[28] common wealth] Translating τὸ κοινὸν ἀγαθόν (*tò koinòn agathón*), 'the common good', as Holland has it; again this shows Barker's interest in the political aspects of Xenophon's text.

[29] soldiers] Barker's terminology for the various military ranks shows strong influences from Latin or Roman tradition, and hints at his use of a Latin translation alongside the Greek. So, too, do some of the names of the peoples Cyrus conquered, for example, the 'Mariandines' in Book 1 (echoing Francisco Filelfo's much-published Latin translation) rather than the 'Magadidae' of modern translations. See Introduction, p. 36.

[30] grand captain] general.

[31] **Marg**] Oration.

our wills cause much loss to the same. But if we were in our enemy's country, we should gladly do him the like displeasure. Furthermore, you do now victual us to your great cost. If we were there, we should be victualled to their pain. But if greater danger might ensue to us there than here, peradventure the more safety were to be chosen. But now they shall be equal to us whether we tarry for them to fight here or go against them thither. And likewise, we shall be equal to fight with them whether we abide till they invade us or provoke them to fight, invading them. But truly we shall have the more courageous and valiant hearts of our soldiers if we invade them, and seem not unwilling to countenance them. And they shall be the more afraid of us, when they hear that we do not linger at home being with fear oppressed, but when we heard of their coming, marched against them that with all speed we may encounter with them, not tarrying till our own country might be endamaged, but prevent them and waste their land. Furthermore' (quoth he), 'if we make them somewhat more fearful and ourselves the more bold, I think it shall be to our great advantage. And by this mean, I suppose that much the less peril shall be our[s], and our adversaries very much more. For my father ever sayeth, and you grant, and all other do accord, that fields be rather tried by the hearts of men than by the strength of body.' Thus he said. And Cyaxares made this answer: 'I would surely, Cyrus, that neither you nor any other the Persians should suspect that I have grieved with the finding of you,[32] notwithstanding I think it most expedient for all things that we should march forward against our enemies.' Then said Cyrus: 'Seeing we do agree, let us prepare ourselves. And if our sacrifice readily do assent to us, let us go on with all celerity.' Then commanding the soldiers to be in a readiness, Cyrus made his sacrifice, first to Jupiter king, then to other gods, praying that they being favourable and merciful would be guides to the army and assured succourers, confederates and counsellors of good affairs. He did also make petition to the avowers[33] of Media, inhabitants and patrons of the same. When he had luckily finished his sacrifice, and the army was assembled at the marches, having lucky tokens they did invade their enemies' land. When he was soon passed the borders, he pacified the lady of the earth with liquid sacrifices,[34] and the gods with offered hosts, and appeased the patrons, avowers of Assyria. Which when he had done, he once again sacrificed to Jupiter father, and if any of the other gods were showed, he did [not] neglect the same. These things speedily proceeding, leading the footmen no great journey, they did encamp. The horsemen ranging abroad did get a great prey of all things and so continuing in camp and wasting the country, they abode their enemies.[35]

[32] finding of you] i.e. providing for you.
[33] avowers] The Greek gives 'heroes and protectors', but Barker returns to the term 'avowers'; Holland uses 'tutelar Deities'.
[34] liquid sacrifices] libations to the Earth.
[35] abode their enemies] awaited their enemies.

When it was said that they came on and were ten days' journey off, Cyrus said: 'It is now time, Cyaxares, to march forward, that we seem neither to our own men afraid to go against them, but rather show ourselves to be glad that we shall fight.' Which thing when it seemed meet to Cyaxares they did set forward, always keeping array, going every day so far as they thought sufficient, and ever supped by daylight. They made no fires in the night within the camp but afore the camp, that if any came by night they might see them by the fire, and not be seen of them. And many times they made fires behind the camp, to deceive their enemies, whereby the espies many times fell into the scout watch because the fire was behind, thinking themselves to be yet far off the camp. The Assyrians with their confederates, the armies being nigh together, did cast about a trench which manner the barbarian kings use at this day, that when they be encamped, they straight way environed the same with a bulwark, because of the huge multitude. For they know that the host of horsemen in the night is troublous and full of disquiet, and as I might say, most barbarous,[36] for they have their horses tied by the feet at mangers, to whom if any man would go it were a pain in the night to lose them, it were pain to bridle them, pain to trap and barb them. And being on the horseback, it is not possible by any mean to ride them through the camp. For these causes, both they and the other the Barbarians do enclose themselves with such munitions, thinking that they thereby are in safeguard and need not to fight but when they list. Thus doing, they were nigh the one the other, and being distant the space of a Persian mile, the Assyrians were so camped as we have said in place entrenched but plain and apert°.

But Cyrus, in as secret wise as he could, did do make rampires° and mounds of earth before his camp, thinking that all shows of war being seen suddenly should be more terrible to their adversaries. And that night, watches and ward[s] as was expedient appointed of either parts, they went to rest. The day ensuing, the Assyrian, Croesus, and the other captains kept their army in quiet within the trench. Cyrus and Cyaxares, being in array, did tarry, looking when their enemies would come to fight. But when it was certain that they would not come forth of their camp, nor intended to fight that day, Cyaxares calling Cyrus and the other captains said thus: 'Friends, I think that as we be now appointed, so should we march to our enemy's camp, declaring that we be ready to fight. For if they will not come forth against us, our men shall be the more encouraged, and they beholding our boldness, shall be the more afraid.' Thus he said. But Cyrus said: 'Cyaxares, for God's sake let us not do so. For if we show ourselves as ye would and do go forward, our enemies shall view us now as we come forth, they being nothing afraid of us, knowing that they be in safe place, where we

---

[36] most barbarous] A misunderstanding; Xenophon refers to the manner in which horses are kept by 'barbarians', which makes the cavalry difficult to manage at night.

can do them no hurt. Then if we doing no good should return and they eftsoons espy our number to be far inferior to theirs they would condemn us, and the day following advance forthwith much more bold hearts. But now knowing that we be prest and not seeing us, ye may be well assured they will not set us light but marvel what we mean and not cease (I dare say) to talk their minds of us. But when they come forth, then it shall be expedient for us to show ourselves as well to them marching straight against them, taking such advantage as we heretofore have desired.' So Cyrus on this wise speaking, Cyaxares and the other accorded. Then taking their supper and appointing watch and ward, and made fires before the watch, they went to rest. The next day early, Cyrus having a garland,[37] did sacrifice and commanded all the other noble gentlemen to have garlands, and to be present at the sacrifice.

When the sacrifice was finished, assembling them together, he said thus:

The Oration of Cyrus

'God (dear friends), as the sacrifice expounders sayeth and I also perceive, do foreshow battle and have[38] granted us the victory, promising health and safety in the sacrifice. Now to advertise you what at this time ye ought to be, surely I am abased: because I know that you be fully expert as myself, and both have exercised and heard and also hear continually of these things, as well as myself. In so much as you may right well teach other the same. But if ye be untaught, now hearken. Such fellows as be come new amongst us, whom we assay to make like to ourselves, you must advertise both for what cause we be here found of Cyaxares, what we have exercised, and for what purpose we have called them, that they may declare themselves to be our assured confederates. And of these also you must remember them, that this day shall declare how worthy every man is. And marvel it is none, though in such things as men learn late, some have need of other teaching. But it is sufficient, if they after admonishment can do like forward men. And in doing of these things you may have experience of yourselves, for he that can in such matter make other men better, he may certainly know how perfect good he is himself. But he that hath only monition° of these things, and goeth no further, he must think himself but half perfect. For this cause I do not speak unto them but command you to speak, that they may be in use to please and content you; for you are nigh unto them, every man in his part. And this know you well: so long as ye show yourselves to them to be of victorious courage, so long shall ye teach them and all other not in word but in deed to be likewise of valiant hearts.' Finally, he bade them go to their dinner and wearing garlands to make sacrifices and go to their companies with

---

[37] garland] i.e. wearing a propitiatory garland about his head.
[38] have] Grammatical error: does foreshow and [that being so] grants us the victory, etc.

their garlands. They being departed, [he] called straight way the tailguides,[39] saying thus: 'Friends Persians, you also be made and elected to the estate of the nobility, being counted in all other things equal with the best and for age to be more wise, for which cause ye be placed equal with the best. For you being last, and marking them that be hardy, by encouraging may make them more valiant. And if any man be faint-hearted, if you perceive it you may in no wise cocker° hi[m], for it is meet for you above any other to get victory both for your age and sober behaviour. Therefore when any of the former sort do call upon you and exhort you to follow, obey them. And that you may not be inferior to them in this thing, exhort you them again to lead on with all speed afore against our enemies. And now depart hence to your dinner, and being decked with garlands, go to your crews.' Thus Cyrus and his army was appointed. The Assyrians after dinner came forth boldly and made a stout show. The king being brought in a chariot did encourage them with this exhortation. 'Friends Assyrians, now must ye show your self men, now must you fight for your lives, for the country in which you were born, for your wives and children and for all that ever you have. If you overcome, you shall be lords of the same, as you have been before. If ye be overcome, ye know well you must leave all to your enemies. Wherefore if ye love victory, abide and fight; for it is a vain thing for them that would have victory to flee away and turn to their enemies, the sightless, armless, and handless part of their body. And he is a fool which would live and intend to flee away, knowing that they that overcome shall be safe and they that flee shall rather die than they that tarry. He is also a fool which being desirous of wealth, seeketh his own destruction. For who do now know that they that do overcome save their own goods and take theirs that be overcome. They that are overcome shall lose both themselves and also their goods.' Thus the Assyrian king was doing.[40]

Cyaxares sending to Cyrus, affirmed that it was meet time to set upon their enemies, saying, 'Though now but few be come out of the trench, yet by that time we join with them, they will be many. Therefore let us not prolong the time till there be more than we, but let us vaunce° forth now, while we think we may easily overcome them.' To whom Cyrus answered: 'Except more than the one half of them be overcome, be ye assured, Cyaxares, they will say that we, fearing the multitude, did set upon a few of them, and not think themselves to be overcome. Wherefore a second field shall be required, when as peradventure they will use more policy than they now do, offering themselves to try it with us with what number so ever we will desire.' The messengers bearing this departed. At which time, Chrysantas a Persian and other of the gentlemen, brought certain runaways, of whom Cyrus having opportunity, asked what his

---

[39] tailguides] The rearguard.
[40] doing] i.e. occupied.

enemies were doing. They answered that they now were come forth in harness and the king being come abroad did array them, encouraging always so many as came out with a great and vehement oration, as they say that heard it. Then said Chrysantas, 'What if you Cyrus assembling your men do eftsoons exhort them, that you may make them of the more courage?' Cyrus said, 'Let not the Assyrian's oration trouble you, for there is no exhortation, be it never so vehement, that can make the hearers in one day of cowards valiant men, neither archers, darters or horsemen, except they have before been trained in the same feats, nor bodies able to travail except they have been before accustomed to pains.' 'It were sufficient' (said Chrysantas), 'to make their hearts by exhortation the more courageous.' 'Can one day's oration' (said Cyrus), 'so ravish the hearers' hearts with shame that they refraining from unfit[41] things will turn to that that is expedient, and for renown's sake endure all pain and peril, thinking this constantly in their minds that it is better to die valiantly than to live cowardly? If such opinions should be engrafted in men's minds and be stable, must not such laws first be given which may pronounce to valiant men a glorious and free life to be prepared; to cowards a base, miserable and wretched life, everlastingly enduring? Teachers also and governors must be appointed over them which may rightly instruct, teach and accustom them to these things, till they may take root in them, to think that valiant and redoubted men be without doubt most happy and to repute cowards and villains of all other most misers. Thus must they be instruct, which will declare their discipline to be better than it that cometh of fear of their enemies. But if a man should go to fight with such soldiers, whereof many had forgotten their old lessons, then a man with a good exhortation might presently make them contagious, in as much as of all other it is the most easiest thing, both to learn and to teach, that manhood is amongst men the most precious thing.[42] And I surely would not believe these our men whom we have exercised with us to be stable and constant, except I had seen you at this present, have given them example, what they ought to do and have taught them that they were ignorant in. But such as be untaught altogether in manhood, I would marvel, Chrysantas, if an oration being goodly pronounced could more profit them to valiantness than a musical song being sweetly sung can profit them that have nothing learned to be cunning in music.' This communication they had. Cyaxares, sending again to Cyrus, said that he did evil to tarry too long and not with all speed to march against his enemies.

[41] unfit] 'unset' in text — probably a compositorial misreading.
[42] the most precious thing] A confusing translation. Holland's is clearer: 'But, if a man, when souldiers are going armed into the field (what time many of them forgoe and forget even their own lessons and principles) were able at the instant, with a subitary speech to make them brave and worthy warriors, certes, it were the easiest matter in the worlde, both to learne and also to teach the most excellent vertue of all others that belongeth to a man' (sig. K2).

Cyrus made answer to the messengers saying, 'Ye must well understand that they be not all come forth that must come. Thus show unto him that all men may hear it. Nevertheless because it is his mind, I will now set forward.' Thus saying, and making prayers to God, he led forth his army. And so soon as he began to lead he went afore apace, and they followed in good array because they had learned and practised afore to go in order, being courageous how the one might exceed the other, both because their bodies were accustomed to labour and also captains were their guides and cheerful because of their cunning they had learned and long afore exercised, how most safely and easily they might encounter with their enemies, specially with archers, darters and horsemen. And being yet without the danger of the arrows, Cyrus gave this privy word: 'Jupiter confederate and captain'. When it was gone through the army, he began to sing to Castor and Pollux a song of triumph,[43] according to the custom, which all the soldiers with devout mind and loud voice did recount, for by such thing being made superstitious, they have the less fear of men. The song being ended the nobles went together with lusty countenance, being well taught, beholding one another, calling by name their friends and governors, saying and that often: 'go to it, loving friends, go to it, valiant men', encouraging one another to follow. Which they that were behind hearing, semblably exhorted the former to march on boldly.

Thus Cyrus's army was full of forwardness, desirous of renown, full of strength and boldness, full of courage, soberness and obedience, which is I think most terrible to a man his enemies. The Assyrians, being come out of their trench when the Persian host approached nigh, leaped into their chariots and went among their other people. The archers, darters and slingers threw their weapons much sooner than they could hit. When the Persians coming on were within the arrow shot, Cyrus with loud voice said: 'Bold friends, let one speedily go forward showing himself and encourage other.' They told this forth to other. And some for prompt courage, for lusty heart, and haste to fight, began to run, whom the whole main battle followed, running. And Cyrus himself forgetting to go softly led the army running and also cried thus: 'Who doth follow? Who is so hardy? Who shall first kill a man?' The other hearing the same cried likewise. And this noise (as he would have it) went through the whole army. 'Who shall follow, who is hardy?' The Persians after this sort, manly gave the onset, their enemies were not able to abide the field but recoiled and fled into their trench, the Persians pursuing them to the entries of the same, slew many of them being thrust on heaps together, and leaping after them which fell into the ditches, killed many both horse and man. For some of the chariots enforced to fly fell into the ditches. The horsemen of the Medes, seeing this, set upon

---

[43] song of triumph] The paean before battle, sung to the Dioscuri (Castor and Pollux).

their enemy's horsemen, which also recoiled. And there began a great chase, both of horse and men, and slaughter of both sorts. The Assyrians being within their trench, standing at the top of the ditch, neither had the wit nor the power to shoot or dart at them that flew so fast, partly for the terrible sight, partly for the great fear. And in short space, perceiving that some of the Persians did murder many of them at the entry of the trench, they turned their back and fled from the front of the ditch. The wives of the Assyrians and their confederates seeing them fight within the camp skriked° out and strayed abroad like folk amazed, some bearing their children, some, and they young,[44] running and tearing their garments, beseeching all that they met with not to flee and forsake them but to defend their children, their wives and themselves. Then the kings in persons with their most trusty men standing at the entry, and climbing up at the height of the ditch, did both fight themselves and exhort other to the same. Which thing when Cyrus perceived, fearing lest if they should make irruption, a few might soon be hurt of so many, he commanded they should retreat out of the arrow-shot and be obedient. Then might a man have seen the goodly education of the noble men, for they straight obeyed themselves, and straight charged other to obey likewise. When they were without the shot,[45] they stood in their places as it had been in a dance,[46] knowing perfectly where every man should be.

The end of the third book.

---

[44] they young] i.e. the younger women too.
[45] without the shot] out of arrow-shot.
[46] dance] Translating χορός (*chorós*), Holland has 'daunce or quire of Musicians' (sig. [K3]), perhaps because of the paucity of early modern knowledge of the performance conventions of Greek drama.

The Discipline of Cyrus, the Fourth Book

Cyrus, tarrying a good while with his army, declared them to be ready to fight if any would come forth, but when none came, he retreated his host so far as he thought good. And when he had encamped, appointed watch and ward, and sent forth the scout watch standing in the middest, he assembled his own soldiers, and thus spake:

The Oration of Cyrus

'Friends Persians, I first do give God so great thanks as I can, supposing that you all do the same, for we have gotten victory and health, wherefore we be bound to render God gifts of thanks with all that ever we have. I truly praise you all at this time for this present feat is achieved to all your honour, but what every man is worthy, when I am certified of such as be meet, I shall be ready to reward the same accordingly, both in word and deed.[1] But as for this captain Chrysantas being nigh me, I shall not need to learn of other: for I myself know what he is, for as he hath done all things as well as you have, even so when I, calling him by name, commanding him to retreat, he driving his sword to strike his enemy heard me forthwith and leaving that he was about to do, did as he was commanded. For he both himself drew back and very readily had other do the same, in so much as he brought his crew without danger of shot, before our enemies could perceive we gave back, or bent their bows or throw their darts. And so he is both safe himself and through his obedience hath saved his men also. I see other wounded of whom, when I know what time they were hurt, I shall then declare my sentence of them. But Chrysantas being valiant in manly prowess, wise and meet both to rule and be ruled, I at this present make a tribune or captain of a thousand. And when God shall give me any other good thing, I will not then forget him. And I will advertise you all that what as ye have seen in this fight, ye never cease to remember the same, that you may judge always of yourselves whether valiantness or cowardice rather saveth the life. And whether they that fight willingly be sooner eased than the unwilling. Finally, what manner pleasure victory bringeth. These things, you may now best judge, having both experience of them and the thing being so late done. And certainly by remembering of these things you shall be the better. Now therefore, as men loved of God, as valiant and wise men, take your repast, making sacrifice to God, and singing a song of triumph, ever providing for that which is commanded.' These being spoken he took his horse and rid till he came to Cyaxares, and rejoicing with him and enquired if he needed anything, returned again to his own army, who at that time having supped and,

---

[1] word and deed] Cyrus makes good on the decision in Book II to reward his soldiers in proportion to their efforts.

appointing convenient watch, went to rest.

The Assyrians because their king was slain, and with him almost all their noble men, were in much dolour and many that night fled out of the camp. Which thing Croesus and the other confederates perceiving were much grieved; and as all things were dolorous, so this most troubled them all, that the chief nation of their army was of no policy nor manner, wherefore they left the camp and departed in the night.

The day being come, and the camp of his enemies appearing to be barren of men, straight he went in with the chief of the Persians. And his enemies had left many sheep, many oxen and many wagons full of treasure. And then came thither Cyaxares with all the Medes, and there did dine. Dinner being ended, Cyrus assembling his captains said thus: 'What and how great goodness of God is offered unto us, do we seem not to regard? For now you yourselves do see that our enemies for fear of us be fled away, which being within a trench leaving the same and fled away, how can a man think they would have bidden by it if they had seen us in the plain? And if they, having no experience what we be, durst not abide us, how shall they now be able to abide us, being overcome and suffering many displeasures at our hands? And if their most valiant men be slain, how shall their cowards dare fight with us?' Then one said: 'Why do we not then with all speed pursue them, seeing so good success is evident?' 'Because' (said he), 'we want horses, for the best of our enemies whom it were most convenient either to take or kill shall be on horseback, whom we be able with God his help to put to flight: but to take them by chasing, we be not able.' Then they said: 'Why do you not go and show these things to Cyaxares?' He answered: 'Follow you all now me, that he may know we be all of one mind.' Then they all followed him, and declared what they thought expedient for the things they requested. And Cyaxares, partly envying that they should first speak of such things, partly peradventure supposing himself to be well enough, would not adventure the second time, for truly both himself was jocund and saw many other of the Medes to be so likewise.[2] Therefore he said unto Cyrus: 'I have perceived, Cyrus, both by report and proof, that you, the Persians, of all men covet never to be satisfied in any one pleasure. I truly think it is much more to be desired, to enjoy that pleasure that is greatest. And what thing can show great pleasure of felicity to men than is now chanced to us? Therefore if now being in happy ease, we soberly can retain the same, we may peradventure without danger, continue in this felicity to our old age. But if we be in this

---

[2] likewise] Xenophon emphasises the difference between the moderate, austere Persians and the wine-loving Medians once again, giving Cyrus the moral high ground here — and demonstrating how Cyrus makes that difference visible to his men.

unsatiable and study still to pursue ever new pleasures, take heed lest we suffer (as they say many have done in the sea) which having good chance, will not leave sailing till they be drowned.[3] And many achieving victory, being desirous of more, have lost the first. And truly if our enemies that be fled were in number fewer than we, we might peradventure safely pursue them; but now remember with what portion of them we, all fighting, have gotten victory. Many there be which struck no stroke, whom if we do not compel to fight, they not knowing neither our nor their own strength, through ignorance and faintness will be glad to escape. But if they know that they shall be in as much peril by departing as by tarrying still, we must beware lest we do compel them against their wills to play the valiant men. And this know for surety: that you are not so desirous to take their wives and children as they are to conserve the same. Consider also that wild swine, though they be many, when they espy the hunter will flee with her pigs; but if a man hunteth any of their young, though perchance there be but one, she will not flee but rage at him that is busied to catch the prey. Now, therefore, if they, enclosing themselves in a trench, suffered us to fight with as many of them as we would, and now would couple with them in the plain, and they severally shall fight with us and shall assail us at the front as they now did, some on the one wing, some on the other, and some at the tail. Consider, lest every of us shall have need both of many eyes and of many hands too.[4] Finally' (said he), 'I would not gladly now, seeing the Medes in such joy, go further with them, compelling them to more danger.' Cyrus made this answer and said: 'Ye shall not need to compel any man, give them only leave to follow me that will and peradventure we shall do such feats as both you and your friends shall rejoice at. And we will not chase the multitudes of our enemies, for how could we take them? But if we may catch any of the remnant or tail of the army, we shall bring the same to you. Consider also, that we at your need have come a long way to do you pleasure; you therefore, being just, must requite the same that at our return we may have some profit, not all looking for it, of your treasure.' Then said Cyaxares, 'Truly if any man will willingly follow you, I would also acknowledge thanks unto you.' 'Send one of your trusty men with me' (said Cyrus), 'which may declare your commandment.' 'Take of these whom ye will', said he. And as it chanced, he was present which said once he

---

[3] they be drowned] A Greek-sounding nautical analogy (especially as there are no sea-journeys involved in the Persian campaigns), Cyaxares here articulates a prophetic critique of Cyrus's imperial appetites, against which Cyrus's own father had warned him at the end of Book I. On the force of the charge of 'insatiability' against Cyrus in Herodotus, see Grogan, *The Persian Empire*, pp. 81–86.

[4] hands too] An awkward translation, syntactically, presented here as two sentences. Cyrus's point is that when the enemy fight from an enclosed or fortified position, the managing of the battle lies with Cyrus's own army, whereas in the open field, the enemy can attack them from several positions, meaning that each soldier must 'have need both of many eyes and of many hands too'.

was his kinsman and kissed him at his departure.⁵ 'This man shall be sufficient', said Cyrus. 'Then let him wait upon you', said he, 'and show thou that who that will may go with Cyrus.' Cyrus, taking this man, departed, to whom he said thus: 'Now shall I prove whether your words were true when ye said ye had a pleasure to behold me.' 'Then I will not forsake you', said the Median, 'if you say so.' 'And will ye encourage other' (said Cyrus), 'to follow me?' Then he swore and said: 'By God I will, and so well that ye shall look merrily upon me.' Then he declared effectually all the cause why he was sent of Cyaxares, and added this, that he would not forsake so noble, so bounteous a man being descended (which was a thing passing other) of gods' lineage.⁶ Cyrus being about this thing, as it were by divine chance, messengers came to him from the Hyrcanians. The Hyrcanians be borderers to the Assyrians, no great country, and therefore subject to the Assyrians. They were counted at that time good horsemen and so be yet. Therefore the Assyrians use them as the Macedonians use the Scyrites, sparing them neither in pains nor in perils, and at this time were charged with the defence of rearward, being a thousand horsemen, that if any danger should be in that part, these should feel it afore them. The Hyrcanians because they should come last of all, had their wagons and their families last also, for the most part of the Asians go to war with their households. Thus at this time the Hyrcanians were used in the warfare. Then considering how they were intreated° of the Assyrians, how their king was slain and themselves overcome, how great fear was in the army and how their confederates fainted and shrunk from them, these things being peised°, they thought it good time to make defection, if Cyrus's host should still invade, and sent their messengers to Cyrus. For his name, by reason of this battle, was most renowned. They that were sent said unto him that they had just cause to hate the Assyrians, therefore if he would go now against them, they would become his confederates and be the forward. And beside these, they declared in what case his enemies were, that they might the rather stir him to take the voyage° in hand. Cyrus asked them, 'Think ye that we may overtake them before they be entrenched? For we' (said he), 'think it a great loss that they have escaped us so privily.' Cyrus spake this because he would have them to take good conceit of themselves.⁷ They answered that if in the morning early they would go with speed, they might overtake them. For they by reason of their multitude and wagons do go very slowly. 'And also', they said, 'that because they had watched the night before, making now a small journey, they were encamped.' And Cyrus said, 'Have ye anything to prove whereby we may believe that you do tell us truth?' 'We will' (said they),

⁵ at his departure] i.e. Artabasus. In Book I (pp. 101–2).
⁶ gods' lineage] The claim that Cyrus was born of the gods.
⁷ good conceit of themselves] i.e. so that the Hyrcanians would think as highly as possible of his own army.

'ride this night and bring you pledges, only do you make us promise before God and give us your right hand that we may declare the same to others as we receive of you.' Then he promised them faithfully to use them as his friends, and assured if so be they performed their promise, and that neither Persians nor Medes should be in more credit with him. And at this day, a man may see the Hyrcanians as trusty rulers and governors as the best of Persians and Medes. Supper being ended, Cyrus set forth his army somewhat before night, commanding the Hyrcanians to tarry and go forth with him. All the Persians, as meet was, speedily came forth, and Tigranes also with his own army of the Medes came forth: some, which being young children when Cyrus was a child, were become now his friends; some being his companions in hunting and delighting in his goodly behaviour, some to give him thanks because he had delivered them from great fear; some for hope, because he appeared a valiant and fortunate man, which hereafter would be a man of mighty power; some because when he was brought up in Media, and had done them some pleasures, would do him now some service; many because through his gentleness, they received pleasures of his grandfather; many because they saw the Hyrcanians, and a rumour was spread that they should be brought to great wealth, were moved that they might have part thereof. So the Medians almost all came forth, except such as did accompany Cyaxares, and they that belonged to them. All other gladly and readily did set forth, not, as it were, of necessity but of free heart and gentle courage.

When they were come forth, first he went to the Medians and both praised them and prayed with great desire that God might be favourable guide both to him and them, and that he at length might be able to give them worthy thank for their good heart toward him. In conclusion he said: 'Let the footmen have the forward' and commanded the horsemen to follow. And if in any place they should rest or stop their pace, he commanded that some of them should make speedy repair to him, that they might ever know what were best to do. And then he commanded the Hyrcanians to conduct the host, which asked of him, 'What, do you not look that we should pledge our pledges as you have commanded, that you, having our truth plight, might go forward?' Who (as they say) made this answer: 'I know that all we have faith and trust in our own hearts and hands, for we be so appointed that if ye be true, we shall be able to do you good; if ye be false, we do not think it will come to pass that we shall be subject to you, but you (God willing) rather thrall to us. Therefore, Hyrcanians, because ye say that your company is last, when you see them give us knowledge that we may spare them.' The Hyrcanians hearing this led the way as he commanded. Marvelling at his so princely courage, neither fearing the Assyrians, the Lydians, nor none other their confederates, and that he did not one iota° esteem neither their absence nor their presence. Thus going forth, night approached, when (as it is said) a light from heaven did glister° on Cyrus and all his army. Whereby every man conceived fear of God and boldness against his enemies. They going forth speedily without let,[8] made that night a great journey, and came very nigh the Hyrcanians' army by break of day: which the messengers perceiving declared to Cyrus that they were their countrymen, which they knew both because they were last and also by the multitude of their fires. Wherefore Cyrus sent one of the messengers to them, commanding him to say that if they were his friends, they should with all speed come and meet with him and take hands. He sent also some of his own men, commanding them to say to the Hyrcanians that as they saw his men give the onset, so they also should do. Thus one of the messengers tarried still with Cyrus, and the other rid to the Hyrcanians. And whilst Cyrus tried what the Hyrcanians would do, he stayed his army in array. Then the chief of the Medes, with Tigranes, came to him to know what they should do. Which said unto them: 'This next host is of the Hyrcanians, to whom one of their own messengers with certain of mine is going to say unto them that if they will be our friends, they shall come and hold forth their right hands. Wherefore if they so do, take them by the hands every man as shall chance, and also embold them, but if they take their weapons or go about to fire, do your endeavour to dispatch them first that none of them escape.' These were Cyrus's admonitions. The Hyrcanians, hearing the messengers, were glad, and taking their horseback, came with all celerity, holding forth their hands as it is said. The Medes and Persians did likewise take them by the hands, bidding them to be of good heart. Then Cyrus said: 'We truly, O Hyrcanians, do now give credit to you, you must do likewise to us. But tell me first this thing: how far hence is the vaward, and the other puissance of our enemies?' They answered: 'Not fully four miles'. Then said Cyrus: 'Now, then, go to it, friends, Persians and Medes, and you also Hyrcanians, for I speak now unto you as to our friends. And you must certainly know that we be in such case that if we trifle, we shall sustain utter displeasure, for our enemies know the cause of our coming. But if we go to it with constant courage, and assault our enemies with martial and vigorous hearts, ye shall see them very shortly, that they shall be found as slaves fugitive, some of them louting° at us, some flying away, some for being discomfited they shall stare on us, and neither suspecting that we be come, neither in array nor appointed to fight, we shall take them prisoners. If then we will hereafter eat our meat and take our rest and lead our life pleasantly, let us give them no respite, neither to consult nor to prepare any good for themselves, neither to know at all that we be men, that they may think nothing else to come amongst them but buckler, sword, battleaxe and blows. And you Hyrcanians advancing toward them, go afore us that by the sight of your armour we may the longer be in covert. When that I am come to our enemy's army, leave with me every

---

[8] without let] without any obstacle.

of you a troop of horsemen which I may use, remaining in their camp, if aught needeth. And you princes and seniors, make the assault in array, many together; if ye will do wisely that you fall not into the throngs and be borne down by violence, suffice your younger sort to chase and kill. For this is now most sure, that few of our enemies do escape and lest fortune (as it chanceth to many conquerors) should change her copy,[9] beware in any wise that ye fall not to pillage, for he that so doth is no valiant soldier but a vile burden-bearer.[10] And it shall be lawful for him to use such a one as his slave. And this also ye must know, that nothing is so available[11] as victory, for he that conquereth doth spoil all things: men, women, money, and all the whole land. Then look only to this, that we may retain our victory, for in it he that spoileth is comprised.[12] And in following this chase, remember that ye return to me by daylight, for the night being come we will receive no man.' Thus Cyrus when he had spoken he sent every man into his crews, commanding them that they should go likewise and signify the same to their decurions, which were in the front of the battle. Who hearing this precept, gave like commandment unto every one of his men. And so the Hyrcanians led the forward, Cyrus with the Persians went in the middleward, placing the horsemen, as it was meet, on either side.

Their enemies, when they could discern the thing, some marvelled at the sight, some perceived the matter, some told it forth, some cried out, some loosed their horses, some prepared themselves, some threw their armour off the wagons, some did on their harness, some leaped on horseback, some bridled the same, some set their wives in the wagons, some gathered together their riches to save the same, some hoarding their money were taken, prepared to fly away and we must think that they did many other diverse things, saving that no man fought, but perished without resistance.[13] Croesus the Lydish[14] king, because it was summer, had sent his women in chariots before by night that they might, by reason of cold air, have the easier journey, and he taking his horsemen with him, followed them. Likewise did the Phrygian which is king of Phrygia that is next Hellespont. When that they had learned and heard of them that fled and other that overtook them how the matter stood, they themselves fled as much as they might make. But the king of the Cappadocians and Arabians being nighest and making resistance unarmed were slain of the Hyrcanians. But the most

[9] change her copy] Barker's use of a metaphor from the world of print (that Fortune might change what's written in her copy-text), rather than the more straightforward reversal of fortune, is revealing.
[10] burden-bearer] A baggage-carrier (for the army).
[11] available] advantageous, beneficial.
[12] comprised] seized.
[13] without resistance] This catalogue of the battle may have encouraged Sidney, Scott and some Italian critical theorists before them to consider the *Cyropaedia* to be an epic or 'an absolute heroicall poem' (Sidney, p. 103).
[14] Lydish] Lydian.

part that were killed were Assyrians and Arabians. For being in their own land, they were earnest[15] in their way. The Medians and Hyrcanians bearing down as they would, continued in this chase. Cyrus commanded the horsemen being left with him to ride about the tents and slay as many as came forth with harness. To other that remained, he did proclaim that so many of his enemy's soldiers as were horsemen, targetmen or archers should bring forth their armour, trussed up, and leave their horses at their tents; he that did contrary should forthwith be [be]headed. They with swords ready drawn stood in order about the tents. The other which had armour came and brought it forth, casting it in one place as he commanded, which he caused to be burned by them whom he appointed. Then Cyrus remembering that he was come without any manner of victual, and that without it he could neither continue his army nor do any other feat, providing for the same both speedily and prudently he thought it needful for all the soldiers that some man should have the charge of the provision that sustenance might be ready at the soldiers' coming. Wherefore perceiving that it was very expedient to present[16] all them that had the provision of victual in the camp, he commanded that all the commissaries should assemble. And where there was no commissary, the most ancient in the tent. To him that disobeyed, all extremity was pronounced. They, seeing their lords obey, did forthwith obey themselves. When they were come together, he first commanded them to sit down which had in their tent more than two months' victual, which being marked, he commanded likewise them that had one month's victual. And of these almost all sat down. These things thus learned, he spake unto them after this sort: 'Go to now, friends, if ye be irk of displeasures[17] and look for any good at our hand, see that ye do your diligent endeavour that you provide in every tent double so much victual for captains and soldiers as ye have done tofore for every day. And see that all other things that may be meet for the good dressing of the victual be ready prepared. Because they that shall have the victory shall soon be here again and be glad of such plentiful purveyance.' They hearing this, did with all diligence as they were commanded. He assembling his captains, said thus to them:

The Oration of Cyrus

'I know (dear friends) that we at this present might prevent our fellows, being absent, in taking our dinner and refreshing ourselves both with meat and

---

[15] earnest] The text suggests that they are slowest in escaping, but Barker may here be using a medieval term to imply a military fervour [*OED* n. 1], a thirteenth-/fourteenth-century term.

[16] present] 'prevent', in the text, probably a compositorial error, found in both 26066 and 26067.

[17] irk of displeasures] Weary or unwilling (to face displeasures).

drink; but methink that such a dinner cannot profit us as to be noted careful for our fellows,[18] nor the good cheer can make us so strong as if we can make our confederates courageous. Therefore if now whilest they be chasing, slaying our enemies and fighting with them that resisteth, we should appear to set them so light that before we know what they have done, we should be noted to have filled our bellies, though we be not reputed unhonest yet we shall in our most need lack confederates. But he that will provide that they, being in pains and perils at their return, may have necessary food, these dainties (I think) should be more pleasant to us than if we did by and by fill our bellies. Consider, furthermore, that though there were no cause of shame toward us for them, yet we ought at no time to overcharge our selves with meat or drink, for we have not yet accomplished our enterprise, but all things have even now need of most care and diligence. We have in this camp many more enemies than we be ourselves,[19] and them at liberty which ought still to be safely kept and so to be kept that there might be some to provide us necessaries. Furthermore, our horsemen be gone, making us to muse where they be, whether they will return or tarry; therefore, friends (I think), such meat and drink ought to content us as a man thinketh most expedient not to be full of sleep and forgetfulness. I know furthermore that there is much money in the camp, which being common as well to them that were at the taking of it as to ourselves, I know we might use at our pleasure and convert to our private substance. But I think it should not so much avail us to take it to ourselves as if we, appearing to be just men, might by this means purchase them our more assured friends than these now be. Therefore I think it good to commit this money to be distributed of the Medians, Hyrcanians, and Tigranes at their return, and to think it our advantage though they distribute less to us. For by gains they will have the more pleasure to tarry with us. And at this time to be aforehand with them, it would minister riches to us but a short space; but to be desirous to possess those things whereof riches ariseth, this (I think) might purchase us and all ours more durable wealth and riches. I suppose' (said he), 'that we being at home do much travail to this end: that our diet might be the finer and our gains the greater, that when need required, we might use both to our weal. Therefore surely I can not see wherein we might learn a lesson to our greater commodity than of these present things.' Thus he said.

Hystaspas, a Persian, and one of the nobility, confirming Cyrus his oration, said thus:

'It were an unseemly thing, Cyrus, if we may times in hunting will continue without meat, to kill a wild beast, not being greatly available to us, now in the hunt of all riches, as it were, we should suffer a thing to be an impediment to us

---

[18] careful for our fellows] i.e. anxious/solicitous for our 'confederates'.
[19] ourselves] i.e. they have more prisoners than soldiers.

as prevaileth in evil men, and is obeisant to good men, for we should appear to be slack in doing our duty.' Hystaspas thus according with Cyrus, all the other did approve the same.

Cyrus then said, 'Go to then, seeing we accord, let every man send of his bond five of his most forward men which shall go about and, whom they see preparing necessary things, them they shall praise, whom they see negligent, them they shall more straitly correct than if they were their own masters.' And they did accordingly. Then some of the Medians, overtaking certain wagons going away, did return and drive them, being replenished with things more for the army. Some of them took and brought away chariots of the most noble women, part being lawful wives, part concubines which were carried about for their goodly beauty, which they took and brought away. For the manner of the warfare of Asia is even at this day to have with them their most precious things, saying that they have the more courage to fight, their most lief things being present for them (they say) of necessity they are enforced manfully to defend. And peradventure it is for this cause, peradventure for pleasure and volupty°. Cyrus beholding the feats of the Medes and Hyrcanians did, as it were, rebuke himself and his train that other men at that time should seem more valiant than they in doing feats, he and his remaining in idle place. They that brought this gear showed what they had brought to Cyrus, riding forth again to pursue the remnant, for so they said they were commanded of their captains. Cyrus grieved with these things when he had bestowed the prey, assembling eftsoons the captains and so standing as they might hear what he spake, said thus:

The Oration of Cyrus

'If we, friends, may achieve those things which we see to be evident, great profit shall redound to all the Persians, and the greatest by reason be ours, that travail for it, we all, I am sure, know. But when we be lords of them, how shall we be able to retain them, except we have Persian horsemen of our own, I truly cannot see. Consider therefore we Persians have armour whereby we may put back our enemies at hand strokes. But they being put to flight, what horsemen, what archers, what targetmen, what darters can we, lacking horse, either take or kill when they flee? And what fear need either archers, darters or horsemen have to do us displeasure, knowing well that by us they shall be in no more danger nor displeasure than by trees fixed in the earth by nature? And if this be so, is it not evident that these present horsemen do think these preys which be taken to be no less theirs than ours? Yea and peradventure more too. Therefore the case standeth in this necessity: if we can prepare horsemen not inferior to theirs, may we not all plainly espy that we shall be able to do all things against our enemies without them which we do now with them? Yea, thereby we may have them of gentler stomachs toward us, that whether they tarry or depart, we shall little pass, being strong though of ourselves without them. I think no man will reply to these but that it were far better that the Persians should have horsemen of their own. But this, peradventure, you do muse at, how we should prepare the same. Let us then consider if we would be furnished with horsemen, what we have and what we lack. As for horses, we have in the camp many already taken, we have bridles to ride them and other things meet for men of arms. Furthermore, we have all things that an horseman should need, as breastplates defensive for our bodies, darts both to cast and to keep.[20] What lack we then? Belike men, but of them we have plenty, for nothing is so much our own as we ourself be ours. Yet peradventure some man will say, We be not cunning, neither any of us was cunning in that we now can do before we learned the same. Then some will say that they learned it when they were children. And I pray you, whether be children more prudent to learn those things that be taught and showed than men? Whether, when the thing is learned, be children more able in body to practise the same or men? Furthermore, we have such opportunity to learn as neither children nor other men have. For we shall not need to learn to shoot, as children, for we do know the feat; nor to dart, for we can do it already. And it is not with us as it is with other men for unto some tillage is a let, unto some occupations, to other, domestical matters.[21]

'But us, not only time or opportunity, but also necessity enforceth to study the feats or policies of war. Furthermore, it is not in this thing as in many other warlike affairs, which as they be difficult and hard, so be they profitable. For is it not more pleasant to ride our journeys than to go them on foot? And for speed, is it not more pleasant to be, if need requireth, straight with a man his friend?[22] And when need is, straight to chase either a man or a wild beast, and overthrow the same? And is not this also a great ease, that when a man must bear harness the horse must help to bear the same? For truly is it all one to wear and to bear? But if any man do fear lest we, enterprising the feat of riding and not attaining to it, should prove neither good footmen nor good horsemen, he feareth in vain. For we may, when we list, soon fight a-foot, neither shall we in learning to ride forget our cunning on foot.' Cyrus thus said. Chrysantas agreeing with him spake on this wise:

The Oration of Chrysantas

'I truly am so desirous to learn the feat of riding, that being once an horseman,

---

[20] to keep] to defend oneself (at closer quarters).
[21] other domestical matters] Cyrus's point is that they have the freedom to learn horsemanship, unlike men who are busy with tillage or other trades or domestic labours.
[22] his friend] i.e. to be able to reach a friend quickly.

I would think myself a winged man.[23] Now I am content, when I contend to run with any man on even ground, only to pass him by the head. And when I see a wild beast outrunning me, if I can so aim mine arrow or dart that I may prevent and hit it before it be very far off. But being a horseman, I may kill a man as far off as I may see him; I may, chasing deer, overtake and kill some at hand, some with dart strike, as though they stood still. For if two things be swift and draw nigh together, they be as though they did stand. Wherefore of all creatures I do most desire to counterfeit the Hippocentaurs, if any such were, which in forecasting used man's prudence and in working that was requisite man's hands, but to overthrow it that fled and drive back it that tarried, they had the swiftness and strength of an horse. Therefore, if I were an horseman, I would translate[24] all these things to myself. For I shall be able to foresee all things, having reason as a man and with my hands I would use mine armour, and with the strength of my horse, I would overthrow that as did resist me. But I would not be so compact of an horse and man, as Hippocentaurs be, for this is better than to be so concorporate°. The Hippocentaurs, as I think, lack many commodities which men have found how to use, and many pleasures which horses by nature know how to enjoy. But if I learn to ride, being on horseback, I shall do the feats of an Hippocentaur; alighting from my horse I shall eat, I shall be clad and take my rest as men do. Therefore, what other thing shall I be than a divided and united Hippocentaur? In this also shall I pass a Centaur: he seeth with two eyes and heareth with two ears, but I shall foresee with four eyes and forehear with four ears, for an horse (they say) foreseeing with his eyes do warn a man of many things, and advertise him no less forehearing with his ears. Therefore write my name as one most willing to be an horseman.'

'And us also, for God his sake', said all the other. Then Cyrus said: 'Seeing we be fully accorded, what if we make a law for ourselves that it shall be villainy for any man to be seen on foot to whom I shall give horses, whether our journey be little or great, that men in all things may take us to be creatures made of horse and man?' Thus Cyrus did ask them. They all accorded to the same. Wherefore from that time, till this day, the Persians have followed this decree in so much that none of the noble and honourable men of Persia in no wise willingly will be seen abroad on foot. Thus they debated their matters, and the day being more than half past, the horsemen of the Medians and Hyrcanians came riding to them, bringing many prisoners both horse and men, for so many as would deliver their harness they did not kill. Being come, Cyrus asked them first if

---

[23] a winged man] A hippogryph (or 'Hippocentaur', below). On this image of the Persian nobles aspiring as riders to be centaur-like, see David M. Johnson, 'Persians as Centaurs in Xenophon's *Cyropaedia*', *Transactions of the American Philological Association*, 135 (2005), 177–207.

[24] translate] Another neat and revealing textual metaphor from Barker. Holland uses the simpler formulation, 'furnished with all these togither' (sig. M2).

they were all safe, which thing affirmed he asked what they had done? They declared everything, setting it forth to the uttermost. He heard them gently what so ever they would speak, and praised them thus:

'Truly, friends, you have declared yourselves to be right valiant men, and surely you seem now far more lusty, courageous and warlike than ye did tofore.' Then he asked them how much ground they had gone over, and whether it were inhabited or no? They said that they had passed through a great ground, and that every place was inhabited, and replenished with sheep, goats, neat°, horses, victual, and all good things. 'Then must we' (said he), 'look for two things: the one to be their lords that have these things, the other that they may remain still, for a place inhabited is a rich possession. And a place desert of men is also desert of other good things. I know well that you have slain all such as did resist, and rightly, for that doth chiefly establish victory, but such as yielded themselves ye have brought prisoners, whom if we deliver, we shall (as I think) do right well. For first it is not meet that we at this time should beware of them or keep them or find them victual. And with hunger truly we will not kill them. Then setting them at liberty, we shall have the more subjects: for if we can achieve the lordship of their country, all the inhabitants of the same shall become our captives, and the others shall the rather tarry if they see these delivered and left alive, and shall rather choose to be obedient than to make resistance. Thus I think if any man judgeth otherwise, let him say his conceit.' They hearing did agree these to be done. Cyrus then calling the prisoners thus said:

The Oration of Cyrus

'Friends, because you have been obeisant, you have saved your lives. Do so hereafter and you shall sustain no damage, saving that he shall not be your king that was tofore. Yet ye shall have the same houses, ye shall till the same land, ye shall accompany with the same wives and rule the same children that ye do now. Neither shall ye fight against us, nor none other, but if any man offer you wrong we will defend you. And that no man should command you to go to war, bring in your harness to us and to them that do bring forth the same, peace is given and other things which we have spoken without deceit. But as many as will not deliver their warlike weapons, against them we must out of hand make war. If any of you will come to us as a friend, to do or show us anything, him will we entertain as a fellow and friend, not as a slave. These things persuade yourselves and declare them to other. If any will make resistance to you, being willing to do thus, bring us to them, that we may rule them and not they us.' Thus Cyrus said. They kneeled on their knees and said they would so do. Being departed, Cyrus said:

'Now it is time (O Medians and Armenians) that we all sup. We have prepared you the best we could get. Therefore go you and send us half your bread that is purveyed, for it will suffice us both, but meat and drink send us none, for of them we have sufficient. And you (Hyrcanians) bring these men to their tents, the chief to the best. For have regard of it, and all other, as you shall think most seemly. And yourselves sup where you shall most delight, for your tents be yet untouched, you being as well provided for as they. And this know ye both, that such things as be abroad we will keep and watch this night; to them within your tents, look yourself and bestow your harness well for they that be in the tents be not yet our friends.' The Medians and Tigranes' men washed for all things was ready, and changing their garments went to supper; their horses likewise lacked no forage and they sent to the Persians half their bread, but sent neither meat nor wine, thinking that Cyrus and his company had had enough because (he said) he had plenty of them, but he meant for meat, hunger, for drink, running water. Cyrus causing the Persians to sup and the night drawing nigh, did send many in bands of five and ten, commanding them to lie in coverture° round about the tents, thinking watch to be needful both lest any man should assail them without, and lest also if they within would flee and convey forth their money that the same might be taken, and so it chanced in deed. For many fled and many were taken. Cyrus suffered them to have the money that took them, commanding the men to be killed in so much that afterward ye could not, though ye would, have taken one going away by night.[25] Thus the Persians did whilst the Medians were drinking, banqueting and using their minstrelsy.[26]

Cyaxares king of the Medes that night that Cyrus went abroad was drunk, as well as his fellows, for their good fortune, thinking the other Medes to have been in their tents except few because he heard so great a noise. For the Medes' servants their masters being absent did riotously drink and make revel, specially because they had taken of the Assyrians' camp wine and many other like things. Day being come, no man repairing to his pavilion but such as supped with him, and hearing say that the camp was void of the Medes and other horsemen, he came forth and saw it was even so indeed. Then he was sore displeased, both with Cyrus and the Medes, that they should depart and leave him desolate. And by and by for (as they say) he was a cruel and inexorable[27] man, commanded one of this men being at hand to take the horsemen that were about him with all haste, go to Cyrus's host, and say thus: 'I thought that neither you (Cyrus) would so rashly have dealt with me, nor that you Medians, though Cyrus were so minded, would have left me thus desolate. Now therefore whether Cyrus will

---

[25] by night] i.e. that you could not have found anyone else trying to escape by night.
[26] minstrelsy] Barker preserves yet another contrast between the hardy, moderate Persians and the luxurious Medians, even while they are united in one army.
[27] inexorable] severe.

or no, come you with all speed to me.' Thus he commanded. The messenger that was appointed to go said, 'How shall I, sir, find them? How shall I know where Cyrus and his men be become? For I hear say that diverse of the Hyrcanians being fled from our enemies and come hither be now gone, being their guides in this voyage.' Then Cyaxares hearing this was much more moved with Cyrus because he would not show him of it. And therefore with much more haste sent for the Medians, as though he would leave Cyrus alone, and with greater threatenings than before, accused the Medians' fact[28] and threatened the messenger if he did not make bold declaration thereof. This messenger went forth having a hundred horsemen, being angry with himself because he went not forth with Cyrus. And going their journey, by reason of diverse ways and paths, they wandered they wist not whither and could not come to Cyrus's host, till they chanced upon some of the Assyrians whom they compelled to be their guides. And so went till they espied the fires about midnight, being come night the camp, the watch (as they were commanded) would not give them passage before day. Day appearing, Cyrus calling his clergy,[29] commanded them to choose out the most precious things to make sacrifice to God. They being about the same, he assembled the nobility and sayeth:

The Oration of Cyrus

'Friends, God foreshoweth much good but we (O Persians) at this present be very few to achieve the same. For when we have achieved it, if we be not able to retain it, it must return to other again. And if we leave part of us for the custody of that we have won, we shall be taken shortly to be of little power or none. Therefore I think it good that one of you should with all celerity repair into Persia, declaring what I say, and commanding them with all speed to send an army, if the Persians desire the dominion of Asia and commodity thereof. Go thou then which are most ancient, go (I say) and thus declare that so many soldiers as they send, when they be come to me, I will care for the finding of them. What we now have you well know, hereof ye keep no secret. And what I may send of these things into Persia honourably and lawfully belonging to God, enquire of my father: concerning the commonwealth, enquire of the princes and let them send some to see what we have done, and to make answer to our requests. And you being well appointed, take a band of men to accompany you.' Then he called the Medians, at which time Cyaxares his messenger came, and in presence of them all declared both his anger toward Cyrus and his menacing toward the Medes. In conclusion he said that he had commanded

---

[28] Medians' fact] the Medians' actions (i.e. having followed Cyrus).
[29] clergy] Translating (οἱ) μάγοι ((hoi) mágoi), the magi. The term 'clergy' was sometimes used to refer to the priestly orders of non-Christian religions.

the Medes to depart, though Cyrus would have them tarry. The Medes hearing the messenger stood in silence, being in perplexity how they might disobey his commandment, and afraid how to obey his threatenings, specially knowing his cruel conditions. Therefore Cyrus said, 'I, messenger and Medes, do not marvel though Cyaxares seeing our enemies them to be many and not knowing what we did, be troubled both for us and for himself. But when he shall know that many of our enemies be slain, and all put to flight, first he shall tease us of his fear, then shall he know that he was not left desolate, because his friends have destroyed his foes. And how can we be worthy accusement rightly doing him pleasure, enterprising nothing of our own brain? For I desired him to license me to take you with me, and you, as men not desirous to go forth, asked of him if you should go. Now you be come hither in deed, but being commanded of him, to go so many of you as were not unwilling to the same. As for his anger, I know well, being appeased with our well doings, it will relent and banish away, with his vain fear. Now, therefore, you messenger, rest ye because ye have travelled. And you, O Persians, because we look for our enemies, either to fight or yield, prepare that we may be in good appointment: for so appearing we must needs much rather accomplish our purposes. You the prince of the Hyrcanians, tarry, commanding your captains to see their soldiers harnessed.' The Hyrcanian going about the same, Cyrus said: 'I have great pleasure (O Hyrcanian) perceiving you not only to declare your assured friendship, but also wit and policy, which at this present shall (I am certain) much avail us. The Assyrians be mine enemies, but now more hateful to you than me. Therefore let us consult for both parties that none of our present confederates do forsake us, but that we may, if we can, get more. You have heard how the Median calleth home his horsemen, which if they depart, then how can we only footmen remain. Therefore both you and I must do our devoirs that this messenger may be desirous to abide with us. You therefore, preparing a tent well apparelled with all necessaries, shall appoint him to the same. I shall devise to occupy him about some such thing, which he had rather do than depart. And declare you unto him what hope of great avail all our friends may conceive if our emprises° have good success. When you have thus done, repair eftsoons to me.' The Hyrcanian departed and brought the Median to his tent. He that should go into Persia was there prest. Cyrus commanded him to say unto them, as he in his former words had declared, and that he should deliver letters unto Cyaxares. 'And I will' (said he), 'that you shall be privy to that I write, that you may know how to make direct answer if he make any demands.' The epistle was thus written.

The Epistle of Cyrus

'"Cyrus to Cyaxares greeting, Neither did we leave you so desolate, for no man that is superior to his adversaries is then destitute of friends, nor we did not depart from you thinking you to be left in any danger. But the further we be distant from you, the more we think we work your safety. For they which remain nighest their friends do not most provide their friends' service, but they that drive their enemies furthest off, they rather set their friends in safety. Consider, therefore, what I am towards you and you toward me, and then appeach° me. I brought you confederates, not so many as you thought but so many as I was able. You granted me, being among my friends, so many as I was able to allure; now being among mine enemies you do call home not him that will but every man generally. Truly I thought then that either of us had ought° thanks to other. But now ye enforce me to put you out of mind and do my part to tender all the thanks I can to them which have accompanied me. Yet truly I cannot be like unto you, for sending now into Persia for an army, I do command that so many as shall repair to me, if you have need before they come to us, ye shall command them to do you service, not as they will but as it pleaseth you. And I will counsel you, although I am of less years, that you will not revoke your gifts, lest for thanks enmity shall be due unto you. Nor do not summon them by menace whom ye would have repair speedily unto you. Nor when ye say you are left alone, then do not menace many lest you teach the same to set little by you. Fare you well. We shall be ready to come to you when we have with speed accomplished those things which, being achieved, we think, shall redound to both our public weal."³⁰ Deliver this to him, and if he do ask you of any of these things been written, affirm the same. And concerning the Persians, I have given ye precepts tofore mentioned.' Thus speaking to him and delivering him the letters, he dismissed him, charging him so to make haste as he knew speedy repair to be profitable. Then he did see that all were in harness, both Medians, Hyrcanians and Tigranes' men, and the Persians were also harnessed. And at this time, certain of those marches brought forth their harness and he commanded the darts to be thrown into that place before appointed and to be burned of them which were assigned, chiefly such as were not needful. But the horses he commanded the bringers to keep and remain till he did otherwise signify unto them. And assembling the captains of the horsemen and Hyrcanians, he said thus:

Cyrus his Oration

'Do not marvel, friends and confederates, though I do oft assemble you, for new matters being in hand be commonly in no due order. And things out of order must needs make business³¹ till they be well placed. We have much treasure

---

³⁰ public weal] This is the first use of 'public weal', translating κοινὰ ἀγαθά (*koinà agathá*).
³¹ make business] i.e. occupy us.

taken, we have many men likewise. And because neither we know what is properly ours, nor they what was severally theirs, a man cannot see very many of them doing that they should do, but all almost doubting what they ought to do. Therefore that this may be redressed, ye shall divide the same, and what tent any man hath taken, being furnished with victual, ministers and apparel, with other sufficient implements for a warlike tent, hereafter he must put no more to it than the receiver may know because he ought to be as circumspect in these as in his proper possession. He that hath chanced on a tent unfurnished, seeing to them that be in it, shall relieve the lack of the same for I know that there be many things superfluous. For our enemies had all things more abundantly than our number can spend. The treasurers of the Assyrian king and of other princes came to me, declaring that they had coined gold, making mention of certain tributes. Therefore proclaim that they bring forth all such things to you wheresoever ye sit,[32] affraying them that do not obey your commandment; you receiving it, give to an horseman double, to a footman single, that you may have to buy such things as you lack. Proclaim a market-place in the camp where no man do other wrong, suffering victuallers and merchants to sell every man his chaffer°, and these things being uttered, to bring other that our camp may be inhabited.' And they forthwith proclaimed the same. But the Medians and Hyrcanians said thus: 'How shall we without you and yours make division of the things?' Cyrus to these words thus replied: 'Do you friends think that when anything is to be done we all must be present at every matter, and that I am not sufficient to provide for your wants and you for ours? And how can it be but that we shall have more matters to do, bringing fewer to pass than we do. But consider, we have kept these things for you, you making us believe they have been well kept. Therefore divide you them now, and we will believe that you have divided well. And so in this matter let us endeavour to do somewhat else for the commonwealth. First consider how many horses we have, and how they be brought to us; if we suffer them to be unrid, we shall have no profit by them but trouble in keeping of them. But if we appoint horsemen to them, we shall be both delivered of business, and they shall augment our strength if you have any other to whom you would give them, with whom you could have more pleasure to adventure when ye need than with us, let them have them. But if ye will ratherest have us to help at a pinch, give them us. For when as alate° you went forth and did adventure without us, we were in greater fear lest ye were not well. And you made us much ashamed that we were not where you were. But if we take horses, we shall follow you. If we seem to do more good being horsemen, we shall lack no courageous diligence to aid you; but if we seem to do more good afoot, we shall alight among you, and straight become your footmen, taking our horses to be kept of some appointed to the same.' Thus he said. And they

---

[32] wheresoever ye sit] i.e. wherever you are based.

made this answer: 'We (O Cyrus) have neither men to set upon these horses, nor if we had we would prefer any man to you, you being willing to occupy the same. Therefore now take the horses and do with them as you think good.' 'I take them' (said Cyrus), 'and with good fortune be we made horsemen. Divide you the common spoil and the first select for God, as the sages[33] shall think good. Then divide for Cyaxares in every thing as you think ye may most gratify him.' They then smiling said that the fair women must also be divided. 'Divide', said he, 'both women and other things as ye list. When ye have made division for him, see that these, O Hyrcanians, which willingly have followed me have no cause to complain. And you Medians, honestly esteem these our first confederates, that they may think to have done well in allying friendship with us, and distribute part of every thing to Cyaxares his messenger, and to them that came with him, exhorting them to abide with us, saying that I would have it so, that Cyaxares may be the better ascertained of everything that is done. To these Persians and my train, that that is superfluous, yourselves having honest portion, shall be sufficient. For we (I tell ye) be not much brought up in delicates but very homely. Therefore you peradventure shall laugh at us, if ye give us any precious thing. And I know well that setting on horseback we shall be the cause of much laughter to you, for I think surely that we shall have many a fall.'[34]

Then they went to make division, having good sport at the riding matter. Cyrus calling the captains commanded them to take horses, horseburdens[35] and horsekeepers, and that in number each man by lot should equally receive them to his ray°. He commanded also to be proclaimed that if there were any slave of the Assyrians, Syrians, Arabians, Medes, Persians, Bactrians, Carians, Cilicians, Grecians' army, or of any other place, they should show them self. They hearing the proclamation very many showed themselves straight [a]way. He choosing the best favoured, said that if they would be free, they must be harness bearers, which he delivering to them, affirmed he would provide, that they should have things necessary. Whom leading to his captains, straight [a]way he bestowed, commanding bucklers and short swords to be delivered them, that they having the same might follow the horses, and that necessaries should be provided as well for them as for his Persians, and that themselves having curets and spears should ever be on horseback. And he began the feat, and to the footmen of the nobility in his place he appointed another captain of the noble men.

Being busied about these things, Gobryas, an Assyrian and ancient man on

---

[33] sages] Barker now translates (οἱ) μάγοι ((*hoi*) *mágoi*) as 'sages' rather than 'clergy'.
[34] a fall] Again, Cyrus exaggerates any Persian lack of facility with horses, and makes a virtue of their 'homely' frugality and lack of appetite for luxury.
[35] horseburdens] i.e. the horses' trappings.

horseback with a company of horsemen having all barbed horses, came at that instant. And they which were appointed to receive harness, commanded him also to deliver his lances that they might burn them as they did other. Gobryas said he would first see Cyrus. The ministers, leaving the other horsemen behind, conveyed Gobryas to Cyrus who, seeing Cyrus, said thus: 'I am (O lord) an Assyrian born. I have a strong fortress and am lord of a large land. And having a thousand horsemen, I served the Assyrian king, with whom I was in high favour. After that he, being a noble man, was slain of you, and his son, my mortal enemy, succeedeth him in the empire,[36] I am come to you, and kneeling on my knees, I recommend myself to you as captive and confederate, beseeching you to revenge my cause. And that you may the better do it, I adopt you to my son, for of the male kind I am childless. For the only son which I had (O lord) both good and goodly, so reverencing and loving me as a child might cause his father to be happy. This my sovereign lord, father to him that now reigneth, sent for my child intending to give him his daughter in marriage. I, looking too high, sent him forth, thinking to have seen my son despoused° to a king his daughter. The king now being, calling him to hunt and permitting him to range as large as one that was counted his most excellent horseman, friendly in the hunt entertained him. A bear being put up, they both followed the chase. The prince picked his dart (alas the while) and missed. My son in even time[37] let drive and overthrew the bear, whereat the other disdaining, kept this hatred secret. A lion again aroused, he eftsoons missed, which as I think was no strange thing. My son again (O unhappy chance) hit the lion and slew him, and said, "Twice have I in order driven one dart, and at each time killed a deer". At that word that wicked man no longer dissembling his hatred, but cruelly taking a spear from one of his men, struck him through the heart and bereft my only and lief son his life.[38] And I, poor miser, instead of espousal° did bring the dead corpse away, and being thus in age, buried my most good son growing to man's estate. This murderer, as though he had vanquished an enemy, neither showed any token of repentance nor did him any honour for his wicked trespass at his funeral, but his father truly both rued for me and showed evidently that he was in anguish for mine so great dolour. I, truly if he had lived, should never have come to you to the hurt of the other, for he was especial good lord to me, and I as faithful servant to him. But the kingdom being revolved to[39] the murderer of my son, I can never be faithful to him, nor can he never be friendful° to me, for he knoweth my heart toward him. And as before I lived a pleasant life, so now being despoiled of my son I waste mine age with pain

---

[36] empire] Barker (and Holland) translate ἡ ἀρχή (hē archḗ), the government/rule as 'empire' here.
[37] in even time] here, likewise.
[38] bereft] 'beraught' in the text (and in Holland (sig. N2v)).
[39] revolved to] Holland uses 'devolved', but 'revolved' also means 'turned to'.

and pensiveness°. If you therefore will take me to your clemency,⁴⁰ I have some hope that through you my dear son's death shall be revenged and myself revive again, neither living with ignominy and reproach nor dying with sorrow and lamentation.' Thus he spake. Cyrus answered: 'If you, Gobryas, think in heart as ye have spoken with tongue, I receive your humble suit and promise you, God being my good lord, the avenging of your son. But now tell me, if we do you this pleasure, suffering you to retain your city, your country, your armour and power as you have heretofore, what service will you do us for these benefits?' He said, 'My fortress at your commandment I will deliver as your house, and the tribute and land that I pay now to him I will translate to you. When you go to war I will go a warfare with you, I will aid you with the force of my country. I have also a daughter a virgin and dear damsel, being now marriageworthy, whom hereto before I thought I had reserved a wife for this new king. But now my daughter, oft kneeling on her knees, hath made humble request unto me not to give her to her brother's queller°, which thing I myself approve. Now therefore I give her to you, so to be provided for as I shall appear to provide for you.' Then Cyrus said, 'In confirming the truth of these things, I give you my right hand and take yours, God being witness betwixt us'. These things being done, he commanded Gobryas to depart to his men in harness, asking him how long the way was to his country. He answered: 'If ye set forth tomorrow in the morning, ye shall the next day lie with me.' Gobryas then departed, leaving a guide behind him. Then came the Medes saying that they had given the sacrificers such things as they could choose out for God his part. And they had selected a most goodly tent for Cyrus, and a Susian woman, being reputed the most goodly creature in all Asia, and two most excellent musician women, and secondarily to Cyaxares the next in price.⁴¹ And furnishing themselves with such like things, that they should want nothing in the time of war, for there was great abundance of all things. The Hyrcanians also took that they needed, dividing equal portions with Cyaxares his messenger. And certain superfluous tents they gave to Cyrus, to the use of the Persians. They said also there was a coin which being collected should be distributed.⁴² And so it was. They thus did and said.⁴³ Cyrus commanded them to take the custody of Cyaxares' portion whom he knew to be most familiar with him. 'And what so ever ye give me, I

---

⁴⁰ clemency] Holland has 'If it will please you therefore, to entertain mee so, as that I may conceive some hope by your meanes to be revenged ...' (sig. N3).

⁴¹ the next in price] i.e. they chose for Cyaxares the second-best tent, after selecting the best tent for Cyrus. The 'Susian woman' is the first reference to Panthea.

⁴² distributed] Barker misses some of the detail here. Holland is closer to the Greek in noting 'As touching the money in coine, they said, they would then make partage thereof when they had gathered in all' (sig. [N3]v).

⁴³ did and said] From here to the end of Book IV, Barker and Holland both include the first few sentences of Book V as the conclusion of Book IV, thus separating the narrative of Araspes and Panthea from this lighter material. See Introduction, pp. 35–6.

take it' (said he), 'thankfully, and he that hath most need among you, he shall use the same.' Then one of the Medes, a great esteemer of music, said: 'I truly, Cyrus, hearing this night past these women minstrels whom you now have, I was greatly delighted. Therefore if ye would vouchsafe to give me one of them, I would think it greater joy to go to war than to remain at home.' Cyrus said unto him, 'I give her thee with all my heart. And I think I ought to give thee more thank for thy request than thou me for my gift, so desirous am I to do you pleasures.' And he that asked the woman had her.

Thus endeth the fourth book.

The Discipline of Cyrus, the Fifth Book

Cyrus calling Araspes, a Median which was his playfellow being a child to whom also he gave the Median robe off his back at his departure from Astyages into Persia,[1] commanded him to take the custody of the woman and the tent. She was the wife of Abradatas king of Susa, which was not present at the taking of the Assyrians' camp, being gone of embassage to the king of Bactria, being sent thither of the Assyrian to treat of confederacy betwixt them and of entire friendship with the king of Bactria. Cyrus commanded Araspes to take the custody of her, who, being so commanded, asked of Cyrus if he had seen her whom he commanded him to keep. 'No surely', said Cyrus. 'Indeed', said he, 'I chose her for you. And at our first coming to her tent, we could not know her for she sat on the ground with all her women about her, being apparelled like her handmaids; we being desirous to know which was the mistress did avise° them all forthwith, and she, although she did sit muffled and beholding the earth, did far exceed the other. Wherefore commanding her to arise, all the other did arise about her. She far did pass them all as well in feature and lineaments of body as nurture and comeliness of the same although she was clad in coarse array, and the tears did distil evidently from [her] eyes,[2] some on her attire, some down to her feet. Wherefore the most ancient of our company said: "Be of good cheer, Lady, we hear that you have a goodly valiant man to your husband, but now know you for certain that we have chose[n] you for a man which neither in beauty nor in valiantness is inferior to him. But as we think, if there be any man, Cyrus is the man most worthy admiration whose, from this time, you shall be." When the lady heard this, she did tear that tirement° off her head, and cried out and all her maids together skriked with her. At which time her face the greater part did appear, likewise her neck and hands. And be ye assured, O Cyrus, that to us all that did behold her, it seemed unpossible that such a creature could be born of mortal parents in Asia. Therefore, sir, see her in any wise.' Then Cyrus said: 'Truly, so much the less, being such a one as you do report her.' 'And why so?', said the young man. 'Because' (quoth he), 'hearing you declaring her beauty, if I should be moved to go and see her, having almost no time, I am afraid lest she should soon allure me to come eftsoons to behold her, whereby I might perchance wax negligent in my weighty affairs, sitting and vizying° her.' The young man smiling said: 'Think you, Cyrus, that the beauty of a mortal creature could enforce a man unwilling not to do for the best? If nature be of such power, she should enforce every man alike, for the fire burneth every man alike because it is his nature. But of beautiful things, some with some be had in price, some not so, some esteeming this, some that. For it is

---

[1] into Persia] In Book I (p. 101).
[2] [her] eyes] 'Our' eyes in the text; a mistake, as the context makes clear, although perhaps also Barker proposing a certain pity felt by Araspes towards Panthea early on.

a voluntary thing and every man loveth what he list.³ The brother is not in love with the sister, another is; the father not with the daughter, another is. For fear and law is sufficient to refrain love. But if there were a law which should enjoin that men should not eat, and yet not be hungry; should not drink, and yet not thirst; and that no man should be cold in winter, or hot in summer, law truly could compel no men to obey these things, for by nature they be conquered of the same.⁴ But to love is a voluntary thing, every man loving his own things, as his apparel and other garments.'

Then said Cyrus: 'If love be voluntary, how can it be but a man may leave it when he list? But I have seen men weep for sorrow because of love, and to the loved would become bond and thrall; and yet before they loved, reputed none evil so great as bondage, they giving away many things which had been better for them to have kept, and have desired to God to be delivered of love, as of any other thing, from the which they could not be released, being bound with stronger durance° than if they had been tied with chains, yielding themselves to the loved, serving them with all obedience, and being in such distress, do not once attempt to make an escape but be rather gaolers of the [be]loved, that they should not escape them.' Then the young man said: 'They do thus', quoth he, 'and therefore they be very misers, and as I think, wishing continuance of their woe, would so die. And whereas there be a thousand shifts to be rid of this life, they do not rid themselves but some of them fall to stealing and robbing of other men. Yet when they have robbed and stolen, you with the first⁵ do see that theft is not necessary, and accusing the thief and robber, do not pardon but punish him. Semblably, the beautiful do not compel men to love them or covet that is not lawful. But the vile shadows of men⁶ be inferior to their affections, and then do accuse love. Honest and good men, although they desire gold, good horses and fair women, yet they can easily refrain from all the same, not being more subject to them than they ought to be. For I did behold this woman which seemed me a most goodly creature, and yet I am now with you, I am on horseback, doing such things as my duty requireth.'

'Peradventure', said Cyrus, 'ye came sooner away than love could fasten in a man. For the fire touching a man doth not straight burn him. And wood is not straight got in flame. Yet would not I willingly neither touch the fire nor

---

³ every man loveth what he list] On the narrative of Panthea and Araspes, and the debate between Araspes and Cyrus on the nature of love, see Introduction. This episode is the most commonly cited narrative from the *Cyropaedia* in early modern England, and forms the main plot of Farrant's dramatic romance *The Warres of Cyrus* (printed 1594, but probably first performed in the late 1570s).
⁴ conquered of the same] Araspes here subtly challenges the arguments of Persian education and justice as Cyrus had learned them in Book 1.
⁵ with the first] i.e. you are the first to (accuse them of stealing).
⁶ shadows of men] Holland has 'silly and foolish folke' (sig. O1).

behold beautiful persons. And I would counsel you, Araspes, not to be busy in beholding beautiful folks, for the fire burneth whom it catcheth and fair folk so enflameth them, yea though they behold afar off, that they burn in love.' 'I warrant you Cyrus', said he, 'though I never leave looking, yet will I not be overcome, whereby I should do anything that I ought not.' 'Ye say well', said Cyrus, 'therefore keep this woman as I bid, and see well unto her, for peradventure this woman is taken in good time.' Thus they talking departed. The young man noting both the singular beauty and perceiving the great honesty of this woman, and having the custody of her, thought he would do her pleasure and by continuance understanding that she was not unthankful, but very diligent on her part to cause her servants that all things at his coming should be ready, and if he were by chance sick, lacked no keeping, he through all these occasions fell in amours° with her, and peradventure there was no marvel in the matter. Thus these things stood. Cyrus being desirous that the Medes and other his confederates should be willing to abide with him, assembled all the chief of them and said thus.

The Oration of Cyrus

'I certainly know, O Medians, and all other here present, that ye come not forth with me, neither for lack of money nor in this behalf minded to please Cyaxares, but for the desire to gratify me herein, and seeking mine honour, ye came forth to travail by night and to adventure yourselves with me. For the which things I thank you. If I did not, I should do naught.[7] But to recompense you accordingly, I am as yet of no power. And so to say I am not ashamed. But to say, if ye tarry with me, I will acquit you I might well be ashamed, for I think I should seem to say for this purpose that you might be the more willing to tarry with me. But instead of it, thus I say: if you depart, obeying Cyaxares, I having good success will do my devoir that you shall have cause to praise me. For I will not depart but, keeping my promise with these Hyrcanians to whom I have made an oath and joined hands, I shall never be found untrue to them. And I will attempt to do so much for this Gobryas, which of late hath given us his town, country and power, as he shall not repent him of his repair to me. And most of all, God so manifestly giving us so good chance, I should be in fear and dread if that I left the thing and did depart unadvisedly. I therefore will thus do. Do you as you shall think good, and declare unto me what your mind is.'

Thus he said. He that once said he was his kinsman[8] spake first in this wise: 'I

---

[7] do naught] Barker ignores the redolent Greek verb ἀδικέω (*adikéō*), 'to do wrong', with its implication that Cyrus would be unjust not to thank them for their support.
[8] his kinsman] Artabasus (in Book I).

truly, O king, for a king ye seem to be no less by nature than a master bee in a swarm of the same,[9] for to him always bees willingly be obeisant, in so much that if he remaineth at home, none goeth abroad; if he goeth forth, none tarryeth behind, such vehement love is engrafted in them to be governed of him. I say that men be semblably affected toward you, for when you departed from us into Persia, who was there of the Medes that did forsake you that did not wait upon you till Astyages did return us? And when ye came from Persia to aid us, we might perceive that, incontinent,[10] all your friends willingly followed you. And now thus we stand that, being with you in our enemy's land, we dare be bold. But without you, even to return I should be afraid. Therefore let other men show what they will do, for I truly, O Cyrus, and all mine, shall remain with you and by the sight of you abide all brunts, firmly trusting to your beneficence.' Then spake Tigranes thus: 'You, O Cyrus, shall not marvel though I say nothing, for my mind is not appointed as a counsellor's, but as a performer of things that you do command.' Then the Hyrcanian said: 'I, O Medians, will think if ye depart that it is the workmanship of God, not suffering you to enjoy so great felicity. For who is well with himself that will recoil, his enemies being fled; and will not receive, they delivering their harness; and will not take, they yielding them self and theirs, especially having such a captain as this is, who I think (God being my record) hath more delight to do us pleasure than to enrich himself.' After him all the Medians said: 'You, Cyrus, have brought us forth, and you, when you think it time to return, shall bring us home.' Cyrus hearing these words, thus made his prayer: 'O Jupiter immortal, grant me I beseech thee, that I may be able in doing them pleasures to surmount their doing me honour.' Then he commanded all the other to have their appointed garrisons about them, and the Persians to take tents seemly for horsemen, and sufficient for the footmen, and so to order that all the ministers should bring all necessary things to the Persian crews and to see that their horses be well trimmed; and the Persians should have nought else to do but attend upon warlike affairs. And thus they spent this day.

Rising early in the morning, they marched toward Gobryas, Cyrus being on horseback and the new-made horsemen of the Persians about two thousand.

---

[9] swarm of the same] Another use of apian metaphor (see drone bees in Book II — p. 123), popular in both classical and early modern writing, and often associated with sovereignty (see Joseph Campana, 'The Bee and the Sovereign: Political Entomology and the Problem of Scale', *Shakespeare Studies*, 41 (2013), 94–113); here, Xenophon emphasises obedience to the sovereign. Barker ignores the feminine gendering of the bee and presents a 'master bee' rather than a queen bee. Xenophon does not term Cyrus a king until after the conquest of Babylon, but Artabasus here anticipates and rationalises it.

[10] incontinent] Holland, too, follows Barker's phrasing about Cyrus's friends' rush to follow him ('we might perceive incontinently' (sig. O1v)). The Greek does not have the usual ἀκράτεια (*akráteia*), however, but ὡρμήθης (*hōrmḗthēs*), aorist passive indicative second person singular of ὁρμάω (*hormáo*), to hurry or rush.

Other[s] having shields and swords followed, these being equal in number, and the residue of the host set forth in array. He commanded every one to say unto their new servants that as many of them as were seen behind the guides of the tail of the army, or before the train, or were taken on either side divided from them that were in array, should be punished. The next day about twilight, they were at Gobryas's fort, and saw a strong trench, and all things prepared within the walls to make strong resistance, and many oxen and sheep to be gathered within the trench.[11] And Gobryas sent to Cyrus, willing him to ride about and see if the entrance were very easy, and that he should send some trusty men to him within, which viewing what there was, might make relation to him. So Cyrus being willing to see at that present if the town might be taken, or Gobryas appear vain, he rode about and saw every thing too strong for him to enter. They whom he sent to Gobryas did report to Cyrus that there was such plenty within as was able to their judgement without want to suffice a man's life them that were within, Cyrus mused what this matter should mean. Then Gobryas himself came out, and brought forth all that were within, some bringing wine, barley meal, wheatmeal, some driving out sheep, neat, goats and swine, and all other victual, and brought forth abundantly that Cyrus with his whole army might sup well. Some being appointed did distribute and serve the supper. Gobryas, when all his men were come forth, moved Cyrus to enter in, that he should think all to be in surety. Cyrus, sending in afore espies, with power entered in himself; being entered the gates which were opened, he desired all his friends and captains about him to do so.

When all were in, Gobryas brought cups of gold, lavers° and flagons with all other kinds of ornaments, and a coin called darics° innumerable, and they all things wondrous bountifully. Finally bringing his daughter, a maid of marvellous goodly shape and beauty, clad in mourning apparel for her brother's death, said thus: 'I give you these riches, and this my daughter, I do recommend to be bestowed as you shall please. We beseech you, I tofore for my son, she now for her brother, that you would be his avenger.' Cyrus thus answered: 'I promised you to avenge your quarrel to my power, if you were true; now finding you so to be, I am bound to keep it; and her I will also promise, that with God his help I shall perform no less. And this treasure I also accept, rendering the same to this your daughter and he that shall be her make°; one gift if I have of you when I depart, I will more joyfully accept than all the treasure of Babylon, which is much, and of the whole world, which is infinite.' Gobryas marvelling what it should be, and suspecting he would name his daughter said, 'What is it, Cyrus?' And Cyrus answered: 'I think, Gobryas', said he, 'that there be many men which by their will would neither displease God nor hurt man nor be found false. But because no man will prefer them to great riches, to dominion,

---

[11] trench] τὰ ἐρυμνὰ (tà erymná, from the adjective ἐρυμνός, 'trenched').

to strongholds, to dear beloved children, they do die before they have declared what they were. But you giving me now strong towns, infinite riches, your whole power and most dear daughter have manifestly declared to all the world that willingly I neither would be cruel toward strangers for many's sake nor vain of my covenants. These things shall I never forget, be you sure, so long as I shall embrace justice, and be thought worthy the praise of men, but shall do my diligence to reacquit[12] your honour by all honest ways. And be not afraid that you shall lack a meet man for your daughter, for I have many honourable friends, of the which some shall marry her, having so much money as you have given, or other much more than it, I cannot truly say. And know you well, that some of them, for the many which you have given, will not a little the more esteem you.[13] But me now they entirely love, desiring of God they may have once occasion to declare that they will be no less loyal and faithful to their friends than I am to mine, and toward their enemies never to be remiss while they live, except God worketh the contrary. But they do not so much esteem all your riches, being joined with all Syria and Assyria, as they do virtue and noble fame. Such men set even here, I would ye should well know.' And Gobryas smiling said, 'For God his sake Cyrus, show me which they bee, that I may request of you one of them to be my son'. 'Ye shall not need', said Cyrus, 'to request of me, but if you accompany with us you shall be able to show any of them to other.' Thus much talking and taking Gobryas by the hand, he rose up and departed, taking all his men with him.

And after much desire of Gobryas's part to sup within, he would not, but supped in his tents, taking Gobryas with him as a guest, thinking most assurance for them in the army that he should be present, no man knowing better how to do if any danger should chance, and setting upon seats of grass, thus demanded of him: 'Tell me, Gobryas, have you more carpets than any of us?' To whom he answered: 'I know well that you have many carpets, and many resting places; your house is far larger than ours which, for your houses use earth and heaven your resting places, be so many as there be caverns on the earth. And you take for carpets not so many as be made of the wool of sheep but so many as the field and mountains do send for the branches.' And Gobryas this first time supping with the Persians and seeing their thin fare thought his more liberal than them. But when he had advertised[14] their moderateness in diet, for there is no Persian of good education that in meat or drink appeareth to be moved in eyes or with ravening°, nor in the mind, but be of as foresight as though they were not at meat. And as horsemen not being troubled with their

---

[12] reacquit] i.e. requite.
[13] esteem you] i.e. that there are many who will not esteem you any more for the money that you give them.
[14] advertised] i.e. observed.

horses can both hear, see and speak on horseback as they ought, even so they at meat think they ought to appear both prudent and modest, and to be moved for meat or drink they think it very gross and brutish.¹⁵ He perceived also that they demanded one of another such questions as were more pleasant to be demanded than not. So jested one with another, as was more pleasant to be jested than not, and so toyed° as was far void of despite°, far off from doing hurt, far off from offending one another. And the greatest thing among them seemed to him that being in warfare, no man should think he ought to be better provided for than other that came to like adventure by chance, thinking that feasting to be the best if they may make their confederates best instruct to war. Therefore Gobryas rising to go home, thus (as it is reported) said: 'I do no more marvel (O Cyrus) though we have more place, apparel, and treasure than you, we being less worthy than you, for all our care is to have most possessions, all yours as I perceive to be best men.' Thus he said. Cyrus answered: 'Then Gobryas, be here tomorrow betimes°, bringing your men of arms, that we may see your strength and that together ye may convey us through your country, that we may know which we should take for our friends, which for our foes.' Thus communing, they departed the one and the other to his business.

When day was come, Gobryas brought his horsemen and led the way. Cyrus, as was the part of a wise captain, did not alonely° mark the way of the voyage, but in his way considered if he might impair his enemies and increase his strength. Calling the Hyrcanians and Gobryas (for them he thought to have most knowledge in those things that he would learn) said: 'I think dear friends that I should not do amiss to debate with you, my most assured friends, concerning this war. For I see it to be more to be regarded of you than of me that the Assyrian do not overcome us. For I peradventure, not going well to work, may have some other refuge.¹⁶ But if he subdue you, I see all that you have shall be another man's. He is mine enemy, not hating me but thinking it is his detriment if we be strong. And for this cause he maketh war against us. But you he hateth, and thinketh he hath injury at your hands.' To this they both answered that every of these things did warn them to be careful because they knew it belonged to them, and also were in great study how this present enterprise should succeed. Then he began thus: 'Tell me, doth the Assyrian think that you only make him war, or knoweth that he hath also another adversary?' 'Surely', said the Hyrcanian, 'his greatest enemies be the Caducians, a nation very great and valiant. The Sacians also, our borderers have sustained much displeasure by the Assyrian, he going about to have them thrall, as he hath us.' 'Think

---

¹⁵ gross and brutish] Further emphasis on the moderation of the Persian diet and appetites.
¹⁶ other refuge] i.e. if I lose against the Assyrian, I will still be able to find another place of refuge.

ye not then' (said he), 'that they both would gladly take our part against the Assyrian?' 'Yes very earnestly', say they, 'if they might confeder° with us.' 'And what letteth them to join with us?', said he. 'The Assyrian's whole country', said they, 'through the which you now go.' When Cyrus heard this, 'What, Gobryas,' said he, 'do not you accuse this young and newmade king of proud and haughty humour?' 'I' (said he) 'have so found him.' 'Is he so, said Cyrus, only to you or to some other likewise?' 'Certainly to many other likewise', said he. 'But to show of his outrage toward poor men, what should it need. For a much more noble man's son than I am, being his companion as mine was, and banqueting with him, he did make an eunuch for because, as some men say, his harlot praised him for his goodly port°, saying "she should be happy that might be his wife". But as the king himself now sayeth, because he would have disparaged his woman. And now he is an eunuch for his labour, but come to his dominion, his father being dead.' 'Do you not think', said Cyrus, 'that he would be glad to see us if he thought we might do him any good?' 'Yes, I know that certainly', said Gobryas, 'but it is hard to see him.' 'Why so?', quoth Cyrus. 'Because', said Gobryas, 'he that will join with him must pass by Babylon itself.' 'And what difficulty is in that?', said Cyrus. 'Because I know', quoth Gobryas, 'that a more puissant power shall issue out of it than you have, and this you must know: that for this cause the Assyrians yield you less harness and bring you fewer horses than they did at the beginning, because your power seemed but weak to them that saw it. And this rumour is very much dispersed. Therefore I think it best that we go forth warily.'

Cyrus hearing Gobryas so say spake thus unto him: 'I think, Gobryas, you saw well, moving me to make my journey more circumspectly. Therefore peising° the matter, I cannot see what way to be more safe and sure than to go the right way to Babylon where our enemy's power is most puissant. And there be very many, as you say. If they be in courage, they will as I think, declare it to us. If they see us not but think we vanish for fear of them, ye know well they shall be delivered of the fear which now they are in, and shall for it gather greater courage, so long time as they see us not. But if we march straight against them, we shall find some yet lamenting their death whom we slew, some wrapping their wounds which they had of us, and all yet remembering the manhood of this our host, and the miserable flight and calamity of theirs. This know also, Gobryas: that a great multitude endued with boldness be very stout and fierce in hearts. The same being in fear, the more they be, the fearfuller and more amazed be the minds, for of many and evil rumours, of many and evil chances, their fear augmenteth; likewise of many cowardly-hearted and amazed men, it is increased. Therefore for the vehemency° of it, it is hard for it to be extinguished with words of a captain or for him to work courage, marching against his enemies, or by recoiling to stir up their manhood; and the more that a man exhorteth them to be bold, the more in peril they think they are. Therefore let us thoroughly debate this matter as it is. For if hereafter the victories in chivalrous affairs[17] shall be theirs which may number most men, then you do not fear for us without a cause. And we at this time be in danger. But if as hereto before, so now also the battles shall be tried by the good fighters, you may be bold and not be deceived yourself. For you shall (God being our help) find more among us that will fight than among them. Therefore, be more bold. And furthermore consider this with yourself: our enemies be very much fewer than they were before we gave them their overthrow, very much fewer than when they fled from us. But we be more now after our victory and stronger through your access. Do not, therefore, dishonour yourselves being now with us, for with conquerors, Gobryas, ye know that even they that hang on be of bold heart to follow. Nor you may not be ignorant of this: that it is expedient that our enemies should now behold us. And ye know well that we can seem no way so terrible to them as to go against them. Therefore my sentence being thus notified, lead us the straight way to Babylon.' So they went on, and came the fourth day to Gobryas his country's end.[18] Being in his enemy's land, he took and appointed to be in array about him both footmen and men of arms, so many as he thought good. The other horsemen he willed to range abroad, charging them to kill so many as did wear harness, the other to bring to him with all the cattle they could take. He commanded also the Persians to range with them. And many came again, thrown of[f] their horses, many bringing great prey.[19] When the prey was brought in, assembling the princes of the Medes and Hyrcanians and the honourable Persians, he said thus:

'Gobryas, loving friends, hath entertained us all after most honourable fashion. Therefore if we, appointing God his part and the residue of the army sufficient, would give him the whole prey we should do very well, showing ourselves so shortly that we in doing pleasures do our most endeavour to surmount them that have done us the same.' When they all heard this, they all praised him, they all extolled him, and one said thus: 'We all (O Cyrus) will do thus, for Gobryas (as I think) did repute us as beggars because we came not full of money and because we drink not in golden cups. But if we do thus, he shall know that men may be liberal without gold.'[20] 'Go therefore' (said Cyrus), 'giving the sages that [which] is due to God, and choosing out necessaries for

---

[17] chivalrous affairs] Translating τὰ πολεμικὰ ἔργα (tà polemikà érga); Holland has 'in the question of warre and martiall exploits' ([O4]v).
[18] his country's end] i.e. to the limits of Gobryas's lands.
[19] great prey] The hunting imagery recalls Persian belief in hunting as training for military campaigning.
[20] liberal without gold] Persian hardiness and poverty are again contrasted with wealth and luxury and its uses, and the potential for virtue and generosity even in such moderation and frugality is emphasised.

the army that as remaineth, call Gobryas and give it him.' So they taking that was meet gave the other to Gobryas, then marched toward Babylon itself, being in array as though the field were pight°. And when of the contrary part, the Assyrians came not forth, Cyrus commanded Gobryas to ride and say, if the king will come forth in defence of the country that he would fight with him; if not to defend his country, or else it must forcibly give place to the conquerors. Gobryas, rode thither where as he might be most safe, uttered the same. The king sent him this answer: 'Thy Lord sayeth (O Gobryas) that it repenteth him not because he hath slain thy son but because he hath not slain thee also. But if ye will needs fight, come thirty days' hence, for now I have no leisure, being about purveyance for the same.' To whom Gobryas said: 'I pray God this repentance never leave thee for it is manifest that I do vex thee, seeing thou art troubled with repentance.'

Then Gobryas showed the Assyrian's answer, which, being heard, Cyrus withdrew his army and, calling Gobryas, said: 'Did not you tell me that he whom the Assyrian did geld would, as ye thought, take our part?' 'I know well he will', said he, 'for we have many times very freely devised together.' 'Then', said Cyrus, 'seeing you think it for the best, go unto him and first so do as ye know he will show you; then after more familiarity, if ye perceive he will be our friend, devise how he may be our covert friend, for no man doth so much avail his friend in war as if he be counted his enemy, nor none doth so much endamage his enemy as he that is counted his friend.' 'Truly', said Gobryas, 'I know that Gadatas would give largely to do this present king of Assyria some great displeasure.' 'Tell me' (said Cyrus), 'do you think that the captain of the fortress which, you say, was built both for the Hyrcanians and Sacians as a defence of the country in all war, will suffice this eunuch to come with his power to the fortress?' 'Yea certainly', said Gobryas, 'if he, unsuspected as he is now, did come unto him.' 'Should he not', said Cyrus, 'be most unsuspect,[21] if I did besiege his holds°, as though I would take them, and he to make resistance as much as he might, and I to take some of ours, to send as it were messengers from me to them which ye say be enemies to the Assyrian? And the captives should say that they were going to the army to fetch ladders to scale the castle, which the eunuch hearing, should feign°[22] to be the cause of his coming to reveal these things.' 'I know well', said Gobryas, 'that if the matter be thus handled, that he will be ready and desire him to remain there till you be passed.' 'Think not then', said Cyrus, 'that being once come, he might cause us to get the castle?' 'Yes, surely' (said Gobryas), 'he going about the same within and you

---

[21] most unsuspect] By now the centrality of deceptions and performance of generosity to Cyrus's military strategy is familiar to readers.
[22] feign] Despite its recurrence in Cyrus's stratagems, the term 'feign' occurs only twice in the text.

sharply assaying it without.' 'Go your way then' (said he), 'and in declaring these things, do what ye can that he may be prest. And as for assurance, utter you nor declare no more to him than you have received of us.'

Thus Gobryas went forth. The eunuch was glad to see him, granting to all things, faithfully promising to do his endeavour. When that Gobryas had reported that the eunuch unfeignedly had taken in hand all that Cyrus willed, the day following he did make assault. Gadatas did resist; the ground which Cyrus took was so much as Gadatas suffered. The messengers which Cyrus sent being tofore instructed whither to go, Gadatas suffered some of them to escape to get ordnance° and fetch scaling ladders. They whom he took were examined before many other. When they had showed the cause of their coming, he straight way being well appointed went that night as it were to reveal the same. Finally being credited, he entered the castle as an aider, and the while with the captain made such preparation as he could. When Cyrus was come, with the help of them that were captives, he took the castle. This done, Gadatas the eunuch, staying[23] out of hand all things within, came forth to Cyrus and doing his homage according to the law, said thus: 'Rejoice, noble Cyrus, even so I do truly', quoth he, 'for you with God do not only command me but also compel me to rejoice. And this ye shall know for certain: that I do much esteem to leave this castle as an help to my confederate friends.' 'The Assyrian as it appeareth, Gadatas, hath bereft your getting of children, but he cannot bereave your getting of friends. For know ye well that by this feat you have made us so your friends that we will to our power do our parts to be no less your assured friends than if you had sons and nephews natural.' Thus he spake. The Hyrcanian straight rejoicing at this fact, came to Cyrus and, taking him by the right hand, said: 'O noble Cyrus, thou great comfort to thy friends, how much thank makest thou me to owe to God that hath allied me with thee.' 'Go therefore', said Cyrus, 'and taking the castle which you now do so rejoice to be mine, so appoint it that it may be most seemly for your friends and other confederates, most of all to this Gadatas which hath taken and yield[ed] it to us.' 'What', said the Hyrcanian 'shall I when the Caducians, Sacians and my countrymen come, call him that we all may use common consultation of matters needful and of the good governance of the castle?'[24] Cyrus assented he should so do. And they being assembled which should have to do with the castle did devise by common assent for the guard of it, that it might be no less commodious than friendful unto them, and an hold of resistance against the Assyrians.

This being done, the Caducians, Sacians and Hyrcanians went on this warfare

---

[23] staying] i.e. settling (things within the fort).
[24] of the castle] i.e. if the Caducians etc. arrive, shall I call them in too to consult on the use of the fortress?

more in number and lustier in courage. And then of the Caducians were assembled twenty thousand footmen and four thousand horsemen, the Sacians ten thousand archers on foot and two thousand archers on horseback. The Hyrcanians sent more, so many footmen as they could, and increased their two thousand for tofore many horsemen were left at home because the Caducians and Sacians were at debate with the Assyrians, all the time that Cyrus sat about the provision of the castle. The inhabitants of the Assyrians adjoining to those places, many brought their horses, many delivered their harness, fearing their borderers on every side.[25] Then came Gadatas, showing Cyrus that messengers were come, declaring unto him that the Assyrian, hearing of the loss of this castle and being grieved with it, was prepared to invade his country. 'Therefore, Cyrus, if you will suffer me, I will do the best I can to save my forts, for of other things I do not greatly pass.' Cyrus said, 'If you do depart now, when shall you be at home?' Gadatas answered, 'The third day I shall sup in my country'. 'And do you think , said he, to find the Assyrian there?' 'Yea, I know surely', quoth he, 'for he will make haste so long as you seem to come so far off.' 'In what time', said Cyrus, 'might I be there with mine army?' To this Gadatas answered: 'You have now (O lord) a great army and you cannot get to my land in less than six or seven days.' 'Then go you with all speed', said Cyrus, 'and I shall come as I may.' So Gadatas departed. Cyrus then assembling all the princes of his confederates who were present at that time very many noble and martial men, said thus:

The Oration of Cyrus

'Friends confederates, Gadatas hath done feats which we all ought much to esteem, and that before he did any pleasure showed him of us. And now the Assyrian (as it is reported) invadeth his land, wherefore it is manifest that he will be avenged of him because he thinketh he hath sustained great displeasure by him. And peradventure he thinketh after this sort that if such as make defection to us be not hindered by him, and they that be with him be so destroyed of us, that shortly none will abide with him. Therefore, friends, I think it shall be a noble act if we cheerfully do aid Gadatas, being so beneficial a man to us, doing but right in requiting thank. And truly as I think, we shall do a feat profitable for ourselves: for if it be apparent to all men that we do intend nothing more than to subdue and displease them which do us hurt, and to exceed in doing well that that do us good, it is like that by this means many will desire to be our friends and none court to be our enemies. But if we seem to forget Gadatas, how can we (I pray you) by other mean allure men to do us good? How can we be bold to praise ourselves? How can any of us look Gadatas in the face if we, being so many, be overcome in doing well of one man being in such case?' Thus said he. Every man accorded that this thing should be done.

[25] inhabitants] 'inhabitance' in both 26066 and 26067.

'Go to then' (said Cyrus), 'seeing you all assent. And let every man now leave for our beasts and carriage such as be most meet to go with the same. Gobryas shall be captain and have the conveying of them, for he both is expert in the way and strong for other occasions. We will set forward with the best both of our horse and men, having victual for three days. The less and homelier we provide now, the pleasanter shall we dine, sup and sleep hereafter. Now, then, let us march forward: you Chrysantas, first take them that be harnessed with breastplates and lead the way which is plain and broad, placing all the centurions in the front. Let every crew follow you, one after another, for being thick together we shall go both more speedily and the more surely. Therefore I will that the curet men shall lead the way because they being the slowest part of the army, and the slowest going before, the lighter must needs easily follow. But when the lighter leadeth the way in the night, it is not to be marvelled, though the army be disparpled°; the same, disparpled, be soon put to flight. After these, Artabasus shall guide the targetmen and archers of the Persians. Next them Adramas the Mede the Median footmen, then Thatamas[26] the Caducians, and all these shall so order that the centurions may be in the front, the targetmen on the right side, the archers on the left, after a quadrat[27] battle. And thus going, they shall be the readier to do their feats. After them all the carriage shall follow, whose captains shall so oversee them all that all things be in the order before they rest, and that early in the morning they with their carriage be ready in due order that they may follow in array. After these carriage, the Persian horsemen shall follow, having likewise the captains of the horsemen in the front. And every captain of horsemen shall lead his troop by itself as the captains of the footmen, then Rambacas the Median with his own horsemen likewise; after you, Tigranes with your men of arms and so forth, all other captains of horsemen with such as ye came to us, with the same set forth. Last of all, according to their coming, the Caducians shall go: you Alceuna leading them, see that you at this time be last of all and that none be behind your horsemen. And remember that you all go with silence, both captains and other sober men, for in the night all must be perceived and wrought rather by ear than by eye. And disarray in the night is more troublous and harder to stay than in the day. Therefore silence must be used and order must be kept. And the watchers of the night when we shall rise by night must be both short and many,[28] that none in the watch, the lack of sleep being long, be hurt in the way. Therefore the hour of departure must be warned

---

[26] Thatamas] Barker's names are somewhat confused, and he misses some of the leaders and groups catalogued in this passage (e.g. Embas with the Armenians and Artuchas with the Hyrcanians). Holland has (more accurately) Artabasus lead the Persians, Andramias the Medes, Embas the Armenians, Artuchas the Hyrcanians, Thambradas the Sacians and Damatas the Caducians. 'Thatamas' is probably a garbling of Thambradas.
[27] quadrat] Named for a square plate with graduated sides.
[28] short and many] The watches should be short and many, not the watchers themselves, as this construction implies.

with a horn. Thus having every man that is necessary be present at the way that goeth to Babylon, he that marcheth must always follow straight at the tail.'

After this every man went to his tent, talking by the way thus together: what a memory hath Cyrus? How many hath he set in order? How many commanded by name?[29] Cyrus did this through great diligence: for it seemed very marvellous to him if artificers° should know the names of every instrument pertaining to their occupation and a physician know the names and tools of medicines which he used, that a captain should be so dull as to have no knowledge of the names of his inferiors whom he must use as instruments when he will prevent anything, when he will eschew°, when he will encourage, and when he will affray.[30] And when he will set forth any man, he thought it a seemly thing to call him by his name. He was also in this opinion, that they which supposed they were known of their chief captain should the rather desire to be seen doing well, and the more refrain to be seen doing evil. It seemed also a foolish thing unto him if he would have anything done in the army, to command it as some masters command in their families: 'let one go fetch water!'; 'let another go rive° wood!'. For he thought if they were so commanded every man would look other in the face, no man doing that was commanded, every man being in fault, and no man ashamed of it, none fearing the displeasure for it because it was generally every man's fault. Therefore he called by name whom he commanded to do anything. And this was Cyrus's opinion in these matters.

The soldiers when they had supped, appointed watches, and prepared every thing accordingly, they went to rest, and about midnight, warning was given with an horn. Cyrus willing Chrysantas to tarry in the way before he setteth forth of the army, he with his ministers went forth, shortly after Chrysantas was present with the curet men to whom, when Cyrus had appointed lodesmen°, he commanded him to set forth quietly till one should come and show him that all were in the way. He, standing in the way, did set forth in order him that came well; to him that slacked he sent to call him forth. When they were all in the way, he sent horsemen to Chrysantas, to show him that all were ready in the way. Then he did set forth faster, he himself riding quietly to the former

---

[29] by name] Popular recountings of Cyrus's marvellous memory for his soldiers' names (although Xenophon only reports that he remembers the names of the leaders of the various troops and allies he commands) earned him a reputation as an exemplar of mnemonic skill, although Xenophon's implication is primarily one of Cyrus's care for his 'friends', the instruments of his empire-building, as the subsequent analogies imply. See also note 51 (p. 98).

[30] when he will affray] J. K. Anderson notes that Xenophon himself cleaves to this practice in the *Anabasis*, often calling on or praising his soldiers by name. Xenophon (London: Duckworth, 1974), p. 127.

part did behold the [a]rray, and whom he saw going in good array and without noise to them he would ride and demand what they were, which thing being known, he would praise them. If he saw any disordered, the cause thereof being considered, he would labour to appease their tumult. One thing only was left in his night's purveyance, that before the whole army he did send few expedite° footmen, which should both see Chrysantas and he them, and give good ear if by any other mean they could perceive anything, they should signify that same to Chrysantas in meet season. And one there was chief and governor which did order them and show what was meet, and without rebuke what was not so. Thus by night he went on. The day being come, because the Caducian footmen came last, he left with them the horsemen of the same that they should not be destitute of men and of arms. The other he commanded to go to the vaward, because his enemies were in the front, that if any should come against him, he being strong and in array might couple with them, and if any flee, they might the more speedily chase the same. For he had always in array, some to chase if need were, some to remain with him, never suffering the whole array to be broken. Thus Cyrus led forth his host, himself not using always one place but riding from place as the battle required, espying and considering what ought to be done. Thus Cyrus's army marched forth.

One of Gadatas's horsemen, a man of power, seeing that he had forsaken the Assyrian, thought if Gadatas might be destroyed that he should have all his land. He therefore sent one of his trusty servants to the Assyrian, commanding him that went if he found the Assyrian army in Gadatas's land, he should declare unto the king that if he would lay in ambushment he might take Gadatas and all his company, commanding him also to show plainly what power Gadatas had, and that Cyrus did not follow, declaring also which way he should come, charging his servants within to yield to the king his castle with all his goods which he had in Gadatas's land, saying also that he would come himself after he had slain Gadatas if he could do it; if not, from henceforth he would be on the king's part. He that was appointed to this thing, riding post, came shortly to the king, declared the cause of his coming. Which being heard, he straight way took the castle, and having many horsemen and chariots, laid ambushment thick in every village. Gadatas being nigh these villages sent certain spies afore; the king perceiving that espies were coming, commanded two of the chariots and a few horsemen to flee, as though they were but few and afraid. The espies, seeing this, fell to chasing, making a token to Gadatas. He being deceived pursued with all his power. The Assyrians perceiving that Gadatas might be taken, came straight forth of ambushment. Gadatas's company, perceiving that, fled; the other pursued. He that privily watched Gadatas struck him, but he missed and gave him no deadly stripe, for he wounded him in the shoulder. That done, he rode till he came among the chasers. Being known what he was, and joining with the king, he spurred his horse and freely fell to the chase. Then such were taken of the light horsemen which had but slow horses and Gadatas's horsemen were in danger all, being tired with their long journey. But when they saw Cyrus coming with his army, a man may think that they were as glad and joyous as it were from a storm to arrive at an haven. Cyrus at the first sight marvelled. But perceiving the matter, and his enemies all making against him, he led his army in order against them, which his enemies perceiving recoiled and fled. Cyrus, seeing that, commanded them that were appointed, to follow the chase. He with the residue went on, as he thought good. Then chariots were taken, some their drivers being overthrown, some in the return, some by other means, some being enclosed of the horsemen which slew very many and him that hurt Gadatas. The Assyrian footmen that besieged Gadatas's castle, being many, some fled into the castle that had forsaken Gadatas, some got away afore to a certain city of Assyria, whither the king was also fled, with his chariots and horsemen.

Cyrus when this was done entered Gadatas's land and appointing what should be done with things taken, went straight to see how Gadatas did with his wound. As he was going, Gadatas, his wound dressed and bound up, met with him, whom Cyrus seeing was glad, and said: 'I was coming to see how ye did.' 'And I' (said Gadatas), 'was coming to behold and see your visage again which hath such a mind that, having no need of me, I know well, neither making me promise, have done thus for me, never receiving any private pleasures at my hand. But because I seemed to you to further my friends, you have so lovingly holpen me, for now by myself I was perished, but by you I am saved. I swear by the gods immortal (O Cyrus) if I were as I was once and had gotten children, I think I should have never have had such a child as you have been to me. For I know many other children and this king of Assyria have wrought his father more grief than he is able now to do you.' Cyrus said to him: 'Gadatas, yourself being a great marvel, do now marvel at me.' 'O', quoth Gadatas, 'what meaneth it that so many Persians, so many Medes, so many Hyrcanians, and all the Armenians, Sacas and Caducians being present, study to do you pleasure?' Then Gadatas thus prayed, 'O Jupiter, o gods all, grant these men all weal and plenty, and specially him which is cause that they be such. And that we may reward them (O Cyrus) whom you praise, take gently these gifts that I am able to give you.' And so brought forth very many, both (if he would) that he might make sacrifice and also to reward the whole army worthily, for this good feat and happy chance.

The Caducian, being governor to the rearward, not being at the chase and being desirous to do some notable feat, making no man of counsel, not showing anything to Cyrus, did range the country toward Babylon. His horsemen being

The Fifth Book   191

scattered, and the king of Assyria coming from that city whither he before fled, met with them having his army well appointed, and perceiving, set upon them, and slew the prince of the Caducians and many other, taking many horses and defeated them of the prey which they do drove.[31] And the Assyrian, chasing so far as he might with surety, returned. The foremost of the Caducians were saved at the camp a little before night.[32] Cyrus, hearing the thing, met with the Caducians; whom he was wounded, he comforted, and sent to be cured as he had been Gadatas, and the other to be received into the tents, being careful that they should have all necessaries, taking the other honourable men of Persia to be jointly overseers to the same. For good men in such things be willing to take pains. And then Cyrus was grieved and it did evidently appear for when the time came that other went to supper, he still tarried with his ministers and surgeons, and with his will leaving no man uncured, but either presently saw the doing himself or if he could not in tend[33] it, every many might see that he did send other to cure them.[34] And so at that time they went to rest. By the break of the day, warning given to the captains to be assembled, he said thus.

The Oration of Cyrus

'Friends and confederates, it is an human thing that that is chanced. For men to err as men, I think it no marvel. Yet it is seeming that we of this thing that is chanced enjoy some commodity: that is to learn never to disparple from the whole power, it being weaker than our enemies yet. I do not speak thus, as though a man might not sometime, the case so requiring, go forth with less power than the Caducian now did. For though a man deviseth with him that is able to help, and do set forth, yet he may be deceived. It may chance him that tarryeth to deceive his enemies, to change his way from them that be already gone. There may be other things to work our adversary's trouble, and our friend's surety, and so be separate that he shall not depart but shall augment his strength.[35] But he truly that departeth, making no man privy, he doth not differ from him that adventureth alone. But for this, God willing, we will be avenged of our adversaries, or it be long;[36] for when ye have made a short dinner, I will

---

[31] do drove] An early use of the verb 'to drove' (to herd animals, here the spoils of the earlier victory), though the tense is poorly handled.
[32] before night] The rest of the Caducians reached camp — and safety — before night. Holland is clearer: 'As for the formost of the Cadusians, they recovered the Campe by the shutting in of the evening and so escaped safe' (sig. Q1).
[33] in tend] i.e. achieve (the curing of some soldier).
[34] to cure them] Highlights Cyrus's ministering care and clemency even to foolish allies who took up an unsanctioned independent action and failed.
[35] augment his strength] i.e. there are ways of having a break-off party from the main army work to your advantage.
[36] or it be long] i.e. 'ere' it be long. A mistake in both 26066 and 26067, corrected by Holland (sig. Q1v).

bring ye where the deed was done and we shall both bury the dead and also show to our enemies that where they think they have overcome, there (God willing) other shall overcome them and shall have no great lust to behold that place where they have slain our friends. If they will not match with us, we will burn their towns and waste their countries that, beholding what they have done to us, they shall not rejoice but beholding their own displeasure they shall be sad. Therefore all other go to dinner; you, Caducians, first choose you a prince, according to your law, which with God his help and ours may see unto you in all your lacks. And when you have dined, send your elect to me.' They did so. Cyrus after he had led forth his army, did appoint him that was elected of the Caducians to his crew, commanding him to lead the same next him, 'that we' (quoth he), 'may encourage our men'. Thus they went forth and coming to the place, they buried the Caducians and wasted the land.

This being done and getting much victual of their enemy's country, they marched to Gadatas's land. And considering that they which did yield unto him inhabiting nigh Babylon should suffer displeasure if he were not present, he commanded all the prisoners that he delivered to say unto the Assyrian (and sent an herald to the same) that he was ready to suffer his husbandmen to occupy the earth, doing them no harm, if he likewise would suffer the tillmen of them which had yielded to him to occupy their ground also. 'And although you can let°, yet shall you let but few. For it is a small country that is given over to me, but I may suffer much of your ground to be occupied; and as for reaping of the fruit, if it be war, he shall reap it that hath the victory. If it be peace, it is plain it shall be yours, for if any of my soldiers ariseth against you, or any of yours against me, we both shall be able to punish the same.' Thus instructing the herald, he sent him forth. The Assyrians hearing these things did the best they could to persuade the king to accord to this request, because very little should be void of war.[37] And the Assyrian, whether it were through the persuasion of his countrymen or that he was desirous, he assented to it, and these conditions were made that the husbandmen should have peace, and the soldiers war. This Cyrus brought to pass concerning tillage. And as for pasture of cattle, he commanded his friends, if they would, to use and lay them in their dominions still. They brought preys from their enemies, so much as they could, that the warfare might be the sweeter to their confederates. For the perils is no less without receiving of necessary victual.[38] And the sustenance taken of their enemies seemed to make the labours of war lighter.

---

[37] void of war] i.e. that there should be little war in those lands. (Holland: 'and to leave as little warre behind as might be' (sig. Q2).)
[38] necessary victual] i.e. Cyrus still allowed his soldiers to take as prey/booty the enemy's cattle, as well as those out grazing.

The Fifth Book 193

Cyrus being appointed to set forward, Gadatas came and brought many other and diverse gifts, as it was meet, from a noble place.³⁹ He brought also many horses which he took from his horsemen whom he suspected of treason. When he was nigh, he said thus: 'I have brought ye (Cyrus) these things that you at this present may bestow them as ye think good. And count' (quoth he), 'that all that ever I had beside to be yours. For I neither have nor shall have of my body begotten to whom I may leave mine inheritance. But with me, all my stock and name must decay. And I take God to witness (Cyrus) which see and hear all things, that I have neither done ne said any wrong or evil wherefore I should so be served.' And this speaking, he bewailed his fortune and could no more speak. Which things being heard, Cyrus, having pity of his distress, said thus: 'I receive your horses, whereby I shall do you pleasure, giving them to your more assured [men] than they which, as it seemeth, before had them, and I shortly shall supply the Persian horsemen to the number of ten thousand, which thing I have long coveted. Your other treasure take and keep it yourself, for it might else be that I in the requital should be inferior to you. And if at our departure you should give more to men than you receive of me, by the gods, I could not but be ashamed.' Then Gadatas said: 'Truly I believe you in this thing, for I see your gentle nature. Therefore I am ready to keep them. For so long as we were in friendship with the Assyrian, my father his possession was most princely, the great city Babylon being so nigh. And what commodity might redound of so noble a city, that did we enjoy, and what encumbrance, we departing home again did not feel of them. But now that we be at discord, it is evident when you be departed that all my friends and family shall be in danger of deceit and, as I can perceive, we shall lead a pensive life, having our enemies so nigh, and seeing them stronger than ourselves. And peradventure some man will say, "why did ye not consider so much before ye made defection°?" Because, Cyrus, my mind through despite done me and anger in me could never consider what was best for me. But I always was, as it were, with child⁴⁰ after this sort: shall I not be revenged on him which is enemy both to God and man, which mortally hateth not only if a man do him displeasure but if he suspect any man to be better than himself? He therefore, I think, being bad, useth their help that be much worse than he, for if there be any that appeareth better than he, be you of good cheer, Cyrus, ye shall not need to fight with any good man, for he is able to provide for this, and take the pain to kill him that is of more price. This is it that grieveth me, and I dare affirm among the evil, he far exceedeth.' Cyrus hearing him thought he spake matter worthy to be weighed, and therefore said: 'Will ye not

---

³⁹ a noble place] This may be a compositorial error for 'palace', though Holland translates it 'having a large habitation, and the same well stored' (sig. Q2).
⁴⁰ as it were, with child] Barker faithfully imitates the image of pregnancy in the Greek too. Holland has 'and ever was with child of these fansies' (sig. Q2v).

then, Gadatas, fortify your holds with strong garrisons, that you may use the same safely when ye repair to them yourself, and going this expedition with us may bring to pass, if God be with us, as he now is, that he shall fear you and not you him? And in as much as ye delight to see your own, take such with you with whose company ye delight. And go forth with me and you shall do me, as I think, much pleasure, and I will do for you the best I may.' Gadatas hearing this sighed and said: 'may I prepare all things before you depart? For I' (said he), 'would have my mother with me.' 'You may prepare', said Cyrus, 'and I will abide on you till ye say that all is well.' Then Gadatas, departing with Cyrus's help, did guard his forts which were strong, furnishing them with all things wherewith great manors may be inhabited, and took with him both his faithful friends in whom he delighted and also many whom he distrusted, compelling them to lead their wives and sisters, being yoked, that by them he might detail them.

Cyrus having Gadatas and his retinue, which should both declare the way, waters, forage and victual, that he might always camp in plentiful places, marched forth. And so going till he espied the city of Babylon, and perceiving there was a way that led to the very wall, he called Gobryas and Gadatas, asking them if there were any other way which did not lead so nigh the wall. Gobryas answered: 'Sir, there be many ways. But I thought now you would have gone nigh to the city that you might show them your army, which is now both great and goodly, seeing that when you had fewer you came to the wall and they did see us to be not many. And though the king be now prepared, as he said to you he would be ready to fight, yet I know if he saw your power, he would think himself still unprepared.' Cyrus to this thing answered: 'I think you marvel, Gobryas, that what time as I having much less power yet vaunced even to the city wall, why now having more power I do not march to the same. But marvel not, for it is not all one to march straight and to march about. For all men march straight which, being well appointed, think it best to fight. They march about which, being forecast,[41] consider how they may march most safely, not most shortly. For we must needs compass by reason of our long going, chariots and other very much carriage contained in our army. These things must be closed with harness men and none of our carriage to appear to our enemies void of harness, wherefore going after this sort, it must needs follow that the strong shall encounter with the weak and feeble. Therefore, if they of the city would rush[42] out by throngs and join with us, they should more fiercely encounter with us, passing by, and where men go in length, there the help continueth the

---

[41] forecast] i.e. spotted in advance by the enemy
[42] rush] Both 26066 and 26067 have 'thrushe', mistakenly; Holland has 'sallie forth thicke out of the City and charge us' (sig. [Q3]).

longer. But being nigh, all they of the city might easily assail us and retreat when they list. But if we march, being no further distant than they may see us, and keep the same length that we now do, they shall see our multitude because of the glistering,[43] all our whole company shall seem more terrible. And if they come orderly against us, thus marching, espying them far off, we shall not be taken tardy but rather, good friends, they shall attempt nothing if they be enforced to range far from their walls except they think they be more puissant than will we, for to depart far is full of fear.' When he had said thus, he seemed to them that were present to say well. Therefore Gobryas did lead, as he commanded, the army thus passing by the city he retired back to strengthen it that was behind. When he had so travelled a certain space, he came to the borders of the Assyrians and Medians, from whence he marched where as were three castles of the Assyrians and assailing one, being the weakest, he took by force. The other two Cyrus affraying and Gadatas persuading, the captains did yield. This being done, he sent to Cyaxares requesting him to come to the army that he might devise with him concerning the keeping of the castles that he had taken, and that he should see his host and be a counsellor in other things as should be thought meet to be done, 'and say if it be his pleasure that I will come to him, there to encamp'.

The messenger went to show him these things. Cyrus commanded Gadatas to deck very gorgeously the Assyrian tent which the Medes had selected for Cyaxares, and beside all other ornaments to bring the women into the parlour of the tent, and with them the women musicians which were chosen for Cyaxares. And they did as they were commanded. He that was sent to Cyaxares, after he had declared his message, Cyaxares hearing him thought it better that the army should remain in the borders (for the Persians were come which Cyrus sent for, being in number forty thousand archers and targetmen), perceiving that they also did hurt the Median land, he thought it better rather to be rid of these than to receive a new multitude. He that conducted the Persian army, demanding of Cyaxares according to Cyrus his epistle if he had any need of the army, who denying, the same day hearing that Cyrus was at hand, went and led the host to him. Cyaxares the day following, with the residue of the Median horsemen, went forth. When Cyrus heard that he was coming, taking the Persian horsemen (which were many) all the Medians, Armenians, Hyrcanians and other his confederates being best horsed and cleanest armed, went to meet and show Cyaxares his power. Cyaxares, seeing so many goodly and brave men accompany Cyrus and so few (and them very base) waiting upon him, he thought it should be much dishonour to him and was very pensive. Cyrus alighting of his horse and coming to kiss him, as the manner was, Cyaxares alighted of his horse but turned his back and would not kiss him but wept that all men saw it.

---

[43] glistering] See the light 'glistering' on Cyrus at p. 158, indicating the gods' favour.

Then Cyrus commanding all other to stand back and stir not, taking his uncle by the hand and leading him out of the way under palm trees, commanding the ground to be covered with carpets, and caused him to lie, and, sitting with him, said thus: 'Tell me on God his [be]half, uncle, why are ye angry with me and what it is that you with so displeasant countenance take so grievously?' Cyaxares answered thus: 'Because, Cyrus, I am reputed by the ancient memory of all men to be lineally descended of old progenitors kings, and that being a king his son and taken as a king myself and now considering how vile and base I am appointed, and with how brave a company both of my retinue and with other power you be with honours present. It would, I think, have grieved a man thus to have been served of his enemies, but so to be entreated of them that have least cause, it is (God wot) a piercing pain. I had rather ten times be buried quick° in the earth than to sustain such villainy, and be louted° and laughed at of mine own servants. I know this, that you are not only of more power than I but that my servants also which come to meet me be more mighty than myself, and so appointed that they may do me more hurt than I can do them.' Which words speaking, he wept much more than he did before, in so much that he enforced Cyrus to fill his eyes with tears. Staying therefore a while, Cyrus said thus: 'Neither do you speak these things truly (O uncle) nor take them rightly, if ye think that in my presence the Medes be appointed as they were able to do you any displeasure. I marvel not though you be angry and in fear. But whether you be rightly or unrightly displeased with them, I will pass over. For I know if I should excuse them, ye would take it grievously. And I think it a great err° that a man in power be offended with all his subjects at once, for he must needs in fearing many be hated of many. And because he is in indignation with all, he causeth all to be of one mind. For the which cause be you assured, I would not send you your men till I came myself, fearing lest something might chance through this anger that should repent us all. But of these things, I being present and God willing, you be clear out from all danger. But whereas ye think that ye be unjustly handled of my part, it grieveth me very much that I, employing my pains to the uttermost part of my power to do my friends most pleasure, should seem to work the contrary. But let us not thus accuse one another but try if we can what mine offence is, and I will avouch that case which in friendship is most narrowly required. And if I be thought to have done evil, I will confess the wrong. But if it shall appear that I have done no fault, nor intended the same, you must confess that ye have had no wrong at my hand. And if it shall be evident that I have done you good, and have been willing with all my power to the same, shall I not seem to you to be worthy rather praise than to be accused?' 'It is but right.' 'Let us then', said Cyrus, 'examine every thing particularly that I have done, and so it shall plainly appear which is well, which evil. And we will begin from the first original, if you think it good.

'When you understood that many enemies were assembled, and they ready to invade you and your land, ye sent straight to the common council of Persia requiring aid, and to me privately to labour to be captain if any Persians should be sent. I was persuaded with your words and came, bringing you men to my power, both many and very meet.' 'It is true', said he. 'Then show me first', quoth he, 'whether in this thing you do take any displeasure by me, or rather friendship?' 'It is manifest', said Cyaxares, 'that by these I have had pleasure.' 'Then', quoth he, 'when our enemies came and you must needs match with them, did you in that thing perceive me either eschewing labour or fearing peril?' 'No surely at all', said he. 'When the victory with God his help was ours and our enemies were fled, did not I desire you that we should with common force pursue them and with common courage avenge them, that if good or harm did chance it might be commonly borne? In these things can you accuse me of any avarice?' At which words Cyaxares held his peace. Cyrus saying unto him again: 'Seeing in this thing you had rather keep silence than make answer, yet show me if ye thought yourself to have injury when as you thinking it dangerous to follow the chase of our enemies, and I, not suffering you to be in any part of that danger, desired you to send some of your horsemen. And if in this request I did you wrong, in especiall[y] doing you the pleasure of a just confederate, I would ye would declare the same.' And when Cyaxares said nothing to this, Cyrus said: 'Seeing it is not your pleasure to answer, show ye now wherein I have done you displeasure. When you did answer me that perceiving the Medians to be in joy, ye would not cease that joy and enforce them to any more danger, if that I seem to have done you displeasure, because not passing of your anger,[44] I did require eftsoons that thing which I knew you might easily grant me, and as easily commanded the Medians to it, for I requested you to give me him that would willingly follow me, which thing being obtained of you, my travail was to persuade them. Then I went and persuaded them. When I had so done, I took them with me, you being well contented. If ye think this worthy to be accused, nothing that you give us and receive, as it appeareth, shall want accusement. Well, we thus marched forth. When we were gone, what feat did we that is not evident? Did we not take our adversary's camp? Be not many of them dead that came against us? Be not they that be alive bereft, many their horses, many their harness, yea and their money, which tofore spoiled and bare away your goods? Do you not see now, your friends having and bringing the same, part for you and part for them that be under you? And that that is the most noble and high feat, ye see your land augmented and your enemies impoverished, ye see their fortress taken, ye see yours which before were in your adversary's possession, to be contrary wise now returned to you. If any of these things be good or if any be evil, I being glad to learn, I know not how to say, yet I would be glad to hear.'

---

[44] passing of your anger] i.e. not exceeding your anger.

This being spoken, Cyrus ceased. Cyaxares made this answer.

'If these things, Cyrus, that you have done be well done, I know not what I ought to say, for ye know well that these good things be of such sort that as the more they appear to be, so much the more they do aggrieve me; for I had rather you had augmented your own land by my strength than see mine so enlarged of you. These things to you the doer be honourable, but to me, the very same bring dishonour. And as for money, I think I give you more freely than I take of you that you have given me, for being enriched with them by you, I perceive the rather how I am made the poorer.[45] And if I did perceive my subjects to have had a little injury at your hand, it should, I think, grieve me less than it do now, to perceive that they have received great pleasure by you.[46] If you think that I unjustly do weigh these things, turn them all from me to you. And then consider what they seem to you. If a man should so handle your hounds which you keep for yourself and your friends' pleasure that they be made more obedient to him than to you, should he delight you with such service? If this seemeth but a trifling thing to you, yet consider this: if a man should so frame your servants, whom you keep to do you service and attend upon your body, that they had rather be his than yours, would you give him any thanks for his beneficence? Let us come to that which men do most love and embrace as their chief propriety. What if a man should so attend on your wife that he could make her more in love with him than with you, would you thank him for this attendance? I think you should have great cause. But this I know well, that he that did thus should, of all other, do you most injury. And to speak a thing most like to my anguish, if a man would so handle these Persians that you have brought that they had rather obey him than you, would ye count him your friend? I think not, but rather your more enemy than if he had slain many of them. If you should lovingly thus say to any of your friends, go and take of mine all that would go, and he hearing, take all that ever he could, he being enriched with your goods, you not having sufficient for your need, could you think him an unreprovable friend? So Cyrus (I think) that I now have sustained though not the very same, yet the like by you. Yet truth it is that you say, that I granting you them that were willing, went forth with my power, leaving me alone.[47] And what so ever ye have now taken with my power that ye bring to me and do enlarge my land with my power, I being no cause of those commodities seem to show myself as it were a woman, you doing pleasures both to other men and also

---

[45] made the poorer] Cyaxares challenges Cyrus's policy, noting that financial debt and social or political debt are different entities with different contractual and political implications.

[46] great pleasure by you] See the similar argument made by the Armenian king's father about Tigranes and his sophist friend stealing his affection away from his father, at p. 139.

[47] alone] i.e. you went forth leaving me alone, after I granted you those men who would follow you voluntarily.

to my subjects.⁴⁸ So you appear to be a man, I not worthy to be a king. Do these seem benefits unto you, Cyrus? Ye know if ye had esteemed me ye would have been well ware to bereft me anything rather than mine authority and honour. For what am I the better to have my country dilated and be myself dishonoured? Nor I did not rule the Medians because I was better than all they, but because they thought me in all things better than themselves.'⁴⁹

He thus still speaking, Cyrus did interrupt him, saying: 'For God his sake (uncle) if I have done you any pleasure, now at my request cease of your complain, and when ye have full experience how we be toward you, and if any doings shall appear to you to be done for your profit, I embracing you and you me, take me as your friend; but if they appear otherwise, then accuse me.' 'Peradventure', said Cyaxares, 'you speak well. And I will so do.' 'What', said Cyrus, 'if I kiss ye?' 'If ye will', said he. 'Will ye not turn from me as ye did alate?' 'No', said he. Then Cyrus kissed him. Which thing when the Medians, the Persians and other many beheld, being all in suspense whereto this matter would ensue, were straight glad and rejoiced. Then Cyaxares and Cyrus taking their horses rode afore. The Medians, as Cyrus winked to them, followed Cyaxares; the Persians, Cyrus. Them, all other when they were come to the camp and they had placed Cyaxares in a tent well apparelled, they that were appointed did minister all things necessary unto him. All the time that Cyaxares was unoccupied before supper, the Medians went to him, some of their own minds, many commanded of Cyrus,⁵⁰ presenting their gifts: one a goodly cupbearer, another a cunning cook; some a baker, some a musician; some cups, some a gallant garment. Every one, for the most part, gave him the preciousest things that they had gotten, in so much as Cyaxares did repent him, both because Cyrus had not withdrawn himself from him nor the Medians were any less loyal unto him than they were tofore. When the time of supper came, Cyaxares called Cyrus, desiring him, because he had not seen him long before, to sup with him. 'Do not desire me, Cyaxares', said Cyrus. 'Do ye not see that these which be present do all tarry on us? Therefore I should do evil if I seem to seek my own pleasure, little regarding them. For soldiers thinking themselves to be condemned, if they be good, be made much the less courageous; if they be evil, they be the more despiteful. But you which have come so far, go now to supper. And if any do you honour, embrace and feast the same that they may have the more affiance°

---

⁴⁸ to my subjects] Cyaxares' point is that Cyrus's success with power borrowed from him puts Cyaxares in the position of a supplicant, Cyrus in the position of the kingly hero, particularly in the eyes of Cyaxares' people.
⁴⁹ better than themselves] Cyaxares repeats the point made in Book I by Cyrus's father, pp. 109–10.
⁵⁰ many commanded of Cyrus] Barker under-emphasises that most οἱ πλεῖστοι (hoi pleîstoi) are, in fact, commanded by Cyrus. Holland makes this clear: '(and those were the greater number)', sig. R1v.

in you. I will depart, going about these things which I have spoken. Tomorrow early all the chief men shall be ready at your gates that we may devise with you what is hereafter to be done. You being present, show your sentence, whether ye think it good to continue this war or to discharge our army.' Then Cyaxares went to supper. But Cyrus assembling his especial friends both in wisdom and valiantness at a need said thus.

The Oration of Cyrus

'Loving friends, that that we first have wished, that (by God his help) we have. For so far as we invaded, so much land have we conquered, that we may see our enemies impaired and ourselves augmented both in number and courage. Now if our friends lately gotten will remain with us we shall be the more able to accomplish both when time requireth force or policy. Now that the most part of our friends may have the mind to abide with us, it must be as well your feat as mine to compass it. And as he which in fighting taketh most men must needs be counted most chivalrous, so when policy must be had, he that can make most men to accord with him seemeth worthily most eloquent in tongue and valiant in deed. Yet do not muse in this matter as though I would show you a form of Oration which I would every one should follow, but so handle them that they may be persuaded by the feats that every of you do. And let this be your study and care. I will diligently see that the soldiers, having necessary things, so much as I may, their advices° may be known concerning this war.'

Thus endeth the fifth book.

The Discipline of Cyrus, the Sixth Book

This day being thus spent and supper ended, they went to rest. The day following early, all the confederates came to Cyaxares' doors. And in the time that he apparelled him and heard so much people to be at his gates, even that time Cyrus's friends brought unto him some the Caducians desiring him to tarry, some the Hyrcanians, another Sacian. Hystaspas brought Gadatas the eunuch desiring Cyrus to tarry. Cyrus perceiving that Gadatas was in great fear lest the army should be dismissed, smiling said: 'I know well, Gadatas, that you, being persuaded by Hystaspas, do think as ye have said.' Gadatas holding up his hands to heaven sware that he was not so moved to think by Hystaspas's persuasion. 'But I know well' (said he), 'that if you were departed, all that I have should utterly be lost. And therefore I come to him demanding if he knew your pleasure concerning the dissolving of the army.' 'Then by like', said Cyrus, 'I do wrongfully charge Hystaspas.' 'Yea surely' (quoth Hystaspas), 'very wrongfully, for I did speak the contrary to Gadatas, that it was not like that ye would tarry, affirming that ye were sent for of your father.' 'What say you' (quoth Cyrus), 'durst you be bold to utter so much, now knowing my mind?' 'Aye, by my troth' (said he), 'for I see that you be desirous to go and show yourself to the Persians and declare to your father what ye have done.' 'Are not you desirous' (said Cyrus) 'to go home?' 'No, truly' (said he), 'but I will tarry so long as a captain till I have made this Gadatas lord of the Assyrian.' Thus they in sadness[1] bourded° one with another. Then Cyaxares being honourably arrayed came forth and sat in a Median throne. When all were come that were appointed and silence made, Cyaxares said thus: 'Dear friends, peradventure because I am present and ancient to Cyrus, it is seemly that I should speak first, and opportunity (as I think) now serveth first to consult of this, whether it is meet still to continue our war or to discharge the army. Let every man therefore say what he thinketh in this matter.' Then first spake the Hyrcanian, saying: 'I think, loving friends, that there is no need of words when the very deeds declareth what is best, for we all know that, abiding together, we shall do our enemies much more damage than receive. But if we be disparpled, they shall deal with us to their most pleasure, and to our most pain.' After him the Caducian said, 'What should we speak of departing home and to be dissevered though we continue the war? For we being warlike and scattering but a while from our company were surely beaten.'[2] Next him Artabasus, which sometime said he was Cyrus's kinsman,[3] spake thus: 'I, Cyaxares, do much dissent from them which have tofore spoken.

---

[1] in sadness] Some misapprehension here; they indulge in half-serious jesting. Holland, for example, has 'thus communed they together betweene jest and good earnest' (sig. [R3]).
[2] surely beaten] The Caducian refers to their failed independent attack on the Assyrians, in Book v.
[3] Cyrus's kinsman] In Book i, as Cyrus was leaving Media for Persia.

For they say that we ought to tarry and continue this war. But I say that when I am at home, I am in war. For I have holpen many times when our goods be driven away, and many times I had business about our forts, being fearful and ware of their trains°. This I did of mine own cost. But now I have their castles and am not afraid of them. I feast with their goods and banquet at mine enemy's cost. Therefore, seeing that to be in war partly is domestical and partly as a feast, I do not think that this common joy should be dissolved.' Then Gobryas said: 'I, friends and confederates, hitherto have cause to praise Cyrus's fidelity for he hath not failed in anything that he hath promised. But if he did depart out of this land, it is evident that the Assyrian will not so cease but be avenged, both as he intended to do you wrong and as he hath already done to me. And I shall afresh be punished because I am confederate with you.'

After all these, Cyrus said: 'I am certain, friends, that if we now dissolve our army, our state shall be feebler, and our enemies again stronger. For all they from whom harness hath been taken shall shortly make new. They whose horses were bereft them shall shortly get other. And for them that be slain, other shall grow and be gotten. Therefore no marvel it shall be though they eftsoons be able to molest us. If it be so, what meant I to move Cyaxares to propound the case of the dissolution of the army? Know ye well that I feared afterclaps.[4] I see our enemies able to match with us, with whom if we use this trade in war, we shall not be able to fight; winter also is at hand, if we had houses for ourselves, yet surely we have none for our horses, our ministers, nor for the multitude of our soldiers, without the which we cannot proceed in war; the victual where we have come is consumed of us, where we have not come, it is conveyed for fear of us into their holds, so that they have them and we can not come by them. For who is so painful or who is so hard that striving with hunger and cold can endure to war? Therefore if we should use this trade of war, I truly affirm that we should rather willingly discharge our army than afterward for want of provision be compelled unwillingly. But if we will continue the war, thus I say we must do with all celerity: our endeavour shall be to take so many of their holds[5] as we can and build of our own so many and strong as we may. If this be done, they shall have most victual which be able to take most and lay it up; they shall besiege other which be more strong. And now we do not differ from them that sail in the sea, for they always sailing and yet that that they have sailed is no more their own than that that they have not sailed. But if we can get the holds, the same shall put our enemies beside their ground and for

---

[4] afterclaps] An unwelcome or unexpected consequence of an affair or incident, or a surprise; (also) a later threat. Barker gives a strong image for something merely hinted at in the Greek. Holland uses the same term (sig. [R3]v).
[5] holds] i.e. strongholds.

the quiet be to us in all things more available. But if any of you peradventure doth fear to be in garrisons, far from his own country, let not this trouble you. For we being furthest from our country will take in hand to keep those holds that be next to our enemies, you shall keep and maintain those which be in the borders of you and the Assyrians. And if we keeping those that be next our enemies can save the same, you being so far off, shall live in much quiet. For they cannot (as I think) set light the harms, being so nigh, and intend to work any wiles with you, being so far.' When these things were spoken, as well all the other as Cyaxares himself rise up and said they were ready so to do. Gadatas and Gobryas both the one and the other said they would defence their holds, where their confederates should determine that they might be succours° to their friends. Cyrus, seeing all to be prest to do as he had said, thus concluded: 'If we then will accomplish all that we have said, we must with all celerity provide such things as we have used, as engines[6] to beat down our enemy's holds, and workmen to build fortresses for ourselves.' Cyaxares promised to provide one engine, Gadatas another, Tigranes another. And Cyrus said he would do his diligence to make one himself.

When these things were thus agreed upon, they prepared engine matters. And every man did purvey things meet for the engines, and such men were appointed as seemed most meet to such purposes. And Cyrus, perceiving that long tarrying must needs be in this matter, did encamp in place which he thought most wholesome and most commodious for things needful. And whatsoever needed defence, he finished it, that they might always remain safe if at any time with their force they did camp far off. Furthermore [he] enquired of them whom he thought to have most knowledge in the country from whence they might best provide for the army, and always encamped nigh pastures, both that the army should have things needful and also be the more in health and strength to endure the labour of their voyage and in their carriage to keep their order. Thus Cyrus was occupied. Many of them renegades[7] and captives of Babylon said that the Assyrian was departed into Lydia, conveying many talents of gold and silver with other riches and treasure infinite. Wherefore the commons of the soldiers reported that he removed his money for fear. But Cyrus considering that he was gone, to make all sure that he could, contrary-wise prepared to be ready to join with him, as though he should go to battle and did furnish the Persian horsemen, taking some horses of the prisoners, some of

---

[6] engines] i.e. siege-engines.
[7] renegades] 'rennagates' here; Holland has 'fugitives' and 'captives' (sig. [R4]). No early modern sense of religious conversion seems to be in play; Barker translates οἱ αὐτόμολοι (*hoi autómoloi*, from the adjective *autómolos*, 'going of oneself', and therefore, as substantive, 'deserter') and οἱ ἁλισκόμενοι (*hoi haliskómenoi*, present participle, used as substantive, of ἁλίσκομαι *haliskomai*, 'to be taken', i.e. deserters and prisoners of war/captives).

other his friends, receiving all men, rejecting nothing, whether any man gave him good harness or horse. He also prepared chariots, some of the captives, some otherwise, as he could, and did destroy all cars° with two horses, being the fashion of the Trojans, and also that manner of driving chariots which the Cyrenians yet useth.[8] For afore time the Medians, Syrians, Arabians and all in Asia did use their chariots so, as the Cyrenians now do. He thought it most expedient that they which were best in the fight in chariots should be in that part where the light-harnessed men were, which to attain to the victory have not very great power. For chariots three hundred bringeth three hundred men and have horses a thousand, and two hundred, governors of the chariots be such as the noble men do think most trusty to the number of three hundred, and such as do no hurt to their enemies. Therefore he did banish this kind of chariots, and for these he did prepare more warlike, with strong wheels, which should not soon be slit, and long axle-trees°, for all things being large be the harder to overturn. And he made for the drivers a seat, as it were a tower of strong timber, the height whereof is five cubits, that the horses may be ruled about[9] the seats. And he did harness the cart-drivers with helmets, all save their eyes; he did also fasten such picks° of iron round about the wheels two cubits in length and other under the axle-tree, declining toward the ground, as though they should assault their enemy's chariots. And as Cyrus then devised them, so they at this day use their chariots which be under that kingdom. He had also many camels,[10] so many as his friends could provide and all the other that were taken. Thus these things were finished.

Being desirous to send a spy into Lydia, and learn what the Assyrian did, Araspes, the which had the keeping of the fair lady, seemed most meet for this purpose. But Araspes had this chance, being caught with the love of the lady, he was enforced to break to her of his lust, which she denied, being faithful to her husband, although he was absent, whom she loved entirely. Yet she did not accuse Araspes to Cyrus, being afraid to set variance betwixt two friends. But Araspes, thinking it a villainy not to obtain his lust, menaced the lady that if she would not willingly she should do it against her will. Then the woman fearing violence kept the thing no longer close but sent her eunuch to Cyrus, commanding him to declare all the whole matter; which when he heard, laughing once again at him which said he was superior to love, sent Artabasus with the eunuch commanding him to say unto him that he should not enforce the woman, but if he could allure her he would not hinder him. Artabasus, being come to

---

[8] yet useth] Persian chariots and Cyrus's innovations with chariot design and use attracted attention from those reading the *Cyropaedia* for its military teachings and models.
[9] about] i.e. from.
[10] camels] Herodotus records the strategic use Cyrus made of camels in the battle against Croesus (I. 80).

Araspes, did rebuke him, calling the woman a thing committed[11] to his fidelity, declaring his untrust, his unrighteousness, and untemperance, insomuch as Araspes wept sore for sorrow, being oppressed with shame and confounded with fear for Cyrus's displeasure. Which thing Cyrus understanding, called him and privily thus said unto him: 'I see, Araspes, that you be afraid of me, and are much troubled with shame. But let it go. For I have heard that gods have been conquered of love. And I know that men being reputed most prudent, have been [be]fore tormented with love. And I have accused myself because I could not contain being in company with beautiful persons, little esteeming them. And of this your fear, I am the causer. For I enforced you to this invincible feat.' Araspes making answer said, 'You be in this thing, Cyrus, even the same man that ye be in all other: that is, merciful and pardoning men's offences. But truly other men do oppress me with pensiveness and seeing the rumour of my mishap is dispersed insomuch as mine enemies rejoice, my friends counsel me to make an escape lest I should be grievously punished of you for my guilt.' Cyrus said: 'Know this well, Araspes, that by this opinion ye may do me high pleasure, and greatly profit our confederates.' 'How can it be' (said Araspes), 'that I can any ways do you acceptable service?' 'If now' (said he), 'ye would feign to make an escape from me, and go to our enemies, I think ye might be credited of them.' 'By God' (said Araspes), 'I am sure that I and my friends might so cause a rumour that I were departed from you.' 'So may you' (said Cyrus), 'return to us, knowing all our enemy's secrets. And I think they will make you privy to all their counsel and devices because ye shall be in credit with them, so that nothing shall be hid from you that we would know.' 'Then', said he, 'I will even now depart, for ye know that this shall be an argument of truth, because it shall be thought that I flee for fear of your punishment.' 'Can you so forsake fair Panthea?', said Cyrus. 'Surely, Cyrus', said he, 'I have two minds,[12] and with the one I have now played the Philosopher with this unjust sophister Love. For there is not one, both good and bad, nor loveth at one time good and evil things, and yet at one time will and will not do one thing. Therefore it is manifest that there be two minds, and when the good is superior, it worketh well; when the evil, it enterpriseth evil. And now because the good hath you his confederate, it doth subdue, and that very mightily.' 'Well' (said Cyrus), 'if ye will now go, ye must so do, that your credit may increase among them, ye shall show unto them what we are about. But so show as our doings may be lets to their emprises. And this shall be a let unto them if you say that we be appointed to invade their land. For hearing this they shall the less gather together their whole power, every man fearing his private part; and ye shall tarry with them a good while. For that that

---

[11] a thing committed] Referring to Panthea's status as spoils of war, Artabasus's reproof is centred on Araspes' disrespect of Cyrus in the discharge of his role as her steward.
[12] two minds] Barker translates ψυχή (*psykhē*) as 'mind'.

they do bring next us, that to know shall be most convenient for us, and counsel them also to be in array when ye think they be most strong. For when you shall be departed and thought to know their order, they must needs keep the same, and be afraid to change it, and if they do change, they shall be troubled with the sudden change.' Thus Araspes departing, taking his most assured servants and uttering to some of them what he would have done in this matter, went his way.

Panthea, hearing that Araspes was gone, sent to Cyrus, saying: 'Be not sorry (O Cyrus) for Araspes his departure to your enemies, for if ye will suffer me to send to my husband, I will promise you that he shall come and be a much more assured friend than Araspes was, bringing you so much power as he is lord of. For the father of the king was his friend. But this king attempted once to have made divorcement° betwixt me and my husband. Therefore knowing that this king doth despite him, I am sure he would gladly incline to such a man as you be.'[13] Cyrus hearing this commanded her to send to her husband, and so she did.

Abradatas, knowing his wife's tokens and perceiving how other things stood, speedily came to Cyrus, having two thousand horsemen. They that were the Persian espies sent to Cyrus, declaring what he was. Cyrus straight commanded that he should be brought to his wife. When the wife and husband saw the one the other, they did embrace each the other as it was like after such despair. Then Panthea declared the goodness, the temperancy and the clemency[14] of Cyrus toward her. Abradatas hearing it said, 'What shall I do, Panthea, to render thanks to Cyrus for you and me?' 'What other thing', said Panthea, 'but to endeavour yourself to be such a one toward him as he hath been toward you.' Then Abradatas went to Cyrus and when he saw him, he took him by the right hand and said: 'For the pleasures that you have done me (O Cyrus), I have no more to say but that I betake myself to you as your friend, as your servant and confederate. And whatsoever I see you desire, I shall do my devoir to the uttermost of my power to aid and help you in the same.' And Cyrus said, 'I accept you. And now I dismiss you, to go and sup with your wife. Then ye shall again be placed in my tent with your and my friends.'

Afterward, Abradatas perceiving Cyrus very studious about forked chariots and barbed horse and horsemen, he intendeth to provide him an hundred

---

[13] as you be] Cyrus's restraint and magnanimity in relation to Panthea makes him a model to later rulers, many of whom are associated with him in the historical record by similar acts (see Jeffrey Beneker, *The Passionate Statesman: 'Eros' and Politics in Plutarch's Lives* (Oxford: Oxford University Press, 2012)). Machiavelli observes Scipio Africanus' restraint with the women of Carthage; Alexander the Great's restraint with Darius III's womenfolk earns him Darius's respect.

[14] goodness, temperancy and clemency] Barker translates σωφροσύνη (*sōphrosýne*) here as 'temperance'. Holland has 'piety, temperance and commiseration' (sig. S1v), but glosses 'piety' as 'integrity'.

chariots of his own, and men of arms like unto his, and appointed himself to be in a chariot captain to the other. And he yoked in his own chariot eight horses in four teams. His wife Panthea had made of her treasure a curet of gold and an helmet of gold, and likewise his vambraces°, and had apparelled the horses of the chariot with barbs of brass. Abradatas thus had done. Cyrus seeing his chariot with four teams thought he might as well devise one with eight teams, in the which a place of engines made very low might be drawn with eight yoke of kyne°, and this was three paces at the most above the ground, wheels and all. Such towers[15] following in order, he thought, might be great succour to his footmen, and great hurt to his enemy's array, he made in these houses circles° and pinnacles°, and placed in every tower twenty men. When all his provision was finished, concerning his towers he did practise experience how they would draw, and the eight yoke did more easily draw a tower with all the men in it than every yoke one load of carriage, for the weight of the carriage was twenty-five talents, and the weight of a yoked tower, like a tragical tent[16] made of the heart of trees, and twenty men and harness, the burden being less than twenty five talents to every yoke. So when he perceived this carriage to be expedite and ready, he provided that these towers should go with the army, thinking that the advantage[17] of war was health, justice and felicity.

There came at this time from the king of India one bringing money, and showed Cyrus that the king did thus greet him: 'Cyrus, I am glad that you have declared to me your want. I will be your friend and send you money, and if you have more need, send unto me, for I have commanded my men to do your commandment.' Cyrus hearing this said: 'I command that certain of you tarry here in our tents for the custody of the money, and to live at your lust. But three of you shall go at my request to our enemies, as it were from the king of India, to treat of confederacy. When ye have learned what they say and do, ye shall with all speed declare the same as well to the king as to us, in the which things if ye do me faithful service, I will give you more hearty thanks for it than for the money that you have brought me. For common spies, being like slaves, can know nor report no more than the common sort, but such men as you be do many times explore the most secret counsels.' The Indians hearing joyfully these things, and being rewarded presently of Cyrus, went forth the next day, promising when they had learned all that they could of their enemies they would return with all the speed they might. Thus Cyrus had provided all

---

[15] towers] i.e. the movable towers of the chariots.
[16] tragical tent] Xenophon makes a comparison with the weight of the timbers on the tragic stage, but 'skenos' ('stage') can also mean 'tent'; Barker seems to be imagining a war-pavilion, despite the counter-evidence of the 'hearts of trees'.
[17] the advantage] Barker misses the full force of 'pleonexia' (wanting more) in the Greek, obscuring the point that Cyrus believes in *seizing* the advantage in time of war, rather than appreciating the advantages of war as such in these terms.

things for the war very princely, as a man intending no small enterprise, and was not only studious for the good doing of his confederates, but also moved emulation among his friends, that they might show themselves most clean in their armour, lusty on horseback and painful in labour. This feat he devised, causing them to show themselves abroad, rewarding such as were most forward. And the princes whom he saw careful to have their soldiers most warlike, them he would with praise provoke, benefiting them with such gifts as he could. When he made sacrifice, kept awake,[18] then would he appoint such exercise as might serve in war, giving royal rewards to them that did best, so that much joy was in all the host.

Now Cyrus had finished all things as he would for this expedition, engines except. The Persian horsemen were the full number of ten thousand, and the picked chariots,[19] which he had prepared, were a just hundred, and those which Abradates the Susian counterfeited° like Cyrus were also as many. And Cyrus caused Cyaxares to change the Median chariots from the Trojan and Libyan fashion after this form, and they also were an hundred. And on every camel there were appointed two men, being archers, and the most part of the army was now in such courage as though they had had already the victory, and their enemies could do nothing. These things being thus furnished, the Indians which were sent of Cyrus in espial[20] came and declared that Croesus was elected captain and conductor of all their enemies. And that it was declared of all the kings being confederated that every man should be present with all his puissance and to bring so much money as could be, which should serve both to hire so many for wages and to reward so many for need as they could; and that many were already in wages of the Thracian sword-fighters, and that the Egyptians were sailing toward them, being in number one hundred and twenty thousand with shields as low as their feet, and great spears such as they now use, and short swords; also that an army of the Cyprians was coming by ship and that all the Cilicians were now present, both Phrygians and Lycaonians, Paphlagonians and Cappadocians, and Phoenicians.[21] And with the prince of Babylon the Assyrians and the Ionians, Aeolians[22] and almost the Grecians inhabitants of Asia were enforced to follow Croesus. And that same Croesus had sent to the Lacedaemonians[23] for aid. And that this army was assembled at the river Pactolus and that they would go in Tymbraia where as now the

[18] kept awake] An addition by Barker.
[19] piked chariots] scythed chariots.
[20] in espial] 'especiall' in the texts, a mistake in both 26066 and 26067.
[21] Phoenicians] Barker omits the 'Arabians' in this list — although this may indicate his concurrent use of Filelfo's Latin text, as Filelfo also omits them.
[22] Aeolians] 'Eoltans' here.
[23] Lacedaemonians] Spartans.

assemblies of the barbarians of nether Syria being under the king be made, and thither every man was commanded to bring his chaffer and ware. And the captives did show almost the same thing, for Cyrus devised that such might be taken as he might learn somewhat of them, wherefore he sent espies like unto slaves, as they had been runaways. When Cyrus his host heard these things, every man was in muse°, as they had good cause, and they went abroad more discouraged than they were wont, few appearing to be merry. They flocked together, being full of questions of these late tidings. Cyrus, hearing such fear to be conceived in his army, called together the princes of the armies and all other by whose discouragement he thought damage might ensue and by their good courage profit, commanding also his servants that if any other of the men of arms would come to hear what was said, they should not prohibit him, to the which being assembled, he said thus:

The Oration of Cyrus

'Friends, I have assembled you because I perceived some of you, after that report was made of our enemy's power, to be very like fearful men. I marvel truly that any of you is in fear, because our enemies do gather together, seeing we be much more increased now than we were when we did discomfit them. And now thanks be to God, we be far better appointed than we were tofore. Seeing these things (O good lord) should you not be bold? If ye be now afraid, what would ye do if the rumour were that all the things which maketh with you were all against you? What if ye heard that they which first had victory upon us did eftsoons come against us still retaining their victory, or that they which tofore did defeat the shot of the archers and darters did now come both the very same and other many like unto them? Furthermore, if they which so appointed the footmen that they got the victory be now so furnished in horsemen that they dare encounter with men of arms; and habergeoning[24] bow and arrow, having every man a strong spear, intending so to come and fight at hand, also vauncing with chariots which be not made as afore, easy to be driven away, but have the horses barbed, the drivers standing in towers of timber, being armed their uppermost part with breastplate and helmet, with scythes of iron fastened to the axletrees, able to disturb in a moment them of the contrary part. Besides forth, they have camels, with which they give the onset every one of the which a hundred horse dare not abide to look on.[25] They have also towers

---

[24] habergeoning] 'haberdouning' in both 26066 and 26067, probably a variant on the rare term 'habergeoned': being equipped with a jacket of mail. Barker may have been distracted by the build-up of terms for weaponry and armour in this passage. But the Greek suggests quite a different sense: now 'abandoning' (ἀποδεδοκιμάκασι [apodedokimakasi]) bow and arrow for a spear.

[25] dare not abide to look on] Herodotus (1. 80) also notes the fear shown by horses of camels

to break the ray,[26] with which they guard and defend theirs, and with their darts drive you from fighting with them in equal ground. If any of you would report that all these things our enemies had, being now afraid, what would you then do? Seeing that now ye be in fear, when it is told that Croesus is chosen grand captain of our host, which was so much more cowardly than the Syrians that when they were discomfited and fled, Croesus seeing them vanquished, instead of succouring his confederates fled himself away. This also is told, that our enemies not being sufficient of themselves, are compelled to have other in wages,[27] which would better fight for them than they for themselves. If any man be of this opinion that these be puissant and ours feeble, I think it meet for such friends that they depart to our enemies, for being there, they shall do us more good than if they were still with us.' When Cyrus had thus said, Chrysantas a Persian stood forth and spake on this wise:

The Oration of Chrysantas

'Do not marvel (O Cyrus) though some hearing these news be of discouraged countenance, for it is not of any fear but of grief, as when men be desirous and in hope to make good cheer, than if any business is showed which must of necessity be done afore the same, no man I think is glad to hear such news. So we likewise thinking now to have been in wealth, and learning that there be yet things undone which must needs be done, we have heavy countenances not for any fear but because we would satisfy our former desires. But seeing we shall not only fight for Syria, whereas is plenty of corn, cattle and fruitful date trees, but Lydia also, whereas is abundance of wine, figs, and oil, the sea flowing to it through the which more goods cometh than any man hath ever seen;[28] remembering I say these things, we be no more grieved, but rather encouraged that we with all speed might enjoy these Lydian commodities.' Thus he said. All other the confederates being delighted with this oration, praised the same. Then Cyrus said: 'I think (friends) it were best for us to go against them with all celerity, that by our speedy coming we may prevent them in such places as they have provided their victual, and the sooner that we go, the fewer shall we find present and the more absent. Thus I think if any of you be of other judgement, either for our safeguard or expedition, let him show his mind.' When as many did accord that it was best to march forth with all speed against their enemies, and no man did reply, then Cyrus began after this wise:

---

as part of the story of this battle with Croesus at Thymbria.
[26] ray] i.e. array.
[27] other in wages] mercenaries.
[28] ever seen] The proverbial (and historical) riches of Lydia still survive in the expression 'as rich as Croesus'.

The Oration of Cyrus

'Loving confederates, our hearts, bodies and harness, which we need to have, be abundantly (God be thanked) provided for us. Now we must provide victual for our voyage, both for ourselves and our beasts, and that no less than for twenty days. I accompting, perceive that we shall have a journey of fifteen days, in the which we shall find no victual, for all is wasted, partly of us, partly of our enemies so much as they could. Therefore sufficient meat must be provided, for without it we can neither fight nor live. And as for wine, let every man have so much as may suffice, accustoming ourselves to drink of water because much of our journey lacketh wine, and though we could provide very much of it, yet it should not suffice. Therefore that we for lack of wine do not fall into sudden diseases, thus must we do: let us straightway begin to drink water with our meat, which thing now doing, it shall be no great alteration. For he that eateth meal cakes, eateth dough mixed with water. And all boiled meat is dressed commonly with much water. Then after meat if we drink wine, nature being well contented shall rest. And yet we must leave that after meat till we have learned to drink water, for mutation by little and little causeth nature to abide every change,[29] and God teacheth us the same, drawing us by little and little from cold to endure vehement heat, and from heat to vehement cold, whom we following must accustom to assay the way before that we may come to our purpose. As for the burden of your bedding, bestow it upon necessary victual, for excess of victual shall not be unprofitable. And though you lack bedding, fear ye not but that ye shall sleep sweetly; if ye do not, then blame me. As for garments, the more plenty that a man hath present, the more shall be help both the whole and sick. And we must provide such victual as is for the most part sharp, tart and salt, for such both be good meat and of longer continuance. When we be come to plentiful places whereas it is like we may get corn, there must we prepare bakehouses to bake us bread, and the instruments of baking be but light. We must also prepare such things as sick men shall have need of, for the burden of them is very little but if there shall happen any such chance, great shall be our lack. We must have also collars° for they be much occupied, both in horse and men, which being worn and rent must needs cause tarryance° except a man have other bindings. And if any man hath learned to plane a spear, he must not forget a chip-axe°, and it is also good to have with him a file, for he that sharpeth a spear's head, he also sharpeth his heart. For a certain shame cometh to him which sharpeth his spear and is himself a coward. We must also have very much timber, both for chariots and wagons, for in many affairs, many things of necessity shall be painful and onerous. And we must have also necessary instruments for all these things, for craftsmen are not to be had in

---

[29] abide every change] i.e. that the soldiers should little by little reduce the amount of wine they drink after dinner.

every place. But to do as chances shall require, a few, and they not very cunning, shall suffice. We must also have in every chariot a pick-axe and a fork, and on every bearing beast a twibill° and an hook, for these be necessary for every man his private use, and also many times profitable for common causes. And what need is of necessary victuals, you the leaders of harness men inquire of the soldiers that be about you, for it must be regarded that they lack not, for we shall have need of them. The drawing beasts which I command to have, you captains of the carriage, search and provide. And him that lacketh compel ye to prepare. You also captains of the vaward, ye have set out by me whom I have rejected both of darters, archers and slingers. They that be darters in this soldierfare° must be compelled to have an axe to chop wood; they that be archers, a fork; they that be slingers, a pick-axe. They which have these things must go before the wagons as wings, that if need be to make way you may readily perform the same. And that I lacking anything may see where to provide and use the same, I will also have of meet age for war ferrours°, carpenters and shoemakers with their instruments, that if anything requireth their art in the army, we shall not lack the same. And they shall be dismissed into the trade of soldiers and doing service in their craft, to him that requireth for money, they shall have their appointed place. And if any merchant will follow for to sell anything, let him have victual for the days tofore spoken. If he be taken selling otherwise, he shall be spoiled° of all. But when those days be expired, then he may sell what he will. And what merchant we shall know to bring most victual, he shall be rewarded and advanced both of me and my confederates. And if any thinketh he shall need money for his occupying,[30] let him bring such as will depose° for him and be his surety that he shall follow the host, and he shall have part of our treasure. Thus I have pronounced my mind in these things. If any man perceiveth any other thing to be needful, let him make declaration to me. And go you forth to make preparation. I will make sacrifice for our setting forward. And when our sacrifices shall be well finished, we shall signify unto you. And let every man be present with these things tofore rehearsed at a place appointed, with their captains; you the captains every man his men being set in array shall all come to me, that every one many know his several place.'

They, hearing these things, prepared themselves. He made sacrifice, which being lucky, he marched forward with his army, and the first day encamped so nigh as he could, that if any man had forgotten anything he might go for it, and if any man knew anything to be wanted he might prepare it. Cyaxares, with the third part of the Medians, abode at home, that the country should not be destitute of help. Cyrus set forward so speedily as he could. The horsemen being in the vaward, sending afore them outriders and espies to have thorough

---

[30] occupying] i.e. buying more merchandise.

knowledge of former places,[31] next them he placed the carriage, and where it was plain ground, he made many several bands of wagons and carriage. In the rearward, the footmen's host followed. If any the carriage were left behind, such captains as chanced to be there did see that they were not stopped in their voyage. Where the way was straight, the carriage being divided, harnessed soldiers went on either sides of it. And if anything did stop, such soldiers as were appointed did see remedy for it. And every hundred for the most part went with their carriage by them, for it was commanded that all the carriage should go every one next his crew, except some necessary chance did let them. And every burden-bearer had a token of a captain, and did go first, that the thing might be evident to them of his hundred. In so much as they went round together and every man very circumspect[32] to his own things that he left none behind. And thus doing, they needed not to inquire one of another for every thing was in more safety and things necessary more ready at hand throughout the whole host.

The espies going forward thought they saw men gathering forage and wood, and they did see other beasts drawing such matter and feeding. And looking further, they thought to espy a smoke or dust araised, of all the which they did gather° that their adversary's army was at hand. Wherefore the captain of the espies sent one in haste to declare the same to Cyrus, who hearing of it, commanded them to abide in the same espials, signifying to him when they saw any new things, and did send a troop of horsemen to outride, commanding them to do their endeavours, to take some of the men that were in the plain that he thereby might have some certain knowledge they did as they were commanded. He separated another crew of his men to provide such things as he thought should need before they did join. And first he willed them to dine, then to remain in their array, foreseeing to things, commanded. After dinner he called the chief of horsemen, footmen and chariots and the captains of the engines, carriage and wagons, and there came together. They that did course the plains brought certain men that they had taken, who being demanded of Cyrus, said that they went before the camp and came beyond the scoutwatch° to provide forage and fuel, for by reason of the multitude all things were very scarce. Cyrus hearing this asked how far off the army was. They answered, 'Two Assyrian miles'.[33] They Cyrus thus demanded: 'Is there any talk of us among them?' 'Yea truly' (said they), 'and that very much of your nigh approach.' 'And be they glad to hear it?' said Cyrus. Thus he asked because of them that

---

[31] former places] Another problematic translation, missing (for example) the sense of ἀναβιβάζων (*anabibázōn*, present participle nominative singular masculine of ἀναβιβάζω, *anabibázō*, going up to a height).

[32] circumspect] i.e. watchful, careful.

[33] Assyrian miles] The Greek text has 'parasangs', previously translated by Barker as 'Persian miles'. (Filelfo's Latin translation uses 'parasangs' throughout.)

were present. 'No, surely', said they, 'they be not glad but rather very sad.' 'And what are they now doing?', said he. 'They do array themselves' (said they), 'and so have done these three days.' 'Who doth embattle them?' (quoth Cyrus). 'Croesus himself' (said they), 'with another Grecian and one Median which as they say fled from you.' 'O immortal Jupiter' (said Cyrus), 'that I might take him as I would.'[34] Then he commanded the captives to be had away, and rose as though he would say somewhat to them that were present. In the meantime came an other from the captain of the espies, saying that a great troop of horsemen did appear in the plain, 'and we think' (quoth he), 'that they be sent to view your army. And before this troop, there be thirty other horsemen riding together which, if they could, would peradventure take us, being espies, and we but ten in this espial.' Then Cyrus commanded the horsemen which were always attendant upon him to ride to the spial°, being quiet and secret from their enemies. 'And when' (quoth he) 'our men leave their espial, arise you and resist the pursuers of our espies. And that you may not be oppressed with the great troop, go you, Hystaspas, with a thousand horsemen and show yourself against our enemy's troop, and see ye do not pursue them in any covert, but providing that your espies may keep their place, go forth. And if any declaring token of love come unto you, receive them gently.' Hystaspas departed and armed himself, the other went forth as they were commanded.

And Araspes with his servants being come with in the spial, chanced to meet with him, who was afore sent as an espy, being keeper of the Susian woman.[35] Cyrus hearing of it leapt from his chair, and running to him, did lovingly embrace him. Other not knowing the thing were much amazed at the matter, until Cyrus said: 'Loving friends, this man most trusty is come unto us. Therefore it is convenient that all men should know what he hath done. He neither distained° with any offence nor afraid of any punishment did depart, but was sent of me that, knowing our enemy's secrets, he might reveal the same to us. Therefore, the promise that I have made unto you, Araspes, I do remember and I with all these will perform it. It is meet, friends, that you also honourably do entertain this honest man, for he for our weal hath adventured himself, and sustained the infamy of an odious crime.' Then they all did embrace Araspes, taking him by the hands. Cyrus said: 'Enough of this. Now what the time requireth, we should know that Araspes declare, diminishing nothing of the truth, nor impairing our enemy's puissance, for it is better that we thinking it more should find it less, than hearing it less should find it more.' Araspes answered: 'That I might know the more certainly their power, I was one that did appoint their array.' 'Then', said Cyrus, 'you do not only know their number

---

[34] as I would] Cyrus keeps up the fiction that Araspes has fled his camp.

[35] keeper of the Susian woman] i.e. Araspes, who returns now to the Persian camp with his attendants, and meets Cyrus.

but also their order.' 'Yea, surely', said Araspes, 'and how they intend to make their fight.' 'But first', said Cyrus, 'declare us briefly their number.' 'They be all appointed thirty a rank, both foot and horsemen, except the Egyptians which be separated as it were forty furlong off.[36] For I was very diligent to know how much ground they did contain.' 'Then show', said Cyrus, 'how the Egyptians be appointed, because you did except them.' 'The captains of every ten thousand do divide the thousand into several hundreds, for this form of array is their country fashion. And Croesus was very loth to grant them this array for he did covet to exceed your army in the main battle of footmen.' 'Why should he covet that?', said Cyrus. 'Because' (quoth he), 'he might environ you with the greater multitude.' 'But they should first know' (quoth Cyrus), 'whether they could enclose other as they intended. But we have heard of you what we for the time needed to learn. You therefore, friends, must work accordingly. Therefore departing hence, look well to the armour both of your horses and yourselves, for many times the want of a trifling thing doth make both man, horse and chariot to be unprofitable. In the morning early when I have made sacrifices, I will that both horse and man be refreshed, that when the time shall require, the travail of both neither shall for lack of food be unsufficient. And you, Araspes, shall guide the right wing, as you are appointed. And you the other captains of ten thousand, continue as ye be already placed, for when the fight shall join, it shall be no time to change horses from one chariot to another. And enjoin the centurions and bandleaders to be placed in the main battle, every band being divided in two parts.' (And a band did contain four-and-twenty men.)[37]

Then one of the captains of ten thousand said, 'Do you think (Cyrus) that we being thus appointed shall be able to match with so main a battle, being so many a rank?'[38] Cyrus said, 'When the battles be so thronged together that they cannot conveniently encounter with their enemies, do you think that they shall do their enemies hurt or confederates good? I rather would that for every hundred, ten thousand were set in a rank for so should we fight with the fewer. I will appoint my main battle that the same, I think, in every part shall avail and defence itself. I will place the darters next the curet men; after darters, the archers, for these may not be placed first, which themselves confess that they can endure no fight at hand. But being forefenced with curetine° they do endure, and some darting, some shooting before all the rest, may annoy their enemies. And when a man doth endamage his adversaries, it is evident by the

---

[36] forty furlong off] A mistake; the size of the army — apart from the Egyptians — covers forty furlongs.
[37] four-and-twenty men] Modern editors suggest that this is a gloss on the manuscript that has been absorbed into the text at some point in its transmission.
[38] so many a rank] i.e. the captain worries that, having fewer men, they may not be able to contend adequately with a force ranged at such depth, their own forces being ranged more widely with less depth.

same that he doth relieve his friends. Also, I will place hindermost such as be called sure behind. For as there is no profit in an house without strong building of stones, and wise workers of the roof, even so there is no profit in an army except both the first and the last be good and forward° men. Therefore do you order yourselves as I do prescribe, you captains of the targetmen, place your bands after this sort. And you, captains of the archers, next the targetmen likewise. And you which are captains of them in the rearward, command that every man have eye to other, encouraging them that do their duties and menacing them that be slow in the same. And if any man would shrink and be traitorous, let him be punished with death. They which be foremost must embold the followers by word and deed. And you which be placed after all must cause that cowards be more in fear of you than of our enemies. And thus do you: you, Abradatas being master of the ordnance, so do that the teams and carriers of the towers may follow immediately next the main battle. And you, Daochus, being captain of the carriage next the towers, conduct all that part of the army. And let your officers sharply chastise them which go or tarry out of time. And you, Caraducus, being captain of the chariots that carryeth the women, appoint the same last next the carriage, for all these things following shall both ease opinion of multitude and also be apt matter for us to work policies.[39] And our enemies if they will enclose us, shall be enforced to fetch the greater compass. And the more ground that they compass, the weaker must they needs be; you therefore thus do. And you, Artabasus and Artagersas, have each your thousand footmen with us next these. And you Pharnucus and Asiadatas, do intermeddle neither of your thousand horsemen in the main legion but behind the chariots severally appoint your army, and then repair to us, with the other captains, for you must so appoint yourself as you may fight with the first. And you which are captains of the men on camels, place them behind the cars, and Artagersas shall appoint; you that be elected leaders of the chariots, let the chief of you be placed with his chariots before the main battle. Every other hundred chariots, one warding the right side of the army, shall follow the legion on the wing and another the left side.' Thus Cyrus did embattle them.

Abradatas the Susian king said, 'I promise you, Cyrus, I would be right willing to be placed against the face of the contrary battle,[40] except it seemeth otherwise to you.' Cyrus rejoicing and commending him, demanded of the Persians being in other chariots, if they could suffer the same, who answered that it should be their dishonesty to grant it. Wherefore he caused them to cast lots. And the lot fell on Abradatas, according to his request, and was placed against the Egyptians. Then they departing and providing the tofore said things, went to supper. Then watch and ward being appointed, they took their

---

[39] to work policies] i.e. to be ready to ambush the enemy.
[40] face of the contrary battle] i.e. to lead the attack, directly in front of the enemy ranks.

rest. The next day early Cyrus did make sacrifice. The residue of the army dining and making oblations°, did harness them sel[ves] with many and goodly coat armours, with many and goodly helmets and breastplates. They did also harness their horses with shaffrons and cremets[41] and barbed as well their coursing° horses as them that did draw the chariots, in so much as the whole army did glitter with harness and shine with orient colour.[42] And Abradatas's chariot with four teams and eight horses was wondrous brave and martial. And he being about to put on a linen breastplate after his country fashion, his wife Panthea brought him an helmet and vambrances of gold, large bracelets about the joints of his hands, and a purple gown down to the foot after robe fashion and a scarlet crest. This had she privily wrought for her husband, knowing the measure of his harness. He marvelled to see it, and asked of Panthea: 'Wife, have not you defaced your jewels in making me this armour?' 'Truly', said Panthea, 'I have a more precious jewel yet, for if you appear to other as you seem to me, ye shall be my most sovereign jewel.' Thus speaking, she did enarm him, and would no man should have seen her, for the tears did distil upon her cheeks. Abradatas being in the front of the army, a goodly man to see, now harnessed with this armour seemed a most galliard° and clear gentleman, his nature being correspondent to the same. Then taking the reins of the chariot governor, he prepared to ascend into the chariot. Then Panthea, all other being commanded to stand back, said: 'Truly, Abradatas, if any other do more esteem her husband than her own life, I think ye know that I am one of them. Therefore what need I to rehearse every thing severally, for my facts, I think, persuade you more than my words. And thus endeavouring myself toward you, as you know I profess to you by love toward you and yours to me, that I had rather be buried quick together in the earth with you, being a noble man, than live in villainy. Thus I esteem you with the best, and myself not with the worst. And I know that we owe great thank to Cyrus, which deigned to entertain me, being a captive and chosen for him, not as a thrall with villainy nor free with the disparagement of mine honour but kept me as I had been his brother's wife. After that Araspes departed from him, which had the keeping of me, I promised him that if he would suffer me to send unto you, that you should become more loyal and assured to him than ever Araspes was.' Thus she said. Abradatas being delighted with her and tenderly touching her head, looking up to heaven made this prayer: 'O most mighty Jupiter, grant me to appear an husband meet for Panthea and a friend worthy Cyrus, who hath so honourably dealt with us.' Thus speaking at the entering of the chariot seat, he went up to the same. He

---

[41] shaffrons and cremets] frontlets and breastplates.
[42] orient colour] The Greek refers to 'Phoenician' colouring; purple dye from Tyre, Phoenicia, was prized in classical antiquity, though it was more commonly known as 'Tyrian purple' in the sixteenth century.

being ascended, and the governor making fast the seat, Panthea having none other thing to embrace, did kiss the chariot seat. And he went forth. Panthea followed him privily till he turned and espied her and said, 'Be of good comfort, Panthea, farewell and now depart'. Then her eunuchs and women conveyed her to her own chariot, and so bestowed her that she was covered with a curtain. Other men, although Abradatas and his chariot was goodly to behold, yet they could not behold him till Panthea was past. When Cyrus had made oblation° and the army was furnished according to his commandment, appointing espies one before an other, he assembled the captains and said thus:

The Oration of Cyrus

'Dear friends and confederates, God hath expressed in our sacrifices the same tokens as they did when they gave us our former victory. I would ye should record things which, I think, if you remember ye shall the more courageously go to the battle. You have been exercised in martial prowess much more than your enemies; you have excelled one another; your enemies have impaired one another. Of both parties there be [those] that have not fought. They that lean to our enemies know that their chief captains will soonest shrink; you that be with us know that with willing confederates, you adventure to fight. And it is like that they which trust one another will abide and fight with one accord. They which be in distrust must needs devise which of them soonest may escape. Then, friends, let us go against our enemies, having harnessed chariots against our enemies unharnessed. And likewise being harnessed, both horse and man, let us fight with them unharnessed. And with such footmen ye shall fight as ye did tofore. For the Egyptians have like harness and keep like array, and shields they have greater than they either can do or see anything. And being disposed into hundreds, it is evident that one shall hinder another, except very few. And if they think by their throngs to oppress us, we must first resist them with horses, and the weapon of defenced horses. And if any of them abide by it, how can he fight at once with our horsemen, with our footmen and our turrets? For they in the turrets shall defend us, and so hurt our enemies that they, leaving fighting, shall not know what to do. And if ye want anything, declare it unto me and with God's help we shall lack nothing. If any man will say aught, let him speak his mind; if not, returning to sacrificing and prayer to God, to whom we have already sacrificed, repair unto your men, every man so exhorting his as I have you. And let every one declare to his men that he is worthy to be a ruler, expressing himself to be manly both in behaviour, countenance and words.'[43]

---

[43] and words] The 1567 edition resets this final leaf of the end of the sixth book, omitting the graduated final paragraph and tag 'Thus ended the sixth book', and incorporating 13 typographic differences in just 49 words.

The Seventh Book of the School of Cyrus's Institution, Containing the Overthrow of Croesus, the Taking of Sardis and Babylon, and the Beginning of Cyrus's Civil Regiment

Having made their prayers to God, they went to their ensigns° and for Cyrus and his company meat and drink was brought, they being yet about the sacrifice; he, standing still as he was, made a small repast and always gave to him that wanted. Then prayers and ceremonies of tasting made, he drunk and so did they that were with him. This done, beseeching Jupiter to be companion and guide, he mounted on horseback and commanded the other to do the same, being all armed as he was with coats of purple, corselets of brass, headpieces with white crests, sword and spear and dart. This only difference was, that their armour shone like gold and his glittering like glass: and the horses were likewise barbed with brass. Being on horseback, and musing which way to take, it thundered on the right side, at which as a lucky token he said, 'We follow the most mighty Jupiter', and so marched, having on the right hand Chrysantas and the horsemen, on the left hand, Arsamas and the footmen, commanding to have good eye to the ensign and to follow in order. The ensign was an eagle of gold,[1] displayed upon a long spear, and this standard do remain with the king of Persia. His army rested thrice before he had sight of the enemies. Then having gone two miles and an half, they began to see their enemy's camp, which they perceived to be much greater than theirs, and saw how they[2] stayed their main battle to fetch a compass and enclose them.

Cyrus seeing this stayed never the more but went on and, considering how much they did stretch along the wings of the battle, he said: 'Do you mark, Chrysantas, what a compass our enemies make?' 'Yea', quoth Chrysantas, 'and I much marvel, for methink they draw their wings too far from the battle.' 'Yea, and from ours too', quoth Cyrus. 'And why do they so?', quoth he. 'Because', quoth Cyrus, 'they fear we would give them the onset on their battle, they[3] being so far from it.' 'And how can they help one another being so far asunder?', quoth Chrysantas. 'Their purpose is', quoth Cyrus, 'so much to environ us as they may in all places give us the onset at once.' 'And do they well?', quoth he. 'For some

---

[1] eagle of gold] The ensign of Cyrus, and the Achaemenids after him, was a golden eagle, according to Xenophon (here and in *Anabasis*, I. 10. 12); Quintus Curtius Rufus (III. 3. 16) describes a similar ensign used by Darius III in the unsuccessful campaign of the last Achaemenid ruler against Alexander.

[2] they] i.e. Croesus's army, who arrest the central section and instead try to surround the Persians 'like a [Greek letter] gamma [Γ]', ὥσπερ γάμμα (*hósper gámma*). Barker tries to provide the general sense, but an error seems to have crept in here: Croesus clearly intends to (en)compass rather than to 'fetch a compass'.

[3] they] Here, the main army, waiting in the centre. Cyrus deduces that Croesus fears that his own flanks will come too close to Cyrus's army and end up engaging with them while the main part of his army is still too far away.

part they do well, for some evil', quoth Cyrus. Then he commanded Arsamas to lead the footmen softly and Chrysantas to follow with the horsemen in order, and that he would go see where were best to begin the battle and consider for all the army. And when he had found the place, he would sing a song of praise which he willed them to follow, because of the noise and escries° that should be made at the giving of the onset, which should be when Abradatas did enter with his chariots, whom he commanded the rest to follow that they might assail the enemies, being in disorder, and that he would not be long from them. This said, he gave the privy word, that was 'Jupiter saviour and guide', and marched, going betwixt the Chariots and the pikemen[4] and spake to them all according to their quality.[5] To some he would say, 'It doth me good to see your faces'; to some, 'Remember, this day's fight is not only for the time present, but for the victories past and the felicities to come'; to some, 'From henceforth we can have no cause to blame God, having given us so great advantage, but we must be valiant men'; to some, 'How could we ever exhort one another to more profit than now? For if we do well, we may greatly help ourselves'; to some, 'Ye be not ignorant what rewards be propounded: to them that conquer, glory, praise, advantage, freedom and rule; to them that be conquered, the contrary. Therefore he that loveth himself let him do as I shall, for I will give none example of cowardice.' To them that had been proved before, he said: 'What should I speak to you? For you know what day the valiant men have in battle and what the cowards.' Then going toward Abradatas who, seeing him, left his chariot and came running to him, and so likewise the other that had charge of the chariots, to whom Cyrus said: 'The immortal God hath given you your request, that is, to have the forward. Ye must remember to do well, for the Persians shall behold you, we shall follow you, and not suffer you to be succourless.' To whom Abradatas answered that for his part he was well enough, but for the sides of the host, he stood in doubt, seeing the enemies defenced with all kind of strength and they only with his chariots. In so much as if he had not taken the charge upon him, he would have been ashamed of it, considering the danger of the rest and safety of himself. 'Well', quoth Cyrus, 'if you be well yourself, for the rest take no thought. For I trust with God's help to order the matter so as you shall give the onset when they shall flee, and then think me to be at hand and set upon your enemies.' Thus he said with lusty words, being otherwise no great bragger, and then he said he should have the enemy coward and the friend valiant. And whiles he had leisure, he should exhort his men to be of good courage, and that they might do it the better to set a contention among them. For by that, every

---

[4] pikemen] i.e. soldiers carrying pikes.
[5] according to their quality] Shakespeare may have drawn on this scene for the words of encouragement his Henry V offers to the various ranks of his army the night before Agincourt.

man would endeavour to do better than his fellow, and all affirm that nothing is so available as virtue.

Abradatas departed and did accordingly. Cyrus went to the left wing where Hystaspas was with half the Persian horsemen, whom, calling by name, he said, 'O Hystaspas, now ye see we need your quickness, for if we can get the advantage of our enemies, we shall without danger of ourselves overthrow them.' To whom Hystaspas, smiling, said, 'Let me alone with them that be in the front. As for the sides, give the charge to other.' 'I will myself do it', quoth Cyrus, 'and which of us soonest by God's help have the victory, let him come to that place where most danger is.' Then coming to the cars, he spoke with the captains of the same, saying he was come to succour them. And when they should hear that he had given the charge, they should do their devoir because they should fight more in safety without at the side than being within at the front. Then he commanded Pharnucus and Artagersas, that with a thousand footmen and as many Persian horsemen they should set upon their enemies when they saw him enter the right wing, and force themselves to break the ray, which they might well do, being strong and on horseback and the enemy's fresh men[6] in the rearward, against whom they should set their camels, and be assured that before they came to the stripes, they should condemn their enemies.[7] Cyrus having spoken thus, went to the right wing.

Croesus, supposing to be nigh enough, gave token that they should no more go forward, but turn against the enemies, and gave the sign to battle, and at once brake in at three places: the front and both sides. At the which Cyrus's host was in great fear, and, as a little stone is enclosed in a great circle,[8] even so was Cyrus's army with all generation of enemies,[9] the hindermost band only except; which thing Cyrus hearing, gave token that they should turn to the enemies, a great silence being among them, because of the peril that was present. Therefore he began the song of praise, the which the whole army followed. Then, they crying to the martial god Mars[10] with the men of arms, he gave the charge upon the wing which by the might of the battle that followed, was soon sparpled°. Artagersas, perceiving that Cyrus had given the onset, with the camels set upon the left wing, according to Cyrus's commandment. The horses could not abide the camels a great way off, but (as their nature is) so soon

[6] fresh men] A scribal or compositorial error for the enemy's 'horse men'. Barker's grasp of the phalanx formation is poor (unlike Holland's).
[7] condemn their enemies] i.e. that the Persian army will see their enemy undone. Holland has 'ye shall see your enemies to become ridiculous and to make you good sport' (sig. V2v).
[8] in a great circle] Barker modifies the Greek text's simile of a small tile, ὥσπερ μικρὸν πλινθίον (hósper mikròn plinthíon), surrounded by larger ones.
[9] generation of enemies] 'Generation' is Barker's addition.
[10] martial god Mars] Holland has 'they sounded *Alala* to Mars', and Filelfo's Latin also has calls to Mars, though modern editions specify that Enyalius, a minor god serving Mars, is the figure invoked.

as they felt them, turned back, leaping and flinging here and there over all the fields. But Artagersas, keeping order, was continually at their backs, and with good courage troubled them on both sides with his cars, in so much as some flying them were dispatched of the horsemen that followed; some avoiding the horsemen were killed with the cars. Abradatas, without any longer tarrying, came on, crying with loud voice: 'O friends, follow me', and with his spurs took up his horse and brake in with the rest of the chariots, and went so far that he came to the Egyptian band and a small company of his trusty friends with him. Whereby it was evident that as in many other places, no battle is so strong as a band of faithful friends.[11] So the day it was proved by him and his assured friends who never shrunk from him but were always about him without fear. The other chariotmen, seeing the Egyptian battle so strong, withdrew themselves and forsook him. He and his little company not being able to break the Egyptian battle, with extreme violence beat some down and caused some to retire, whom with their hooked carts they broke a pieces, both horse and man and every thing. Abradatas in this wonderful revolution and tempest of war, passing with his car over the heaps of so many dead bodies, fell from his cart to the ground, and so did the rest of his companions who, freely fighting as was meet for noble men, died most valiantly. The Persians seeing this danger of Abradatas came whole together and brake upon them that had slain him, and slew many of them. Notwithstanding the Egyptians did valiantly, being many in number, and well armed with strong and large pikes, and shields bigger than the Persian targets that covered their whole bodies, being also good to punch at hand, and so fiercely coming on that the Persians gave back, still fighting till they came to their towered chariots, with the which the Egyptians were afresh so handled that there began a new fight, cruel to behold, with the murder of so many men, with the noise of so many cries, and fall of so many weapons as was pity to hear.

Cyrus being come, and seeing the Persians put back, was grieved, and perceiving none other way to win but by coming upon them at the back with his band, he gave a turn and (unlooked for) came upon them behind, and did so much harm as the poor Egyptians amidst the wounds and blows were fain to turn back to back[12] to resist their enemy. And with a cry that enemies were on their backs, they fought so manfully that Cyrus himself was unhorsed, his horse being wounded in the belly with a sword, at the grief whereof, being in a rage, fell and threw Cyrus to the ground. There might a man have seen how worthy a thing it is for a prince to be beloved of his subjects. For by and by making a

---

[11] band of faithful friends] Again, it's possible that Shakespeare borrows Henry V's rhetoric of comradeship and the 'band of brothers' idea from here.

[12] back to back] i.e. the Egyptians are forced to turn around to face Cyrus, who now attacks them from the rear.

great shout altogether, manly fighting for to save Cyrus, after much murder on both parts, one alighted off his horse and set Cyrus upon the same; who, seeing the Persian bands of Hystaspas and Chrysantas to be come and the Egyptians beaten down on every side, he went up to one of the chariot towers where he saw all the enemies flying away on every side, saving only the Egyptians who, being determined to die in the place, covered them self with their shields and resisted to the death. Wherefore marvelling at their virtue and pitying their calamity, commanded them that fought against them to withdraw and sent a trumpet unto them, demanding whether they had rather die for them that had forsaken them or be saved of him and be reputed valiant men. The Egyptians said, 'How can we be saved and reputed valiant?' Cyrus answered, 'Because we see you only remain and fight.' Then the Egyptians: 'And what honesty shall it be to us to be saved?' And Cyrus: 'In that ye do not betray your friends, but yield to us that rather seek your life than death.' The Egyptians asked: 'If we become your friends, what service will ye have of us?' And he said, to be his true liege men,[13] and receive benefit. 'And what benefit?' quoth they. 'In giving you' (quoth Cyrus), 'greater stipend than ye now have for the time of war and in peace. If you will remain with me, I will give you land and cities to inhabit.' Then the Egyptians desired they might not be compelled to fight against Croesus, and to the rest they consented and gave their faith, and remained ever after trusty people, and had given them two cities beyond the flood Cyme at the sea coast, Larissa and Cyllene, which be still possessed of their offspring and called the Egyptians' cities.

In this fight, the Egyptians had the price[14] of the Assyrians, of Cyrus's camp the Persian horsemen, whereby the duty of the service remaineth in price with the Persians. The hooked carts were also much praised, and remaineth also in estimation. But as for the camels, because they did only affray the horses and did none other hurt, and no gentleman use to keep any for to ride, they were restored to their kind and used for the burden. After this victory, Cyrus hearing that Croesus was fled to Sardis,[15] and the other nations gone as far as they could, he took his voyage toward Sardis where, being arrived, encamped and set his artillery against the town. And the night following, with the Chaldeans and Persians, by the help of a Persian slave, servant to a captain at the castle, knowing a way through the water, he got the fortress, which thing being known, the Lydians forsook the walls. Cyrus abiding till day, entered with the rest of his

---

[13] his true liege men] An elaboration by Barker in specifically feudal terms; the Greek simply promises εὖ ποιεῖν — i.e. to do (someone) good. Holland follows Barker: 'I will doe well by you, and look for the like at your hands, as of true liege men' (sig. [V4]).
[14] had the price] Holland's phrasing is clearer: 'In this battaile, the Aegyptians alone of all the enemies bare themselves courageously and wonne renowne: and of those on Cyrus side the Persian horsemen seemed to performed the bravest service' (sig. [V4]).
[15] Sardis] Capital of Lydia.

army, commanding every man to keep array. Croesus had fled into the palace and cried for Cyrus. He, leaving a guard about him, went to see the castle which the Persians kept, and seeing the harness of the Chaldeans being on the ground, they being gone to sack the town, he called their captains to him, commanding them to depart the army. For he in no wise would that they that had broken order and been disobedient should get the spoil from them that were obedient and in order; and that he had purposed to make them notable above all the Chaldeans, which they through their greediness had lost. The Chaldeans were in great fear and besought him to cease his anger, and that they would render everything. He answered, he had no need of them, but if they would have his favour, they should deliver to the Persians the things that they had got. For thereby his army should be made the more obedient. The Chaldeans did accordingly. When Cyrus had set things in order, he commanded Croesus to be brought before him, to whom Croesus said: 'All hail my lord, fortune[16] having granted you so to be.' 'And you also', quoth Cyrus, 'for we both be men.' Then Cyrus asked him if he would give him any counsel. Croesus answered, with all his heart if it might be good counsel, for it should be good for himself also.[17] 'Then', quoth Cyrus, 'ye shall understand that whereas my soldiers have taken great pains in my service, and I hitherto not rewarded them, it seemeth a thing of congruence that I should give them this city to be sacked which, next Babylon is the most rich in Asia. Loth I were to have them disobedient, and sorry to see so noble a city sacked.' Croesus thus answered: 'Give me leave to say to the Lydians that I have obtained of you that the city shall not be spoiled, neither women nor children hindered, and that they for this benefit shall present to you the chief jewel they have, and so shall you have riches infinite, and the city still in good case; whereas if ye sack it, ye shall destroy all arts and sciences, which be the fountains of all good things; and when this is done, ye may consult of the sack[18] hereafter. And as for my treasure, send your officers and let them take possession of it.'

Cyrus liked his advice and followed the same. Then Cyrus willed him to tell what answers he had of Apollo at Delphos,[19] because he had great affiance° in them, and was in great credit with Apollo. 'I would it had been so', quoth Croesus, 'but it came otherwise to pass.' 'And how?', quoth Cyrus, 'for methink ye speak strangely.' 'When I came first to Apollo I did but to prove him. And not only God but man also cannot abide to be discredited. Wherefore when I

---

[16] fortune] On Croesus's verbal challenge to Cyrus and Xenophon's careful reworking of the Herodotean narrative of Cyrus, Croesus and Solon, see Tatum, *Xenophon's Imperial Fiction*, pp. 146-59.
[17] for himself also] Barker's use of indirect speech where his source uses direct speech breaks with his habit in the first six books.
[18] consult of the sack] i.e. you can still decide to go ahead and pillage the city.
[19] at Delphos] The oracle at the temple of Apollo at Delphi.

sent unto him concerning my sons, he would give me none answer. But after I had pleased him with gifts of gold and silver, and purging myself of my former mistrust, he said I should have children. And it was true, but without any consolation to me, for the one died in the flower of his age and the other never spake.[20] Being oppressed with the calamity of this misfortune, I sent again to him to know how I might live the rest of my life in felicity. He answered, if I knew myself,[21] I should live happily. By which answer I was greatly comforted, thinking it to be an easy matter for a man to know himself, but to know another man I thought an hard thing, and so I lived without mischance till this time. Then being persuaded by the Assyrian to come against you in camp, I fell into all kind of peril, and yet am saved, I cannot tell how, without any evil, and cannot be angry with God. For knowing myself to be too weak to meddle with you, I went my way and had no hurt. But now,[22] waxing proud by my riches and being allured by the persuasions of them that comforted° me to take the matter in hand, affirming that I should be lord of all and they my subjects, I took it upon me, not knowing myself in that I did not consider how far unlike I was to match with you, being of the line of God and of most noble virtues, whereas the first of my ancestors[23] was at one time made a king and a freeman; wherefore of right and skill I am for my ignorance punished, and now I know myself indeed, and confess the answer of Apollo to be true, humbly beseeching you to have pity upon me, for only you may make me happy.' Cyrus answered that he himself knew best what was to do, and that for his part, he was sorry for his misfortunes. And in some recompense, he restored him his wife, children and familiar friends, and only forbade him use of arms. Croesus answered, if he did so he should make him have that happy life that he was wont to attribute to other. 'And who be they?', quoth Cyrus. 'My wife', quoth Croesus, 'who being in continual pleasures and delicacies with me doth not taste the cares that I find in war and other governments, but I hereafter shall live as she doth, through your benefit, and therefore am bound once again to give great thanks to Apollo.' Cyrus, hearing his talk, much marvelled at his modesty, and from that time forth had him always with him, either for to have profit by him or to

---

[20] never spake] Herodotus tells of the first time the son spoke, to plead for mercy for his father who was about to be killed by one of Cyrus's army, following the conquest of Sardis, in the Herodotean account (1. 85).

[21] knew myself] 'Nosce te ipsum', inscribed at the temple of Apollo at Delphi. In the Holland version, two versions of the declarations of the oracle at Delphi are set off from the text in Greek and Roman capitals: 'know thyselfe Croesus, and thou shalt surely be happy' and 'Croesus know thy selfe, and thou art he that to thy last shall happy be'.

[22] But now] i.e. lately/recently.

[23] first of my ancestors] Croesus refers to his ancestor Gyges, a bodyguard to King Candaules, and the man to whom uxorious Candaules secretly revealed his wife, naked. Following this, Candaules' wife persuaded Gyges to kill Candaules for his transgression, and to become king himself (Herodotus, 1. 8–12).

be the more in safety for him.²⁴ The day following, he gave the money to some to keep, and appointed some to take the treasures that Croesus should deliver them, and give the clergy to offer as much as they would desire, and lay up the rest in his coffers, and appoint wagons to bear it from place to place that they might have the use thereof at their need.

    This being done, Cyrus asked when any of them saw Abradatas, marvelling that he had no sight of him, being wont most diligently to resort unto him. One of the servants answered that he was slain, valiantly fighting with the Egyptians, and how he was forsaken of the most part of his men, and that his wife had taken him into her chariot and brought him to the flood Pactolus,²⁵ accompanied with her maids and eunuchs, being about to make a grave to bury him there, his wife sitting on the ground dressing the dead body, having his head in her lap. Which when Cyrus heard, he struck his thigh and by and by mounted on horseback and took with him a thousand horse, commanding Gobryas and Gadatas that they should prepare so rich ornaments as they could get to honour the body of so worthy a friend, and provide herds of cattle to sacrifice at his funeral. Being come where he saw the sorrowful wife sit by the corpse of her noble husband, he wept and said: 'O faithful and good heart, wherefore hast thou forsaken us?'²⁶ And took him by the right hand, which being cut off of the Egyptians, dissevered from the body, whereat he was much more grieved. The wife shrieked pitifully and took the hand of²⁷ Cyrus, kissed it and set it again in the place, saying, 'The rest of his body is in like case, but to what purpose should I show it you? And this hath he done and suffered as well for your sake as for mine. For I always comforted him to do so valiantly, as he might appear a worthy friend for you; and [he] hath done no less, not to obey me but to serve you. And he now is dead, and I that was occasion thereof am alive.' At the which words, Cyrus not being able to keep him from weeping, after a certain space, when he could speak said, 'O Panthea, your husband being victoriously dead, hath gotten an immortal name. And now you shall take these ornaments for his funeral which Gobryas and Gadatas have brought; and I promise you that in other things nothing shall be wanted²⁸ to do him honour,

---

²⁴ safety for him] The Herodotean account differs significantly: in it Cyrus has Croesus placed on a pyre, and is only rescued, and then listened to, by Cyrus, when it rains — a sign of Apollo's favour for Croesus.
²⁵ Pactolus] The river of King Midas, whose touch turned everything to gold, as Ovid presented it.
²⁶ forsaken me] Echoes of Psalm 22, although closest to the later King James version, 'My God, my God, why has thou forsaken me?'. Barker's endorsement of the reading of pagan classical writers in the service of strengthening Christian faith is explored in the preface to his translation of St Basil the Great's well-known sermon 'To Young Men on the Use of Greek Literature' (*An exhortation of holye Basilius Magnus to hys younge kynsmen* (1557)).
²⁷ took the hand of] i.e. took [Abradatas' dissevered hand] from.
²⁸ wanted] 'vanted' in 26066 and 26067; a compositorial error.

for every one of us shall leave some monument in his memory. And as for yourself, ye shall not be abandoned, for I will honour your wifely chastity and virtue and bestow you upon whom you request me.' Panthea answered, 'I will not hide from you upon whom I will be bestowed.' This being spoken, Cyrus went his way, having pity of the woman that was bereft such a man, and the man that should no more see such a wife. Then she commanded her eunuchs to depart, that she might bewail her fill, and her nurse[29] abide and when she was dead to fold her and her husband in one cloth.[30] The nurse besought her not to commit any such folly, but when she saw that would not prevail, she sat her down and wept. Then Panthea took a sword that she had prepared for the purpose and killed herself, and reposing her head upon her husband's breast she died. The nurse cried out, and wrapped them together as she was commanded. Cyrus, hearing of the woman's act, returned with speed to see if there were any hope of life. The three eunuchs, knowing their lady to be dead, drew their swords and killed themselves. And there was made a monument[31] for them all that remaineth to this day, and letters in the Syrian tongue set upon the high pillars and the statues of Abradatas and Panthea. Cyrus, hearing no remedy, marvelled at the stoutness of the woman, and weeping at her calamity, departed, and caused sepultures to be made according to every man's degree, with letters on the lower pillars of them that bare the sceptres.

In this mean time, a discord arose between the Carians, being a civil debate, and keeping the forts of the countries and both parts, called to Cyrus for aid who, being at Sardis about artillery to batter the walls of them that would not obey, sent Cadusius, a Persian, a man skilful in war, and of great humanity, with an army appointed unto him; with whom the Cilicians and Cyprians went on their voluntary will, wherefore he never sent Persian governor over them[32] but suffered their natural kings to rule and pay him a tribute and find him men at his need. Cadusius came into Caria and both parts came unto him, promising to receive him into their town if he would be enemy to their enemies. Who answered that either part had reason to lament of their adversary, and that they should so order the matter as the adversaries should not know that they had conference with him, that the device might have the better effect. Then they gave their faith on both sides, the Carians to receive him without fraud to the weal of Cyrus and the Persians, and he to enter without guile for the weal

---

[29] nurse] 'Nourice' in Barker, changed throughout to 'nurse'.

[30] in one cloth] Echoes here of Desdemona's instructions to her servant that she and Othello are to be buried in their wedding sheets, as their winding sheet?

[31] monument] Cyrus's order for huge, grand tombs for Panthea and Abradatas provides the ending for Richard Farrant's *The Warres of Cyrus*, a stage romance based on this Panthea and Araspes subplot (only in Xenophon).

[32] over them] i.e. Cyrus, as a mark of appreciation for their volunteering in this way, never thereafter sent a Persian satrap but trusted their own kings to rule over them.

of them that received him. Thus devising with both parts, he that same night entered their castles and forts. That done, the day following he called both parts before him, thinking themselves deceived, and thus said: 'O Carians, I did swear to enter into the weal of them that should receive me. Now if I should destroy you both, I think I should be entered to both your hindrance, but if I make peace and cause you to till your land, I think I am entered to both your profits. Therefore from this day forth ye shall have friendly conversation together, you shall without fear labour your lands, you shall make parentages and matrimonies, and if any of you goeth about any injury, Cyrus and we shall be his adversary.' From that day forth, the ports[33] were opened, the ways full of people, the fields full of labourers, feastful days celebrated and all things with peace and joy replenished.

In this time, messengers came from Cyrus demanding if he had need of any army or artillery. Cadusius answered that he might spare his own army. And having finished those things, he left garrisons in the forts and departed with his army. The Carians besought him to tarry, which he refusing it, sent to Cyrus requesting him if he did appoint them any governor it might be Cadusius. At this time, Cyrus sent Hystaspas with an army against Phrygia that joined with Hellespont,[34] and willed Cadusius to accompany him that they[35] might the rather obey Hystaspas. The Grecians that inhabit the sea[36] gave many gifts, and agreed to go where Cyrus should appoint, to pay tribute and receive no barbarian soldiers into their towns. The king of the Phrygians prepared himself to stand at his defence, but being abandoned of his captains, he rendered himself to be judged as Cyrus would. Hystaspas left many garrisons and departed, taking away with him many Phrygian horsemen. Cyrus gave commission to Cadusius that he should suffer those Phrygians to bear armour that had been obedient; the other he should spoil of their horse and harness and make them slingers. This done, Cyrus leaving great garrisons in Sardis, he removed his camp toward Babylon, having many carts of treasure and Croesus in his company, who had the just account of the treasure and gave the same in writing to Cyrus that he might know who did faithfully and who no. Cyrus took

---

[33] ports] i.e. gates.

[34] Phrygia that joined with Hellespont] The Ionian Greek cities flourished under Persian rule, but would eventually revolt, setting off the Greco-Persian wars in 499 BCE. Traditionally the border between Europe and Asia, the Hellespont retained its currency as a key border in the early modern imagination, thanks in part to the classical legacy but also to the contemporary status of the Bosphorus in Ottoman territory, on the edges of Europe. See, for example, the significance of crossing the Hellespont in Christopher Marlowe's *Hero and Leander*.

[35] they] i.e. the Phrygians (hearing another army to be on its way, might therefore submit to Hystaspas).

[36] Grecians that inhabit the sea] i.e. Greeks who live by the sea.

the writings and said to Croesus he had done very warily,[37] notwithstanding they that did take any of the money should take their own, for he had it for the use of all and gave the bills to his friends that they might know who did well and who not. The Lydians that went willingly with him he received them in the army; they that did the contrary, he took their horses from them and gave them to the Persians and burned their harness and compelled them to bear slings, which is esteemed most vile service.[38] But yet with other company they do good, whereas being alone they be worth nothing.

In his voyage to Babylon he subdued great Phrygia, Cappadocia, and Arabia, and increased his camp forty thousand men, and gave many horses to his confederates. So he arrived at Babylon with an huge puissant army, and environed the city with his army, he with certain horsemen viewing the city about; and having considered the walls, he intended to withdraw the army when a runaway of the city came and told him that they w[ith]in would set upon him if he retired, for they thought his battle very small; and it was no marvel because the compass was so great, that the host seemed very little. Which Cyrus hearing, commanded the soldiers that were about the walls and seemed very weak because of the length, to return into their places and both ends to repair to him that was in the middest, and by doubling their ranks they that went were the bolder, and they that stood the less in fear. And so united, they approached the walls within a bow shot, and went with courage beholding their enemies, the best being on both sides and the worst in the middest, which order is best to fight and worse to fly. And so they received at their pleasure without damage of the enemy and camped about the city.[39]

When they had well considered the same, then he called the captains and principal men of the army and said, 'Companions, having considered the quality of this city, I can not see how it can be got by force (the walls being so strong and high) but by siege. I think it the more sure and easy way to win it, there as be so many sorts of men, they shall the sooner be oppressed with hunger. Therefore they must either fight it out, which thing we desire, or perish by famine, which I think will prove. This is mine advice; if any of you can show me better way, I will follow it. If not, I will begin the siege.' Chrysantas answered that it was best so to do because the city was not only strong by the walls but also by the flood Euphrates that came through the middest of the city and was a quarter of a mile broad and two men's height deep.[40] Which opinion Gobryas

---

[37] warily] 'warely' in the text, i.e. carefully.
[38] vile service] Compression by Barker of Xenophon's more involved account of why and how slings are considered only fit for slaves.
[39] camped about the city] Barker omits some additional manoeuvres that Cyrus has his army perform before camping at a safe distance away from Babylon.
[40] height deep] Once again, Barker shifts the translation into indirect speech where direct speech is clear in the text.

confirmed, being practised in the city. Then Cyrus made a great trench[41] and deep for the more safety of his host, and with good measure of the ground, left so much space as might serve to build a tower, compassing the city with a great ditch and did cast the earth toward his camp, and erected towers over the flood, of an acre of bigness every way: that is, forty foot in h[e]igh[t] and the half in breadth, making the foundation of palm trees (which in that place be very great, and their nature such that if they be pressed down, they crook° up again).[42] And this he did to make the Assyrians to understand that he would endure the siege, and though the flood did bear down the trench yet it should do no hurt to the towers. The Babylonians having victuals for twenty years made a mock of all this gear, which when Cyrus understood, he divided his army into twelve parts, that every part might serve one month in the year. Which when the Babylonians heard, they made eftsoons a greater mock at the matter, considering that if the Phrygians, Lydians[43] and Arabians and Cappadocians did serve their course, they would be more enriched to them than to the Persians.

The trench and towers being furnished, Cyrus had learned that there was a feast in the town at which the Babylonians used to revel and riot all the night. Wherefore when night was come, he opened the trench and suffered so much water to pass as the flood might be waded over. Which being done, he commanded tribunes of the Persians that they should bring their bands two in a rank and the rest of the army to follow in like order. Then he commanded certain to prove whether it were passable.[44] Which being known, he called the captains and conductors and thus said: 'Friends, seeing we may with commodity enter the city by the flood, let us boldly do it and fear nothing. For having overcome them, when they were well friended, watchful, sober and in good order, now being the more part oppressed with sleep and wine and all without armour, what shall hinder or stop our victories? Which hearing that we be entered the city, shall not only not be able to fight against us, being astonished and amazed, but scarcely able to stand upon their feet. Now peradventure, some men may think that at the entry of the city we shall suffer a sharp assault, being beaten with stone and tiles that shall come from the houses' tops upon us. But this is not to be weighed: for we have Vulcan the god of fire for our debtor,[45] because

---

[41] a great trench] Cyrus's strategy of digging a trench draws praise from the Roman author Sextus Julius Frontinus (*The Stratagems of War*, III. 7. 3), an important figure in early modern political and military theory.

[42] palm trees] Barker omits Xenophon's comparison of the trees crooking-up again to the backs of pack-animals (unlike Holland).

[43] Lydians] 'Lycians' in the text, mistakenly; interestingly, Holland follows Barker's 'Lycians' but glosses it as 'Lydians' (sig. Y1).

[44] passable] Barker's account of Cyrus's great stratagem for breaking the siege at Babylon is curiously underplayed here, not just compressed but deprived of the supporting shape provided by Xenophon's punctuation and syntactical organization.

[45] debtor] Uncertain — 'dellsour' in the text; a compositorial error? Holland has simply 'a

the porches of their houses be overlaid with sulphur and their gates made of palm tree plastered with rosin, and we have flare and pitch and fire-brands enough to make sudden and great fire, so that with little labour, we shall make them either forsake their houses or be burned in the same. Therefore with lusty heart and courage, take your armour and follow me, who, with God's help will conduct you into the city, and by the help of Gobryas and Gadatas, who can guide us well the way, and they shall bring us straight to the palace.' 'That' (quoth they), 'shall not be hard to do, the gates of the court being open, and the keepers drunken as the rest of the city is.'

Cyrus said the thing was not to be delayed but to go on with all speed to take their enemies tardy. And this said, they entered in and of them that they met, some they killed, some fled into their houses, some made shouts and cries, to the which they that were with Gobryas answering with little noise, because they might seem to be drunk as they were, they together with the band of Gadatas went to the palace where, finding the gate shut, they killed the keepers, being drinking and sleeping. At the noise and tumult whereof the king, being moved, commanded the gates to be open to see what it might be, at the which Gadatas and his company rushed in and killed as many as came in their walk till they came to the king, whom they found standing with his sword drawn, and manfully set upon him and the other that, with such things as they could get, stood at their defence, and slew the king and all his men. In this time, Cyrus had sent the horsemen to make a cry in the city by them that could speak the Syrian tongue that as many as were taken out of their houses should be dead and charged them to kill so many as they found abroad.[46] Then came Gobryas and Gadatas, thanking God that they were revenged of the wicked king, and weeping for joy, kissed Cyrus's feet.[47]

When it was day, and they that kept the fortresses understood the city to be taken and the king slain, they rendered the castle to Cyrus, into the which he put other men and caused the dead to be buried and the living to bring their armour forth, and if any did the contrary, to dispatch him without more ado. Which being brought forth accordingly, he bestowed in the forces for munition, and to the sages gave the first fruits of the spoil to be offered to God, and to the rest of the camp for their travail he divided house and money accordingly; and if any man thought he were not well served, he might come and show his grief. He commanded the Babylonians to till the land, to pay tribute, and serve them

God to help us'.
[46] found abroad] Barker collapses two sets of orders: the cavalry have orders to kill anyone found outside, while those who spoke Assyrian were to convey to those in their houses that they should stay there or be killed if found outside.
[47] kissed Cyrus's feet] They kiss his hands and feet, but Barker may be thinking of *proskynesis* here: the doing of homage to ancient Persian kings by prostrating oneself at the king's feet.

to whom they should be given, and that the Persians and other companions that would there abide with him should be called lords of the things that they had.[48]

Then minding to order his court and princely state, he thought it good to do it with the counsel of his friends, that he might be less seen without envy and with more majesty, to the which purpose he devised to come abroad and show himself to all that would come unto him and give them audience; which thing being known, infinite people came about him, thrusting and fighting, that his servants could have no rule among them although they did the best they could to keep back the multitude; for every man thrust in afore other to get to Cyrus, who, seeing any of his friends, would hold forth his hand and reach them toward him, desiring them to tarry till the multitude were gone.[49] They tarried, and the people resorted more and more, so that night was come before he had any time for his friends. Wherefore he said unto them: 'It is now time to depart', having endured all day without meat. The next morning Cyrus came betime to the same place, and perceived greater confluence of people to be than was before, wherefore having a great guard of Persian soldiers about him, commanded them to keep back all other till the princes and captains had been with him, to whom being come, he spake in this wise: 'Friends and companions, we cannot complain of God[50] that we have not had our desires in all our enterprises unto this day, but after so many noble victories, if this be our life that we cannot repose ourselves nor enjoy our friends, I bid this felicity farewell with all my heart. Yesterday from morning till night I did nothing but gave audience to the people, and now I see as many or more to trouble us after like sort, whom, if I suffer to come unto me, we shall never have done. And one thing makes me smile, that these homely fellows that knows not me nor I them, do presume to be before you that have so long travailed in my service.[51] Whereas I think it meet that they that would have ado with me should first have the favour of you. But some man might haply say, "What meaneth this sudden alteration? Why did ye not so at the beginning?" The answer is ready: that in war the prince must be abroad, he must be doing of this thing and that thing; in pains he may not be inferior to his soldiers, nor in virtues, and many occasions he loseth except he be in sight himself. But now the great travail of war being ceased, methink we should seek for some quiet.[52] And because I cannot tell

---

[48] that they had] Cyrus's concern here is to show that the Babylonians whom he has defeated are not to be co-opted as allies but as slaves to the Persians.

[49] till the multitude were gone] An example of Cyrus's ostensibly being available to all and all his men being equal, but actually favouring his intimate friends, including those not of his class, such as Pheraulas.

[50] God] Barker more consistently translates 'the gods' as 'God' in books VII and VIII.

[51] homely] Barker adds a touch of colour to another long and convoluted sentence.

[52] some quiet] Following the conquest of Babylon, Cyrus's leadership style and lifestyle change significantly, becoming more private, despotic and luxurious, respectively.

which way to bring it about, and would be glad to do for the best, I am come to know your advice and counsel in the matter.'

When Cyrus had spoken, Artabasus (that said he was his kinsman) said thus: 'Cyrus, when you were young I was desirous of your friendship, and not bold to show it. But after I had been your messenger to Cyaxares, I thought I should have had more leisure and opportunity to have been with you, being for that travail well commended of you; but then came the Hyrcanians with new business so that we for your sake did our best to show them all manner of courtesy. Then after our enemy's camp was broken, ye had no time to pass the time with me, and I was well content therewith. After came in Gobryas, Gadatas, Cadusius and the Sacian, and all were honourably entertained and hard for me to have access unto you, then[53] going about the furniture° of Persian horsemen, cars and engines of war. I thought I might have had a time to enjoy with you. When the terrible news came that all generation of men were assembled against us, though the thing were horrible, yet I thought that God giving you the victory[54] there should remain no let to our conversation. But now, our enemies overcome, Sardis taken, Croesus prisoner, Babylon won and all ours, I thought, I might have free access unto you. Yet I swear that yesterday and I had not played the man and laid about me with my fists, I should not have gotten to you, nor then nother,[55] had not you drawn me with your hand and commanded me to abide; and so I did the whole day without meat or drink. Therefore if we that be chief about you may have access unto you, so it is; if not, I would counsel all to forsake you, except such as from their childhood have been brought up with you.' Cyrus and many other smiled at this talk. When Chrysantas arose, and thus said, 'It hath been very wisely done of you, Cyrus, to show yourself to every man, suffering them to speak unto you, because you have had to do with so many sorts of men who in camp time[56] be most allured by the presence of the captain. But now that ye have got all things as you would, and be in so good state ye may at all times furnish yourself of men, and yourself ought to seek from repose and not be without an house and family, the greatest comfort in the world, being shame to us to have our houses and you to be without'; all the other according to Chrysantas.

[53] then] tha[n] in the text, but 'then' makes more sense in this context.
[54] God giving you the victory] Barker inserts God into this passage where Artabasus simply envisages success in their campaigns.
[55] nor then nother] A compositorial error? '[N]or then nigher' seems to be the sense, though the translation of the whole sentence is quite muddled. Like Filelfo, Barker has left out the oath 'by Mithras', the only direct reference to a Persian god in the *Cyropaedia*; Holland retains it ('so help me Methres', sig. [Y3]), though he glosses it 'That is, the Sunne', preserving a faint Zoroastrian connection.
[56] in camp time] Further compression here; Chrysantas spells out the necessity of Cyrus motivating the multitude to fight for him, which becomes less visible in Barker's comment about 'in camp time'.

Cyrus entered the palace, receiving the treasure that was brought from Sardis, and after the counsel of his clergy, sacrificed to Jupiter and the god of household,[57] bending his mind to settle his state. And pondering what a charge he had to govern a city, the chief of the world, lately conquered and not well affected toward him, he thought it necessary to have a guard about his person. And considering that princes many times be betrayed by their meat, drink, sleep and bed, he thought it good to provide for the same; and thinking that no man can be faithful that loveth another better than his lord, and that they which have children, wife or woman be constrained of nature to love the same, he concluded that eunuchs should be most meet for his purpose, being deprived of these matters, and he able to advance them to honours wherewith they be most won. For being a generation of men most vile, they stand only upon the favour of their prince, and every man thinking himself better than they, they bear their hearts to him alone that accept their service. But it might be thought that they were weak and effeminate, whereas the truth is not so, for by example of other beasts, as horses, fierce and untractable, being gelded, leave their wildness and yet be meet for the war; bulls gelded be not so savage, and yet more meet to till the land; dogs gelded wait on their masters, not straying abroad, be meet to keep a guard[58] and not the worse to run. Men likewise, in this case, though they be bereft of voluptuous instinct, yet they be not the less unmeet to serve, in riding, in shooting, in obeying, in diligent doing of their duty, and no men more desirous of honour than they, as appeareth in war and warlike chases. Their fealty in their lords' perils is so well known as it needeth no more proof, whose lack of nature is recompensed by use of weapon. Wherefore he appointed all the guard of his person to be of gelded men. Yet considering that this was not sufficient, he purposed upon a great number to rule so great a multitude, and remembering that the Persians at home in their country had but bare livings for the barrenness of the country, which with continual toil they could not make very fruitful, he thought they would be contented to lead a better life with him. Wherefore he ordained ten thousand of them to ward the palace when he was within, and go about his person when he went abroad. And that nothing might be wanted, he bestowed many other garrisons throughout Babylon to remain whether he were at home or abroad, and caused the Babylonians to pay them their stipend whom he intended to keep low, and of all other to make most poor. And this order for the guard of his person, and of the city, yet remaineth.

Then weighing how he might maintain his empire achieved,[59] and enlarge the same by further conquest, and considering how little the number of his

---

[57] god of household] Barker does not name Vesta, as he had in Book I.
[58] guard] 'yearde' in the text; the later books contain more compositorial or scribal errors than the earlier ones.
[59] empire achieved] This is only the second use of the term 'empire'; it first appeared in Gobryas's account of the Assyrian prince's inheritance of his father's empire in Book IV.

soldiers were in respect of his subjects, he thought good that they with whom, by God's help, he had gotten so famous victories, should be still trained in virtue, not leaving their accustomed uses and living licentiously in idleness, but so in use with goodness as, uncommanded, they might do any noble virtue. Wherefore he called the nobles and chieftains,⁶⁰ and said unto them: 'My friends and companions, we be greatly bound to the immortal gods, who have granted us to have the things that we desired, a country fertile and abundant, houses well apparelled, and slaves at commandment, which things I would no man should think he hold them injustly or of another man.⁶¹ For by ancient law among all men, it hath from the beginning been confirmed that cities taken, and all things in them, as men and money, be the reward to victory. Therefore let no man think he possess anything unjustly, but if he leaveth anything, that it cometh of humanity. Mine opinion is, O friends, that if we give ourselves to ease and pleasure after the rate° of them that thinks to be none other felicity and none other misery but to take pain, we shall of necessity set little one by another, and be deprived of all our weal. For it sufficeth not to be good a while, except a man continueth in the study thereof to the end. And as other arts despised be of less price, and strong bodies turned to idleness fall into diseases, even so prudence, temperance and fortitude their exercise being less, be turned into vice. Wherefore methink that we in no wise should leave the use of virtue to follow vice. To begin well is a great matter, but to bring to good end is all.⁶² Many a thing is well begun by rashness, but not ended but with prudence and diligence. Wherefore seeing this to be manifest, we ought to apply virtue more than ever we did, knowing that the more goods a man have, the more envy and danger he hath also, specially in a kingdom gotten by force, as ours is. Of the which yet we need not doubt, we having come by it by martial prowess and not by treachery. Wherefore let us endeavour ourselves to that may be our avail, thinking we that be rulers ought to be better than they that be ruled, whom we will make partakers with us of heat, cold, meat, drink, sleep and labour; but in knowledge and art of war, they shall not meddle with us but be kept under as tributaries and subjects, we being only worth[y] those arts whom God have given to use as instruments of felicity.⁶³ And as we have taken from them their armour, so we may never be without armour, for they that have weapon in hand have all things that they list. Now if a man would say, what are we the better for

---

⁶⁰ nobles and chieftains] Barker omits a significant sentence in which Cyrus decides not to be seen to command this course of action but rather to ensure that his men would choose it, such that they would be more willing and obedient to this desire.
⁶¹ **Marg**] Oration.
⁶² to bring to good end is all] The follow-through from Cyrus's education to his acquisition of an empire is matched by his keenness to ensure that that empire now be maintained.
⁶³ instruments of felicity] Barker shifts these gifts of freedom and felicity to the ruling classes rather than being the gifts to all men that Xenophon acknowledges.

our victories if we must still labour and suffer hardiness as we did tofore? Ye must know that those goods be the sweeter that be gotten with the more travail, and wise men take labours for sauces to meat; no dish never so dainty can be pleasant if a man have not a need thereof. And if God would give us the thing that we most desire, and a man obtain that he would ratherest have, yet should he take no pleasure thereof except he had a need, for hunger maketh meat good, and thirst drink pleasant, and labour rest sweet. Wherefore I conclude that we ought still to embrace virtue, that we may taste the sweetness of it and avoid that is counted most grief: that is, to lose the good that we have got. For it is not so grievous never to have had our desire than after we have had it, to forego it. What reason can we have to be worse than we have been, because we have rule? And what a shame is it to be worse than our subjects? Or because we be more happy than we have been? And is happiness wont to engender vices? Or because we have many servants whom we may punish at our pleasure? And how can we punish them, being worse than they? Will we have a guard of strangers, and will not be a guard to ourselves? One thing we must know, that there is no guard so strong as virtue and he that lacketh it, lacks all other things, which how ye ought to practise and use, I need not to rehearse, for as ye see the nobles of Persia do, even so I determine that you shall do.[64] And if you see me continually doing my duty, follow me, and I shall see you doing yours and reward ye. Children that shall come of us must be brought up here, for seeing our example, they shall be made the better.[65] And they, although they would, shall not incline to vice because they shall neither hear nor see any vicious thing, but be evermore trained in the studies of virtue and honesty.'

---

[64] you shall do] A key passage in Cyrus's so-called 'Medization': abandoning his Persian principles of moderation for the more extravagant appetites he had first seen at the Median court.
[65] made the better] Cyrus sets up in Babylon the Persian structure whereby children learn virtue by observing the ancients as they all share the same public space.

The Eighth Book of the School of Cyrus's Institution, Containing his Civil and Princely Estate, his Expedition into Syria and Egypt, and his Exhortation Before his Death to his Children

When Cyrus had thus spoken. Chrysantas arose and spake after this sort: 'Friends Persians, I have considered many times that a good prince differeth nothing from a good father: the father always providing that the child should never lack.[1] Cyrus being our prince, hath been always careful for our weal and felicity. But because he of his modesty hath not altogether uttered his conceit, I will express the thing at large to such as do not well understand the same. Consider with yourselves what city have ever been taken of the enemies by them that have not obeyed their prince? And what city of the friend[2] have ever been preserved of disobedient people? What army did ever get the victory by soldiers without obedience? What thing is greater cause of loss of field than when every man followeth his own way? What good thing in all the world can stand where men do not obey their betters? What city can be inhabited by law and skill where every man will have his will? What private house be safe where servants disobey their lord? What ship arrive at port desired where mariners will rule the master? We that now be come to wealth, whereby have we attained to the same but by obedience to our prince? We have been always prompt and ready to do the will of him, both day and night. Things that have been commanded us, we have done them at full, him we have followed and idle contentation we have eschewed, and thereby have we finished our enterprises. Then if to obey the prince be the only way to get lordship and empire, think there is none other way to save the same but that self obedience. Before this time we obeyed many, and none obeyed us; now we command and be obeyed of other. Therefore as you think meet to command them that be under you, so think it convenient to obey them that be above you, and so much the more as there is a great difference between you and servants, they obeying for fear, and you for love.[3] Therefore if we will be thought worthy to enjoy this liberty, let us obey our prince, for the city that obeyeth not one prince but followeth the rede° of many, is soon made thrall to one enemy or other. Therefore let us wait at the court as Cyrus exhorteth us; let us exercise those virtues that hitherto have holpen us, and now may save us. Let us be pressed to serve Cyrus in all his affairs, letting you to know that the profit of the one cannot be divided from the other, having still the same friends and the same enemies that we have had heretofore.'

When this was spoken, many Persians and other the confederates arose and agreed to the same, and accorded that the nobles should be present at the court

---

[1] Marg] Oration.
[2] city of the friend] i.e. ally.
[3] you for love] On the doctrine of obedience espoused by Cyrus and here developed by Chrysantas, see Introduction.

and wait till Cyrus dismissed them. The which thing then observed remaineth yet in Asia, and the things from time to time followed the order that then was taken, in the which and all other things it fareth alike. For if the prince be good, the manners of the country be the better; if he be evil, they be the worse.[4] After this order taken that the nobles should wait at the court with horse and harness, Cyrus created officers for his customs and tolls, for his works and household, and for every other thing necessary for his state, not omitting keepers for his horse and hounds. Of them that he chose for the ward of his felicity, he did not commit the care[5] to other but made it his own care, that they might be made the better. For he considered that of them he must choose, when any war was to be made, captains, and with them have conference of most weighty affairs; and if he must send any armour in his absence, he must take of them. He considered furthermore that he must use them for governors and presidents of countries, ambassadors of princes, to treat of matters and to avoid war, wherefore he thought if these were as they ought to be, his things should go well. If they were otherwise, that all should go to wrack, wherefore he was diligent in this behalf. He considered furthermore that he himself ought to practise virtue, for he knew well enough that it should be hard for him to entice other to virtue if he did not embrace the same himself.[6] And to bring all this to pass, he perceived he had need of time, and that the principal care ought to be for the revenues of his empire, because the charge of the same should be of great importance. And if he did attend only upon these things, he should have no time for other things of the commonwealth; he thought it best both for his own quiet and for the good order of the thing that he should appoint the captains of bands to have the care of the same, the alpheres°, the sergeants and masters of the camp, as he did in war.[7] And if he had need of any service, it was enough to speak to one of them.

And after this sort, he appointed his household matters so that he needeth not but to speak to one man to have many things done, whereby he had more quiet in this empire than some man have in his private house. He appointed further what kind of life they should have that should keep him company, whom he would call if they were not at the court, because in his presence he was sure they would do nothing that should be unseemly, and being absent, he could not be persuaded but that they were evil occupied and ordained that they that were present, should have the wages of them that were absent. Whereby they

---

[4] they be the worse] Machiavelli, for one, noted the disparity between the declared philosophy of rule and the more manipulative reality of Cyrus's kingship.

[5] care] 'cure' in the text.

[6] the same himself] As his father had advised him at the end of Book I.

[7] in war] Again, 'care' appears as 'cure'. Note Barker's changed terminology for the different groups and ranks of Cyrus's army. On the Spanish/Arabic term 'alpheres', which appears here for the first time and helps date the translation of books VII and VIII, see Introduction, p. 41.

resorted very many to Cyrus, lamenting of their injury. He would hear them, and give them fair words, but delay their requests, whereby they were the more diligent upon him and he in the surer case by that he did not suddenly chastise them. This way he used to make them well occupied that were present, and to check them all that were absent, being the best way to allure them with easy gain that served, and to affray them with great loss that served not, and give none audience to their complaint.[8] And by this mean he made them good that else would have been nought, having espies[9] to mark who was away and ask for them, which thing is yet used of the kings that be in empire, praising them that be present and blaming them that be absent, himself being example of virtues to his subjects, thinking that as men be made the better by laws written, so by the good customs of a prince, who is a seeing law, they be enhanced that do well and they corrected that do evil.[10] Wherefore above all things he bent himself to embrace religion, even in his happy time, and ordained ministers[11] that at the break of day should sing hymns to God, and appoint what days should be made feastful. Which order then taken, remaineth with the kings of Persia, the which manner the other Persians followed, thinking to be thereby the happier, because he that so did was of all other the most happy Prince, and that they in so doing should be the more dear to him, and he indeed was glad thereof, because he knew that men be more willing to go to the sea or to do any other enterprise with them that be religious and godly, than with the other. And he considered that if his men were well affected toward God, they would be better fashioned toward him and themselves. And one thing he would have known, that he in all his affairs never did any injury to friend nor confederate but by the way of justice sought to govern and benefit them; whereby the other left unlawful ways, and sought to come up by lawful means. And he thought that he should cause all men to have shamefastness if he showed himself to be ashamed at any uncomely word or deed, because men esteem more not only a prince, but also other of whom they have no fear, being indued° with bashfulness.

And women they have in most reverence whom they see most maidenlike; and he thought he should cause his men most obedience if he praised obedience in all things above all other virtues, and so he did. And the like in temperance, he provoked his men to be temperate. For when men see the prince void of

[8] their complaint] Compression by Barker, who omits the third and most important 'device' of Cyrus's to compel attendance at court: the transfer of absent nobles' goods to those present, a system of 'favourites', as Holland deems it (sig. Z2v).
[9] espies] The role of spies in Persian statecraft, specifically as the 'eyes' and 'ears' of the ruler, was a familiar idea in early modern England.
[10] do evil] By rendering two sentences as one, Barker shows how the exemplary virtue of Cyrus is also (and importantly) a disciplinary one, re-describing his surveillance of his subjects as an initiative of public reform.
[11] ordained ministers] Xenophon describes the institution of a college of the magi. Once again, Barker replaces 'the gods' with 'God'.

despite and outrage, the low sort be afraid to use any distemperance. And this difference he put between a bashful and a temperate man:[12] the bashful flee the evil in the presence of other[s], the temperate flieth the same even in secret; and supposing that either would be the more continent, if they saw him[13] never for any pleasure to be withdrawn from virtue. But evermore embracing honesty he ordained that the worse should obey the better and that they all should wait at the court with marvellous order and comeliness, with civility one to another, with moderate mirth and pastime. And for to retain them in warlike pastime, he took them that seemed most meet to go a-hunting with him, wherein he thought the best exercise for the war and truest for the feat of riding, for they must ride in every place, they must match with every beast, they must be quick and learned to manage their horse, they must endure pain and hunger to follow their game, which things the kings still useth. And he himself did exercise all these feats because he thought no man worthy to rule except he were better than them that be ruled. And if he could not go abroad, he would hunt wild deer at home, and used for an ordinary never to go to meat but when he had sweat before, nor gave his horse no provend° except they were well chased before. His officers he would have a-hunting with him, and them and all other he laboured to pass in all honest exercise. And as they exceeded in virtues and goodness, so did he promote them to offices and dignities, wherefore every man did his best to do well, that he might be so esteemed of Cyrus.

And not only in these things, Cyrus thought meet to be better than his subjects, but also in apparel and array of his person, wherefore he wore[14] a Median robe, and comforted his friends to do the same, for by this they should hide such defaults of body as they had, and by their garments seem the goodlier. He would have such shoes as they might put somewhat under to seem the taller. He would have them paint their faces to seem the fairer, and to rub their skin to seem the better coloured. He trained them so as they did never spit nor snite the nose before company, nor to turn to look at any man as they that marvelled at nothing; and all this he did, to be in more veneration with his subjects.[15] Whom he minded to make officers and rulers, them he framed to be like himself in all things, and more sage than the other. Whom he made servants, from them he took away the use of arms and all exercises appertaining to free men, providing

---

[12] a bashful and a temperate man] The contrast in the Greek is between αἰδώς (aidós, a 'sense of honour') and σωφροσύνη (sōphrosýne), with an additional contrast between οἱ αἰδούμενοι (hoi aidoúmenoi, present participle, nominative masculine plural of αἰδέομαι, aidéomai, 'to be ashamed') and sōphrosýne.
[13] him] i.e. Cyrus (who gives example to both sorts by his own self-control).
[14] wore] 'ware' in the text.
[15] with his subjects] Cyrus's emphasis on appearance, make-up and high-heeled shoes is part of the 'Medization', a turn to the Median ways held up for critique in Book 1. But the Persian social regulation of bodily habits such as blowing one's nose or urination remains in place.

so for them as they lacked neither meat nor drink. When he went on hunting and had them to chase the deer out of the woods into the plain, he suffered them to bear meat with them, which the gentlemen might not do. When he made any voyage, he used them to drink water as other cattle,[16] and at dinner time let them have their meat sufficiently, wherefore they as well as the gentlemen called him 'Father'[17] because he provided for them as for the other. And by this mean he established the Persian empire, and provided that his person was without all danger. For by taking away the use of arms from the nations won, he made them effeminate and cowards,[18] neither meet to make war, nor rebel; there was none might come about him except they were very excellent in their feats, whom he used in the war to be leaders of men of arms or footmen; or in peace for the government of the guard of his person. Whom because he had to do in many matters, he suffered to have oft repair unto him, and devising how he might live in most security by them, he entered into many cogitations. Sometime he thought it good for his safety to take their armour from them, but then he could not see how he could long endure if they were made unmeet for the war. Therefore the only way was to make the nobles and chief men more assured to him than to themselves, which thing how he brought to pass, methink it convenient to write.

In all his life afore all others things, he used so much humanity as was possible, supposing that as it is hard to love him that hate thee, or to will well to him that will evil to thee, so impossible to be hated to them that loveth thee. Wherefore whiles he was poor and had no thing to give, he used much courtesy of words among them; he was as ready in labours as they be provided for their wants; he rejoiced at their well doing, and lamented at their evil chances. But after he was of ability to do them good, he considered that no benefit was more acceptable to men than to be in company together at the table. Wherefore he had the same service for his friends at his table that he had for himself, and for them that were absent he would show himself mindful, and send them some reward from his own table, declaring that he favoured them although they were from him about their offices, to whom particularly he would send, being in the ward or in other service,[19] and praise them openly at his board°, whereby he won their hearts and benevolence. And if he had any other friend that he

---

[16] as other cattle] Barker reinforces the analogy Cyrus makes between the serving-men and animals by adding 'other'.
[17] 'Father'] See also Chrysantas's description of Cyrus acting paternally at p. 237.
[18] effeminate and cowards] An interpolation by Barker, evoking the story (in Herodotus, Book I) of the Lydians' second rebellion, after which Cyrus (on the advice of Croesus) removed their arms and encouraged them to dress in tunics, play the harp and engage in luxurious or effeminizing behaviours, as he has it. (It is contradicted a few sentences later here.)
[19] in the ward or other service] i.e. on garrison duty, or serving his household.

would set forth, he sent him meat from his table.[20] For even at this day, the people think it a great matter to see a present sent from the king, and him to whom it goeth, they have in great reverence and suppose him able to do them good at their needs. And indeed, presents sent from kings' boards be not only for these causes delectable, but also for their fine making most pleasant to be eaten, of the which there is no marvel for as all other sciences be most perfect in cities, so the fare of the King is most delicate. In little towns one man makes a bed, a door, a plough and a table, yea and many times the same man buildeth an house and is glad he can of all these pick out a living, such a master of many acts cannot do them all well; but in great cities, because many men have need of every art, one is sufficient for a man's living, and sometime less than one, for one makes women's shoes, and another men's. And sometime one getteth his living by shaping and another by sewing, wherefore he that doth one act alone must needs do it best. The like reason is in dressing of meats. For when one makes the bed,[21] covers the table, and playeth the cook, and other things he cannot do them all well; but where as one is about the boiled meat, another about the roast, one makes the bread that apperteineth only to his art, and so forth, of necessity every thing must needs be well done, and therefore the fare of the court exceedeth all other.

Now I will show how Cyrus passed in other things. For as he surmounted all men of revenues and entrate°,[22] even so he exceedeth all other in giving and in liberality, which thing beginning with him, hath continued with all the kings of Persia. Who hath so rich men as the king of Persia? Who hath so well and rich arrayed men as he? Whose princely gifts be rings, bracelets and horses trapped with gold? For these no man may have, except they be given of the king. Who hath ever brought to pass by great munificence of gifts to be preferred in love to parents, brethren, and children? Who so easily could subdue his enemies so far from him as he? Who, after the conquest of so many nations, could get at his dying day the name of a father, but he which is the name not of a taker away of others' good, but of a giver to other of his own? Furthermore, they that now be called the king's eyes and his ears[23] were begun by none other mean but through

---

[20] meat from his table] Barker omits another comparison between servants and animals here, about having all servants' food served from his table in order to inculcate goodwill, as happens with dogs.

[21] the bed] Here, the dining couches. I have omitted a repetition of this sentence, presumably a compositorial error.

[22] entrate] See Introduction.

[23] king's eyes and his ears] Holland glosses these as 'Intelligencers' (sig. [2A1]v). Here, Cyrus's spies are construed as dutiful and grateful subjects within his economy of virtue and liberality. Steven Hirsch contests the historical truth of this network of spies, but acknowledges that the inheritors of the Achaemenid empire show signs of 'a syndrome of spy-paranoia' which they may also have inherited. *The Friendship of the Barbarians: Xenophon and the Persian Empire* (Hanover and London: University Press of New England,

his liberality and largesse. For rewarding them with great honours that advised him of things appertaining to his state, he brought to pass that many did both hear and see things meet for the king to know, whereof the saying was that he had many eyes and many ears. He that thinks it better that one man should have the office alone to be the king's eye, he thinks not well. For one man can not see nor mark many things. And if one man had the commission, the other might not meddle. Who being known, men would be ware enough of him, whereas it is expedient for a king to hear many things of many men, whereby men be afraid to speak anything against him, as though he were present to hear, and to do any treason toward him, being among them to see it. And so not only no man did speak any villainy or outrage against him, but also evermore spake most honourably of him. And nothing made men's hearts to be so knit unto him as that for little things he would give great gifts. And marvel is none, though he in gifts did excel all other, because he excelled all other in riches.

But this is to be marvelled, that he being a king, did pass all other in humanity and courtesy, and nothing grieved him more than to be overcome in doing well, insomuch as he was wont oft to say that the office of a pastor and a king were like;[24] for a pastor ought to see that his sheep be well kept, and a king that his people well governed; the one and the other being the felicity of both, wherefore being of this mind, it is no marvel though he laboured to pass all others in gentleness. Of the which he showed an evident proof when Croesus advertised him to leave his large giving that would soon make him poor, whereas he might be made most rich if he would attend unto it. Cyrus asked him how much money he thought he might have had if he had spared after his counsel.[25] Croesus named a great sum. And Cyrus prayed him to send one of his trusty servants with his man Hystaspas, whom he commanded to go to all his friends and on his behalf to desire them that they would serve him of so much money as they could spare, because his present necessity required no less; and that they should give the account to Croesus's man, with their bills of the same. Thus sending him away with letters of credit, he went and did his message, which thing being fulfilled accordingly, and the letters of account given to Croesus's man, he returned to Cyrus and showed him what riches he had gotten by his journey, besides the money that was brought for him. Wherefore Cyrus said unto Croesus: 'Here is one of our treasures, the other you may see and count what money I have if I would use it.' Croesus took the count and found it to be much more than he said it should have been. The which Cyrus perceiving said,

---

for Tufts University, 1985), pp. 101–39 (p. 129).
[24] were like] Cyrus's parallel between a shepherd and a king is important in light of a tradition of commentary, largely growing from the positive biblical reports of Cyrus, connecting him to shepherd-kings such as David. Holland, interestingly, hedges his bets, using both 'heardman' first and 'pastour' in this passage (sig. [2A1]v).
[25] his counsel] Another example of Greek direct speech Englished as indirect speech.

'You see, Croesus, that I have treasure when I need. Whereas you would have me hoard them up at home and get envy and hatred abroad, and hire strangers to have the keeping of them. And now I have my friends in good case, which be my treasures. I have them my keepers of my person and my goods, a great deal more faithful than hired guard men, and one thing I will tell ye: that I have that affection that all men have, for I am desirous of money.[26] But whereas I know that money is the cause of much trouble and anguish to them that cannot use it, but hoard it up, tell° it, lock it, weigh it, and dieth in desire of it, and albeit they have their houses full of money, yet they can eat no more than they can bear, for they should burst; nor clad them more than need, for they should be choked. I honour God with my money, I desire much, and I distribute much. I help my friends, I enrich my men, and I get benevolence of all sorts: the fruits of my riches is my sickerness°, my good name and glory, which the greater it is, the better it is and more easy to bear, and many times makes them light that bears it. And one thing, Croesus, I would ye should know that they that have most money be not most happy, for then the keepers of town walls should be the happiest men because they keep all that is in the cities. But he that hath a way to get much money and spend it well, him I think happy indeed.'[27]

And thus Cyrus reasoned effectually with Croesus. Understanding furthermore that every man hath regard to his health, and prepares things to increase the same, and to avoid sickness, no man took no keep.[28] He thought good to see for this lack and called the most skilful physicians unto him, devising with them for medicines, instruments and other things appertaining to the same. And if they healed any of his friends, he would thank them and reward them. These things he devised for to have the good hearts of his trusty men. And among all other things he propounded plays[29] and warlike pastimes and rewards convenient for them to endure his court to contention and gear of noble feats.[30] Furthermore he ordained that in all matters of controversy, men should choose them judges. They studied on both parts to choose their most friends, he that was overcome had envy at them that did overcome, and hated them that gave sentence against him. He that did overcome, pretended to have overcome by right and therefore bound to no man. And they that would be most in favour with Cyrus, as it fareth in all cities, bare envy one at another,

---

[26] desirous of money] Barker's translation seems mild; modern editions translate the Greek term ἄπληστος as 'insatiate'.

[27] happy indeed] Xenophon tacitly rewrites Herodotus here, in having Cyrus teach Croesus a lesson about happiness (specifically about it not being found in great wealth) that Herodotus had Croesus learn from the Athenian lawgiver Solon in Book I of the *Histories*.

[28] took no keep] i.e. that when in good health, men try to increase their fortunes as if they will always be healthy, but that nobody makes provision for sickness.

[29] plays] Not drama but games and contests of a military nature.

[30] gear] 'gare' in the original, but no clear sense here. Perhaps an archaic sense of 'gear' as 'goings-on'; the context is military games.

in sort that many had rather receive a loss than have a benefit that should help his fellow. And this was a cast° of Cyrus, that they that were so great about him should all be occasioned to love him rather than one another.

Now among the declaration of many of Cyrus's acts, methink it good to show how he came abroad the first time to make his sacrifice, because it is one of the arts that princes use to be in the more reverence. Before he went forth, he took about him all the Persians and other nobles, and gave them Median robes to wear. And this was the first time that the Persians wore them. And when he had distributed them he told them he would go visit the temples, and desired them to be at the court by break of day, and he ordered as Pheraulas should appoint them, and that they should mark what way might be better done, and tell him at his return. For he would follow that that seemed most for his honour. After he had given the best robes to the noblest men, he brought forth other of diverse colours, and gave among them, and willed them to clad their men as he had clad them. Then one asked him how he[31] would be decked. To whom Cyrus answered that he thought himself well armed when he saw them in so good order, and that he apparelled with mean garments should think himself richly vestured°, being beneficial unto them. Then they went and called Pheraulas, a Persian of the common sort but diligent, modest and ready to serve, and that once judged that every man should be rewarded according to his desert,[32] saying unto him that he would go forth in most comely order that might be pleasant to his friends and fearful to his enemies. According together how it might best be done, Cyrus gave the charge thereof to him for the day following, and that he might be the better obeyed, he gave him coats to distribute among the pensioners°[33] and the guard belonging to his person, who said to Pheraulas that he was become a great man in that he commanded them in their offices; who answered, it was nothing so, but that he was rather become their cloak-bearers. And having given the choice of the coats to the principal, he went his way, appointing the order against the morning.[34]

The guard they stood on either side the way that none might come to Cyrus but the noble men, and there were tipstaves° to beat them that were out of order. There were four thousand spearmen, four a rank, and on every side of the court gate two thousand. And all the horsemen were come and alighted off their horses with their hands out of their sleeves, as they be wont to do in the king's sight. The Persians stood on the right hand and the other companions on the left hand, and the chariots likewise on every side. When the court gate was opened, there was brought out four white bulls to be sacrificed to Jupiter

---

[31] he] i.e. Cyrus.
[32] according to his desert] In Book II.
[33] pensioners] First usage of this term for elders/officers. Holland has 'Captaines of the Guard', but glosses 'Pensioners', probably following Barker (sig. [2A3]v).
[34] the morning] Compression of narrative colour in this passage.

and other gods, as the clergy did appoint, which the Persian esteem above all other.[35] After the bulls were brought horses to be sacrificed to the sun. After this came forth a chariot of gold to be offered to Jupiter, and another to the sun, then the third cart with purple covers, whom men followed with fire in their hands. Then came out Cyrus with a Persian hat[36] on his head, and a coat pain[t]ed with white and red[37] (which none may wear but kings) and a pair of Median britches down to the knees, and a warlike cloak of purple. And he had a crown upon his hat and so had all his kinsmen, and so have at this day.[38] His hands were bare, his chariotman followed him not so high as he, either because it was so indeed, or because it was made so. Cyrus seemed the most goodliest and as he passed they honoured him, either being so commanded or because they wondered at his goodly and rich array. Before this day, no Persian did ever kneel to Cyrus.[39] The four thousand went afore him and about him: three hundred sceptre-bearers on horseback, then was brought forth two hundred spare horses for Cyrus, saddle[d] with traps of gold, then two thousand lancemen, an hundred on a rank, of whom Hystaspas was captain. Then the two thousand horsemen that were first made, whom Chrysantas governed. After them other ten thousand of whom Datamas[40] was captain. Then the Medians, the Armenians, the Hyrcanians, the Caducians and other followed, of which Gadatas had the charge. After their horsemen followed the chariots, four abreast, of whom Artabates,[41] a Persian, was overseer.

[35] above all other] Compression of detail here creates confusion; Xenophon notes how the Persians most esteem the magi as their guides in religious matters.

[36] Persian hat] A curiously careless translation of τιάρα (tiára). Much more common in early modern English is the term 'tyre' or 'tire'. Randle Cotgrave's *A Dictionary of the French and English Tongues* (1611) helpfully defines 'Tiare' as 'A round and wreathed ornament for the head (somewhat resembling the Turkish Turbant) worne, in old time, by the Princes, priests and women of Persia' (cited in Patricia Parker, 'Barbers, Infidels and Renegades: *Antony and Cleopatra*', in *Center or Margin: Revisions of the English Renaissance in Honor of Leeds Barroll* (Plainsboro, NJ: Susquehanna University Press, 2006), pp. 54–88 (p. 67)).

[37] white and red] Some careless compression here; over his scarlet trousers, Cyrus wears a tunic of purple and white, and it is this colour that none but kings may wear.

[38] at this day] Barker's translation is confusing. Holland has 'turbant' for Barker's 'hat', and with a 'Diadem' on it, which Holland glosses as 'Regall bande' (sig. [2A4]). Holland may take his cue from the common expression 'even at this day' (νῦν, *nŷn*) to link Cyrus's headwear directly to the headwear of Islamic Persia: 'About his turbant aforesaid he had a Diadem, the very badge and cognisance, that all his kinsmen likewise be known by, and even at this day they retaine the same Ensigne' (sig. [2A4]). See also note 9 (p. 135).

[39] kneel to Cyrus] Xenophon dates the habit of *proskynesis* (prostration) to Cyrus's new-founded imperial style, showing the importance of conspicuous and courtly displays of deference and obedience. In a later age, the gesture became a European shorthand imputing Persian tyranny.

[40] Datamas] Dutamas, mistakenly, here.

[41] Artabates] Despite the similar name, Barker and modern editors agree that this man, who only turns up in Book VIII ('Artabatas', in modern editions) is a different person to Artabasus, the Median. See note 42 (p. 247).

In his going forth, many men came over the rails to make their suits to Cyrus, who commanded of the pensioners that went about him and his chariot to bid them tell their suits to his officers and captains. Of the which calling some of them to him that he would have most honoured, commanded to hear the requests, and if they were of any importance, to make relation of him. And they went earnestly about the matter, saving only one Daiphernes, a man of proud and haughty nature, thinking to be esteemed the jollier fellow, went very slowly about the matter. Which when Cyrus perceived, he sent him word not to meddle in the matter, for he would no more trouble him; and to another that was ready in his service, he gave an horse, and caused one of his mace-bearers to lead him whither he would, whereby the people gave him ever after great honour. Being come to the place where they should sacrifice, he offered the bulls to Jupiter, and the horses to the sun, and to the gods of the earth and patrons of Syria, such beasts as the sages did appoint. When the sacrifice was done, he appointed a place of two mile length where he commanded the horsemen to run their horse, divided into three parts, and he himself ran with the Persians and did best; of the Medians, Artabates[42] had the prize; of the Syrians, Gadatas; of the Armenians, Tigranes; of the Hyrcanians, the colonel's son; of the Sacians, a private man outwent them half the race length. Cyrus asked the young man if he would give his horse for a kingdom.[43] The young man answered, 'For a kingdom I would not forego it, but to a good man, I would gladly give it.' Cyrus answered that he would show him where he should not miss a good man, though he were blindfold. 'Show me the place', quoth the Sacian, 'that I may hit him with this clod.' Cyrus showed him a company of his friends. The young man threw the clod and hit Pheraulas who was going about Cyrus's business and did not stay for all the blow.[44] The Sacian opening his eyes demanded whom he had struck. Cyrus answered, 'None of them that were present'. 'Why', quoth he, 'is it any of them that be absent?' 'Yea', quoth Cyrus, and showed him where he rode among the chariots. 'And why doth he not turn?', quoth he. 'Belike', quoth Cyrus, 'he is not well with himself.' Then the young man went to see and found it was Pheraulas, his beard being bloody and with a blow of his nose. When he saw him he asked him if he were struck.[45] 'As ye see', quoth Pheraulas. 'Then', quoth he, 'I give you this horse.' 'And why so?',

---

[42] Artabates] An understandable error (that may derive from another one in Filelfo) this close to the appearance of Artabates; Xenophon's text has the Median, Artabasus, win the contest between the Medians.

[43] for a kingdom] This episode is the source of Shakespeare's Richard III's famous final words at the battle of Bosworth. See Cherchi.

[44] did not stay for all the blow] i.e. did not stop, despite the blow. On Pheraulas see Nadon, pp. 71–75, 150–52; Tatum, *Xenophon's Imperial Fiction*, pp. 204–06; Gera, pp. 173–83; Johnson, p. 184; Tuplin, 'Xenophon's *Cyropaedia*', pp. 81–82.

[45] struck] Here 'stroke[n]'.

quoth Pheraulas. The Sacian told him all the matter and said, 'I think I have not missed a good man'. 'It had been better for you', quoth Pheraulas, 'to have given him to a richer man; notwithstanding I accept your gift', and prayed God who suffered him to be hit that he might prove a good man indeed, that his gift might not be frustrate. And so they changed horses and rode forth.

The chariot had run also, and to the victors there was given an ox and wine, to make merry after the sacrifice. Cyrus was rewarded with certain cups which he gave to Pheraulas, because he had so well ordered the matter. And the kings of Persia useth this manner of riding to the temple at this day. This being ended, they went into the city, and Pheraulas desired the Sacian to supper, and gave him his rewards and other too. And he, perceiving goodly appurtenance[46] and rich array and many servants, said: 'Be you of the order of rich men?' 'What rich men?', said Pheraulas. 'Even of the order that got their living with their hands.' 'My father se[n]t me to school, and with his labour found me poorly. Being come out of my childhood and he not able to find me, he made me labour the land as he did, and so I found him to his ending day, labouring a poor little land, but so good as rendered me double fruit.[47] And after this, coming to Cyrus's service. I have obtained these things that ye here see.' 'Happy you', quoth the Sacian, 'as well for other things as for that ye be made rich of a poor one. For I think the getting of goods is very sweet unto you.' 'Well', quoth Pheraulas, 'if ye think me the merrier because I am richer than I was, ye be deceived. For I ensure[48] you that I eat and drink with less repast than when I was poor, for now I have much. But I spend much, I care for much, my servants' livings, their liveries, alms, provision for my cattle, shepherds for the same, loss when the rot cometh among them. So that I have more care now than ever I had.' 'Yea', said the Sacian, 'but when ye see every thing in good case, ye be the gladder and so enjoy your riches.' 'Not so', quoth Pheraulas, 'for there is no such grief as to fear to become poor when a man hath been rich. In proof whereof it hath not been seen that any rich man hath been constrained to watch for pleasure of riches, but many that have lost their riches could not sleep for sorrow.' 'Nor no man sleep', quoth the Sacian, 'when he getteth anything for joy.' 'That is true', quoth the other, 'for it were as sweet a thing to have as to get, the rich should be a great deal more happy than the poor. But he that hath much, must spend much upon his friends, upon strangers, and upon the service of God. Therefore he that hath much delight in money hath much grief when he is at any expense.' The Sacian

---

[46] appurtenance] Here 'apporuiance' — a compositorial error confusing 'purveyance' (provisions) with 'appurtenance' (belongings), perhaps?

[47] double fruit] Barker compresses Pheraulas's elaboration of the 'honesty' of the land and labour which usually yielded a little fruit, but sometimes twice as much. Further narrative detail and colour is excised from Pheraulas's account of his household tribulations soon after.

[48] ensure] Misreading of 'assure'?

answered he was not of that opinion, but thought him most happy that hath much and spend much. 'Then for God's sake', quoth Pheraulas, 'make yourself happy and me too. Take all that I have, spend it at your pleasure, use me as ye would do a stranger, and worse too if ye will, for I shall be content with a small portion.' 'Ye do but dally with me', quoth the Sacian. Pheraulas sware he meant good faith. 'And that beside this, I will obtain of Cyrus that ye shall not wait at the court nor be in no garrisons, but be at home and enjoy your riches. For I will do all for you and me too. And if I get anything at Cyrus's hand, or by my service in war, you shall have it to make you happy and me without care. For if I be discharged of this business, I shall the better serve Cyrus.'[49] So both agreed; the young man thought himself most happy because he was lord of so much riches, and Pheraulas thought himself more happy that he was delivered of care, and set at large to do his pleasure. Pheraulas was a man of gentle nature, glad to help his friends and to do for all men. Because he thought a man to be the most worthy creature, most thankful toward them that showed him pleasures, praising them that deserved it, loving them that were kind, reverencing the father and mother and most mindful of the quick and the dead.[50] So Pheraulas was very joyful to be at liberty among his friends, and the Sacian was glad to be so wealthy a man. He loved Pheraulas well because he was ever bringing somewhat home, and Pheraulas loved him because he kept his gear so well. And thus they two lived.

After the sacrifice, Cyrus called to a banquet as his friends that were most careful for his empire and most trusty, as Artabasus the Median, Tigranes the Armenian, the colonel of the Hyrcanians and Gobryas. Gadatas also, who was made master of the pensioners, and when Cyrus had no strangers[51] he sat with him at the table; when he had, he waited, and Cyrus having him in great estimation and so had the rest of the court. Being come to supper, they were placed accordingly, and the most worthy sat on his right hand, and the next on his left hand, which he did to signify whom he esteemed best, that they without contention might know one another, and every man see that virtue is the cause of honour. Thus by setting at the table, they had estimation, but not so as they exceeded in virtue, so he advanced them in honours. And they that degenerated from virtue were brought to more base place. And thus he appointed his men.[52] Having supped, and Gobryas considering every thing of

---

[49] serve Cyrus] Pheraulas replays Cyrus's recent demonstration to the Sacians of the benefits of having one's goods in (or held by) one's friends.
[50] quick and the dead] Further compression of Xenophon's comments about the moral observations made by Pheraulus in his social philosophy, beyond simply the reverencing of parents.
[51] strangers] i.e. guests.
[52] appointed his men] More compression here; Barker is missing the sense of the mobility of men through these places and Cyrus's show of great favour according to setting, including

his behaviour that, being so mighty a prince, did not have the company of his friends but vouchsafed them at his table, sent them presents that were away, he did no more marvel at his great feats in war but at his unspeakable gentleness in peace.[53] And therefore when all was done, he said, 'Cyrus, I protest before God that I thought you the most worthy warrior alive, but now I think you pass yourself and all other in humanity'.[54] 'By my troth', quoth Cyrus, 'and I had rather show the virtues of humanity than of chivalry because chivalry is cause of many men's hurt and humanity of many men's good.'[55] Then Hystaspas, demanding if he would be displeased if he asked him a question. Then he asked him, if he had not been obedient to him and ready at all his commandments.[56] Cyrus said he could not blame him. Then he asked him why he had placed Chrysantas more honourable than him. 'Shall I tell you the truth?' quoth Cyrus. 'Yea', quoth Hystaspas. 'And will not you be angry?', quoth Cyrus. 'Rather I would', quoth he, 'rejoice to know the truth and not to have no injury.' 'Then ye shall understand', quoth Cyrus, 'that Chrysantas without any commandment would do things accordingly as appertained to me. I never troubled to call him to this or that. Further, if there were anything needful to be spoken to our companions, he would advertise me to do it. If for modesty I left anything unspoken, he would expressed to them with much prudence.[57] He was always content with the present fortune, the thing that might do me good he would gladly do it. Of my good fortune, no man was so joyful; in sort that of my felicity I think he was more merry than myself.' Then Hystaspas answered that he was glad he had demanded the question. 'And why?', quoth Cyrus. 'Because I', quoth he, 'will do my diligence to follow the same way to please him.' But of one thing he stood in doubt: how he should rejoice at Cyrus's good fortune, either by clapping of his hands or by laughing or by other mean. 'No', quoth Artabanus, 'but by dancing after the Persian fashion.' Whereat all they laughed.

When the banquet was brought in Cyrus demanded Gobryas if he had not now rather give his daughter to marriage to one of his friends, than at his first coming. 'Shall I tell the truth?', quoth Gobryas. 'Yea', quoth Cyrus, 'for no need of lie is to be where a question is demanded.' 'Then', quoth Gobryas, 'I had

the observation that this habit endures to this day.
[53] unspeakable] 'unspeable' here; it seems to anticipate the meaning of the next sentence.
[54] humanity] Translating φιλανθρωπία (*philanthrōpía*). Barker's 'chivalry' in the subsequent sentence translates στρατηγία (*stratēgía*, generalship).
[55] troth] 'trought' here. Barker replaces 'by Zeus' in the Greek.
[56] commandments] More direct speech rendered as indirect speech.
[57] prudence] Barker compresses extensively here. Holland's translation makes this clear: 'Moreover, if at any time a matter was to be delivered by speech unto our Allies and Confederates, whatsoever he thought decent for me to say, thereto he would advise me: But whatever he perceived, I was desirous that our Associates should know, but yet upon a bashfull modesty, loth my selfe to utter unto them, hee would declare the same in such termes as if it had beene his owne opinion' (sig. 2B3).

rather give her now than afore.' 'Can ye tell why?', quoth Cyrus. 'I can', quoth he. 'Say on', quoth Cyrus. 'Because', quoth he, 'I saw them here tofore with good heart abide the labours and dangers of war, and now I see them bear in equal mind the favour of fortune, being an harder thing to use well the prosperous state than the contrary. For pride and contempt is wont to rise of good fortune, and desperation of adverse.' At the which words, Cyrus said to Hystaspas, 'Have ye heard the sentence of Gobryas?' He answered, 'Yes, and that he spake many such sentences he[58] would rather be a suitor to his daughter than for a great dowry of gold.' 'And I can give thee many of these sentences', quoth Gobryas, 'if ye will have my daughter. And because ye set not by gold nor silver, ye shall give it to Chrysantas because he is placed above you.'[59] Then Cyrus said, 'If any of you would have a wife, make me of your counsel, for I know the art of wooing.' Then Gobryas said, 'If a man would marry his daughter, with whom must he confer?' 'With me', quoth Cyrus, 'because I know the art.' 'What art?', quoth Chrysantas. 'The art', quoth Cyrus, 'to know what woman is meet for every man.' Then Chrysantas asked what woman he thought meet for him. 'A little woman', quoth Cyrus, 'because you are little. Or else when you would kiss her ye must leap like a spaniel.'[60] 'It is graciously considered', quoth Chrysantas, 'for I am unmeet to leap.' 'Further', quoth Cyrus, 'ye must take one with a flat nose because you have an hooked nose.' 'Then', quoth Chrysantas, 'one that have well dined should lie well with another that is fasting.' 'Very true', quoth Cyrus, 'for a full belly is hooked and an empty, flat.' 'Well', quoth Chrysantas, 'what woman is good for a cold king?' At the which word Cyrus laughed, and so did the other. Chrysantas then said that he marvelled much at Cyrus's nature that, being cold, and still could be merry and frolic. Cyrus said for that conceit he should get a name of a pleasant merry fellow. Thus with like mirth and pastime, they passed away the time together.

Then Cyrus took a woman's vesture and commanded Tigranes to give it his wife, because she had so constantly followed him in the war; to Artabasus he gave a cup of gold; to the Hyrcanian he gave an horse and many other gifts, and to Gobryas he said he would give him an husband for his daughter. 'Ye must give her to me', quoth Hystaspas, 'that I may have his sentences.'[61] 'Are you able to find[62] a wife?', quoth Cyrus. 'Yea, that I am, I thank God', quoth he. 'Where

---

[58] he] i.e. Hystaspas.
[59] above you] A misreading; Gobryas will himself give the gold to Chrysantas, if he gives his daughter to Hystaspas.
[60] spaniel] Translating the Greek κυνάριον (*kynárion*, small dogs).
[61] sentences] i.e. *sententiae*, proverbial wisdom (in Greek, τὰ συγγράμματα, *tà syngrámmata*) — that which first attracted Hystaspas to the thought of marrying Gobryas's daughter (above).
[62] find] i.e. support.

is your substance?', said Cyrus.⁶³ 'Here', quoth he, and pointed to Cyrus. 'I am content', quoth Gadatas, and held forth his hand. Cyrus took it and gave it to Hystaspas, and so they accorded. And Cyrus gave Hystaspas many gifts to send to the young lady, and last of all kissed him.⁶⁴ Then said Artabasus, 'O Cyrus, ye do not give me such gifts and a kiss as ye have given Chrystantas.' 'But I will give ye', quoth he. 'And when?', quoth the other. 'Thirty year hence', quoth he, 'therefore see ye die not in the meantime.'⁶⁵ And thus ending the feast, he brought them to the gate, and the day following he gave licence to all his friends and companions to go home to their houses, except such as voluntarily would tarry, to whom he gave house and land to them and to their heirs. And they were the most part Medians and Hyrcanians. To them that departed, he gave great gifts, that no man had cause to grudge or complain. And besides this, he gave the soldiers that warded his person the money that he got at Sardis. And further to the colonels and captains he gave great gifts, according to every man's worthiness, and gave moreover to the chief captains to distribute among the sergeants, alpheres and other soldiers. At the which largesse, some said he must needs have much money that give so much. Some answered, 'His nature is rather to give and enrich other than to keep himself'. At the which words, he taking comfort assembled his friends and thus said unto them: 'I know that many men desire to be counted richer than they be, thinking thereby to be thought the more liberal and free, in which their opinion, methink, they be deceived. For he that is counted to have much money, and doth not accordingly distribute unto his friends, by and by getteth the name of a covetous man. Another sort there is that desire to keep close their riches, and them I take to be unnatural to their friends, for because it is not known what they have, their friends in their lack do not make their mone° unto him, but be deceived. I think him the good and plain man that showeth what he hath, and helpeth as he may. I will show unto you indeed my riches that can be showed, that that cannot I will tell it by mouth.' And even so he did, with these words: 'Friends, I would you should think these to be no more mine than yours. For I do not gather this riches for mine own use alone but for all them as shall do their duty and embrace virtue, and to succour them that shall at any time have need.'

Having well settled his state at Babylon, he thought good to go again into Persia, and signified his departure. Which voyage how he made, what train he had, how he harboured, what way he kept in going into his country, we think meet to declare. Wheresoever he camped, his tent was set toward the east, and

⁶³ substance] 'that wealth of yours' is what Holland has (sig. [2B4]).
⁶⁴ kissed him] Barker's haste misses that Cyrus kisses Chrysantas, not Hystaspas, in another demonstration granting greater public honour to the more esteemed of the two. The point seems to be Cyrus's constancy to his own principles.
⁶⁵ in the meantime] Barker credits the quip to Cyrus rather than to Artabasas, as Xenophon does.

about it all the guard and pensioners had their lodging. On the right side he placed the bakers, on the left side the cooks. Likewise on the right side, the horses, and on the left, the beasts of carriage. Other things were so bestowed as every man in every place knew his plat° and ground. The carriage was borne partly by men and partly by beasts. Every man came to his appointed place, and at set hours each man went busily about his office. At one time pavilions were pitched and carriage discharged. At one time tents were raised and sumpters° laden. Every thing that was to be done was done in order and due time. Even as in an house where all things is well bestowed, so in his camp nothing was out of order. Provision for things necessary, preparation for their victuals and place, meat for the same, the good appointment of the munition and place for the same, the ready a-lodging of every man. And as in an house well bestowed, all things is so disposed as is easy to be had when need requireth, even so much more in a camp ought an order to be had that things may be done without trouble. Because the occasions of war be more sudden than other, so the disorder there more dangerous than other. Negligent dealing in the war bringeth much care, and wise government great avail. Wherefore Cyrus was very circumspect, that his things were done in order. He had his own tent in the middest of the camp, because it was most sure place. Next about him he had his most trusty men, as he was ever wont to have, about whom the men of arms and the captains of the cars did lodge. The which he placed so because if any alarm were given, they might have time to arm themselves, which was long a-doing. Before and behind the which the archers had their place, then the darters and all these compassed with the pikemen that they being able to abide a good brunt might hold out till the other were in order. He would have every captain's ensign set upon his pavilion that as servants in a city knoweth every man's house, specially the great men's, so in his camp every man should understand where he ought to repair and not need to go about seeking here and there, because every nation and their captain had their place by themselves.

Having thus appointed his things, he thought thus most meet to provide against sudden invasions and tradiments,[66] that the doers thereof might be taken with their own traps. And he esteemed it a feat of war not alonely that the battles° could march and tarry by it manfully, resisting the enemy on either side, but also to know how to retire and leave the battle in place and time to stay, to turn, to come in succours when time was, to prevent and foresee the drifts of their enemies. And after this sort, he proceeded in journey with great order, that he might be always ready against sudden chances. Being arrived in Media, he a-lodged° with Cyaxares king of the same. And after many salutations and

---

[66] tradiment] treachery or betrayal. The *OED* has just three examples, two from Henry VIII's state papers, one from Hoby's Castiglione (1561). The term has Italian origins ('tradimento') and is another relic of Barker's Italian travels.

embracements, Cyrus told him he had provided a palace for him in Babylon where he might lie as in his own house, and gave him many noble gifts, which being received, Cyaxares sent his daughter a crown of gold and other chains and bracelets, commanding her to set the crown upon Cyrus's head. Which being done, he came and said, 'I give thee this maid my daughter to your wife. And as your father Cambyses had to wife the daughter of my father, Astyages, of whom you are born, so I give you this my daughter, with whom being a child you were wont to sport and play, in so much as she being demanded whose wife she would be, she said, "Cyrus's wife". And for her dowry, I give you all that realm of Media, having none heir male to inherit the same.' To whom Cyrus thus answered that he did accept the parentage, he liked the young lady, and praised the dowry and everything contented him, but he would make no contract of matrimony without the consent of his parents. Wherefore giving many tokens unto her, as he thought might please her father, he took his leave and went toward Persia.

And being arrived at the confines°, he left his army there and with his friends went to the city with things sufficient to sacrifice and banquet among the Persians, and presented his father and mother, the ancients and noble men and women with gifts accordingly. Which fashion the kings use at this day when they return from a strange country. Wherefore Cambyses calling together the chief of the Persians and the most ancient and Cyrus with them, he spake unto them in this wise: 'I bear my good heart to you, O Persians, and to you my son Cyrus accordingly.[67] For to you I am a king, and to thee, O son, I am a father. Wherefore it seemeth I ought of congruence to give counsel faithfully to you both. You Persians did honour Cyrus my son, he through God's help hath made you honourable among all men and most renowned in Asia. The nobles that have served with him he hath enriched. The other he hath truly paid and made the Persians of footmen valiant horsemen and increased their dominion; if you in time to come shall continue in this state, all things shall come to pass prosperously. But if you, Cyrus, being swelled in good success of fortune shall go about to be lord of the Persians as of other nations, drawing all things to the private commodity, or you Persians being envious of his glory go about to dissolve his empire, you shall be occasion of much trouble and displeasure, the which to avoid, I think ye ought now in this public sacrifice to accord and call the gods to witness of your consentment, that thou, O son Cyrus, shalt be always ready with all thy power to resist them that shall bring any disturbance to the Persians' laws. And you, O Persians, if any man goeth about to bereave Cyrus his kingdom, or any subject shall rebel from him, shall be ready to aid him and yourselves according to his commandment. I shall be your natural lord and king so long as God shall lend me life. After my death, Cyrus shall be your king

---

[67] **Marg**] Oration.

if he be alive, who, when he comes among you, if he will do well, must make your sacrifices[68] even as I do. But when he shall depart, it shall be convenient that you take one of our family to be your lord and governor, and your minister to God immortal.' These words spoken, they agreed fully together, and after the ceremonies made, called God to witness, and so departed.

Cyrus took his leave, and went into Media, and by the consent of his parents, wedded the daughter of Cyaxares, a very fair maid, although some men write he married his mother's sister, who was too old for him. Being returned with his wife to Babylon, he thought good to send governors into every province, and besides them, captains of the castles and fortresses, supposing that if any of the governors would go about any novile[69] through their riches, these should be always against them.[70] Wherefore purposing upon the same thing, he thought it good to call the chief gentlemen and captains, to utter the thing unto them and signify what way they should take in their provinces, to whom, being assembled, he spake on this wise: 'Friends, such garrisons and captains as we left in cities which we won, be still remaining there, to whom we committed none other thing to do but faithfully to ward the town that they kept, which thing they having accomplished, we will not displace them.[71] Nevertheless, for other considerations, we perceive it meet to send civil governors that may have authority to command the rest and to appoint orders appertaining to the state. And to them that I shall send thither, I think it convenient to assign them house and land, that they may live honourably and dwell quietly, where they may give audience to suitors, and at their arrival find their places ready.' When he had thus spoken, he appointed many cities and provinces to diverse of his friends, the children of the which did possess the lands and possessions that he then gave them. And when he had given this order, he willed them to send evermore to him such things as were the chief commodities of their provinces. He assigned to every man that province that he[72] best liked, as Megabisus into Arabia; Artabatas into Cappadocia; Artacaman into great Phrygia; Chrysantas to Ionia and Lydia; Cadusius into Caria; and Pharnucus in Phrygia by Hellespont and Aeolia. To Cilicia, Cyprus and Paphlagonia he sent no Persian governors because they, uncalled, served him in his wars at Babylon; only he appointed them to pay a tribute and live free. The which order then made still remaineth, the governors of the cities and provinces, the

---

[68] your sacrifices] i.e. sacrifices on your behalf.
[69] novile] An adjectival form, somewhat awkwardly meaning 'novelty' in the sense of new enterprises — another example of a rushed translation. Holland takes more care, noting Cyrus's specific fear that the newly armed and wealthy governors 'should beare themselves insolently, and shake off the yoke of their allegeance' (sig. 2C2v).
[70] against them] Cyrus sends out not just satraps but garrisons who are to keep them in line.
[71] **Marg**] Oration.
[72] he] i.e. Cyrus.

captains of the castles and fortresses whose names remain in writing with the king. And he admonished them to keep those orders in their offices as they had seen him keep at home: that they should have horsemen ready of Persians and their companions, cars and rulers of the same, and that they that had provision should be attendant at the gate of court and be prest and ready at the governors' commandment, and that their children should be trained at the court after the manner of Persia, and that they should wait on the governor a-hunting, and other warlike pastime.[73] Protesting to consider and reward him as an increaser and preserver of the Persian empire that should have in a readiness most men of arms, skilful in their feat, most cars meet for the service and most men trained in knowledge of war, he also advertised them that they should prefer the noble men[74] before all other in their assemblies. And that their diet should be like his, sufficient for their family and seemly for their friend. And that they should have garden parks with deer in them to pass the time, and never go to meat before they had laboured, nor give their horse provend without some exercise. Affirming though he himself were never so good he could not by any human power provide for the weal of all, except he were holpen with the favour of them that were good, the which being good ought to favour the good and be companions of their travail. And that they should not think that he commanded them these things as unto slaves, but that he himself would be the first to do anything that he had commanded them, and that they should be example to their inferiors as he was to them. And these orders then made, were from time to time[75] observed, in waiting at the court, in keeping of the forts, and in placing of the noble men, and in training up their children.

Having spoken and appointed these things, he commanded them to be ready all the year following, for he intended to make an enterprise and before he so did, he would take a muster of men, horses and cars. Which order the kings of this time follow, and cometh forth with his army, that if any governor have need, he is aided; and if any rebel, he is subdued. And it is occasion that every man is the better kept in his office, the laws be the better observed and the rents the better paid which, when the governor cannot bring to pass by himself, he showeth the king and he takes order in the matter by his power, as they soon be dispatched. Thus they went forth, and some were called the king's son, some his brother, and some his eyes.[76] To know what was done in every place,

[73] warlike pastimes] Cyrus instates the Persian education system more widely across his empire.

[74] noble men] Slightly wide of the mark: Barker emphasises the nobility, whereas Cyrus's point is that his governors should also follow the habit of publicly favouring the most deserving at their tables, just as he does.

[75] from time to time] Some confusion with the compression; Xenophon means that these things are still observed (not that they are occasionally observed).

[76] some his eyes] Barker erroneously implies that it is the governors who gain these names.

being so far separated his provinces, one from another, he[77] took this order. Knowing by experience how far a man might ride every day by fresh horse, he appointed places accordingly that the fresh man, taking letters of the weary, without let might bring the news in most short time, riding day and night without stop.[78] Wherefore it was said then of the people that his posts went as fast as cranes. Which saying although it was false, yet this was true that it was no small space that they rode, and that things could not have been so well stayed if speedy quickness had not been used. At the end of the year, every president came to Babylon with his men, and Cyrus took the muster in which was one hundred and forty[79] thousand horses, two thousand cars armed, footmen five hundred and forty thousand, with which army he went forth and subdued all the lands betwixt Syria and the Red Sea. Then returning back, he won Egypt and confined his empire from the east by the Red Sea, from the north with the Euxine Sea,[80] from the west with Cyprus and Egypt, from the south with Ethiopia. Of the which confines some for heat, some for cold, some for water and some for drought be inhabitable.[81] But Cyrus, in the middest of them, led his life as seven months at Babylon in winter, and in the spring three months at Susa, and the two months of summer in Bactria, avoiding both extreme cold and heat, lived as it were in a continual spring.[82] And so well beloved in every place that the people contended to present him with most noble gifts. Every city and every private man thought themselves happy if they might present him, and he rewarded them with things that were rare in their countries.

His father and mother being dead, and he somewhat old, he returned into Persia the seventh year of his empire,[83] where after the manner he sacrificed, and danced his country dances, and gave rewards after the manner thereof. And sleeping on a time in the palace, him thought a creature far goodlier than

---

[77] he] i.e. Cyrus. Holland is clearer: 'Moreover we are given to understand of another invention of Cyrus (which concerneth the greatnesse of his Empire) whereby he quickly had intelligence brought unto him, how the State of things went' (sig. [2C3]v).

[78] without stop] Indeed, the Persians are thereby sometimes accredited with inventing the postal system.

[79] one hundred and forty thousand] Some errors in the figures; 120,000 is the correct figure, and 540,000 foot-soldiers rather than 600,000 (Holland gets it right, and it seems likely to have been caused by a misreading of Roman numerals).

[80] Euxine Sea] The Black Sea. The 'Red Sea' in both cases here implies the Indian ocean.

[81] inhabitable] i.e. uninhabitable.

[82] continual spring] Llewelyn-Jones and Robson note, in *Ctesias's History of Persia*, that the peripatetism of the Persian court is a constant across various accounts of it over the centuries, and suggests a deep link to pre-Achaemenid Iranian nomadic culture.

[83] the seventh year of his empire] A mistake; Cyrus now returns to Persia for the seventh time during his reign. Occasionally in compilations or to round out vernacular translations of other works of Xenophon, the following account of the death of Cyrus is excerpted; see, for example, the 1582 French translation of the *Memorabilia*, which concludes with a translation of the 'treseureuse' (very happy) death of Cyrus.

any natural man appeared unto him[84] and said, 'Prepare thyself, O Cyrus, for thou shalt shortly go to God'. Being waked with the vision, he thought his time at hand, and made perfect sacrifices to Jupiter his country patron, to the sun and to the other gods, with this oration:

'Jupiter father, sun and all your gods, accept these last sacrifices for so manifold benefits received of you, having been by you told what to do and what not to do by sacrifices, by stars, by signs and tokens in all mine affairs.[85] Of one thing I most humbly thank you, that in all my victorious and triumphant state, I never exalted myself more than became a mortal man. The which felicity I humbly beseech you to grant my wife, my children, and my friends. And to me grant a present death, convenient to my passed life.'

These done and said, he went to his chamber and rested quietly. When time was that he was wont to be bathed, the servants appointed to that office came. He had them go their way for he would repose himself; after when time was to eat and the meat brought, he refused all meat and took a little drink. Thus continuing the second and third day, he called his children and friends, and said thus unto them:

'Children, and you my entire friends, I perceive evidently by many conjectures that the end of my life is at hand, which being so, you must speak and do of my death as of a mortal man most happy.[86] To the which I have attained from my youth by that I was in my childhood trained in, most honest education, and in youth with the practice of virtuous things, and in the age of man in matters meet for a man, and with the increase of time so increased in strength of body as I have not found mine age weaker than my youth, nor never enterprised matter but that I have accomplished. My friends I have made lords, and mine enemies slaves. My country, that sometime had no rule in Asia, is now most famous of all other. I never got thing valiantly but I have kept it quietly. The time[s] have passed as I have desired, the fear of adverse fortune have not suffered me to be proud of my felicity or rejoice too much of my prosperity. Now at the time of my death, I leave you my children alive; my country I leave in happy case, and

---

[84] appeared unto him] Xenophon's account of a dream-vision warning Cyrus of his imminent death counters Herodotus's account of Cyrus's bloody death at the hands of Tomyris, queen of the Massagetae (I. 204ff), as well as the accounts of Justin, I. 8; Diodorus Siculus, *A Right Noble and Pleasant History of the Successors of Alexander*, trans. by Thomas Stocker (London: Henry Bynneman, 1569), II. 44; Strabo, *Geography*, trans. by Horace Leonard Jones, 8 vols (Cambridge, MA: Harvard University Press, 1917–1932), XV. 8. 413–14; and Berossus (*Berossos and Manetho*, intro. and trans. by Gerald P. Vergrugghe and John M. Wickersham (Ann Arbor: University of Michigan Press, 2003), p. 61), all of whom have Cyrus die on the battlefield.

[85] **Marg**] Oration.

[86] **Marg**] Oration. For 'conjectures' Holland has 'signes' (sig. [2C4]v). Cicero paraphrases this passage in *De Senectute*, 22. See Cicero, *On Old Age. On Friendship. On Divination*, trans. by W. A. Falconer (Cambridge, MA: Harvard University Press, 1989).

my friends in good estate, wherefore I may well count myself an happy man. Now I will declare to whom I leave my kingdom, that there be no business for it when I am gone. Children mine, lief[87] and dear, I love you both alike, but reason and skill requireth that he that is first born should have the first place, being more able to govern in that he hath more counsel and intelligence. I have been taught by my country use to give place not only to brethren but also to our citizens as they were in age, reverencing them in all seemliness; and I have brought you up in knowledge to honour your superiors and to be honoured of your inferiors, which thing follow, not because I speak them, but because your country command them. You, son Cambyses, take mine empire, which with all my power I give you, and trust that God will therein confirm you. You, son Tanaoxares, I leave prince of Media, Armenia and Cadusia; the greater empire and royal name I leave to your brother, but an happy life with less trouble I leave to thee. For thou shalt not want that felicity that man can have, but enjoy all the things that may bring happiness to man. To be desirous of glory, to be careful for state, to be enforced to follow thy father's virtues, and to live in continual suspect, things that takes away all delight, be associate with him that hath a kingdom. Cambyses, I tell thee this for truth, that this sceptre of gold is not it that preserveth a kingdom, but assured friends be the sickerness of a prince. Think not that men be born friends but be made by benefits, for then every man should be faithful, as natural things can not swerve from their creation. But friends be gotten not by force but by benefit. If thou wilt make thy friends for thine assurance, thou ought to begin with none so soon as with thy brethren, and thy countrymen brought up with thee in one place must be preserved to other that be strangers. They that be born of one seed and nourished of one mother, brought up in one house, loved of all one parents, and calling one father and mother, how can they not be of more entire friendship than all other? Therefore, for God's sake, do not lose the occasion of amity that God and nature have given ye, but rather seek to increase it by brotherly amity, which is a charity that cannot be broken, for he that helps his brother helps himself. To whom is the honours of the brother so dear as to the brother? Who is more honoured of the brother in high estate than the brother? Who ought so soon to help the brother against the injury of other as the brother? No man ought to be so obedient to thy brother as thyself; no many so ready to do his pleasure. For his state, either prosperous or adverse, toucheth no man so much as thee.[88] Thou canst look for no such faithful service as of thy brother, neither in peace nor war. What thing is more in hate than not to be loved of the brother?[89] What thing is more worthy than to prefer thy brother? If Cambyses the elder brother

---

[87] lief] 'lef' here.
[88] thee] 'theye' here.
[89] the] 'thee' here; 'thy' seems the more likely word (as it is in the following sentence).

shall honourably entertain his younger brother, no man shall bear you envy. For the which considerations, I beseech you children, for God's sake, to esteem one another, if ye will do anything that may content me. Think not when I am dead that I shall no more be,[90] because now ye cannot see my soul but of the operation thereof, ye know not.[91] The minds of them that have suffered wrong have ye not seen with what fear they suppress murderers, and with what furies they affray the wicked? Such honours should not be given to the dead if they thought the soul did perish with the body. Children, I never thought in all my life that the mind should live so long as it was in the body and then, being separate, it should die, because I see the bodies receive life of the souls. I think not the soul after death to be a dead thing, although it hath been in a dead body,[92] but as a mind pure and void of contagion is much more clear than ever it was. Because everything at the death of man do return to his natural course, but the mind is except, and can neither be seen present nor absent. This is certain, that nothing is more like death than sleep. When as the mind is most free and doth enjoy the divine contemplation, and foresight of things to come, therefore as the soul separate from the body is immortal, so honour you my soul and keep well my words. And though it were so, that the soul and body did die together, yet fear the gods, who is immortal and liveth everlastingly and governeth all things with such order as they see and can do all things, and refrain from wicked act, whose majesty and beauty cannot be expressed.[93]

'Next to God, fear the kind of man which is perpetual.[94] God hath not placed you in obscure or hidden state but so as your deeds must be manifest to all men, which if they be just and good, they shall be commendable to all men; if ye be evil affected one toward another, ye shall be slandered of all men, and no man will trust you when they see that they, among whom it were convenient

---

[90] no more be] Cyrus on the immortality of the soul.

[91] ye know not] Bond suggests that Barker had Lodovico Domenichi's 1548 Italian translation of the *Cyropaedia* before him in translating this passage on the soul ('very loosely rendered', according to Bond, in Barker, *Nobility*, p. 9, note 2). However, it was a particularly well-known passage, partly because it was also closely paraphrased in Cicero's *De Senectute*, for example, and Barker may just as well have been thinking of that. See Humble, '"The Well-Thumbed Attic Muse".

[92] in a dead body] Plato's *Phaedo* described the immortal soul tacked to the mortal body. In fact, Louis leRoy adds a translation of Cyrus's deathbed speech to his 1553 French translation of Plato's *Phaedo*, probably suggested by this image. Cicero, too, cited Cyrus's dying words on the immortality of the soul by way of conclusion to his essay 'Of Old Age' (*De Senectute*, 22). Johannes Sleidan picks out the argument for the immortality of the soul here, and notes that Cicero translated this section, *A brief chronicle of the Four Principall Empyres* (London: Rouland Hall, 1563), sig. C2.

[93] cannot be expressed] A case of compositorial eye-skip? The final clause clearly belongs to the description of the universe ordered by the gods.

[94] perpetual] i.e. respect the race of men, 'which in a continuall succession is perpetuall', as Holland puts it (sig. 2D2).

that love should be, bear hate and contend one against another. If I with these words have showed you sufficiently what ye ought to do, I am very glad; if this be not sufficient, learn of examples past, and with the doctrine that is esteemed best, choose the makes[95] for you. You shall find many fathers to have loved their children and many brethren loved one another, and ye shall find as many that have done the contrary, seeking occasion of discord and novile, and of all these you may choose that makes best for you. And thus my mind ye know. As for my body, sons, when it shall be passed out of this life, ye shall neither put in gold ne silver nor any other thing but immediately in the earth.[96] Nothing can be more precious than to be laid with the earth, which is the mother and nurse of all good thing. I have been always beneficial and now I return to that thing that is most beneficial to all mortal men. Now methink, I begin to faint, wherefore if any of you will take me by the hand, or see me whiles I am alive, let him draw near; but when I am once dead, I charge you that no man look upon me. Call the Persians and other confederates unto my funeral, make my feast with joyful exequies, for I shall shortly be in sure place where I shall feel no pain, being with God or being nothing. Be courteous to them that shall come, as is convenient to the memorial of him that is a blessed man, and take this for my last lesson: if ye be beneficial to your friends, ye shall be the more able to overcome your enemies.' Having said these words and taken every man by the hand, he ended his life.[97] It is evident that Cyrus's empire was most ample by the confines that we have showed tofore, all the which was governed by his counsel and prudence.[98] For all that were under his jurisdiction, he governed and honoured as his children, and they him as their father. But so soon as he was dead, his children fell out, cities and nations rebelled, and everything went to ruin, the occasion whereof I will show, and first concerning matter appertaining unto God. The kings and presidents that governed under him did evermore keep their oath, never failing of their promise made were they otherwise never so wicked; whereas now for their disordered life no man have them in credit. Had not this been, many captains and governors would not have come to have done homage to Cambyses, whom he cruelly caused to die, and many barbarian soldiers, in trust to find the son like the father, were one way or other dispatched.[99] And whereas tofore any man that took any service of charge

[95] the makes] the like (thing).
[96] in the earth] Several versions later sprung up of the narrative of Alexander the Great visiting the tomb of Cyrus, either in respect or to pillage it.
[97] ended his life] Barker omits the farewells to his family and friends at the end of Cyrus's dying speech.
[98] counsel and prudence] The first sentence of what critics regard as the Epilogue, but which Barker (like other early modern editions) coalesces into Book VIII without a break.
[99] dispatched] Much inaccuracy here in the digesting. Xenophon refers to the Greek and Persian mercenaries of his own generation who came to the aid of Cyrus the Younger, but Barker misses the reference and assumes it refers to an expedition to Cambyses, laying the

in hand, or won any province, was greatly honoured of Cyrus, now no man is in estimation with the king but traitors and flatterers,[100] being like to Leonicus who, leaving his wife, children and friends for hostages with the king of Egypt, esteemed his oath and promise no more than served for his commodity.

Wherefore the Asians perceiving this iniquity in the king became of all other most wicked men. For as the rulers be, even so be the subjects, and from day to day devised all kind of mischief to get money, punishing not alonely the offenders but also spoiling the innocents, so that now the good men be more afraid of the king than the evil, wherefore they will no more come at his commandment to serve in war or peace; rather they think it lawful to rebel from them for their impiety toward God and cruelty toward man. And as their minds became infected, so the honest exercise of their bodies they no more regarded. There was a law that no man should spit or snite the nose, not because they would retain the moisture of the body, but that they would by labour and exercise consign the same. Nowadays, this law is no more regarded, and the exercise of the body is utterly abandoned. It was an order to eat once a day, that they might be the more ready to the service of the commonwealth, and now indeed they eat but once a day, but they hold on from morning till night. There was an use that no great pots should be brought to their tables, lest by overmuch drink they should overlade° themselves; and now they bring no great pots but handle the matter so that instead of bringing in great pots they are borne out drunken souls. There was a manner that in their journeys they should bear nothing with them to eat or drink, and now they bear nothing with them, for their journeys be so short that they need not. They were wont to exercise hunting so much as was sufficient for them and their horses' exercise, and when that Artaxerxes and his family began to set their mind in drinking, they went no more on hunting but were angry with them that did go. The custom of the children coming to the court they yet use, but the use of riding or hunting to be made meet for the war is dispatched. The children used to hear causes rightly judged, and thereby to learn justice; now he speedeth best that hath most money to spend. The children did use to learn the power of things hid in the ground, to know the good from the evil, and now they learn the same to do hurt to other.

---

blame for the deterioration of the Persian empire heavily at Cambyses' door. (Holland, by contrast, includes the passage in full, correctly identifying and glossing Cyrus the Younger.)

[100] traitors and flatterers] Much compression of this passage. Holland renders it in full: 'For, in times past if a man had either put himselfe into daunger for the King; won a City; subdued a Nation, or otherwise exploited any brave service for the honour of the King: these were the men who had honours heaped upon them. But now adayes, if any like unto Leomythres (who leaving his wife and children, his friends children also as hostages with the Aegyptian King, transgressed and brake the greatest sacraments of security that were) doe that which seemeth advantageous onely for the King: such as they are most highly advanced, and goe away with the greatest dignity. Which the people of Asia seeing, are themselves also fallen all to impiety and injustice' (sig. 2D2v).

For in no place so many perish of poison as there.

Now they be more delicate than in Cyrus's days, for then they lived after the temperance of Persia and now they use the excess of Media: the one they forsake, the other they embrace and join more to it. It is not now enough to have soft beds but also their beds' feet clad with carpet, that the ground should make the less resistance. Of the fine diet of the table they have diminished nothing of the old but have added a great deal new. He is now in most price that can invent a new dish. In winter they do not only cover their heads, bodies and feet, but also their very fingers' ends with thick furred gloves. In summer it is not enough to seek the shadow of trees and hills, but devise other artificial shadows. And he that hath most silver plate is most esteemed, which, though a man gets wrongfully, he passes not of it but increase[s] his desire of unlawful gains. Every man was wont to be on horseback, not for none other cause but to prove good horsemen; now they make so soft saddles to their horse as they use still the thing not for good riding but for soft sitting, so that no man ought to marvel though chivalry[101] be decayed in Persia. They were wont that had anything in gift of the king to have in readiness horsemen and other to serve in the war, and they that warded the palace and had provision were such as most valiantly might serve their country at all assays. And now cooks and butlers and caters° be the men at arms, meet to make good cheer at all assays, a great number surely but unprofitable to the war and noisome° to the people, which thing is evident enough, for in the country they do more hurt to friends than enemies. Cyrus put down the use of fight far off with darts and instituted men at arms with barbed horse, and to set foot to foot; now they use no more the dart and dare not meet at hand. The footmen bear still the target, pike and sword, but they dare not approach to the nigh fight.[102] Cyrus invented piked cars[103] furnished with men and governors, which did good service in the field; but now they know not their chariotmen, nor who is practised, nor who ignorant, and so going to the war, before they can abide the brunt of the enemy, some fall down of purpose, some go their way, knowing the reward of their service, and so their cars do more hurt to themselves than to their enemies. Nowadays, they dare make no war without the aid of the Grecians,[104] neither in their civil nor foreign war. And therefore to end my tale,[105] I dare say that no nation is of such impiety toward the gods, of such wickedness toward their natural kin, of such unjustice toward all sorts of men, and of such cowardice in the war as the Persian is. From the which opinion, if perhaps any man do dissent, let him consider their doings as I have and he will affirm as I do.

---

[101] chivalry] Translating τὰ πολεμικά (*tà polemiká*, military matters).
[102] the nigh fight] i.e. not daring to combat up close.
[103] piked cars] The infamous scythed chariots.
[104] the Grecians] i.e. Greek mercenaries.
[105] my tale] Barker interpolates this notion of a tale told.

Thus endeth the eighth book.

Imprinted at London in Paul's churchyard by Reginalde Wolfe.

GLOSSARY

abroad	out(side)
accusements	accusations
adventure	(as verb) to venture, risk oneself
advices	opinions
affiance	trust/faith in a person/thing
affraying	frightening, terrifying
afore	before
alate	of late
allodge	pitch a tent/encampment
alonely	only
alpheres	ensign/standard-bearer (anglicization of 'alferez' — 'horseman' in the original Arabic)
ambushment	a disposition/arrangement of troops, concealed, ready for attack (ambush)
ancients	elders
apaid	satisfied
apert	open, manifest, unconcealed
appeach	charge with a crime, impeach
appointment	equipment
armature	armour
artificer	makers of particular objects (here, military)
assay	attempt (especially in military context)
available	availing, worthwhile etc.
available	effectual, of advantage
avails	advantage, benefits
avaunt	speak boastfully
avise	look at
axle-tree	the beam of wood between the opposite wheels of a carriage
band	troop
barb	a covering for the breast and flanks of a war-horse
barbed	of a horse: armed or caparisoned with a barb
battle	battalion in array
benison	something one receives, blessing
betimes	at an early hour
bewray	expose
board	table

botchers	menders of garments
bourded	jested, made game with
brake	i.e. broke
brunt	a sharp blow
buckler	small round shield
careful	thoughtful, full of care for
cars	chariots
cast	trick
cater	a buyer of provisions
chaffer	merchandise, ware, traffic, trade
champaign	open country/a plain
chip-axe	a tool for cutting timber or planing objects
circles	here: the compass of a place; 'loft' (Holland) or 'gallery' (Loeb)
cloining	acting deceitfully
clouters	cobblers, patchers
cock	water-cock
cocker	indulge
collars	leather thongs, either for fixing things onto animals (as Holland implies) or the part on which the drawing power of the harness is concentrated
comforted	with the sense of 'encouraged'
concorporate	united into one body
confeder	enter into an alliance/league (intransitive sense)
confines	boundaries
conject	figure out, devise
conquery	conquest
conveyance	linguistic expression or utterance
countenanced	watched
coursing	free-running, pursuing
cousin	kinsman
covert	lying in wait, hidden 'in covert' (in hunting)
coverture	covered
cremet	an ornamental bridle for horses
cresses	water-cress, or any other cruciferous plant (usually in pl. in the period)
crew	group of soldiers
crook	curve
cuirass, or curet	a piece of armour for the body (originally of leather), consisting of fastened breast-plate and back-plate

curetine	a group of curet-bearing soldiers; 'curet' is a common sixteenth-century variant of cuirass
curtolax	a single-edged blade
cutlass	a short, broad sword
daric	a Persian coin
darter	targeteer, a foot-soldier armed with a light, round shield (target)
defection	falling away from a leader, party or cause
depose	stand guarantor (here)
despite	disdain, contempt
despiteful	contemptuous, opprobrious
despouse	promise in marriage
devoir	duty, business
diligence	constancy, assiduity in service
disparple	disperse, scatter
distained	dishonoured
divorcement	the act of divorcing, or severance of a close relation
dolour	pain, punishment
drove	a noun form of the verb for driving out a crowd/multitude of animals
durance	constraint
eftsoones	afterwards, soon afterwards (*OED* sense 3; 'again' [1, 2] and 'from time to time' [4])
embassage	embassy/delegation of ambassadors
embold	embolden
emprises	enterprises
enmured	walled
enprinted	printed
ensign	troop
entrate	that which comes in/a revenue; from Italian 'entrata'
entreated	dealt with/treated of
err	error/fault
eschew	avoid
escries	outcries, or battle-cries
espies	spies
espousal	nuptials
espy	spy
except	unless
expedite	nimble, ready (soldiers, here)

favour	appearance/countenance
feign	pretend
ferrour	a worker in iron
fined	refined
forcause	because
forecast	forethought, prudence
forthink	have a change of mind
forward	ardent, ready
friendful	friendly, well-disposed
froward	difficult to deal with, disposed to go counter to what is demanded
furniture	equipping, provisioning
galliard	valiant, hardy
gather	deduce, understand (here)
gear	equipment, armour
glister	glitter, shine
guerdons	rewards
habilite	capability/capacity to do something
hallow	a loud shout to hounds (in hunting)
halt	limping, lame
hand stripes	close fighting
haply	perhaps, by chance
harness	military gear/armour/weapons
haviour	behaviour
herbigage	foraged greens, herbage
herds	animal herders
hereon	herein
high-stomached	of high courage/spirit, haughty
holds	strongholds
holpen	helped
host	army or armed company of men
hunting	hunt [noun]
importable	that which cannot be borne/too grievous to be bearable
in amours	in love
in muse	absorbed in thought
indued	brought up/educated with
inexorable	[of a person] incapable of being persuaded or moved by entreaty

Glossary

inhabitance	dwelling, abode
intreated	treated
iota	the least particle (in figurative sense)
irk	weary, tired, troubled
jade	an inferior horse
kyne	cows/cattle
laver	water-jug or vessel for washing
let	prohibit
lewdness	badness, ignorance
lief	precious
list	like (e.g. what I list' = 'what I (would) like')
lodesmen	guides
longeth	belongeth
louted	mocked
louting	submitting (here)
lucre	gain, advantage
lybards	leopards
marches	borderlands
marches	boundary or borderlands
marches	'marches of Wales' = the part of England bordering on Wales, but more generally 'marches' = borders/boundaries
masters	schoolmasters
matchly	likewise
measurable	moderate
meeter	more fit
ministers (of the camp)	quartermasters
ministers	attendants, persons subordinate to another
mone	to make one's mone = to grieve/complain
monition	prompt, warning, admonition
neat	cow
noisome	disagreeable
nourice	one who is responsible for the bringing-up of a child, especially a wet-nurse or foster-mother
oblation	sacrifices presented to a god
occupations	toil, exercise, having one's time or attention occupied

ordinance	ordaining, decree
ought	owed
out of hand	quickly
overcharge	supply to excess
overlade	to load with too heavy a burden
painful	take pains
painture	a painting
pastance	recreation
peised, peising	weighed, considered
pensioner	bodyguard
pensive	sorrowful, or full of thought
peradventure	maybe, possibly
pick at large	to fight from far off (e.g. with lances or javelins)
picks	scythes (on the carriages Cyrus devises)
piece	a cask for alcohol (in Book 1)
pight	planned, organised (of a military encounter)
pinnacle	any vertical construction on top of an object, sometimes meaning a turret in architecture
pith	force, power, energy (in words, here; *OED* sense 5b)
plat	location
port	bearing, carriage, demeanour
praisably	laudably
prest	ready for action/use
price	an expression of commendation/honour/esteem; appreciation, prized
proponed	put forward, proposed
provend	provender
purveyance	supply of food or necessities
put up	in hunting, the beasts provided
queller	a person who kills someone, executioner
quick	alive
quod	sixteenth-century form of 'quoth', occasionally used here
rampire	rampart, defensive wall/earthworks
rate	after the estimated worth of an individual/thing
ratherest	most rather
ravening	eating voraciously, with connotations of plunder/spoil
ray	military order/ranks
rearward	of the army, the part stationed behind the main host

Glossary

reave	rob, pillage
rede	counsel or advice, usually of one person to another
redound	return
repining	complaining
rive	split/cleave (e.g. wood)
scoutwatch	sentinel, watch
semblably	similarly
severally	separately, individually
shifts	ingenious devices
sickerness	certainty
skrike	shriek; to utter a shrill, harsh cry
sleights	trickery
slinger	someone who casts missiles of some sort using a sling
sluggardy	slothfulness, laziness
snite	to clean/wipe (the nose)
soldierfare	military service or experience
sometime	sometimes
sophister	sophist
sparpled	dispersed/scattered (i.e. 'disparpled')
sparsed	scattered, dispersed
spial/espial	spy or spying
spoiled	despoiled
straitly	rigorously
straits	a narrow or confined place
streight	narrow
stripe	blow, stroke
succours	help/assistance, or one who helps
sumpter	pack-horse
surety	certainty, security, safety
Susian	from Susa, of a native of Susa
tarryance	delay
tillmen	ploughmen
tipstaff/tipstaves	a staff with a metal tip, carried as a badge by certain officials
tirement	garments, attire
tofore	heretofore
toyed	made sport/amused oneself
trains	a succession of moving people or things
travail	labour

travailous	industrious, laborious
twibill	an axe with two edges
unshamefastness	immodesty, indecency
unware	unwary, incautious
unwares	unaware
vambrace	defensive armour for forearm
vaunce	advance
vaunt	boast/show off
vaward	vanguard (military)
vehemency	physical force, intensity
vestured	clothed, dressed in vesture
vizying	looking closely, examining (or, visiting a person)
volupty	pleasures, delight
voyage	military expedition
ward	watch/watchman
ware	wary, careful
waste/wasting	laying waste to
wasters	a wooden sword used in sword-exercise and fencing, or a cudgel
whelp	hound (here)
wise	way (e.g. 'in/on this wise' = 'in this way')
wittily	cleverly
wot	knows (e.g. 'God wot')

NEOLOGISMS

alpheres	anglicization of Spanish 'alferez' (ensign/standard-bearer), originally from Arabic 'al-faris' (horseman). First use in *OED* is in 1581; here in 1567 edition
appointment	here, equipment, provisions (earlier than the ?1578 *OED* instance of this usage)
cremet	an ornamental bridle for horses (not in *OED*)
curetine	a coinage; a group of curet-bearing soldiers (where 'curet' is a common sixteenth-century variant of 'cuirass')
curtolax	a single-edged blade (precedes *OED*'s ascription to Sir Thomas North's 1579 translation of Plutarch as the first usage)
daric	a Persian coin (usage in 1552? edition; predates 1566 *OED* first usage)
drove	a noun form of the verb for driving out a crowd/multitude of animals (noun form not in *OED*)
enprinted	printed (not in *OED*)
entrate	from Italian 'entrata'; that which comes in/a revenue; significantly earlier than *OED* first usage (1670)
expedite	nimble, ready; one usage here for lightly-equipped soldiers precedes the *OED* first usage (1609) in that sense
forward	ardent, ready (in this sense, precedes *OED* first usage (1587))
iota	the least particle (in figurative sense); precedes *OED* first usage (1636)
matchly	likewise (not in *OED*)
novile	novel (precedes *OED* first usage (1586))
soldierfare	military service or experience (precedes *OED* first usage (1579 North's Plutarch))
unshamefastness	immodesty, indecency (not in *OED*)

BIBLIOGRAPHY

Primary

ARIOSTO, LUDOVICO, *Orlando furioso in English heroicall verse*, trans. by John Harington (London: Richard Field, 1591)
ASCHAM, ROGER, *The Scholemaster* (London: John Day, 1570)
—— *Toxophilus* (London: Edward Whitchurch, 1545)
—— *The Whole Works of Roger Ascham*, ed. by J. A. Giles, 2 vols (London: John Russell Smith, 1865)
ASTLEY, JOHN, *The Art of Riding* (London: Henry Denham, 1584)
BARKER, WILLIAM (trans.), *An auncient historie and exquisite chronicle of the Roman warres* [Appian] (London: Henry Bynneman, 1578)
—— *Epitaphia et inscriptiones lugubres* (London: John Cawood, 1566)
—— *An exhortation of holye Basilius Magnus to hys young kynseman* (London: John Cawood, 1557)
—— (trans.), *The Fearfull Fansies of the Florentine couper*, by Iohn Baptista Gelli (London: Henry Bynneman, 1568)
—— (trans.), *The Nobility of Women*, ed. by R. Warwick Bond, 2 vols (London: Roxburghe Club, 1904-1905)
BEAUMONT, FRANCIS, and JOHN FLETCHER, *A King and No King* (London: for Thomas Walkley, 1619)
BEROSSOS, *Berossos and Manetho*, intro. and trans. by Gerald P. Vergrugghe and John M. Wickersham (Ann Arbor: University of Michigan Press, 2003)
BOND, R. WARWICK, *Addenda, Glossary, and Index to William Barker's 'Nobility of Women'* (London: Roxburghe Club, 1905)
BROOKE, CHRISTOPHER, *Two Elegies, consecrated to the never-dying Memorie of* [...] *Henry, Prince of Wales* (London: for Richard More, 1613)
BRYSKETT, LODOWICK, *A Discourse of Civill Life* (London: for Edward Blount, 1606)
BULTEEL, JOHN, *Birinthea: A Romance* (London: Thomas Mabbe for John Playfere, 1664)
CARDINI, ROBERTO (ed.), *Cristoforo Landino: Scritti Critici e teorici*, 2 vols (Roma: Bulzoni, 1974)
CARION, JOHANNES, *The thre bokes of cronicles* (London: for Gwalter Lynne, 1550)
CARTWRIGHT, WILLIAM, *The Royal Slave* (Oxford: for Thomas Robinson, 1639)
CASTIGLIONE, BALDESSARE, *The Courtyer of Count Baldessar Castilio*, trans. by Thomas Hoby (London: William Seres, 1561)
CICERO, *An Epistle or Letter of Exhortation*, trans. by Goddred Gilby (London: Rouland Hall, 1561)
—— *The Letters of Cicero*, trans. by Evelyn S. Shuckburgh, 4 vols (London: George Bell and Sons, 1908-1909)
—— *Marcus Tullius Ciceroes thre bokes of duties*, trans. by Nicholas Grimald (London: Richard Tottel, 1556)
—— *On Old Age. On Friendship. On Divination*, trans. by W. A. Falconer (Cambridge, MA: Harvard University Press, 1989)

CLELAND, JAMES, *Heropaideia, or the Institution of a Yong Noble Man* (Oxford: Joseph Barnes, 1607)
COOPER, THOMAS (ed.), *Bibliotheca Eliotae* (London: Thomas Berthelet, 1552)
COTGRAVE, RANDLE, *A Dictionary of the French and English Tongues* (London: Adam Islip, 1611)
DENHAM, JOHN, *Cato-Major: Of Old Age* (London: for Henry Herringman, 1669)
DOMENICHI, LODOVICO, *La Nobiltà delle Donne* (Venice: Gabriele Giolito, 1549)
DIODORUS SICULUS, *A Right Noble and Pleasant History of the Successors of Alexander*, trans. by Thomas Stocker (London: Henry Bynneman, 1569)
DIOGENES LAERTIUS, *Lives of the Eminent Philosophers*, trans. by R. D. Hicks (Cambridge, MA: Harvard University Press, 1925)
DU BARTAS, GUILLAUME, *The Triumph of Faith, The Sacrifice of Isaac. The Ship-Wreck of Jonas*, trans. by Joshua Sylvester (London: Richard Yardley and Peter Short, 1592)
ELYOT, THOMAS, *The Book named The Governor*, with introduction by Foster Watson (London: J. M. Dent, 1907)
GELLI, GIOVANNI-BAPTISTA, *I Capricci del Bottaio* (Florence: [Lorenzo Torrentino], 1548)
HAKLUYT, RICHARD, *Principall Navigations, Traffiques and Discoveries of the English Nation* (London: George Bishop and Ralph Newberie, 1589)
HOBY, THOMAS, *The Travels and Life of Sir Thomas Hoby […] 1547–1564*, ed. by Edgar Powell (London: Royal Historical Society, 1902)
HOLLAND, PHILEMON *Cyrupaedia, or The Institution and Life of Cyrus, King of Persians*, ed. by Henry Holland (London: for Robert Allot, 1632)
ISOCRATES, *Evagoras, etc.*, trans. by La Rue Van Hook (Cambridge, MA: Harvard University Press, 1945)
—— *To Demonicus. To Nicocles, etc.*, trans. by George Norlin (Cambridge, MA: Harvard University Press, 1928)
JAMES VI OF SCOTLAND and I OF ENGLAND, *Basilikon Doron* (London: Edward Allde for Edward White, 1603)
JOSEPHUS, FLAVIUS, 'The Antiquities of the Jews', in *The Works of Flavius Josephus*, trans. by William Whiston (London: [William Bowyer], 1737)
JUSTIN, *The Historie of Iustine*, trans. by G. W. (London: William Jaggard, 1606)
—— *Thabridgement of the histories of Trogus Pompeius*, trans. by Arthur Golding (London: Thomas Marshe, 1578)
MARLOWE, CHRISTOPHER, *Tamburlaine* (London: Richard Jones, 1590)
MULCASTER, RICHARD, *The First Part of the Elementary* (Menston: Scolar Press, 1970)
—— *Positions (1581*, ed. by Robert Hebert Quick (London: Harrison & Sons, 1887)
NEWTON, THOMAS, *A View of Valyaunce* (London: Thomas East, 1580)
PAINTER, WILLIAM, *The Pallace of Pleasure* (London: Henry Denham for Richard Tottell and William Jones, 1566)
PEACHAM, HENRY, *The Period of Mourning* (London: Thomas Snodham for John Helme, 1613)
PLATO, *Plato in Twelve Volumes, Vols. 10 & 11*, trans. by R. G. Bury (Cambridge, MA: Harvard University Press; London: William Heinemann Ltd, 1967 and 1968)
PUTTENHAM, GEORGE, *The Arte of English Poesie*, ed. by G. D. Willcock and Alice Walker (Cambridge: Cambridge University Press, 1936)

RALEGH, WALTER, *The History of the World* (London: William Stansby for Walter Burre, 1614)

RAMUSIO, GIOVANNI (ed.), *Navigazioni e i viaggi*, 3 vols (Venice: Giunta, 1555–1559)

RICHE, BARNABE, *Brusanus* (London: for J. Oxenbridge, 1592)

ROBINSON, RICHARD, *The Auncient Order, Societie, and Unitie Laudable of Prince Arthure...* (London: John Wolfe, 1583)

SCOTT, WILLIAM, *The Model of Poesy*, ed. by Gavin Alexander (Cambridge: Cambridge University Press, 2013)

SCUDERY, MADELEINE DE, *Artamenes, or The Grand Cyrus*, trans. by F. G. (London: for Humphrey Mosely, 1653)

SHAKESPEARE, WILLIAM, *Richard III*, ed. by Janis Lull (Cambridge: Cambridge University Press, 2018)

SIDNEY, PHILIP, *Apology for Poetry*, ed. by Geoffrey Shepherd (Manchester: Manchester University Press, 1977)

—— *The Countess of Pembroke's Arcadia*, ed. by Maurice Evans (New York: Penguin, 1977)

SLEIDAN, JOHANNES, *A brief chronicle of the Four Principall Empyres* (London: Rouland Hall, 1563)

SMITH, SIR THOMAS, *De Republica Anglorum*, ed. by Leonard Alston (Cambridge: Cambridge University Press, 1906)

STERNE, LAURENCE, *The Life and Opinions of Tristram Shandy, Gentleman* (York, 1759–1766)

STRABO, *Geography*, trans. by Horace Leonard Jones, 8 vols (Cambridge, MA: Harvard University Press, 1917–1932)

STRYPE, JOHN, *Memorials of [...] Thomas Cranmer* (London: for Richard Chiswell, 1664)

TATUM, JAMES (ed.), *The School of Cyrus: William Barker's 1567 Translation of Xenophon's Cyropaedeia (the Education of Cyrus)* (New York and London: Garland Publishing, 1987)

TAVERNER, RICHARD, *The Second Boke of the Garden of Wysdom* (London: Richard Bankes, 1539)

WALSH, OCTAVIA, 'The Princely Persian led his warlike Host', in Bodleian Library MS Eng. poet e.31

WILSON, THOMAS (trans.), *The Three Orations of Demosthenes* (London: Henry Denham, 1570)

—— *Wilson's 'Arte of Rhetorique' (1560)*, ed. by G. H. Mair (Oxford: Clarendon Press, 1909)

WOLFE, DON M., ET AL. (ed.), *Complete Prose Works of John Milton*, 8 vols (New Haven: Yale University Press, 1953–1982)

XENOPHON, *The Education of Cyrus*, trans. by Wayne Ambler (Ithaca and London: Cornell University Press, 2001)

—— *The historie of Xenophon [Anabasis]*, trans. by John Bingham (London: John Haviland for Raphe Mabb, 1623)

—— *Kyrou paideia: or The Institution and Life of Cyrus the Great*, trans. by Francis Digby and John Norris (London: for Matthew Gilliflower and James Norris, 1685)

—— *Xenophons Treatise of Householde [Oeconomicus]*, trans. by Gentian Hervet (London: Thomas Berthelet, 1534)

Secondary

AHN, DOOHWAN, 'The Politics of Royal Education: Xenophon's *Education of Cyrus* in Early Eighteenth-Century Europe', *Leadership Quarterly*, 19 (2008), 439–52

ALLEN, LINDSAY, 'Chilminar *Olim* Persepolis: European Reception of a Persian Ruin', in *Persian Responses: Political and Cultural Interaction with(in) the Achaemenid Empire*, ed. by Christopher Tuplin (Swansea: Classical Press of Wales, 2007), pp. 313–42

ANDERSON, J. K., *Xenophon* (London: Duckworth, 1974)

ASCHAM, ROGER, *The Schoolmaster* (1570), ed. by Lawrence V. Ryan (Washington, DC: Folger/University Press of Virginia, 1974)

AZOULAY, VINCENT, 'The Medo-Persian Ceremonial: Xenophon, Cyrus and the King's Body', in *Xenophon and his World*, ed. by Christopher Tuplin (Stuttgart: Franz Steiner Verlag, 2004), pp. 147–73

BALDWIN, T. W., *William Shakspere's Small Latine and Lesse Greeke*, 2 vols (Urbana: University of Illinois Press, 1944)

BALL, LOUIS, 'The Background of the Minor English Renaissance Epics', *ELH*, 1 (1934), 63–89

BARTLETT, KENNETH R., 'The Creation of an Englishman Italified: William Barker in Italy 1551–1554', *Bollettino del Centro Interuniversitario di Ricerche sul "Viaggio in Italia"*, 20 (1989), 209–17

—— 'Thomas Hoby, Translator, Traveler', in *Travel and Translation*, ed. by Carmine G. diBiase (Amsterdam and New York: Rodopi, 2006), pp. 123–41

—— 'William Barker', in 'Sixteenth-Century British Nondramatic Writers', *Dictionary of Literary Biography* (first series), ed. by D. A. Richardson (Detroit: Gale, 1993), pp. 48–52

BATES, CATHERINE, *On Not Defending Poetry: Defence and Indefensibility in Sidney's 'Defence of Poesy'* (Oxford: Oxford University Press, 2017)

BENEKER, JEFFREY, *The Passionate Statesman: 'Eros' and Politics in Plutarch's Lives* (Oxford: Oxford University Press, 2012)

BINNS, J. W., 'Latin Translation from Greek in the English Renaissance', *Humanistica Lovaniensia*, 27 (1978), 128–59

BLAYNEY, PETER, *The Stationers' Company and the Printers of London, 1501–1557* (Cambridge: Cambridge University Press, 2013)

BOTLEY, PAUL, *Learning Greek in Western Europe, 1396–1529: Grammars, Lexica, and Classroom Texts* (Philadelphia: Transactions of the American Philosophical Society, 2010)

BRADNER, L., 'The Xenophon Translation Attributed to Queen Elizabeth I', *JWCI*, 27 (1964), 324–26

BRENTJES, SONJA, and VOLKMAR SCHUELLER, 'Pietro Della Valle's Latin Geography of Safavid Iran (1624–1628)', *Journal of Early Modern History*, 10 (2006), 169–219

BRIANT, PIERRE, *From Cyrus to Alexander: A History of the Persian Empire*, trans. by Peter T. Daniels (Winona Lake, IN: Eisenbrauns, 2002)

—— 'History and Ideology: The Greeks and "Persian Decadence"', in *Greeks and Barbarians*, ed. by Thomas Harrison (Edinburgh: Edinburgh University Press, 2002), pp. 193–210

BURROW, COLIN, 'Reading Tudor Writing Politically: The Case of *2Henry IV*', *Yearbook of English Studies*, 38 (2008), 234–50

BUSHNELL, REBECCA, *A Culture of Teaching: Early Modern Humanism in Theory and Practice* (Ithaca: Cornell University Press, 1996)

CARLIER, PIERRE, 'The Idea of Imperial Monarchy in Xenophon's *Cyropaedia*', in *Xenophon*, ed. by Vivienne J. Gray (Oxford: Oxford University Press, 2010), pp. 327–66

CAMPANA, JOSEPH, 'The Bee and the Sovereign: Political Entomology and the Problem of Scale', *Shakespeare Studies*, 41 (2013), 94–113

CAVANAGH, DERMOT, 'Political Tragedy in the 1560s: *Cambises* and *Gorboduc*', in *The Oxford Handbook of Tudor Literature, 1485–1603*, ed. by Cathy Shrank and Michael Pincombe (Oxford: Oxford University Press, 2009)

CHERCHI, PAOLO, 'My Kingdom for a Horse', *Notes and Queries*, 46 (1999), 206–07

CLARK, M. L., *Classical Education in Britain, 1500–1900* (Cambridge: Cambridge University Press, 1959)

CLEGG, CYNDIA SUSAN, *Press Censorship in Elizabethan England* (Cambridge: Cambridge University Press, 2004)

COOPER, CHARLES HENRY, *Athenae Cantabrigienses*, 2 vols (Cambridge: Deighton, Bell and Co., 1858–1861)

COSTELLO, WILLIAM T., *The Scholastic Curriculum at Early Seventeenth-Century Cambridge* (Cambridge, MA: Harvard University Press, 1958)

CRAMSIE, JAMES, 'The Philosophy of Imperial Kingship and the Interpretation of James VI and I', in *James VI and I: Ideas, Authority, and Government*, ed. by Ralph Houlbroke (Vermont: Ashgate, 2006), pp. 43–60

CUMMINGS, R., 'Recent Studies in English Translation, c. 1520–c. 1590', *ELR*, 37 (2007), 274–316

D'ALESSANDRO, A., 'Prime ricerche su Lodovico Domenichi', in *Le corti farnesiane di Parma e Piacenza (1546–1622)*, ed. by A. Quondam, 2 vols (Rome: Bulzoni, 1978), I, pp. 171–200

DANZIG, GABRIEL, *Apologizing for Socrates: How Plato and Xenophon Created our Socrates* (Lanham, Boulder, New York, Toronto, Plymouth: Rowman and Littlefield, 2010)

—— 'Big Boys and Little Boys: Justice and Law in Xenophon's *Cyropaedia* and *Memorabilia*', *Polis*, 26 (2009), 271–95

DE KEYSER, JEROEN, 'Elucidation and Self-Explanation in Filelfo's Marginalia', in *Self-Commentary in Early Modern European Literature, 1400–1700*, ed. by Francesco Venturi (Leiden: Brill, 2019), pp. 50–70

—— (ed.), *Traduzioni da Senofonte* (Alessandria: Edizioni dell'Orso, 2012)

DENNY, JOANNA, *Anne Boleyn: A New Life of England's Tragic Queen* (Philadelphia: Da Capo Press, 2007)

DOHERTY, M. J., *The Mistress-Knowledge: Literary Architectonics in the English Renaissance* (Nashville: Vanderbilt University Press, 1991)

DUE, BODIL, *The 'Cyropaedia': Xenophon's Aims and Methods* (Aarhus: Aarhus University Press, 1989)

DUFF, E. GORDON, *A Century of the English Book Trade* (London: for the Bibliographical Society, 1905)

Encyclopaedia Iranica, online edition (New York: 1996–) <http://www.iranicaonline.org/>

GADD, IAN A., '"A Suitable Remedy?" Regulating the Printing Press, 1553–1558', in

Catholic Renewal and Protestant Resistance in Marian England, ed. by Elizabeth Evenden and Vivienne Westbrook (Burlington, VT: Ashgate, 2015), pp. 127–42

GARAVELLI, ENRICO, 'Lodovico Domenichi, nicodemista?', in *Il Rinascimento italiano di fronte alla Riforma: Letteratura e Arte. Sixteenth-Century Italian Art and Literature and the Reformation. Atti del Convegno internazionale di Londra, The Warburg Institute*, ed. by C. Damianaki et al. (Manziana: Vecchiarelli, 2005), pp. 159–75

GERA, DEBORAH LEVINE, *Xenophon's 'Cyropaedia': Style, Genre, and Literary Technique* (Oxford: Clarendon Press, 1993)

GILBERT, ALLAN, *Machiavelli's 'Prince' and its Forerunners* (New York: Barnes & Noble, 1938)

GOLDGAR, ANNE, *Impolite Learning: Conduct and Community in the Republic of Letters, 1680–1750* (New Haven: Yale University Press, 1995)

GRAFTON, ANTHONY, *New Worlds, Ancient Texts: The Power of Tradition and the Shock of Discovery* (Cambridge, MA: Harvard University Press, 1995)

—— 'Renaissance Readers and Ancient Texts', *Renaissance Quarterly*, 38 (1985), 615–49

GRANDE, TRONI V., and GARRY SHERBERT (eds), *Northrop Frye's Writings on Shakespeare and the Renaissance* (Toronto: University of Toronto Press, 2010)

GRAY, VIVIENNE J. (ed.), *Xenophon* (Oxford: Oxford University Press, 2010)

—— (ed.), *Xenophon On Government* (Cambridge: Cambridge University Press, 2007)

GROGAN, JANE, 'Ancient Persia, Early Modern England, and the Labours of Reception', in *Eastern Resonances in Early Modern England: Receptions and Transformations from the Renaissance to the Romantic Period*, ed. by Claire Gallien and Ladan Niayesh (Basingstoke: Palgrave Macmillan, 2019)

—— *Exemplary Spenser: Visual and Verbal Pedagogy in 'The Faerie Queene'* (Aldershot: Ashgate, 2009)

—— *The Persian Empire in English Renaissance Writing, 1549–1622* (Basingstoke: Palgrave Macmillan, 2014)

—— '"A Warre … Commodious": Dramatizing Islamic Schism in and after *Tamburlaine*', *Texas Studies in Language and Literature*, 54 (2012), 45–78

GUNDERSHEIMER, WERNER L., *The Life and Works of Louis Le Roy* (Geneva: Librairie Droz, 1966)

HALL, EDITH, *Inventing the Barbarian: Greek Self-Definition through Tragedy* (Oxford: Clarendon Press, 1989)

HARDISON, O. B., *The Enduring Monument: A Study of the Idea of Praise in Renaissance Literary Theory and Practice* (Chapel Hill: University of North Carolina Press, 1962)

HASLER, P. W., *Commons, 1558–1603*, 3 vols (Woodbridge: Boydell and Brewer, 2006)

—— 'Great Yarmouth', *The History of Parliament: British Political, Social & Local History* <http://www.historyofparliamentonline.org/volume/1558-1603/constituencies/great-yarmouth>

HENINGER, S. K., *Sidney and Spenser: The Poet as Maker* (State College: Pennsylvania State University Press, 1990)

HIRSCH, STEVEN, *The Friendship of the Barbarians: Xenophon and the Persian Empire* (Hanover and London: University Press of New England, for Tufts University, 1985)

HIGGINS, W. E., *Xenophon the Athenian: The Problem of the Individual and the Society of the Polis* (Albany: State University of New York Press, 1977)

HOBDEN, FIONA, and CHRISTOPHER TUPLIN (eds), *Xenophon: Ethical Principles and Historical Enquiry* (Leiden and Boston: Brill, 2012)

HOSINGTON, BRENDA, '"A Poore Preasant off Ytalyan Costume": The Interplay of Travel and Translation in William Barker's *Dyssputacion off the Nobylytye off Wymen*', in *Travel and Translation in the Early Modern Period*, ed. by Carmen G. diBiase (Amsterdam: Rodopi, 2006), pp. 143–55

—— ET AL., *Renaissance Cultural Crossroads* <http://www.hrionline.ac.uk>

HOUSTON, CHLOË, 'Persia and Kingship in William Cartwright's *The Royal Slave* (1636)', *SEL*, 54 (2014), 455–73

HUMBLE, NOREEN, 'The Limits of Biography: The Case of Xenophon', in *Pleiades Setting* (Cork: University College Cork, 2002), pp. 66–87.

—— 'Parallelism and the Humanists', in *Plutarch's Lives: Parallelism and Purpose*, ed. by Noreen Humble (Swansea: Classical Press of Wales, 2010), pp. 237–65

—— '"The Well-Thumbed Attic Muse": Cicero and the Reception of Xenophon's Persia in the Early Modern Period', in *Beyond Greece and Rome: The Ancient Near East in Early Modern Europe*, ed. by Jane Grogan (Oxford: Oxford University Press, 2020)

HUTSON, LORNA, *The Usurer's Daughter: Male Friendship and Fictions of Women in Sixteenth-Century England* (London: Routledge, 1994)

INGRAM, WILLIAM H., 'The Ligatures of Early Printed Greek', *Greek, Roman and Byzantine Studies*, 7 (1966), 371–89

JOHNSON, DAVID M., 'Persians as Centaurs in Xenophon's *Cyropaedia*', *Transactions of the American Philological Association*, 135 (2005), 177–207

KELLER, WILLIAM J., 'Xenophon's Acquaintance with the History of Herodotus', *The Classical Journal*, 6 (1911), 252–59

LAWRENCE, JASON, *Who the Devil Taught Thee so Much Italian? Italian Language Learning and Literary Imitation in Early modern England* (Manchester: Manchester University Press, 2005)

LAZARUS, MICHA, 'Greek Literacy in Sixteenth-Century England', *Renaissance Studies*, 29 (2014), 433–58

LEEDHAM-GREEN, ELISABETH, *Books in Cambridge Inventories: Book-Lists from Vice-Chancellors' Probate Court Probate Inventories in the Tudor and Stuart Periods*, 2 vols (Cambridge: Cambridge University Press, 1986)

Leo Strauss Stranscripts (The Leo Strauss Center, University of Chicago) <http://leostrausstranscripts.uchicago.edu/navigate/8/?byte=547471>

LESSER, ZACHARY, *Renaissance Drama and the Politics of Publication: Readings in the English Book Trade* (Cambridge: Cambridge University Press, 2004)

LLEWELLYN-JONES, LLOYD, and JAMES ROBSON, *Ctesias' History of Persia: Tales of the Orient* (London and New York: Routledge, 2010)

LOW, ANTHONY, '"Plato, and his Equal Xenophon": A Note on Milton's Apology For Smectymnuus', *Milton Quarterly*, 4 (1970), 20–22

MARSH, DAVID, 'Xenophon', in *Catalogus Translationem et Commentariorum*, ed. by Virginia Brown, 9 vols (Washington, DC: Catholic University of America Press, 1992), VII, pp. 75–196

McDIARMID, JOHN F., 'John Cheke's Preface to *De Superstitione*', *The Journal of Ecclesiastical History*, 48 (1997), 100–20

—— (ed.), *Sir John Cheke and the Cambridge Connection in Tudor England*, St Andrews Studies in Reformation History (Leiden: Brill, 2019)

McKerrow, R. B., *A Dictionary of Printers and Booksellers [...], 1557-1640* (London: for the Bibliographical Society, 1910)

Michaelides, Chris, 'Greek Printing in England, 1500-1900', in *Foreign Language Printing in Britain, 1500-1900*, ed. by Barry Taylor (London and Boston Spa: British Library, 2002), pp. 203-26

Milne, Kirsty, 'The Forgotten Greek Books of Elizabethan England', *Literature Compass*, 4 (2007), 677-87

Moore, Helen, 'Gathering Fruit: The "Profitable" Translations of Thomas Paynell', in *Tudor Translation*, ed. by Fred Schurink (Basingstoke: Palgrave Macmillan, 2011), pp. 39-57

Moore-Smith, G. C., *Gabriel Harvey's Marginalia* (Stratford-upon-Avon: Shakespeare Head Press, 1913)

Murdin, William, et al. (ed.), *A Collection of State Papers Relating to Affairs in the Reign of Queen Elizabeth* (London: William Bowyer, 1759)

Myers, Robin, Michael Harris and Giles Mandelbrote (eds), *Owners, Annotators and the Signs of Reading* (London and Boston Spa: British Library, 2005)

Nadon, Christopher, *Xenophon's Prince: Republic and Empire in the 'Cyropaedia'* (Berkeley: University of California Press, 2001)

Newell, Walter R., *Tyranny: A New Interpretation* (Cambridge: Cambridge University Press, 2013)

Niayesh, Ladan, 'Shakespeare's Persians', *Shakespeare*, 4 (2008), 127-36

Nohrnberg, James, *The Analogy of The Faerie Queene* (Princeton, NJ: Princeton University Press, 1976)

Pal, Carol, *Republic of Women: Rethinking the Republic of Letters in the Seventeenth Century* (Cambridge: Cambridge University Press, 2012)

Parker, Patricia, 'Barbers, Infidels and Renegades: *Antony and Cleopatra*', in *Center or Margin: Revisions of the English Renaissance in Honor of Leeds Barroll* (Plainsboro, NJ: Susquehanna University Press, 2006), pp. 54-88

Parks, George B., 'William Barker, Tudor Translator', *The Papers of the Bibliographical Society of America*, 51 (1957), 126-40

Plomer, H. R. (ed.), *Abstracts from the Wills of English Printers and Stationers, 1492-1630* (London: The Bibliographical Society, 1903)

Pollnitz, Aysha, *Princely Education in Early Modern Britain* (Cambridge: Cambridge University Press, 2015)

Prior, Mary, 'Reviled and Crucified Marriages: The Position of Tudor Bishops' Wives', in *Women in English Society, 1500-1800*, ed. by Mary Prior (London: Routledge, 1985)

Pryor, Felix (ed.), *Elizabeth I: Her Life in Letters* (London: British Library, 2003)

Rasmussen, Paul J., *Excellence Unleashed: Machiavelli's Critique of Xenophon and the Moral Foundation of Politics* (Lanham, Boulder, New York, Toronto, Plymouth: Lexington Books, 2009)

Rex, Richard, 'The Sixteenth Century', in *St John's College, Cambridge: A History*, ed. by Peter Linehan (Woodbridge: Boydell & Brewer, 2011)

Rhodes, Neil, *Common: The Development of Literary Culture in Sixteenth-Century England* (Oxford: Oxford University Press, 2018)

—— 'Marlowe and the Greeks', *Renaissance Studies*, 27 (2013), 199–218
—— 'Pure and Common Greek in Early Tudor England', in *The Culture of Translation in Early Modern England and France, 1500–1660*, ed. by Tania Demetriou and Rowan Tomlinson (Basingstoke: Palgrave, 2015), pp. 54–70
ROOD, TIM, 'A Delightful Retreat: Xenophon and the Picturesque', in *Xenophon: Ethical Principles and Historical Enquiry*, ed. by Fiona Hobden and Christopher Tuplin (Leiden and Boston: Brill, 2012), pp. 89–121
—— *The Sea, The Sea! The Shout of the Ten Thousand in the Modern Imagination* (London: Duckworth, 2004)
SANCISI-WEERDENBURG, HELEEN, 'Cyrus in Italy: From Dante to Machiavelli — Some Explorations of the Reception of Xenophon's *Cyropaedia*', in *Achaemenid History 7*, ed. by J. W. Drijvers and H. Sancisi-Weerdenburg (Leiden: NINO, 1990), pp. 31–52
—— 'The Death of Cyrus', *Acta Iranica*, 25 (1985), 459–72
SANDRIDGE, NORMAN, *Loving Humanity, Learning, and Being Honored: The Foundations of Leadership in Xenophon's 'Education of Cyrus'* (Washington, DC: Center for Hellenic Studies, 2012)
SASEK, LAWRENCE A., 'Plato, and his Equall Xenophon', *English Language Notes*, 7 (1970), 260–62
SCHURINK, FRED (ed.), *Tudor Translation* (Basingstoke: Palgrave, 2011)
SHARPE, KEVIN, *Reading Revolutions: The Politics of Reading in Early Modern England* (New Haven: Yale University Press, 2000)
SPENSER, EDMUND, *The Faerie Queene*, ed. by A. C. Hamilton, et al. (Harlow: Longman, 2007)
SPINGARN, JOEL (ed.), *Critical Essays of the Seventeenth Century*, 2 vols (Oxford: Clarendon Press, 1957)
STADTER, PHILIP, 'Staying Up Late: Plutarch's Reading of Xenophon', in *Xenophon: Ethical Principles and Historical Enquiry*, ed. by Fiona Hobden and Christopher Tuplin (Leiden and Boston: Brill, 2012), pp. 43–62
STILLMAN, ROBERT E., *Philip Sidney and the Poetics of Renaissance Cosmopolitanism* (Aldershot and Burlington, VA: Ashgate, 2008)
STREETE, ADRIAN, 'Francis Quarles' Early Poetry and the Discourses of Jacobean Spenserianism', *Journal of the Northern Renaissance*, 1 (2009)
TATUM, JAMES, *Xenophon's Imperial Fiction: On 'The Education of Cyrus'* (Princeton: Princeton University Press, 1989)
TILLEY, A., 'Greek Studies in Early Sixteenth Century England', *English Historical Review*, 53 (1938), 221–38
TUPLIN, CHRISTOPHER (ed.), *Xenophon and his World* (Stuttgart: Franz Steiner Verlag, 2004)
—— 'Xenophon's *Cyropaedia*: Education and Fiction', in *Education in Greek Fiction*, ed. by Alan H. Sommerstein and Catherine Atherton (Bari: Levante Editori, 1996), pp. 65–122
VENN, J., and J. A. VENN (eds), *Alumni Cantabrigienses Part I*, 4 vols (Cambridge: Cambridge University Press, 1922–1927)
VICKERS, BRIAN, 'Epideictic and Epic in the Renaissance', *New Literary History*, 14 (1983), 497–537
VIRGOE, ROGER, 'Barker, William (c.1520–aft. Feb. 1576), *The History of Parliament*:

    British Political, Social & Local History <https://www.historyofparliamentonline.org/volume/1558-1603/member/barker-william-1520-1576>

WAKELIN, DANIEL, *Humanism, Reading and English Literature, 1430–1530* (Oxford: Oxford University Press, 2007)

—— 'Possibilities for Reading: Classical Translations in Parallel Texts *ca* 1520-1558', *Studies in Philology*, 105 (2008), 422–36

WATSON, FOSTER, *The English Grammar Schools to 1660: Their Curriculum and Practice* (Cambridge: Cambridge University Press, 1908)

WILLIAMS, NEVILLE, *A Tudor Tragedy: Thomas Howard, Fourth Duke of Norfolk* (London: Barrie & Jenkins, 1964)

WOOLFSON, JONATHAN, *Padua and the Tudors: English Students in Italy, 1485–1603* (Toronto: University of Toronto Press, 1998)

—— (ed.), *Reassessing Tudor Humanism* (Basingstoke: Palgrave Macmillan, 2002)

—— 'Thomas Hoby, William Thomas, and Mid-Tudor Travel to Italy', in *The Oxford Handbook of Tudor Literature*, ed. by Michael Pincombe and Cathy Shrank (Oxford: Oxford University Press, 2009), 404–17

WOUDHUYSEN, HENRY, *Sir Philip Sidney and the Circulation of Manuscripts, 1558–1640* (Oxford: Clarendon Press, 1996)

INDEX

'Attic bee', 10n, 66
Abradatas, 59n, 64, 65, 175, 206-7, 216-18, 220-22, 226, 227
Accademia Fiorentina, 18, 69
Achaemenid Persia, 1, 44, 45, 132n, 219n, 242n, 257n
Achilles, 74
Adramas, 187
Aeneid, 43, 50, 51, 56, 57, 59, 61
Aeolia/Aeolians, 208, 255
Agamemnon, 55
Agesilaus, 4n, 6, 35, 81,
Aglaitadas, 121-22
Ahura Mazda [Zoroastrian god], 105n
Alceuna, 187
Alexander the Great, 54, 55, 57, 74, 75n, 206n, 219n, 258n, 261n
Alexander, Gavin, 61
Alexander, William, 48
Alexis (from Virgil's second eclogue), 68
Ambler, Wayne, 70
Apollo, 224, 225, 226,
Appian [*Iberika*], 19, 22, 26-27, 32, 33, 41
Arabia/Arabians, 85, 102, 115, 159, 160, 171, 204, 208n, 229, 230, 255
Araspes, 64, 65, 69, 173n, 175-77, 204-6, 214-15, 217, 227n
Arbaces [Panthea's brother in *A King and No King*], 65
Argalus, 64
Aribeus [king of Cappadocia], 115
Ariosto, 2n, 57, 61
Aristippus, 50
Armenia/Armenians, 53, 65, 116, 130-35, 137-38, 140-43, 165, 187n, 190, 195, 198n, 246, 247, 249, 259
Artabasus [Median friend and ally], 101n, 156n, 177n, 178n, 187, 201, 204, 205, 216, 233, 246n, 247n, 249, 251, 252
Artabates, 246, 247, 255
Artacaman [king of Phrygia], 115, 255
Artagersas, 216, 221, 222
Artaxerxes, 3, 79n, 262

Asiadatas, 216
Assyria/Assyrians, 1, 5, 71, 85, 98-100, 102, 115-16, 129-30, 144n, 146-47, 149-52, 154-57, 166-68, 170-72, 175, 180-86, 189-95, 201-4, 208, 213, 223, 225, 230, 231n, 234n
Astley, John, 55
Astyages [king of Media, grandfather of Cyrus], 86, 90-102, 134, 136, 143, 175, 178, 254
Azoulay, Vincent, 115n

B.R. [translator of Herodotus, 1584], 29
Babylon, 1, 2,6, 29, 43-44, 58, 68, 73, 74, 85, 98n, 116, 178n, 179, 182-84, 188, 190, 192-94, 203, 208, 219, 224, 228, 229-36, 252, 254, 255, 257
Bactria/Bactrians, 85, 102, 171, 175, 257
Banks, John, 49
Bannister, Lawrence, 24n, 26
Basil, St, of Caesarea, *De legendis gentilium libris*, 22, 32, 40, 82n, 226n
Basilikon Doron, 46-7, 53, 94n
Basle, 8, 31, 34, 35-6, 69, 85n
Bates, Catherine, 60n
Beaumont, Francis and John Fletcher, *A King and No King*, 65
Belshazzar, 63
Berthelet, Thomas, 10n, 12n, 29, 63n
Bingham, John, 34n, 75n, 80n
Bodin, Jean, 43
Bodleian Library, 65, 70
Boemus, Johannes, 29
Book of Common Prayer, 39, 49n
Botley, Paul, 6n, 7n, 9n, 10n, 54n
Boulogne, 50
Brandisby, John, 34
Brende, John, 36
Brooke, Christopher, 48
Brylinger, Nikolaus, 34, 36, 69, 85n,
Bryskett, Lodowick, 46
Bullinger, Heinrich, 31
Bulteel, John, *Birinthea*, 49, 51, 52n, 65

Butts, William, 14
Bynneman, Henry, 17n, 19n, 26–7, 32, 39n, 258n

Caducians, 181, 185–92, 201, 246
Cadusius, 227–28, 233, 255
Cambyses [eldest son of Cyrus], 85n, 259, 262n
Cambyses [father of Cyrus], 85, 86, 100, 102, 105–14, 254,
Camden, William, 69
Candaules, 225n
Cappadocia/Cappadocians, 85, 102, 115, 159, 208, 229, 230, 255
Caraducus, 216
Caria/Carians, 85, 102, 115, 171, 227–28, 255
Carion, Johannes, 43–4, 63
Carthage, 71, 75, 206n
Cartwright, John, 45
Cartwright, William, *The Royall Slave*, 45n
Caselius, Johannes, 36n, 69
Castelvetro, Lodovico, 59
Castiglione, Baldessare, *Il Cortegiano*, 5, 41, 43, 51, 55, 75n, 253n
Castor and Pollux, 151
Cawood, John, 19n, 22, 31–2, 82n
Chaldeans /'Chaldees', 138–43, 223–24
Charles I, King, 43, 48,
Charles II, King, 65
Charles V [Holy Roman Emperor], 12, 39n
Chrysantas [Persian friend to Cyrus], 122–23, 125, 131–33, 149–50, 153, 163–64, 187–89, 210, 219–20, 223, 229, 233, 237, 241, 246, 250–51, 255
Cicero ['Tully'], 1, 10, 29, 33, 35, 39, 46, 52n, 54, 56–8, 59, 61, 63, 75n, 79n, 80, 90n, 258n, 260n
Cilicia, 85, 102, 115, 171, 208, 227, 255,
Cinthio [Giovanni Battista Giraldi], 46
Cleland, James, 47
Cooper, Thomas, 44, 63
Corydon [shepherd in Virgil's second eclogue], 68
Cramsie, James, 47, 94n
Cranmer, Thomas, Archbishop of Canterbury, 31, 34n, 39, 52
Cratander, Andreas, 34, 36
Croesus [king of Lydia], 54, 102, 114n, 115, 147, 154, 159, 204n, 208, 210, 214, 219, 221, 223–26, 228–29, 241n, 243–44
Croke, Richard, 14
Ctesias, *Persika*, 3, 79n, 257n
Cyaxares [Median uncle to Cyrus, son of Astyages], 99–100, 102, 106–8, 115–16, 118, 120, 128–31, 138, 143–50, 153–57, 166–68, 171, 173, 177, 195–203, 208, 212, 233, 253–55
Cyllene, 223
Cyme, 223
Cyprus / Cyprians, 38n, 85, 208, 227, 255, 257
Cyrenia/Cyrenians, 204
Cyrus the Younger, 3–4, 54, 75, 79n, 80n, 261n, 262n

Daniel (Book of), 2, 43, 44
Danzig, Gabriel, 94n, 135n
Daochus, 216
Darius I, 74
Darius III, 206n, 219n
Datamas [Dutamas], 246
David [biblical], 243n
de Nicolay, Nicholas, 45
de Scudéry, Madeleine, *Le Grand Cyrus*, 48, 65
de Vintemille, Jacques, 28n, 50n
della Valle, Pietro, 45
Delphos [Delphi], 224, 225
Demosthenes, 9, 12, 25, 35, 39
Denham, Sir John, 63
Denys, John, 35
di Varthema, Ludovico, 9, 44
Digby, Francis, 48, 55n
Diodorus Siculus, 63, 258n
Diogenes Laertius, 4, 50, 54
Dionysius of Syracuse, 50
Domenichi, Lodovico, 69, 260n
Dorking, Surrey, 20, 26, 27
Dryden, John, 49
Du Bartas, Guillaume, 62
Dudley, John, First Duke of Northumberland, 28, 77n
Dyx, William, 26n

Egypt/Egyptians, 6, 29, 73, 85, 208, 215, 216, 218, 222–23, 226, 237, 257, 262
Elyot, Sir Thomas, 37–40, 45, 63, 87n

Epitaphia, 19, 22, 32
Ethiopia, 257
Euphrates [river], 229
Euxine Sea, 257
Ezra, 2, 43

Farrant, Richard, 65, 176n, 227n
Fitzalan, Henry, 32
Fitzalan, Mary, 32n
Florio, John, 49
Foxe, John, 29, 34n
Frankfurt Book Fair, 31, 69

Gabeus, 115
Gadatas [Assyrian ally of Cyrus], 184-6, 189-95, 201, 203, 226, 231, 233, 246, 247, 249, 252
Gardiner, Stephen, 16
Gascoigne, George, 81n
Gelli, Giambattista, 17-18, 21, 23, 26, 32, 82n
George, St, 60
Gilby, Goddred, 57n
Gobryas [Assyrian ally of Cyrus], 171-3, 177-85, 194-95, 202-3, 226, 229, 231, 233, 234n, 249-51
Gray, Vivienne J., 3n, 10n, 58, 66n
Greece/Greek studies, 1, 2, 3, 6-16, 18, 22, 23, 25-7, 28, 31-41, 46n, 49, 52, 54, 55, 63, 66, 68, 69, 70, 73, 75n, 79, 80, 81n, 83n, 85, 86n, 87n, 88n, 89n, 90n, 96n, 108n, 111, 112n, 115, 124, 145n, 156n, 152n, 155n, 173n, 177n, 178n, 193n, 202n, 207n, 209n, 213n, 217n, 229n, 221, 223n, 225n, 226, 228n, 240n, 243n, 244n, 250n, 251n, 261n, 263
Greek New Testament, 9, 34n, 39, 41
Grey, Jane, 28
Grey, Katherine, 28
Grogan, Jane, 10n, 58n, 59n, 60n, 64n, 155n
Gyges, 225n

Hakluyt, Richard, 44
Hannibal, 71, 75
Hebrew, 8, 14n, 15, 28, 31, 46n, 68
Heliodorus, 57, 61
Hellespont, 115, 159, 228, 255
Henri II, King of France, 50
Henry V, 64, 220n, 222n
Henry VII, 74n

Henry VIII, 12n, 14n, 22n, 23, 38, 42, 74n, 253n
Henry, Prince of Wales, 8, 43, 46n, 47, 48, 63, 69,
Herbert, Henry, 28
Herbert, William, first Earl of Pembroke, 28, 29n, 45, 71, 76n, 77, 80n, 82n
Herodotus, 3, 4, 29, 34, 36n, 37, 51, 52, 63, 74n, 86n, 93n, 144n, 155n, 204n, 209n, 225n, 241n, 244n, 258n
Higford, Robert [secretary to Thomas Howard], 24n, 26
Hipparchicus [Xenophon], 81n
Hippocentaur (hippogryph), 164
Hirsch, Steven, 242n
Hoby, Philip, 18
Hoby, Thomas, 16, 17, 18, 19n, 37, 41, 43n, 55, 75n, 253n
Holland, Henry, 43n, 48
Holland, Philemon, 8, 34, 36, 40, 43n, 48, 68. 69, 85n, 86n, 87n, 88n, 89n, 90n, 97n, 100n, 103n, 108n, 117n, 120n, 123n, 125n, 129n, 132n, 134n, 135n, 145n, 146n, 150n, 152n, 164n, 172n, 173n, 176n, 178n, 183n, 187n, 191n, 192n, 193n, 194n, 199n, 201n, 202n, 203n, 206n, 221n, 223n, 225n, 230n, 233n, 239n, 242n, 243n, 245n, 246n, 250n, 252n, 255n, 257n, 258n, 260n, 262n, 266
Hosington, Brenda, 17n, 18n, 23n
Howard family (Dukes of Norfolk), 13, 14, 20, 21, 22n, 23n, 27, 29, 32,
Howard house, 29, 76,
Howard, Muriel, 38n
Howard, Philip (later St), Earl of Surrey, 20n, 21, 29, 32, 74, 76n, 80n
Howard, Thomas, fourth Duke of Norfolk, 14, 19, 20, 24, 25, 26, 29, 32, 74n,
Howard, Thomas, second Duke of Norfolk, 74n, 76n
Howard, Thomas, third Duke of Norfolk, 14, 20
Humphrey, Laurence, 23
Huntington Library, vii, 59, 68, 70, 84n, 93n
Hutson, Lorna, 78n
Hyrcania/Hyrcanians, 85, 102, 156-62, 164, 166-71, 173, 177-78, 181, 183-87, 190, 195, 201, 233, 246-47, 249, 251-52

Hystaspas [Persian friend to Cyrus], 120, 122, 161–62, 201, 214, 221, 228, 243, 246, 250–52

Iden, Henry, 82n
Iliad, 55, 57, 75n
Illyria/Illyrians, 85
India/Indians, 85, 102, 128–29, 143, 207–8, 257
Ionia/Ionians, 208, 228n, 255
Isaiah, 2, 43
Isingrin, Michael, 8n, 34, 35, 36, 69
Islam, 23, 135n, 246n
Isocrates, 5, 9, 14n, 22, 28n, 32, 35,

James VI of Scotland and I of England, King, 34, 43, 46, 47–9, 53, 65, 69, 94n,
Jupiter [Roman ruler of the gods], 104, 121, 131, 146, 151, 178, 190, 214, 217, 219, 220, 234, 245, 246, 247, 258
Justin, 62, 63, 258n

Landino, Cristoforo, 43n
Lanquet, Thomas, 44
Larissa, 223
Lazarus, Micha, 9n, 10, 14n
Lee, Edward, Archbishop of York, 40
Leo VI, *Taktika*, 39
Lepanto, 19, 48n
LeRoy, Louis, 28n, 50, 260n
Leslie, John (Bishop of Ross), 19, 24, 26
Lesser, Zachary, 65
Leunclavius, Johannes, 36n, 69
Lever, Thomas, 15
Livy, 4, 35, 37
Lloyd, Lodowick, 63
London, 10, 15, 16, 19, 22, 31, 32, 37, 61, 68, 264
Lucian, 37, 38, 57
Lydgate, John, 37
Lydia/Lydians, 85, 102, 114n, 115, 144, 157, 159, 203, 204, 210, 223, 224, 229, 230, 241, 255
Lyly, John, 63

Machiavelli, Niccolò, 17n, 43, 46, 47, 50n, 55n, 66, 100n, 111n, 136n, 206n, 238n
Mandane [mother of Cyrus], 86, 90–95, 93, 102, 126, 134, 254, 255, 257
Maragdus [king of Arabia], 115

Mariandines, 85
Marlowe, Christopher, *Tamburlaine*, 45n, 57, 64, 228n
Mary I, Queen, 20n, 28, 29n, 31, 32, 38n, 40, 42
Mary, Queen of Scots, 21, 24, 26
Maximus the Confessor, 39
Media, 9, 49, 58, 68, 86, 90, 94, 100, 102, 104, 115, 116, 117n, 129n, 134n, 143, 146, 153n, 156, 157, 160, 161, 162, 164–71, 175, 177, 178, 187, 195, 197, 199, 201, 204, 208, 212, 214, 236n, 240, 245, 246, 247, 249, 252–55, 259, 263
Megabisus, 255
Merchant Taylors' School, 10, 11, 46, 53, 60
Meres, Francis, 60
Midas, 226n
Minadoi, Giovanni-Tommaso, 45n
Mirror for Magistrates, 61, 64
Mithras [a Persian god], 233
Montaigne, Michel Eyquem de, 49
Moore, Helen, 42
More, Sir/St Thomas, *Utopia*, 5, 23n, 43, 50, 51, 61
Morison, Sir Richard, 12, 39
Moxsay, Nicholas, 68
Mulcaster, Richard, 11, 13, 42, 46, 51, 52–4, 60,
Muscovy Company, 9, 44

Nadon, Christopher, 46n, 49n, 58, 66n, 247n
Naples, 18, 41
Nebuchadnezzar, 63
Niayesh, Ladan, 85–86n
Nicoll, John [translator of Thucydides], 37
Norris, John, 48, 55n,
North, Sir Thomas [translator of Plutarch], 116n, 273

Oeconomicus, 9, 10n, 29, 37, 78n, 80n, 107n
On Horsemanship, 35, 55, 81n,
Orlando / *Orlando furioso*, 2n, 57, 62,
Ovid, 37, 226n

Pactolus [river], 208, 226
Painter, William, 64
Panthea, 36, 64–5, 69, 173n, 175n, 176n, 205–7, 217–18, 226–7

Paphlagonia/Paphlagonians, 85, 102, 115, 208, 255
Parks, G. B., 13n, 38n
Parthenia, 64
Paul III, Pope, 18
Peacham, Henry, 48
Perseus, 86
Pharnucus, 216, 221, 255
Pheraulas [friend to Cyrus], 125–7, 245, 247–49
Philip II, King of Spain, 8n
Philip, king of Macedon, 25n
Phoenicia/Phoenicians, 85, 208, 217
Phrygia/Phrygian, 85, 102, 115, 159, 208, 228, 229, 230, 255
Plato, 1, 2, 6, 9, 33, 38, 39, 44, 50, 51, 54, 57n, 60, 66, 75, 79n, 260n
Plutarch, 1, 6, 7n, 34, 37, 39, 69, 116, 273
Pollnitz, Aysha, 12n, 39
Polybius, 80
Preston, Thomas
Preston, Thomas, 85–6n
Puttenham, George, 2n, 60

Quarles, Francis, 63
Quintus Curtius, 36, 219n
Quintus Tullius Cicero, 56, 58

Ralegh, Sir Walter, 2, 44, 60n,
Raven, Edward, 35
Record, Robert, 8n, 31n
Red Sea, 68, 257
Redcrosse, 60
Regius Professorship in Greek, 14
Rex, Richard, 13n, 14n, 15n, 16n
Rhodes, Neil, 9n, 11n, 14, 16n, 23n, 37, 40, 41, 42n, 57, 64n
Rich, Barnabe, 62n
Ridolfi, Roberto/Ridolfi Plot, 17, 19, 24, 76n
Robinson, Richard, 52n, 134n

Sabaris [youngest son of king of Armenia], 133
Sacas [cup-bearer to Astyages], 92–3, 96, 190
Sacia/Sacians, 85, 181, 184–86, 187n, 201, 233, 247–49
Safavid Persia, 1, 3n, 9, 23, 44, 45
Sambaulas, 124

Sambucus, Johannes, 8n, 54
Sandridge, Norman, 66n
Sardis [capital of Lydia], 219, 223, 225, 227, 228, 233–34, 252
Savile, Sir Henry, 8, 38–9
Scaliger, Julius Caesar, 59
Scipio Africanus, 11, 55, 56, 75, 79n, 80, 206n
Scott, William, 56, 60–62, 159n
Scythia/Scythians, 84, 116n
Semiramis, 63
Seymour, Edward, First Duke of Somerset, 12, 28, 77n
Shakespeare, William, 63–4, 85–6n, 125n, 220n, 222, 247
Sidney, Sir Philip, 10, 43, 51, 55, 56, 57–62, 64, 159n
Siena, 16n, 17, 18
Sleidan, Johannes, 34n, 44n, 260n
Solinus, 63
Solon, 54, 224n, 244n
Spartans [Lacedaemonians], 4, 66, 81n, 208n
Spenser, Edmund, 2, 5, 10, 43, 51, 56, 58, 60–61, 63, 81n
Spinola, Benedict, 19
St John's College, Cambridge, 12–17, 23n, 25, 26, 30, 31, 34, 35, 37, 38, 41, 42, 69
Stationers' Company, 31, 32
Sterne, Laurence, 66
Strabo, 45n, 258n
Strauss, Leo, 58, 66
Suetonius, 34, 69
Susa, 175, 257, 271
Sylvester, Joshua, 62

Tanaoxares [younger son of Cyrus], 259–60
Tatum, James, 66, 70, 224n, 247n
Taverner, Richard, 64
Taylor, Andrew, 16
Taylor, John (Master of St John's), 15n
Terence, 35
Thatamas, 187
Thrace/Thracians, 85, 208
Thucydides, 4, 34, 37, 52, 60n
Tigranes [eldest son of king of Armenia], 65, 133–41, 144, 157, 158, 161, 166, 169, 178, 187, 198n, 203, 247, 249, 251
Tomyris, 63, 258n
Trinity College, Cambridge, 16n, 30, 70

Tymbraia, 208

Ulysses, 54
Ussher, James, 43

Valerius Maximus, 63
Vesta [Roman goddess of the hearth], 104, 234n
Virgil, 37, 43, 50, 51, 56, 57, 59, 61, 62, 67, 68
Vulcan [Roman god of fire], 230

Walsh, Octavia, 65
Warner, William, 61
Watreman, William, 29
Whythorn, Peter, 37
Wilson, Thomas, 12, 13, 16, 25, 49n, 98n
Wolfe, Joan, 31, 32
Woolfson, Jonathan, 13n, 18n, 20n, 44
Woudhuysen, Henry, 21, 22n

Zeus [ruler of the Greek gods], 250n
Zopyrus, 74

www.ingramcontent.com/pod-product-compliance
Lightning Source LLC
Chambersburg PA
CBHW061434300426
44114CB00014B/1682